MENSIS	MENSIS	MENSIS
IANVAR	FEBRAR	MARTIVS
DIES · XXXI	DIES XXVIII	DIES XXXI
NON QVINT	NON QVINT	NON SEPTIMAN
DIES HOR VIIIS	DIES HOR X S	DIES HOR XII
NOX HOR XIIII	NOX HOR XIIII	NOX HOR XII
SOL	SOL AQVARIO	AEQVINOCTIV
CAPRICORNO	TVTELA IVNONIS	VIII KAL APR
TVTELA	SEGETES	SOL PISCIBVS
IVNONIS	SARIVNTVR	IVLI MINER...
PALVS	VINEA...	VINEAE PEDAM...
AQVITVR	SVPER...	IN CASTIN...
SALIX	HARVNDINES	PVTANT...
HARVNDO	INCE...	...
CAEDITVR	PALINVRIA	...
SACRIFICANT	IVLI...	...
DI...	CARAGOGNA...	...

Greece and Rome

With 376 illustrations
95 in color
281 photographs, engravings,
drawings and maps

EDITED BY MICHAEL GRANT

Greece and Rome

THE BIRTH OF WESTERN CIVILIZATION

Texts by

MICHAEL GRANT   A.R. BURN   H.C. BALDRY

W.K.C. GUTHRIE   JOHN BOARDMAN   F.R. COWELL

R.A.G. CARSON   MORTIMER WHEELER

BONANZA BOOKS
New York

Copyright © 1964 and 1986 Thames and Hudson Ltd., London.
All rights reserved

This 1986 edition published by Bonanza Books, distributed by
Crown Publishers, Inc.

Printed in Yugoslavia
h g f e d c b a

Contents

I INTRODUCTION

The tradition that holds us in thrall

MICHAEL GRANT

'Then the god drew away from the shore by easy
stages, first planting his hooves in the surf at the
water's edge, and then proceeding further out to sea.
The girl was sorely frightened, and looked back at
the sands behind her, from which she had been carried
away. One hand grasped the bull's horn, the other
rested on his back, and her fluttering garments floated
in the breeze'.

OVID, METAMORPHOSES, BOOK II

Europa, princess of Tyre,
was one of many earthly women beloved of the god Zeus. In order to win her, he changed himself into a beautiful bull and lured her to sit on his back. Then, plunging into the sea, he carried her far away to the island of Crete, where she eventually gave birth to Minos. In this Archaic Greek relief (mid 6th century BC) she grasps the swimming bull by the horn as Ovid describes; two dolphins at his feet symbolize the sea.

Myths such as these are still strangely compelling. In Greek and Roman culture they occupied a central place; in religion, in art, in literature, in the whole fabric of the people's lives, they were fundamental and all-pervasive. Yet until sixty years ago they were inadequately explained as the inventions of poets, as allegories of the processes of nature or as legends based on historical events. Modern psychology, anthropology and comparative religion have given us new insights by showing the myths as survivals, often associated with ritual, of largely unconscious ways of thought, images of forces in man's mental life that are still anything but outgrown. 'Most of them', wrote Jung, 'can be found everywhere and at all times. They occur in the folklore of primitive races, in Greek, Egyptian and ancient Mexican myths, as well as in the dreams, visions and delusions of modern individuals entirely ignorant of all such traditions.'

Europa lived on through the transforming vision of the ages: to the Romans a tale of pathos and charm (fresco from Pompeii, *left*); to the early Renaissance, an evocation of springtime and magic (Francesco di Giorgio, *right*); finally (*extreme right*) to the 18th century, the subject for a piece of gay Rococo decoration (Coypel). But beneath them all still lurks the primeval image of the bull-god, amorous and untamed.

The history of the female nude in painting could almost be told in terms of the Three Graces (*far left*: Roman fresco) and the Judgment of Paris. For Cranach (*left*) many conventions are still medieval—the men's costumes and the hint of embarrassment in the goddesses. Rubens' hefty Graces (*right*) contrast with the girlish figures in the Roman example, but the traditional grouping is retained.

Myths in disguise pass from one culture to another. The folklores of many peoples, for instance, contain strikingly similar stories in which a hero fights and kills a lion with his bare hands. The examples illustrated (*upper row*) show how close these resemblances can be. First: the Babylonian hero Gilgamesh, from a cylinder seal of the 3rd millennium BC. Second: Heracles, from a Greek coin of the 4th century BC; the strangling of the Nemean lion was the first of his Twelve Labours.

Condemned, suppressed or explained away, the worship of Dionysus—the intoxicated surrender to ecstasy, the abandonment of the reason—stands for a constant factor in human affairs, from the overwhelming *Bacchae* of Euripides to survivals of the original classical tradition in 7th-century Constantinople (*below left*) and the sophisticated hedonism of 18th-century France (*below right*: a group by Clodion). Even today, the words 'Bacchic' and 'Dionysiac' are part of everyday parlance.

The hero under other names. *Left*: Samson, a Tuscan relief of the 12th century AD—'and behold, a young lion roared against him. And the spirit of the Lord came mightily upon him, and he rent him as he would have rent a kid, and he had nothing in his hand'. The sculptor is clearly following the same iconographical tradition, though he is less interested in anatomy. Finally (*right*) Michelangelo goes back to the myth of Heracles in order to display the human body under stress and the power of muscle in action.

No myth from the ancient world has accumulated more meanings than that of Orpheus, who entered Hades in search of his dead bride. For seven months he sang his song of lamentation, charming even the animals and birds (*above left*: a Roman mosaic from Palermo), to be torn to pieces in the end by maenads. The early Christians transformed him into the Good Shepherd (*above right*: a sarcophagus of the 3rd century). Later still he can be recognized in King David (*left*: a 10th-century psalter from Byzantium). For Zadkine (*right*) he becomes 'the poet', the self-absorbed singer doomed to a brutal destruction.

'**King Oedipus,** who slew his father Laius and married his mother Jocasta, merely shows the fulfilment of our childhood wishes', wrote Freud. Before he came to Thebes, Oedipus encountered the Sphinx—a monster, half-lion and half-woman, who could be subdued only by one who could answer her riddle—the subject of the painting by Ingres (*below*). His reward was the throne of Thebes and the hand of Queen Jocasta—unknown to them both, his own mother. When they learned the dreadful truth Oedipus blinded himself and Jocasta committed suicide, a scene illustrated in a 15th-century manuscript of Seneca's Latin play *Oedipus* (*bottom*). The Sphinx herself (*right*, from a Romano-British cemetery), according to Jung, symbolizes the incest-prohibition which Oedipus, instead of accepting, defies.

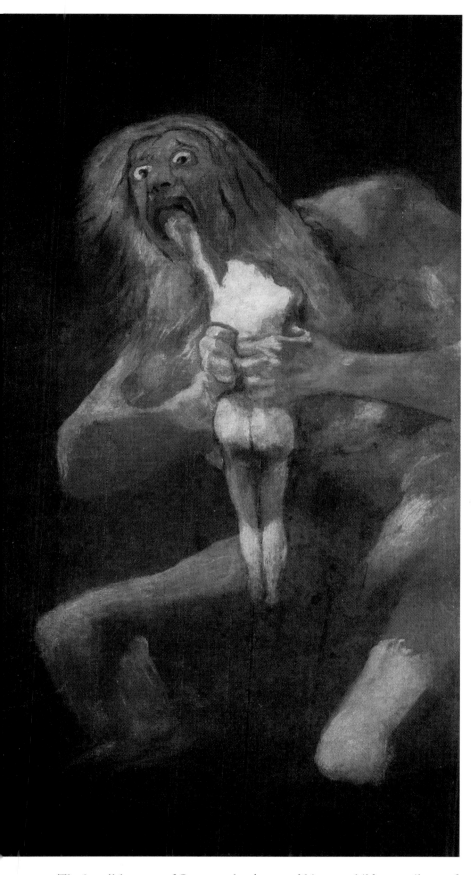

The horrible story of Cronos, who devoured his own children until one of them, Zeus, defied and mutilated him, has continued to hold a fascination for artists and writers throughout history—this nightmare painting by Goya is one of its most telling expressions. What is the source of its power? One answer is provided by psycho-analytic theory. 'You will no doubt be surprised to hear', wrote Freud, 'how often little boys are afraid of being eaten by their father—and you may also be surprised at my including this fear among the phenomena of the sexual life.' But in the eyes of the child, according to Freud, the father is his rival for the love of the mother; the child hates him and wishes to destroy him. This led Freud to formulate his most important hypothesis, the Oedipus complex.

Imperial power has always dressed itself in the trappings of the greatest of all empires. The first coin (*right*) is of Constantine; next to it is Frederick II Hohenstaufen, the 13th-century emperor whose works show a self-conscious ambition to restore the glories of Rome; and finally Napoleon, in the same incongruous toga and wreath, inspired by the same vision.

When Charles II of England wanted a symbol for 'Britannia' he commissioned a design from a coin of Antoninus Pius (AD 138–161) (*far left*). The model for the new Britannia (*left*: a halfpenny of 1673) was the Duchess of Richmond.

The eagle as the symbol of national pride derives from the Roman standard. It appears (*far left*) on a coin of Trajan, on the seal of the United States (*centre*) and as the emblem of the German Federal Republic.

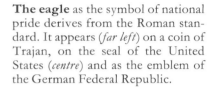

Imitation Romes were built in wood and stucco for great occasions during the Renaissance. This painting by Andrea Vicentino shows the temporary structures erected for the state visit of Henry III of France to Venice in 1574. They were designed by Palladio and included a temple with twelve huge Corinthian columns and a triumphal arch carefully copied from that of Septimius Severus at Rome.

INTRODUCTION

The tradition that holds us in thrall

MICHAEL GRANT

WITHOUT GREECE AND ROME, for better or for worse—and almost certainly, despite all our faults, for worse—we should not be what we are. Their significances crowd in upon us with an insistence that is far too many-sided and complex to be satisfied by simple metaphorical phrases indicating the debt, legacy or heritage that we owe to these sources.

For one thing the influences which, whether we like it or not, hold us in thrall have reached us in many different times and ways, and at every level of consciousness and profundity. In some matters—the classical contribution in the political field, or certain central aspects of the messages of Virgil or Cicero—impingement on the world has been continuous, so that a direct chain of inheritance can be traced all the way through the intervening centuries until the present moment. And yet, even in such basic themes, there have also at many periods been revivals that are due in a larger degree to intentional resuscitation than to the bonds of continuity. When Cola di Rienzi, in the 14th century, tried to restore the antique Roman Republic, this was not only because he was heir to a continuous tradition (though he had the stones of Rome to remind him of this) but because he had 'rediscovered' Livy. Others—Petrarch is perhaps the most famous of them—have often made similar rediscoveries of ancient authors: which really means that they cast the contemporary spotlight upon some part of the almost inexhaustible store, and reinterpreted it in the light of topical preoccupations. For example, the American and French Revolutionaries were to invoke most fervently the same Republican tradition again. And then it was too much to expect that the classically trained British would not equate Salamis and Plataea with Trafalgar and Waterloo, and the *Pax Romana* with their own nineteenth-century empire. In the words of a very late Roman in Gaul, Rutilius Namatianus, echoing Virgil in his praise of the imperial people:

> You brought the nations one great fatherland,
> You raised the savage with your taming hand,
> Broke him, but gave him laws to be his aid.
> A City of the scattered Earth you made.

But when a British colonial civil servant thought of the *Pax Britannica* in the light of his recollections of a classical schooling, he was not, of course, so deluded as to suppose that the parallel between the two sets of empire-builders was exact. The same applies to literature and art: slavish imitation has only been the result of bad classicism; good classicism, from Homer onwards, has meant not the suppression of originality, but its intense stimulation by the disciplinary influence of a fertilizing tradition. Never has this tradition been more determinedly invoked than by Italians of the 15th and 16th centuries. 'Draw near the monuments of the ancients', Jerome Vida (c. 1550) appealed, 'scan them with your eyes, peruse them with your spirit, scrutinize them again and again.' That is an echo of Horace, but Horace, like others who understood what the classics really mean, had added that one can and must modify and improve on what one has found. Greece and Rome are, or ought to be, exciting and provoking, not the dead hand of a restrictive past.

The Stuff of History

When, therefore, we find some sort of an echo of the ancient world in modern times, the process that has brought it into being may well be a fascinatingly complex one. And this is just the sort of historical process that is worth understanding, because this is the real stuff of history, what history is about. Your apparent parallel may represent indebtedness incurred at one of many possible epochs, or it may represent conscious or half-conscious or unconscious imitation—or, in some cases, not so much imitation as reaction. (Or it might even be fortuitous, since there is only a limited number of ways of doing certain things, in politics or art or in many other fields.) And then, when you seem to have proved in any particular case that indebtedness to the ancients exists, is it really a matter of fundamental substance or structure, or may it, perhaps, be something much more superficial? For, as well as authentic debts and links, there are also situations when identical or similar phrases or artistic themes are, out of convenience or nostalgia, made to exploit or enrich what are really quite distinct phenomena. Thus Charlemagne and Frederick II Hohenstaufen, with startling deviation from contemporary artistic norms, deliberately portrayed themselves on their coinage as ancient imperial Caesars and Augustuses—which they were not. In so doing, they foreshadowed even closer imitations of classical models by despots such as Francesco I da Carrara of Padua; and in the same sort of spirit Charles II, requiring a 'Britannia' for his coinage, asked a friend (the Duchess of Richmond) to pose for a design closely based on the 'Britannia' of Antoninus Pius.

Sometimes then the debt is profound, sometimes it is superficial and artificial, and there are many nuances betwixt and between. Sometimes, again, it is quite unconscious—the total unawareness with which one can live on a legacy and yet forget, or never even know, who the testator was. At all these levels the ancient world has been a catalyst, and with varying degrees of intensity has influenced and guided ways of thinking and events.

The Living World of the Myths

I would like to illustrate this vital matter of transmission, and how it comes about, from the field of myth. Classical mythology provides many short-cuts to our knowledge of what the Greeks and Romans were like. Yet it does not figure independently in the following chapters; and this is because its special historic role is that of a link or bridge between a wide variety of different branches of human activity. It is therefore particularly relevant to the question of transmission, between the ancient world and ourselves, which I am here discussing. The peoples of the ancient world depended upon their mythology for an enormous proportion of their art, literature, religion and education. Accordingly these myths were not only the subject of prolonged ancient study, but have become the keen concern today of classicists, anthropologists, theologians and psycho-analysts alike. For this reason, in spite of many false trails and excessive claims, the subject has, during the present century, advanced in a more definitive and revolutionary fashion than almost any other aspect of the studies of Greece and Rome.

The giant Prometheus figures in early mythology as the loyal friend of mankind, for whom he is said to have stolen fire from heaven. A later version of the myth even made him the creator of the human race. Horace alludes to it, and at Panopeus (in Phocis) Pausanias was shown by the local people two lumps of clay—'not earthy clay, but such as would be found in a ravine or sandy torrent, and they smell very like the skin of a man. They say that these are the remains of the clay out of which the whole race of mankind was made by Prometheus.' On this Roman sarcophagus Prometheus is seen meditating before bringing man to life; Zeus, Poseidon, Hermes and Hera watch. To the early Christians the myth symbolized rebirth in the after-life, and iconographically it passed into Christian art as the Creation of Man by God.

Greek and Graeco-Roman myth emerges from this process as infinitely rich and variegated in origin, development and character. Often even a single myth is told in ten diverse and irreconcilable forms; and the attitude of ancient people to every such story was different at every step and level (vertical in time or horizontal in class) of their cultural development. Besides, the myths cannot be understood at all if our researches into their character are restricted to the Greeks and Romans themselves. Not only they, but vast numbers of other peoples, have found the same stories gripping, compulsive and unforgettable. For very many of these narratives, very many indeed, are amazingly paralleled, often down to minor details, in a hundred or sometimes several hundred different cultures far outside the classical world, from Lapland to Melanesia, from North America to Zululand. These unmistakable similarities, which to those innocent of anthropology seem almost incredible, raise a cardinal question: are they caused by C. G. Jung's 'collective unconscious'—creating identical myths in peoples at similar stages of evolution even if they are so utterly remote from one another that no previous contact seems possible—or were the stories in some way actually *transmitted*, perhaps through many intermediaries and over a great period of time, from one culture to another? As the years go by, and more and more direct links, however surprising, are discovered, we must conclude that transmission probably occurred much more often than we can so far trace.

There is the problem of transmission from place to place; there is also the problem of transmission from epoch to epoch. This theme operates backwards as well as forwards from Greece and Rome; the question is first how did *they* get their mythology, and only then how has it come down to ourselves. If we first look far backwards into time—and even if we bear in mind, as we should, that prehistoric beliefs cannot be deduced with any certainty from such material objects as may survive—we can, occasionally, at least guess at Palaeolithic anticipations of anthropomorphic concepts, such as that of the Great Mother, which were later to appear among the Greeks in developed mythological form. Much later, Mesopotamia, Crete and Mycenae left more easily recognizable ancestors—or older cousins—to classical tales. Then, in what (for want of historical knowledge about it) we must still call the 'Dark Age', the beginnings of truly Greek myth are to be found. Many stages of this early development are enshrined in the Homeric poems, and above all in the *Iliad*, which led the way for poets and artists of its time and all other times to come.

The age-long processes of transmission, ever adapting, reviewing and reinterpreting, were already at work. They are clearly operative in the 'Orientalizing' period of Greek art, and then again—as the visual arts came to equal contemporary literature in beauty and vigour—in the archaic and classical epochs of Hellenism. Now, indeed, in an age when shame had been replaced by guilt as the basis of men's moral actions, mythology underwent corresponding changes, and became in the process the indispensable staple material of that Athenian tragedy which, like so many other branches of classical literature, gave us the foundation of what Europe has achieved since. Later, again, the same stories were adapted to the different though cognate cultures of Etruria and Rome.

Meanwhile, throughout ancient history, the Near and Middle East hardly ever ceased to exercise a powerful impact on the Mediterranean world; and eastern motifs and stories continued to find their way, together with the predominant Greek themes, into the artificial mythology which the non-mythically minded Romans created for their own purposes of patriotic antiquarianism and entertainment. And then large segments of the traditional corpus proved suitable for retention to mirror the new spiritual aspirations of the Christian era. The Creation of Man by Prometheus comes to symbolize rebirth in the after life, and Orpheus, the enchanter of animal creation, is depicted as the Good Shepherd by the fresco-painters of the Roman catacombs.

Startling and Productive: the Impact on the West

Ever since then, this same mythology has repeatedly exercised a revivifying effect upon the visual arts of Europe. The first classical miracle had been the brilliance and variety of its achievement, the second has been its subsequent impact, startling and productive, upon quite different civilizations. This is abundantly true of myth: for in literature and art alike this traditional framework has time after time been the medium through which, often in conditions far removed from classical antiquity, even the most strikingly independent minds have felt it necessary to express their ideas and artistic talents.

The guise of the Good Shepherd, for example, was very far from the only role of Orpheus during the Middle Ages. Boethius (c. AD 480–524) handed his story (like many others) on to subsequent generations, and one indirect result was Orpheus' reappearance, much altered, in French and English fairytales. Dante cites him again as a prime illustration for the process of allegory, that style of saying one thing to mean another which, usually in anachronistic fashion, so many medieval writers read into the classics. The Orpheus who emerges would scarcely have been recognizable to the Greeks, but it is to them that he owes his origins, and theirs is the inspiration which cast his story into a mould so deeply influential upon century after century. He owes part of his survival to King David, for it is in the guise of Orpheus that David is portrayed on a 10th-century Byzantine psalter. Likewise Hercules, the last mythological figure to leave western art and literature at the end of the ancient world and the first to return to it early in the second millennium, owes much of his persistence to Biblical comparisons with Samson.

In eastern Europe, the gods and heroes scarcely disappeared at all. Splendid silver plates from Constantinople, now mostly at Leningrad and Nicosia, went on showing classical scenes as late as the 7th century; and they continue to occur in the designs adorning Byzantine caskets three or four hundred years after that. The great 9th-century patriarch Photius still found it necessary to inveigh against pagan mythology; rather as in 1199 Orléans was denounced as a centre of pagan studies in danger of losing its way to Paradise. By then, the Carolingian revival had long since ensured the survival of the classics, and Ovid had become the best-seller he was to remain.

Another great means of transmission came from the capture of Toledo by the Spaniards from the Moslems in 1085. Through this channel, as well as through Arab Palermo, came the Greek culture which had for centuries been preserved at the Islamic Universities of Asia such as Jundai-Shapur. In 12th- and 13th-century Toledo, as well as in Cordova and Seville, the Greek classics were translated into Latin for the western world. This was the decisive time for those Aristotelian studies which dominated western thought until the Platonic Academies of the 15th century. The part played by Islam in this transmission explains why, in the Latin astronomical and astrological treatises which were popular at this as at all other times of crisis, the mythological figures are sometimes shown with Moslem or other oriental attributes.

A New Art and a New Meaning

Yet such medieval survivals, and even deliberate revivals such as we find in artists of the Carolingian age, are slight beside the force with which Graeco-Roman myth burst upon Italian painters and sculptors from the 15th century onwards. The Renaissance love of story-telling found much of its best narrative material in these myths. The tales which Ovid had brought to life from his gleanings of innumerable Greek intermediaries, and which Boccaccio had called to the notice of Italian writers and painters, were brilliantly adapted to a succession of current fashions and personal moods and styles, often far removed from the classical atmosphere. Brueghel, for example, selects the *Fall of Icarus* as the vehicle for a startlingly idiosyncratic revelation—possibly with topical overtones—of his own rough philosophy. What fascinated Michelangelo, on the other hand, about Greek mythology was not so much their stories but their humanism, their demonstration of the potentialities of the human form and spirit at their greatest, struggling—like the Hercules of many a heroic drawing or statue—against the monstrous forces of evil. Through him, myth inspired the Renaissance creation of the male human body—just as through other artists it inspired that other great Renaissance theme, the female nude.

But it was at Venice, in the art of Michelangelo's younger contemporaries, that classical myth underwent one of its most successful and original transformations. Through the opulent, sombre sensuousness of Titian's sometimes frightening mythological pictures moves a strangely fresh and direct personal experience of the classical tradition. Tintoretto contributes his exciting restless vistas, while Veronese lowers the tension to an urbane and colourful pageantry. Then the Narcissus of Caravaggio, again technically superb, displays a harsh and truthful realism which makes a break with all interpretations of mythology that have gone before. For here the figures of the myths, whose behaviour had always been depicted at one remove from humdrum reality, are reduced—as Caravaggio also reduced the figures of Biblical story—to the status of fallible pathetic human beings.

In the 17th century the myths were reborn by new sorts of magic in the great French tragedies, in the new baroque Italian opera, and in the fresh and splendid sculpture and painting of richly differing geniuses: the statues of Bernini, and the pictures of Rubens, Poussin and Claude. Once again the familiar tales had proved begetters of many things unknown before. In the next

The myth of Europa and the Bull (Zeus in disguise) has been illustrated by artists down the ages. The Archaic frieze shown on p. 9 is one of the earliest versions; this red-figure vase-painting of c. 490–80 BC represents a more classical treatment.

century Tiepolo and Boucher, with their rococo dedication to gracefully luxurious femininity, represented only minor facets of the compulsive tradition: though it is amusing and startling to contrast, say, Boucher's or Coypel's *Rape of Europa* with the treatment of the same theme on an Archaic Greek frieze, noting the versions of various great masters along the way.

We have come a long distance. Yet now again a new era, emancipated from this pre-revolutionary prettiness, was heralded by Goya and Blake. Their own mythological paintings, it must be added, can hardly be regarded as typical of this romantic revolution which broke with the past, for they are a law unto themselves. Yet even they, for all the directness of their vision, felt this need for the classical framework.

A Key to the Unconscious?

Then Macaulay, Kingsley and Hawthorne brought the myths, variously adjusted to English and Americans, into every nineteenth-century home; and this gain of breadth, as usually happens, carried compensating losses of depth. Nevertheless further reinterpretations, as profound and personal as any in the past, were to follow in the poetry of Rilke and Cavafy, and the plays of T. S. Eliot, Eugene O'Neill, Gide, Giraudoux, Cocteau, Camus, Sartre: who between them illustrate—as Corneille and Racine had illustrated three centuries earlier—the inextinguishable capacity of mythological Greek tragedy for survival and ever-original adaptation. Their contemporaries in the fields of sculpture and painting, too, depended no less strongly upon classical themes as vehicles for their own imaginations. Outstanding artists of myth such as Picasso, Braque, Lipchitz, Zadkine and Dali have shown a growing tendency to portray the unconscious dream-images which have inspired Freud and his followers to seek mythical prototypes, such as Oedipus and Narcissus and Prometheus, for the psychopathic experiences of mankind. Although Freud's theories have been shown by anthropologists and others to be less universally applicable than he claimed, he has made Oedipus, and classical themes of ritual and crime, part of our own structure of behaviour; and has again shown how ancient myth continues to make itself indispensable to mankind—or at least unavoidable.

As Mircea Eliade puts it, 'every primordial image is the bearer of a message of direct relevance to the condition of humanity'. He was thinking of myths, but the application can be extended to the whole of the complex miracle by which Greece and Rome have been handed down to us. Many, indeed, are the messages which they are able to convey to us, if we are able to receive them. If we try to do this, there is the prospect or danger that we shall become wholly riveted to the Greek and Roman past. This is easy because of the extraordinary wealth of fascination and enjoyment which it provides. The process can, if you like, be called escapism, which has given many people a relatively happy life. But the same process of withdrawal can also add to the store of useful knowledge. Such an increase has never been more necessary than today—and innumerable examples from the past warn us not to dismiss any increase of knowledge, however apparently remote from the present day, as lacking potential usefulness. But in any case, whether researchers into the subject continue to enlarge the frontiers of knowledge or not, escape into the past is one of the means of that healing, invigorating, liberating release which Goethe felt when he read the Homeric Hymns. By coming upon the ancient world at so early a stage, he seemed to experience, at least momentarily, a sense of emancipation 'from the terrible burden which the tradition of many hundreds of years has rolled upon us'.

Goethe was right to see that tradition can be evil as well as good, needing from us a measure of denial as well as acceptance. The traditions are behind us, whether we want them or not. If we remain unconscious of them, we are their woodenly dependent victims. If we understand them, they free us from the bonds of this historical necessity; they enhance our lives instead of deadening them, for we have become their masters rather than their slaves. Greece and Rome are uniquely able to help us in this way, because theirs are the only past civilizations, or jointly the only civilization, spread out for our detailed inspection all the way from beginning to end—from the birth of the west, not until its death, but until its first major change.

In 1450 the humanist Alberti was commissioned to remodel the church of S. Francesco at (Tempio Malatestiano) Rimini. As the basis of his design he took the Arch of Augustus (left), a few hundred yards from the church, and multiplied it by three. Ten years later, on the west front of the church of S. Maria Novella, Florence, (below) he used a pediment, a range of half-columns and pilasters at ground level and scroll-buttresses (their first use in architecture) to link the two storeys together.

The Witness of Architecture

As to what happened after that change, and particularly what happened to the ancient classics, the complicated process of continuity and reaction which I have briefly illustrated from myth can also be illustrated by an art which, though lacking in its very nature this narrative framework, has nevertheless throughout the centuries persistently born witness to its classical ancestry: namely architecture.

At many times during the intervening millennia, buildings have continued to display classical orders and motifs, sometimes in functional and wholly essential roles, but sometimes again in purely detachable positions upon otherwise quite unclassical buildings. You can find themes of Greek and Roman origin in every possible degree of indispensability or dispensability between these two extremes. Almost at the outset of the post-classical era, knowledge of the great domed or vaulted structures of antiquity, such as the Pantheon and Basilica of Constantine or Maxentius at Rome, blends strangely with many Near and Middle Eastern themes to produce that miracle of mathematics, illusion and mystical beauty, the Church of the Holy Wisdom (St Sophia) at Constantinople. From that, again, there is a very direct path to the superb mosques of 16th-century Istanbul, and particularly to the architecture of Sinan, a Christian from Caesarea, whose masterpiece, however, lies inland, at the Turks' first European capital Edirne (Adrianople)—the Selimiye or mosque of the Sultan Selim I. At the other end of Europe, meanwhile, the same transmission from the ancient world to Islam via Christianity had been at work. For the Caliph Abd al-Rahman III's Medina Azzahra palace at 10th-century Cordova showed horse-shoe arches, themselves of disputable origin, supported by capitals which (like many other features of this great but mostly vanished building) directly echo Byzantium and the whole classical world which had preceded it. Islam repaid the influence later.

Meanwhile, throughout the West, extraordinary developments came from the Roman innovation, displayed in the House of Fortune at Pompeii and then Severus' Forum at Lepcis Magna, by which arches were made to spring direct from the capitals of columns. After many years of small churches in Italy, France, Spain and elsewhere, the formula achieved in the 11th century that grandiloquent, varied, cosmopolitan efflorescence which records its origins by the title 'Romanesque'. But then, while Abbot Suger and the Ile de France deduced from its rounded forms the verticality of 'Gothic', the Italians continued to build in varieties of 'Romanesque': of which the 15th-century Florentine Renaissance is seen to be the heir. The continuity behind the Renaissance, as well as its striking originality within that tradition, can be seen by comparing the architectural styles of three churches at Florence. S. Miniato al Monte, started in the 11th century on Roman models, leads on to Arnolfo di Cambio's monumental Cathedral (begun 1296); and it is with such forerunners in mind that the genius of Brunelleschi devised his geometrical masterpiece of the early Renaissance, S. Spirito (c. 1436).

Building Upon the Classical Foundation

Italian textbooks, and then those of France and other countries, tell how the architects of the 15th and 16th centuries wrestled with the ancient motifs and converted them to novel uses and themes; and the results can be seen in the memorials that they have left behind them. Augustus' triumphal arch at Rimini, and Trajan's at Ancona, were mobilized by Alberti to the very different functions of a façade, at the Rimini Tempio Malatestiano and Mantua church of S. Andrea respectively. The cardinal problem, was the adaptation of classical motifs to the unclassically shaped frontages of basilica churches, with their naves higher than their aisles. For these, two-storey façades had to be devised. S. Maria Novella at Florence shows the first hesitating use of the scroll motif to link the two differing elevations, thus leading on to a whole host of west frontages all, in divers forms, exploiting the vocabulary of ancient Greece and Rome. Occasionally there are strange and unconscious echoes, in church façades, of ancient 'baroque' frontages such as Petra's two-storey 'Temple of Isis'.

Michelangelo, in his twin Capitoline palaces integrates and unifies the two storeys by lofty columns, such as are to be seen at Baalbek's late Roman 'Temple of Bacchus', illustrated on a later page. He also utilizes the three-tiered arcades of the Colosseum for his courtyard of the Palazzo Farnese. In his later years, even these inspired variations upon classical themes were not enough for him, and just as his *Last Judgment* in the Sistine Chapel and his paintings for the Cappella Paolina leave the Renaissance far behind, so in the architectural sphere his Laurentian Library at Florence is a startling illustration of what can be done if the antique motifs are retained but deprived of the architectural function which had brought them into being.

Baroque artists steered this process of exploitation *plus* partial, though never total, rejection out of a tortured mannerist phase—characteristic of the 16th century—to a glorious fulfilment which reveals how classical antiquity has produced some of its best results by reaction rather than imitation. The forms which Borromini uses in his Roman churches S. Carlo alle Quattro Fontane or S. Agnese in Agone can nearly all be paralleled, individually, in the ancient world, and yet one could hardly believe, when seeing them, that the classical orders had been linear and horizontal, so dominant now is the oval and the dynamic curve. And yet Borromini himself reminds us that the Romans, too, had been a people who supplanted Greek horizontality by the vault and dome, and indeed that they too had produced a baroque movement: for the lantern of his breath-taking little church S. Ivo alla Sapienza is very closely and deliberately based on the 3rd-century Temple of Venus at Baalbek. In the same way Spanish baroque architects, such as Leonardo de Figueroa at S. Luis at Seville, took up from Bernini and adapted to their own tasks another late Roman 'baroque' motif, the barley-sugar column or *salomōnica*; classical still, technically speaking—it had appeared on Constantine's tabernacle in the old St Peter's—and under a quasi-classical capital, yet how profoundly un-Greek in its dynamic spirality.

But the process of adaptation reaches its superb climax in the 18th-century late-baroque of Balthasar Neumann in the Main valley, and Johann Michael Fischer and Jakob Prandtauer on the Danube. When such church-designers were great architects as well as great decorators—as these men of genius were—the exhilarating rhythms to which they gave expression depended upon the tension between a virile, classically composed structure and the tumultuous decoration which so unclassically overlays it. Whatever the baroque tendencies of Hellenistic sculpture and late Roman architecture, these south German sinuosities (despite the ancient origins of many of their motifs) have moved far away and ahead of any such models. And yet their vehement self-expression was only possible by building upon, and then so excitingly drawing away from, the antique framework. One of many symbols of the process is the broken pediment (already to be seen on the 1st-century Arch of Tiberius at Orange). Pediments were not meant to be broken, but once you have decided to break them, an infinite series of possibilities follows; you can have broken pediments swinging away from each other, as in Pöppelman's Zwinger at Dresden; you can even turn them upside down. But before you can indulge in these stimulating processes, you need the ancient world and its pediments as your starting point.

To the court of France, the process of elaboration, or departure from classicality, seemed to have gone too far, and to have become too emotional; France never went wholly baroque, and just as Le Brun supervised the monumental classicism of Louis XIV, so again, when the 18th century was approaching its last quarter, neo-classicism from the same country began to embark upon its world-wide career. Perhaps it is at its most attractive when it is a little idiosyncratic as in Leningrad, or not too monumental as in Copenhagen or the Hague or Sweden or Virginia. When not at its best, neo-classicism hinted that the heritage of antiquity would, before long, be exhausted; rather as the heritage of antiquity's offshoot of Gothic came to have a defunct look in the nineteenth century. And exhausted, now, the classical idiom is, in its more superficial aspects. Yet exhausted the basic phenomena of classical architecture can never be, for they taught us almost all we know, and for millennia have displayed incredible fertility.

The 'Colonna Santa', preserved in a chapel of St Peter's, was part of the Constantinian Basilica, and was traditionally supposed to have come from the Temple of Solomon in Jerusalem (whence its name, 'salomōnica'). Its sinuous shape, as well as its associations, appealed to the Baroque; Bernini copied it in his great bronze baldachino. In the background of this drawing can be seen the chapel in St Peter's where the column now stands, with the Baroque details of Maderno, including reversed pediments.

The 'Most Subtle Doctor'

To the Romans, building construction was not only an art but a part of government, of which their aqueducts and roads provide formidable evidence. Our debt to Rome in respect of this and other branches of administration is far too manifold and diverse to be covered by any brief generalization. But a very large part of the governmental inheritance may be summed up by the single word, law. Indeed this summing up is often done, but in a somewhat perfunctory manner seeing that law is a technical subject and those who know it are not often the same people who speak or write in more general terms about the ancient world. I would limit myself here to recalling three extraordinary stages in the great history of the transmission of Roman law to modern times. First, in the 6th century Justinian set up, at Constantinople, a commission which produced a *Corpus* of Civil Law *(Digest, Institutes, Novels)* straightening out and bringing up to date all the numerous complications of that Roman legal system which was one of the most massive and permanent achievements of classical antiquity. About the repercussions of this and later Byzantine codes among the Slavs nothing can be said here, but the second great epoch which has to be mentioned is that of Roman law's rediscovery and development—that is to say, the renewal of interest in Justinian's code, amid new circumstances—in 12th-century Italy. In the intervening epochs Rome, Pavia and Ravenna had been centres of legal studies; but at the risk of oversimplification it is with Bologna—prototype with Paris of modern Universities—and with the name of Irnerius, 'a most subtle doctor' who had worked for the German Emperor Henry V and is linked by tradition with the beginnings of Bologna's law school, that the revival of legal science can be associated. And then let us here take for granted the developments and vicissitudes of seven more centuries, and pass to the Code Civil des Français of 1804, called the Code Napoléon in 1807. This blended with customary law, and with the recent laws of the revolution (which themselves claimed inspiration from the Roman Republic), an enormous additional heritage from the laws of ancient Rome, which thus through the new Code exerted perhaps a wider influence than ever before upon the legal institutions and thought of the civilized world; and that influence remains.

Not long before the Code was drawn up, Cicero, who with Virgil has played the greatest part of all in transmitting ancient values, had through Thomas Jefferson infused the American Declaration of Independence with his Natural Law and 'unalienable' rights of man. Cicero, like Tacitus and Thucydides and many others, has throughout the centuries been mobilized by political parties of every conceivable shade of opinion in support of their contradictory views and proposals. The classical world, bequeathing through its incomparably eloquent orators and historians an experience of enormous wealth and variety, has taught us a great deal of our politics. But, at the risk of doing scant justice to various experiments, it must be added that the ancients never fully grasped representative government. Nineteenth-century attempts to see Greece and Rome as the ancestor of our 'democracy', but not equally of the more autocratic systems of modern times, are misguided. Western parliamentary government, it is true, can be traced back (with Teutonic admixtures) to ancient evolutionary processes, but so can almost every sort of authoritarian system including Marxian communism. Or, to put the same point in geographical terms, western Europe's link with the ancient world is no closer than the influence that east Europeans have derived through Byzantium, and then the Muscovite 'Third Rome', and now the modern heirs of Tsarism at the Kremlin.

The Divided Heritage of Christendom

Catholicism and Orthodoxy alike go back, as their Latin and Greek languages show, to the Christianity of the Roman empire. The textbook date of their division is 1054, but for centuries before that the growing division can be traced in the increasing differences imposed by diverging psychology, history and culture; and many of these differences stem from those ancient times in which the Greeks and Romans had never really made friends. The ominous line thus drawn through European Christendom condemned to wishful thinking all medieval attempts to equate Christendom with Europe—even if there were not also many Moslem Europeans, both Turks and Arabs. And this line was the fore-runner of other such demarcations down to the Iron Curtain of our own times. Europe is on both sides of these lines; and so is the heritage of classical antiquity.

Nor does study of this heritage greatly assist to bridge this gap, or for that matter any gap existing between one country and another. However rich our political legacy from the ancient world may be, in international politics it has been for the most part catastrophically inadequate. The Greeks with their aggressive inter-city squabbling, the Romans with their aggressive force-imposed empire—which only briefly under Hadrian's influence showed signs of becoming a commonwealth—provided inadequate schools for their successors the nation-states. Moreover, as the events of the last fifty years have all too clearly shown, these have throughout the centuries shamefully failed to improve upon what they learnt. True, it was through the Graeco-Roman world, and the Roman peace, that Christianity obtained the conditions which enabled it to survive and spread. But Christianity, in international politics, has rarely or never been acted upon.

The Purpose of this Book

The days are past when we can happily set aside the most agreeable elements of this great complex inheritance from Greece and Rome and claim that *these* only are our portion. Our portion is multitudinous and inescapable, good and bad, marvellous and horrible. The purpose of this book is to try to show something of these essential features of the ancient Greeks and Romans who set these intricate and never ending processes in motion.

I am indeed grateful to my fellow-contributors for joining me in this attempt, on a wide front, to describe what happened. There are advantages in having a single author for a book, but that does not mean that there is nothing to be said for multiple authorship. On the contrary, as Stuart Piggott remarked in our predecessor *The Dawn of Civilization*, benefits emerge from this variety, since our evidence for the past yields truths of more than one sort, and needs more than one mind or speciality to interpret it.

Yet the task of these writers has not been an easy one. It has been harder than that of people who wrote about this same subject in Britain even thirty years ago, because the classics have now ceased to be a common background of any social or educational group. 'The fabric of reference and inner recognition on which most of western literature was founded from Dante to Tennyson is receding from our general awareness.... Ours is a culture severed by ignorance or specialization from its moorings in the past.' Yet without the past, and some appreciation of what it has done to us—of where the ingredients in our present life have come from, and how they have come—we can only with difficulty comprehend the meaning of what we do, and what we are

going to do. For without some knowledge of the past we are blindfolded in our efforts to grapple with the future: we can answer the human and intellectual and practical problems that it will pose if we know something of our roots, and so many of those roots lie in the ancient world.

So the need to make the essential values of Greece and Rome more completely and more widely understood is a challenging one. On the whole, it is in America, where the classical languages have been less taught, that this need for reinterpretation has been most fully appreciated. Ezra Pound once said:

> The thought of what America would be like
> If the Classics had a wide circulation
> Troubles my sleep.

Nowadays, they do circulate widely—in translation and description and interpretation. In respect of profundity knowledge of the classics has perhaps declined. Yet this is also an epoch when their essential values are being sought after more passionately, and by more people, than ever before. An intense desire to plumb the secrets of the classical past is abroad; the *Oedipus*, on television, was seen by millions. It is in response to that feeling that the present book has been launched. The subject is without end, and needs to be endlessly relived. For it is eternal, and eternal things, as Gilbert Murray once said, can only be reached and enjoyed by somehow going through the process again; a short-cut or a fast car are not the way to get value from a scenic walk. A book like this is, I hope, not so much a shortcut as an incentive to longer and more comprehensive journeys. For everyone who looks, with any degree of pertinacity, at the ancient world will find that it reveals to him many things not only about the ancient world but, most of all, about the circumstances of his own life, and the men and women who form part of it, and about himself.

Acknowledgements

The editor's task has been made easy and pleasant by the close co-operation of all the authors, who have answered queries, given specialist advice and provided information on the pictures (and often the pictures themselves) with unfailing readiness. To Dr. F. R. Cowell we are especially indebted; his continual help in planning, in research, with the chronologies and with many queries has been invaluable. The final responsibility, however, for the choice of illustrations and for the captions remains with the publishers. The editor wishes to record that it has been a pleasure to work with them.

In collecting the photographs and assembling material for the maps and plans, we have once more relied on the generous help of institutions and individuals all over the world. We should like especially to express our most sincere thanks to the following: The American School of Classical Studies, Athens; the National Archaeological Museum, Athens; the Royal Greek Embassy, London; the Department of Greek and Roman Antiquities, British Museum, London; Dr. J. Dörig, Deutsches Archaeologisches Institut, Athens; Dr. E. Rohde, Dr. Greifenhagen and Dr. N. Kunisch, Staatliche Museen zu Berlin; Herr Lind, Martin von Wagner Museum, Wurzburg; Dr. Gose, Rheinisches Landesmuseum, Trier; Dr. E. Auer, Kunsthistorisches Museum, Vienna; Mrs. J. Switalski, Oriental Institute, University of Chicago; Professor J. L. Caskey, University of Cincinnati, Ohio; Dr. J. de Sola Price, Yale University; M. Georges de Loÿe, Musée Calvet, Avignon; Dr. H. Speier, Musei e Gallerie Pontificie, Vatican; Dr. H. Sichtermann, Deutsches Archaeologisches Institut, Rome; Dr. N. Alfieri, Museo Archeologico, Ferrara; Prof. A. de Franciscis, Soprintendenza alle Antichità di Napoli; Col T. Chiantia, Italian Embassy, London; Mr. R. W. Hamblyn and Mr. H. W. Catling, Ashmolean Museum, Oxford; Mr. A. G. Woodhead, Corpus Christi College, Cambridge; Dr. H. N. Savory, National Museum of Wales; Mr. R. C. Sansome, Somerset County Museum; Mr. R. Merrifield, Guildhall Museum, London; Lady (Olwen) Brogan; Miss G. Farnell; Miss D. Ashcroft; Miss P. Jacobson; Miss N. Lord; and the librarians of the Institute of Archaeology (Miss G. Talbot and Miss Joan du Plat Taylor), the Warburg Institute and the Societies of Roman and Hellenic Studies, London.

II THE TROUBLED BIRTH OF A NEW WORLD

The struggle of the city states

A.R. BURN

'Greece united will be strong and a match for the invader;

but if some of us betray and others stand aside

and the loyal are few,

then there is reason to fear that all Greece may fall'

HERODOTUS, BOOK VII, 157

Strife between the Greeks

was their ruin; Herodotus, writing in the mid-5th century, was to prove a true prophet in the hundred years to follow. The pattern of Greek history was made almost inevitable by her political pattern. The characteristic unit was the *polis*, the autonomous sovereign state consisting of a single town and the land surrounding it, and usually well under 100 square miles. It was a system regarded by the Greeks as the guarantee of their liberties; they contrasted their own freedom with the bondage of those living under an absolute monarchy like Persia. It gave every citizen an urgent sense of responsibility and independence; it made democracy—the rule of *all* the people—possible: but the price paid was division, weakness and civil war. Clearly evident though it had always been to all intelligent Greeks that their crying need was for peace and agreement, they were never able to reconcile themselves to the compromises and adjustments necessary to achieve it.

Local pride, pride in the history, the gods, the heroes of one's own *polis*, pervades Greek literature, and since Greek literature is very largely Athenian literature, it is with the city and story of Athena that we are most familiar—her miraculous birth fully armed from the head of Zeus; her owl, serpent and olive tree; her sacred rock, the Acropolis; her festival, the Panathenaea; and her temple, the Parthenon, shrine of Athene Parthenos, Athena the Virgin. One of the loveliest portrayals of her was discovered only in 1959 at Piraeus (right). It is of bronze, mid-4th century BC. It is symbolic of a whole people's devotion to their patron goddess; symbolic too of the truth that what the Greeks created in the interludes of almost constant warfare, despite the sufferings they inflicted and endured, is indeed the Greek Miracle.

The threat of extinction by the mighty Persian empire spurred the city-states to their one great act of national unity. In 499 the Ionian cities rose in rebellion against the 'tyrants' kept in power by Persia, and received aid from two Greek states, Athens and Eretria in Euboea. Persia was provoked. In 492 an army reached Macedonia but its attendant fleet was wrecked by storms. Two years later, in 490, a fresh expedition was mounted, this time sailing straight across the Aegean, reducing the islands as it went, and landing first at Eretria, which was plundered and burnt, and then on the coast of Attica north of Athens at Marathon.

The Persians disembarked at the northern end of the bay (furthest in the photograph). The Athenians probably arrived along the coast from the opposite direction and took up their position in the southern valley (thick white block) where they were joined by a contingent from Plataea. Here they waited for three days, while the generals debated the situation. Eventually the advice of Miltiades to offer battle was taken.

Miltiades' aim was not to push the enemy back into the plain (where their numbers would tell) but to restrict them further by drawing them forward between the hills. He accordingly made the Greek centre relatively weak and the wings strong. The Persians, who had their best troops in the middle, broke through the centre but were caught by the Greek wings which now converged from behind. The Persian wings (consisting of non-Persian conscripts) fled back to the ships, but those in the centre were surrounded and massacred. In all the Persians lost 6,400 men, the Athenians 192. The bodies were cremated and a mound (arrowed) raised over their ashes.

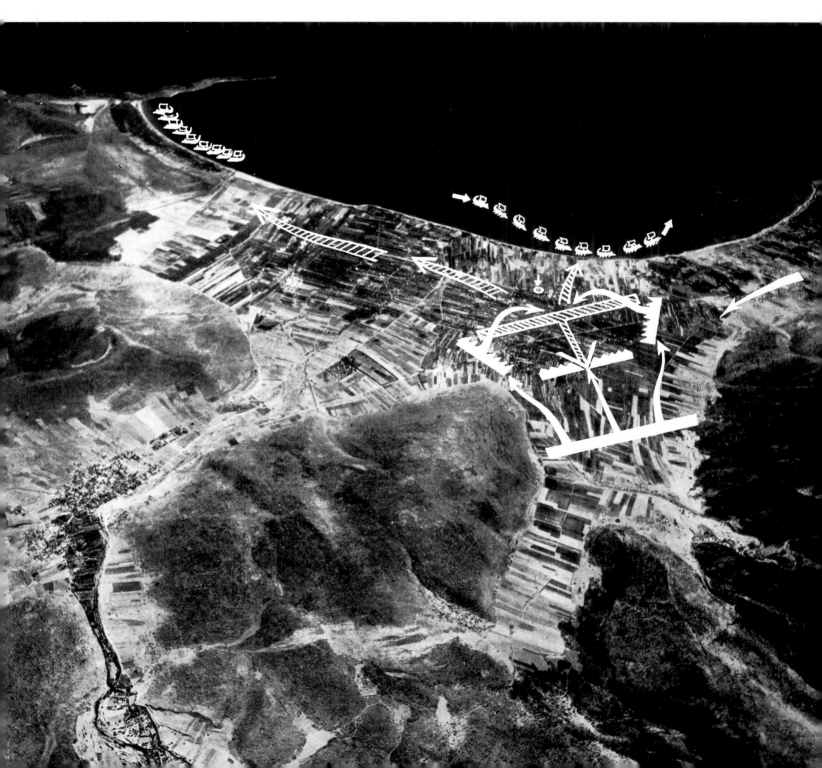

Greece had been saved at Marathon, but it was a respite only. In 480 BC, under Darius' son Xerxes, a new expedition was launched. Xerxes led his huge army across the Dardanelles by a bridge of boats and then round the northern coast of the Aegean. At Thermopylae they were met by a Greek force under King Leonidas of Sparta (*right*), who held the narrow pass between the mountains and the sea for three days. Leonidas' heroic stand against overwhelming odds has passed into legend. Dismissing most of his army he remained with 300 Spartans, who fought to the last man, and 1100 Boeotians.

Miltiades dedicated this helmet (*below*), inscribed with his name, to Zeus after Marathon.

The sea-battle of Salamis, a few weeks after Thermopylae, was one of the most decisive in the history of the world. Technically the navy was commanded by a Spartan admiral, but the moving spirit was Themistocles, the Athenian, who not only planned to fight in the straits but also succeeded in getting the agreement of the allies.

The three crucial phases before the fighting actually started are shown in the reconstruction *above*.

Phase 1: during the night the Greek ships lay in three beaches facing east. Their disposition is not certainly known, but it has been thought probable that in the northernmost bay (furthest away) were the Corinthians and part of the Athenians; in the next, partly hidden by the island of St George, was the main body of the Greek force, Athenian and Peloponnesian; and in the southern-

most bay, next to the town of Salamis, about 40 or 50 ships from
Aegina and Megara.

Phase 2: at dawn the Persian fleet (foreground) sailed confidently straight up the channel into the narrows. The Greeks
came out to meet them from the northern and central beaches and
formed into line behind the island of St George. Simultaneously,
the Aeginetans emerged from the southern bay ready to strike at

the Persian left flank. The Corinthians, at the extreme north, went
through a manoeuvre to make the enemy think they were running
away. They sailed *north*, to wheel round and return when the
Persians had committed themselves in the narrows.

Phase 3: the Persians crowded into the narrows, some 400 ships
in a strait a mile wide, and the Greeks moved their fleet of 300 to
contain them.

The bitter tragedy of the Peloponnesian War threw away all the fruits of victory. The causes of this long thirty-year struggle between Athens (mercantile, expansionist, intellectually brilliant but increasingly imperialist) and Sparta (conservative, militarist, anti-democratic, skilfully uniting the opposition that Athenian policy was provoking) were analysed by the great historian Thucydides, who also noted with cold objectivity the deterioration in political morality and the terrifying spread of brutality that marked its course. Part of the responsibility rests with Pericles (*left*), who stiffened Athenian determination to resort to war.

The struggle spread to the Greek cities in Sicily in 415 BC. The Athenians launched a disastrous expedition against Syracuse, which was friendly to Sparta. The siege failed; the Athenians, after enduring incredible hardships, were utterly defeated and either massacred or enslaved, the Syracusans celebrating their triumph with an issue of coinage (*right*) showing Victory crowning a charioteer, with captured Athenian armour beneath.

The cruel suffering of the fighting is not made explicit in Athenian art. Even in the funeral monuments to those who fell in the war, which often show the dead man triumphing over an enemy, both victor and vanquished are placed on a universal plane (armour, for instance, is not shown realistically; the figures are like gods or heroes). The monument *below* is from early in the war; the other (*below right*) extols Dexileos, killed at Corinth in 394 BC.

The tide of victory ebbed and flowed. One Athenian success, the capture of 120 Spartans at Sphacteria (425 BC), may be celebrated by the famous Nike of Paeonius (*right*). But Athens failed to use her advantage and within months lost 1000 men killed in Boeotia. The war dragged on for another twenty years. It was not until 404, when the Spartans succeeded in destroying the beached Athenian fleet, that she was finally beaten.

The battles which finally broke the Persian power were fought at the Issus and at Gaugamela on the northern Tigris in 333 BC. They are celebrated in the famous mosiac from Pompeii, a Roman copy of a Greek painting, from which this detail is taken. Alexander, his eyes avid for victory, spurs his horse forward; Darius, panic-stricken, takes the fatal decision to flee; a great dynasty is destroyed, and the way is open for the expansion of Greek civilization to the edge of the known world.

The struggle of the city states

A. R. BURN

THE LEGACY OF GREECE is the legacy of her intellectual and artistic achievements, described in the following chapters. Here our task is to present the brilliant but tempestuous world of the city states—the political, social and economic background which stimulated and at times impeded those achievements—and to introduce the chief cities, the leading characters, as it were, in the tragic drama of Greek triumph and failure.

An End and a Beginning

First, then, to recapitulate: the fall of the Mycenaean palaces, like the collapse of Roman government in the west later, was followed by a 'dark age'. The contact with the Levant, which enables us to date the phases of Mycenaean civilization, is broken after 1200 BC; the burned palaces lay in ruins and deserted, some of them, as at Pylos, unto this day; and while invaders or survivors may have built their huts nearby, the remains of their much poorer settlements have in many areas not yet been discovered.

But it would be rash to say, as some have believed, that whole areas, previously settled, were left uninhabited. Absence of evidence (so far) is not evidence of absence. On the positive side, what can be seen is that, probably within a century, and probably first at Athens, which, with her strong acropolis and late Mycenaean covered way to a water-supply, had outridden the storm, there are clear signs of returning social vitality. The tokens of this are the pottery decorated in the style known as Protogeometric; pottery surviving as usual, even if in fragments, where textiles have perished and metal-work has, for the most part, been melted down; pottery decorated in a strong, simple style, not far removed from peasant art; a style which has been hailed as the first truly Hellenic art. It is the art of a still poor, but intelligent and vigorous population, which had survived the great raids and had been emancipated by them, not without much destruction and misery, from the rule of the palace-dwellers and from the prestige of their over-ripe Mycenaean art.

The Protogeometric and the many local schools of mature Geometric art which evolved from it had, altogether, a career of nearly four centuries. The phases, in the absence of writing (an art which had been lost in the great wreck) and of contact with the still literate east, are difficult to date; but from its increase in quantity in the later phases, we can trace the slow process of consolidation. Protogeometric pottery found at old Smyrna must have been brought by settlers—the first Greeks to cross the Aegean and found the mainland settlements which, with the island of Lesbos, became known as Aeolis. Ionia, with Chios and Samos, came a little later. Asian Dōris included the peninsular cities of Cnidus and Halicarnassus, with Rhodes and Cos, islands, which, unlike the others, are represented as already Greek in Homer's Catalogue of the Mycenaean fleet at Troy. The Cyclades also, unmentioned in Homer's Catalogue, were Greek in time to have their own schools of Geometric art; and their people in historic times spoke dialects akin to those of Ionia and of Attica and Euboea, from which many of the colonists of Ionia were believed to have come.

South of these, stretching from the kingdoms of Argos, Sparta and Messenia in the Peloponnese, in a wide arc through Crete and the southernmost islands to the Asian Dōris, lay the Dorian states,

founded according to tradition by the north-Greek invaders who had sacked Pylos and Mycenae; and the tradition appears to be sound. Throughout this area the populations are found divided into the same three Doric 'tribes' (sometimes together with others, founded to include pre-Dorian survivors). They spoke varieties of a common Doric dialect, more archaic than the Ionic, and marked, for instance, by the broad ā sound (as in *father*), which in Ionic changed to e (French è or ê). And in the central Peloponnese, in highland Arcadia by-passed by the invaders, there survived a still more archaic and quite different Greek, whose only near relative in historic times was the dialect of Cyprus. We may infer that throughout this area there had once been spoken a Greek ancestral to Arcadian and Cypriote, the language, as Ventris thought, of the Mycenaean world; a speech surviving only in Arcadia, cut off from the sea by the Dorian invaders, and in distant Cyprus, which the invasion did not reach. A further inference is that the invasion or invasions were not the work of mere savages in search of pasture, but of organized warbands which made deliberately for the south in search of palaces to plunder.

This point is of some importance. The Greeks at the dawn of their recorded history, in the 8th century, were not in any strict sense primitive. All, even the Dorian late-comers, had been to some extent affected by the Bronze-Age civilization; even they had been, in the course of their migrations to new homes, to some extent *detribalized*. It may not have been for anyone's immediate good; but it helps to account for the readiness with which, in the following centuries and under the stimulus of new economic conditions, they adopted and invented new ways. Also the Bronze Age, though the traditions of the Greeks show that they remembered little about its civilization, had left a legacy; a legacy of *techniques*. Writing and palace art had perished, but in the mundane matters of mixed farming, building, carpentry and boat-building, spinning and weaving, metallurgy and the potters' craft, the Greeks of the Geometric period did not begin again where Minoan Crete had begun, but where Mycenae left off.

The life of a farmer about 750–550 BC is well-known through the writings of Hesiod and through illustrations on early Attic vases. Here the farmer drives forward his ox pulling a wooden plough, while his wife scatters seed in the furrow.

The 'Works and Days' of a Greek Farmer

Daily life at the dawn of history in Greece, about 700, is known to us especially from the poem of Hesiod called the *Works and Days*. Starting as a kind of verse letter of expostulation to his unsatisfactory brother, who had quarrelled with him about the division of their inheritance, this poem branches out into a highly interesting exposition of sound mixed farming, on a subsistence basis but with disposal of surpluses by barter, sometimes involving a boat voyage. Hesiod is not a poor man; he has a draught ox, a cart and an iron-shod plough, and can employ a hired man seasonally; but he is definitely of the people, and grumbles about the 'gift-devouring kings' (local chieftains), to whom his brother had resorted, as to a court, for the satisfaction of his claims. Most interesting is the fact that he is not afraid to grumble so, and that his poem survived. His culture includes some astronomical lore, important for getting farm operations started in good time, but he attaches equal importance to observing lucky and unlucky days of the month; he issues warnings against wasting time, against cutting one's nails on a holy-day (an early appearance of the world-wide superstition about nail-parings), and against letting a boy sit on a tombstone, lest it cause sterility. But he is no 'primitive peasant'. His father was not even a native of Boeotia, where he

The potter's craft did not entirely die out during the Dark Age, though much of the artistry of Mycenaean work was lost. This vase-painting of the early 5th century BC shows a potter at his wheel adding handles to a crater-like vessel.

settled, but a 'retro-migrant' from Cyme in the Asian Aeolis, where he had found seafaring an unsatisfactory career, and returned to the old country to take up a farm (perhaps on uncleared and unoccupied land) in a valley-head, alternately draughty and sun-baked, under Mount Helicon. Hesiod heartily approves of competition between craftsmen (potter and potter, bard and bard), and a reward that he holds out for good farming is 'that you may buy another man's farm, and not he yours'. Nothing could be less primitive than this fact, that in Hesiod's world land could be freely bought and sold.

Hesiod gives a unique glimpse of the life of a working farmer in the early Iron Age; but the tone of society was set by local aristocracies, those chieftains whom he disliked and mistrusted: members of the oldest-established families, who held with family tenacity the best land in each of the fertile but limited plains between the Greek mountains. These were the people who could best afford hired men and slaves, often originally prisoners of war, to do the heavy work, and female slaves for housework, including the endless spinning and weaving; or to buy purple cloth or trinkets from Phoenician traders. They could afford the expensive bronze armour, and a horse, or in the earliest days a chariot, to carry them swiftly and untired over the plain to repel a border raid. Their houses were inside the compact, walled 'city' which grew up in a handy position near every good piece of plain-land; so their wealth, unlike the possessions of outlying farmers, was not exposed to plunder. They could best afford time to listen to travelling bards with tales of the ancient heroes, or to pedlars' or the same bards' accounts of their journeys and of foreign parts; or to travel themselves to festivals, at Delphi in central Greece or Olympia in the Peloponnese, or to Apollo's sacred islet of Delos, a great centre of the Ionian world, where there were athletic sports and the most elaborate bardic recitations; among them, especially at Delos, those from the work of the great Ionian, Homer.

Most famous of all such festivals was the four-yearly athletic meeting at Olympia. Here, in the fertile and well-watered western lowland called by Athenians Hollow Elis, but in the local dialect *Wālis*, the Vale, invaders, not Doric but akin to the Dorians, had established a sanctuary of the Father-God, whom their ancestors in Thessaly had associated with Mount Olympus. There had already been there a sanctuary of the Mother-Goddess of the older folk, who, as Hera, the wife of Zeus, kept her place and temple; and perhaps already in the Bronze Age she had been worshipped by girls with competition in a foot-race; for the length of the course for the girls' race, which still existed, much shrunken in glory, in historic times, was exactly one side of the sacred Grove, the *Altis*. Here—it is not clear why especially here—athletes assembled from all the western Peloponnese; presently also from Sparta and the new western colonies; then from all the Greek world. Other events were added: boxing, wrestling, long-jump, discus, javelin, longer running, a race in armour.

To be an Olympic victor was the highest glory known to early historic Greek society; so much so as to call forth from intellectuals some acid remarks about athleticism. And because the four-yearly meeting was an 'international' event, it was found more convenient than (say) the lists of annual magistrates of even the

most important cities as a means of dating historic events. Thucydides, in the 5th century, is the first historian known to us to do this. In his time a learned man of Elis, named Hippias, studied the inscriptions on victory monuments and other records of Olympia, set the names in what he regarded as a probable order, and found that there were enough, allowing one foot-race every four years, to extend back to 776 BC, in terms of our era. This has ever since been reckoned as marking the beginning of the Greek historic era; though whether 'historic' is strictly the right word is another question.

'Phoenician Marks': The Birth of the Greek Alphabet

Homer's poetry is treated elsewhere; but it may here be remarked that the preservation (not the invention) of his great artistic epics may have been rendered possible by the recent introduction of the 'Phoenician marks', as Greeks called them, that is the letters of our alphabet, with their Semitic names (alpha = *aleph*, 'ox', originally an ox-head, thus ⌒; it was the Greeks, who, knowing nothing of the meaning, thought it would look much better 'standing up'; beta = the familiar *beth* of Bethel, Bethlehem, meaning 'house', and in the east was originally written something like ⌂). The 24 letters, some of them switched by the Greeks from representing unneeded Semitic sounds to provide the chief Greek vowel-sounds, represented the best of several simplified writing systems recently developed in the commercial world of the Levant, in the effort to produce, for business men, something better than the old syllabaries, which required the services of a professional scribe. Another, much inferior, was the 33-letter syllabary of Cyprus, formed by selecting (quite arbitrarily) from the 200-odd signs of Minoan Linear B. That Greeks became aware of a need for writing was a sign that communications were becoming more important again, beyond the limits of the parish or the home glen; but in Greece they were used not only for business but for preserving poetry.

The earliest specimens of Greek alphabetic writing in the new script that we have belong probably to the lifetime of Hesiod, and are on fragments of Geometric painted pottery, found near Athens. That is why the prehistoric period in Greece ends at this point.

The cities prospered; they tamed local hillmen; they formed local leagues, as in Boeotia, Phocis and Ionia, or the more powerful established their supremacy over lesser settlements, as did Argos and Sparta; and as security increased, in most places the rich families, the *aristoi* or Best People as they called themselves,

The earliest examples of Greek script are found on fragments of Geometric pottery. This jug, from the end of the 8th century BC, was (no doubt with its contents) a prize in a dancing contest. The inscription reads 'He whose performance is best among all the dancers shall have me'.

reduced the powers of the city king who had been essential as a war-leader in the bad times, and took to directing the affairs of the city through annually elected Regents or Presidents. A 'king' sometimes himself (as at Athens) annually appointed, often continued to supervise the chief sacrifices; it was safest to give the gods what they were accustomed to. Sometimes the right to elect and to be elected was confined to a clan descended from the old kings; sometimes, as at Cyme, it was soon extended to every man who could afford armour and a war-horse. Dandified and sophisticated, the *aristoi* everywhere greatly despised the outlying farmers and hill shepherds, with their skin coats and dirty feet, who bore themselves meekly when they had occasion to come into town. The very idea that such people might have political rights lay still in the future.

The Merchant Colonists Look West

By about 750 BC, two factors were preparing the revolution which was to transform the Greek world. First, in many regions the available, cultivable land was filling up; the more so since the great families engrossed what the poor resentfully considered an unfair share of it. The tradition never died among the Greek poor that in the 'good old days' some founder-king had divided the city's land fairly, and that, since the division had become very unequal, a *new division* was due. The phrase was to become a revolutionary slogan. To avert the reality became the great political object of aristocratic governments. The only other alternatives for the poor, as they multiplied, were greater poverty, or infanticide, which Greek mothers resisted as passionately as any others would, or conquering a neighbour's land, as Sparta before 700 conquered the lower-lying plain of Messenia; an event which was to be fateful for the whole of classical Greek history.

A way out (literally) seems to have been revealed by merchants; not Hesiodic farmer-traders, but long-distance seafarers, who made a living out of the fact that, in a world still largely bronze-using, not only Greece but the great kingdoms of the east had an insatiable desire for the rare metal, tin. Midas, King of Phrygia, a great figure (Midas of the golden touch, round whose name folk-tales cluster), fought the Assyrians on his eastern frontier, went into alliance with Agamemnon, King of Cyme and dedicated a throne at Delphi; and a merchant of Cyme, Midacritus ('Approved of Midas') was said first to have brought tin from a 'Tin Island' somewhere in the unknown west. It looks like a deliberate effort to establish a metal-trade from Asia Minor, in competition with the Phoenicians, who had already reached Spain along the coast of North Africa. This is the context of the epoch-making event, the foundation of the first Greek colony in the west (archaeology confirms a date soon after 750 BC), by Cyme together with Chalcis, the 'bronze-town' in Euboea, famous for its metal-work; it too was called Cyme (in Greek, Kume), a name more famous in its Latin dress, the Cumae of Virgil.

Cumae, planted far afield on the Bay of Naples, looks like a trading outpost, like its Phoenician contemporary, Carthage ('New Town') in Tunisia; but it was soon followed by a whole series of new ventures, which went less far and seized the best coastal land (not always the best harbours) from weak native populations in eastern Sicily and south Italy. Chalcis, probably recruiting land-hungry men also from other cities, such as Naxos, founded a new Naxos, near Taormina, the first Greek town in Sicily, and a base for the conquest of more roomy sites further south (Catana, Leontini); she also founded Rhegium (Reggio-Calabria), and reduced to order an unofficial pirate settlement of Greeks on the Straits, now Messina.

Corinth, already with an eye for harbours, founded Syracuse and colonized Corkyra (Corfu island), a useful half-way house. The Achaeans of the northern Peloponnese, who were not traders but lacked land at home, got the best agricultural sites of all, at Sybaris, Croton and Metaponto in south Italy; Sparta, 'reconstructing' after the conquest of Messenia, planted out 'war-babies' and other dissatisfied elements at Taras (Taranto); Rhodians and Cretans, already accustomed to trade with the Levant, but unable to colonize there in face of the Assyrian Empire, came to Gela on the south coast of Sicily. All this is said to have been done between 735 and 690 BC (the real dates are perhaps a little later).

A Greek merchant ship of about 540 BC, from a black-figure cup. It was on ships like these that the great colonizing movements of the 7th and 6th centuries depended; they were higher in the water than warships, with larger sails but slower and more difficult to manoeuvre.

There was a long pause before the expansion to western Sicily. Then Megara, a small colony near Syracuse—founded when its mother-city, old Megara, was a vassal of Corinth—sent out men to Selinus (Selinunte), after 630, and Gela to Acragas (Agrigento of the splendid temples), half-way to Selinus, about 580 BC. By this time also the Asian Greek Ionians of Phocaea, a neighbour of Aeolic Cyme, which seems to replace Cyme in the western trade (we do not know why), were colonizing from the Riviera (Nice, Antibes, Monaco) to Spain; Massalia (Marseille), their chief success, was only the greatest among many colonies; and their early walls at Ampurias (Emporiae, 'the Trade-posts'), about 520, are the westernmost considerable remains surviving of any Greek city.

South Italy became known as Greater Greece, Magna Graecia. In the west, thousands of Greeks enjoyed for the first time the sense that there was land enough and to spare. On the miniature scale of the Greek world, it was to the old country as America to Europe. Its cities grew larger and richer than any in classical Greece—except Athens in her prime—and made their own contributions to art, literature, philosophy, medicine and engineering.

Colonization in other areas was important, but all of it together not so important as the west. Cyrene, founded by the Dorian island of Thera (Santorin), and later reinforced from all over the Aegean, alone could compare with such cities as Sybaris. Founded a few miles inland, it exported corn and the medicinal herb silphium (now extinct), founded daughter-cities westward to Euhespericae (Benghazi), and long preserved the hereditary monarchy (c. 630–450 BC).

The Rich Eastern Seaboard

Colonization in the north Aegean began later than in the west, surprisingly at first sight; but the large, blond Thracians were a different proposition, as opponents, from the western Sicels. Only perhaps, when Corinth began to monopolize trade with Sicily, did Chalcis and Eretria in Euboea turn to the three-pronged peninsula, later known as Chalcidice, and Megara, now independent of Corinth and on bad terms with her, to the Sea of Marmara. The coast of the Troad and some sites in the Chersonese (Gallipoli Peninsula) had already been occupied by a coastwise spread of settlements from Lesbos and continental Aeolis; Mytilene, largest of the five cities of Lesbos, kept those in the Troad dependent when she could. Megara looked further, and founded two famous cities astride the Bosphorus, Chalcedon and, in 657 or later, Byzantium.

Ionian traders had already visited the Black Sea coasts; but the great outpouring of colonists thither seems to have begun only after events in Asia Minor had cut off the cities there from the hope of expanding by land. The Phrygian kingdom was destroyed, about 676, by migrating barbarians, the Cimmerians, driven south by the coming of the horse-archer Scythians, like Goths before the Huns; and its western successor-state, Lydia with its capital at Sardis only a day's ride from the sea, first drove out the Cimmerians and then pressed Ionia hard, destroying Smyrna (about 600 BC) and attacking Miletus at the mouth of the Maeander valley. However Gyges (c. 678–648), founder of the Lydian military dynasty, while he may have cut short Miletus' territory at home, allowed her to colonize Abydus, on the narrows of the Dardanelles, opposite Sestus; and thereafter Miletus (with recruits, we may guess, from other cities) directed a remarkable colonizing enterprise; she was said to have founded seventy cities in the Black Sea and its approaches. Among the most important were Sinope, probably c. 630, though some Greek computations (which also grossly antedated Cyrene) made it much earlier; Trapezus (Trebizond), a daughter-colony of Sinope; Olbia ('Prosperity'), not far from modern Odessa in the Ukraine. Megara also took part in this movement, with several colonies; her largest was Heraclea in Bithynia, which included many settlers from Boeotia.

These Black Sea and northern colonies were of enormous importance to classical Greece, as sources of foodstuffs and raw materials (grain, fish, timber, leather) and of slaves; but in culture, unlike those of the West, they seem to have remained 'colonial'; in literature and art they followed the mother country; and when they produced famous intellectuals, such as Aristotle from Chalcidice, or Diogenes (of the Tub) from Sinope, they not only went to study in the old country, but tended to stay there.

In the Levant, Woolley's excavations at Al-Mina have shown that a Greek trading colony was established before 700 on the coast of north Syria; its name was probably Posidium. But, like Greek ventures into Cilicia, it was unable to make good its hold permanently against Assyrian and Phoenician hostility. The easternmost typical Greek colony here (not counting the Mycenaean foundations in Cyprus) was Rhodian Phaselis in Lycia. But the Levant trade (Greek metals, wine, pottery and other manufactures against spices, purple, oriental metalwork, ivory and apes and engraved ostrich-eggs—peacocks only later) remained important, despite intermittent warfare. Its impact on the newly expanding culture of Greece was tremendous, as may be seen in the orientalizing movement in Greek art.

Particularly stimulating to Greek intelligence was the contact with Egypt, where thousands of Greeks went, 'both to trade', says Herodotus 'and to see the country', and many of them to serve in the armies of the Twenty-Sixth Dynasty. Some of them carved their names on a leg of one of Rameses II's colossi at Abu Simbel. The extraordinary character of the country, 'gift of the Nile' (Herodotus again) stimulated geological speculations; its wholly alien culture opened Greek eyes to the fact that customs were not necessarily as they were at home; its vast antiquity opened new vistas of time. These successful foreigners were not popular in Egypt, and presently there was an anti-foreign movement; but its leader Amasis, who reigned as Pharaoh 569–529 BC, permitted the Greeks to continue trading through one port, Naucratis ('Sea-Power'), seized as a fort by Miletus long before. Here Greeks from many cities collaborated in the administration of the city and its temples; it was a unique 'treaty-port', presenting analogies to the Shanghai of recent times.

The Age of Revolution

In the transition from 'medieval' or Hesiodic to 'modern' or classical Greece, the period from about 660 to 500 BC is an age of renaissance and revolution. Traders in metal and valuable goods, we saw, had probably pioneered where colonists followed; but colonization itself gave rise to a far more massive trade. Cities had colonized because their peasants needed land on which to grow food; now, the new western colonies, with their good land, could produce a surplus, while on the other hand they wanted the luxury goods, such as the best pottery, metal-work and textiles, which were in short supply under 'frontier' conditions. Few new colonies were planted after about 500, partly because the best sites were occupied, and because in the west the Phoenicians, led by Carthage, went into alliance with native peoples to hold back the Greeks; but also because it was now possible to import food in exchange for manufactures (also oil and wine to the Black Sea), instead of exporting men.

The aristocracies had organized the great colonizing movements, because the best way of keeping their land at home was to provide for the land-hungry abroad; but they were less successful in meeting a new challenge, that of the new trading and manufacturing classes and of peasants, grown more prosperous, so that many of them rose into the 'armoured' class. These new middle classes were increasingly unwilling to submit to the direction and the arrogance of the old, closed oligarchies.

The new age is an age of individualism. Art, in the new mood of confidence, bursts the bonds of Geometric convention, and artists begin to sign their works; it is an age of personal poetry, personal religion, original thinking (the first philosophers), and, in most of the trading cities (not in areas which, like Thessaly and Arcadia, remained agricultural), of personal government.

The great characters of the new age often belonged to the unprivileged classes, or stood near the aristocracy but were not of it. Archilochus of Paros, the first great name in the new poetry, was the son of a noble who had led the colony to Thasos—but by a slave-woman; a man with a chip on his shoulder. Cypselus of Corinth, who overthrew the aristocracy there, came of the ruling and formerly royal clan through his mother; but she, because she was lame, had found no husband within the clan and had been married off to a non-Dorian farmer. Cypselus rose in the army, and overthrew the government (657, traditionally), a few years after it had failed in an attempt to assert overlordship over the colony at Corfu.

Orthagoras of Sicyon, Corinth's neighbour, who about the same time founded a dynasty that lasted 100 years, is said to have been the son of a cook. His descendant Cleisthenes raised the non-Dorian population, organized in a tribe called the Coast-men, to a status equal or superior to the Dorians, and re-named their tribe 'Rulers'. Such revolutionary despots were called 'tyrants', a word not originally hostile; it is not Greek, nor apparently, as used to be thought, Lydian; but *serens*, the biblical name of the lords of the Philistines (who had come from the Aegean or from the nearby Asian coast in the great migrations of about 1200) may perhaps show a common origin.

Corinth, whose fine 'proto-Corinthian' pottery at this time dominated if it did not monopolize the western markets, is the best-known city of this age. Cypselus ruled it for thirty years, popular except with those whom he had overthrown; his son Periander for forty-four—but by now the 'honeymoon period' was over, and he had to surround himself with guards. He subdued Corfu, and founded other colonies on the north-west coasts of Greece, which, exceptionally among Greek colonies, always remained dependent on the mother-city; and he patronized the Lesbian poet Arion. Money—a Lydian invention, first brought into Europe by the trading island of Aegina about 625 BC (not earlier, as used to be thought)—was first struck at Corinth in his time. But his later years were darkened by family quarrels; his sons died before him—one in a new colony at Potidaea in Chalcidice, one in a chariot-accident, one murdered at Corfu—and his successor, a nephew Psammetichus (named, it is interesting to see, after a pharaoh of Egypt) was overthrown after three years, traditionally in 581 (the real dates for the dynasty may be as much as 30 years later). Corinth became a *bourgeois* republic; but, as membership of the governing class seems to have been open to anyone with a moderate property qualification, it was a very different republic from that ruled exclusively by the old royal Bacchiad clan.

No other tyrannies were as durable as those of Corinth and Sicyon. At Megara, Corinth's other neighbour, Theagenes, who had led the peasants in rebellion, was himself driven out before he died, and the city's strength was sapped by bitter and prolonged class-struggles (the background to the poetry of Theognis). Something of the same kind happened at Miletus, and at other cities of which less is known. To the question, what was to be done if the Greek states were not thus to ruin themselves, two opposite answers were given by the two cities that were to dominate the classical period, Sparta and Athens.

The Grim Community of Sparta

Sparta, to judge by her archaeology, was in the 7th century an opulent, aristocratic state, her nobles grown rich on the surplus extracted from serfs, the Helots, in Laconia, and from the farmers of Messenia, reduced to Helot status. But attempts to expand further led to defeat by Argos; and late in the century the Spartans found themselves fighting for their lives against a desperate Messenian rebellion with support from Arcadia (Tyrtaeus' war).

The name of Sparta was proverbial even in ancient Greece for austerity, discipline and prowess in war. Few Spartan works of art have come down to us, but one of them is this small bronze of a soldier wrapped in his cloak and wearing a Corinthian helmet. It dates from about 490 BC, the year of Marathon, ten years before Thermopylae.

It was after this that Sparta became 'Spartan', bringing back into full vigour and further elaborating the 'laws of Lycurgus' (a mythical figure) including archaic customs, such as the rest of Greece was discarding or had discarded. That these customs now resuscitated were part of the old Dorian tribal heritage is suggested by the fact that the Dorian nobles of Crete, the better to control their own serfs, the *Mnoïtes* (Minoans?) had taken similar steps rather earlier. This gave rise to a theory, mentioned by Herodotus, that Lycurgus introduced his laws from Crete. In both areas, the laws included restrictions on individualism and family life; the men, for instance, took their meals in military messes. The sequel, in both areas, was that local art, after showing early promise, wilted and died; nor did either Sparta or Crete make any contribution to Greek thought or literature. In both, society had been 'frozen' in an archaic form, in the interests of military efficiency and the maintenance of privilege.

Peculiar to Sparta was the severe military and athletic training of the boys, who were taken from their mothers at the age of seven and brought up in 'packs', each under a selected young man for whom the boys 'fagged', the whole being under the direction of a respected older citizen. They plucked their bedding of reeds from the River Eurotas; they had no extra clothes for winter, and food was of the plainest, a kind of wheat porridge; they were encouraged to supplement it by stealing from the farms, and punished if caught, being held to deserve it for bad scouting. Any weakly babies, who looked unlikely to survive this treatment, were not brought up at all; they were put out to die on mount Taygetus. Men continued to live a 'Spartan' life, in their messes; failure to be elected to a mess was social and political death. They passed their time in military training, hunting and supervising the helots on their farms, visiting their wives in the log-cabins that were their sole houses, only by stealth. Sparta never coined money, keeping for currency the prehistoric system of iron currency-bars, too cumbersome for anyone to accumulate. Trade and manufacture were left to the 'dwellers-around', the free but non-Spartiate men of other villages and townships in the plain and on the coasts of Laconia. Girls also underwent an athletic training, intended to fit them to be the mothers of warriors.

The government of this grim community was a limited monarchy: limited, first by the curious fact that Sparta from the first had two royal families, which were usually in rivalry; secondly, by a council of twenty-eight aristocrats, elected when over sixty, for life (some of them therefore always senile); and thirdly, and more effectively, by the five Ephors (Overseers), elected annually by and from among the whole body of some 8000 male Spartiates. Originally these represented the Spartan people's safeguard against despotism; but as time passed, they acquired more and more power, until they were in a position to call kings to account for misconduct and even to exile or depose them. The kings' chief sphere of activity was in the command of the army (only one at a time, after a serious quarrel between two kings in the field, in 507), and in foreign affairs, in which they often showed, it must be said, wider views and more generosity than were characteristic of the Spartan assembly and ephors.

The Lycurgan system gave Sparta a professional army (the only one in Greece), which could be reinforced with useful though non-professional forces of the 'dwellers-around'. With it, though still, fortunately for herself, unable to conquer Arcadia and saddle herself with still more helots, Sparta humbled her old rival, Argos, and organized the rest of the Peloponnese—including Arcadia, Elis in the west, Corinth, Megara, Sicyon and the smaller neighbours of Argos—into a League of allies, pledged to follow Sparta in foreign policy. The League was an element of stability in Greece, and was to do good service against the great danger that soon threatened from the east; but it was a stability of conservatism and reaction. The whole Peloponnese contributed relatively little to the constructive classical Greek achievement. This achievement was, in many of its greatest triumphs, the work of Athens.

Athens: the Struggle for Democracy

Athens' history in the 7th century is almost a blank; but this does not mean that she was a negligible quantity. Her art—her Geometric pottery and, later, her first monumental sculpture—was already the best in all Greece. The fact was simply that she did not colonize and had no revolution. With 1000 square miles of territory, much more of a 'country' than that of most Greek states, her population had not yet reached saturation-point.

But that point was reached about the end of the century, and with the coming of coined money and the facilitation thereby of usury and debt, there was, here too, a formidable social crisis. More and more of the poorer farmers fell into debt to the rich nobles; and unpaid debt meant that, in the last resort, not only the debtor's land but his body and those of his family belonged to the creditor. His usual fate, rather than to be kept as a resentful servant, was to be sold oversea, e. g. to the slave-economy of Aegina, a fate from which even Sparta's helots were exempt. There was bitter discontent, and while the rich, with the best arms, could probably have crushed any revolt, they could also see that the elimination of the middling peasantry, or their depression into the ranks of those who could not afford armour, weakened the whole state.

In these circumstances the Athenian nobles showed more wisdom than those of most states. They agreed to the election of Solon, a noble of royal descent but modest wealth, who had seen the world abroad as a merchant, and whose outspoken political verses had made him *persona grata* to the poor, as head of state in the year 594 or 592 BC, with dictatorial powers; and all Athens swore to obey whatever measures he should introduce. Solon then proceeded to cancel all debts outstanding; to lay down that no man should ever again be enslaved for debt; and to buy back with public funds all those enslaved abroad who could be traced. He also forbade the export of corn, thus keeping at home the grain that might otherwise have commanded a higher price in Chalcis or Aegina, and lowering the home price.

Next, Solon drastically reformed the constitution. He laid down that all free men, even the landless, should be admitted to the Assembly (not, as in some states, only those who could afford armour), and that the nine annual Archons (chief Archon or Regent, 'King' for religious affairs, War-chief and six junior judicial archons), though they still had to belong to the equestrian class, should be elected by that Assembly; further, that after their year they should be accountable to the Assembly; and that only if the account was accepted should they pass for life into the august council of ex-archons, which meeting on (or perhaps rather, under) the Rock of Ares, the war-god, was called the Council of Areopagus. Further, the Assembly could also function as a People's Court, to hear complaints against or on behalf of individuals; and Solon provided that 'anyone who wished' might take up the case of anyone wronged; a safeguard of the rights of the poor and inarticulate, and especially of the orphan and widow.

If, however, all the preliminary discussion of public affairs and the decision as to what business should be laid before the Assembly and how, and when, continued to be the business of the 'best people', that is to say of the Areopagus, it would usually be possible for the 'best people' to get their way in the Assembly, as the Senate long did at Rome. Solon saw this, and with great acumen provided against it. He introduced (so later tradition said, and there is no reason to reject it) a new, second or people's council, commonly called The Council, for the express purpose of preparing the Assembly's business. It consisted of 400 (later 500) citizens, selected annually *by lot* from among all who volunteered to serve and who passed a summary scrutiny to ensure that they were citizens in good standing. The Areopagus was left with the function of 'protecting the laws'; it was the supreme court for homicide (preventing blood feuds) and could proceed against revolutionaries; but it lost for ever the power of controlling the Assembly by acting as its steering-committee. Also, the laws were written up in public; they were no longer to be known only to aristocratic judges.

Jurors in the Athenian law-courts gave their verdict by dropping ballot-discs into a box. There were two kinds—those with solid 'hubs' in the centre stood for acquittal, those with hollow for condemnation.

This was not yet democracy; the Archons still had to be rich men, and in practice usually belonged to the old families; but the people gained some control over their government, and the name of Solon was rightly revered by later democrats.

Solon's laws did not give Athens peace. They were followed by faction struggles between 'Coast' and 'Plain', the commercial section against inland aristocrats, and between great men contending for the archonship or, in one case, for re-election to it. In the end, Athens had a 'tyrant' after all: Pisistratus, a popular nobleman and general, who organized a third party among the still poor upland peasants. After many adventures he seized power for the third time about 546 BC, and held it till his death in 528. He ruled from a 'back seat', controlling elections, while the Assembly continued to function, under the Laws of Solon. He raised a direct tax of 10 per cent on farm produce, made loans to peasants on easy terms for the improvement of their equipment, and had the satisfaction of seeing production soar; and he secured outposts for Athens on both sides of the Dardanelles, on the way to the great source of grain supplies on the Black Sea.

His son Hippias remained in power until 510; but as usual, with the revolution's most pressing work done, the new despot's popularity waned. His brother was assassinated in a private quarrel, and Hippias was finally turned out by Sparta, after another Athenian nobleman-turned-businessman, Cleisthenes (he took the contract for rebuilding the temple at Delphi after a fire) had used his influence at Delphi to get the oracle to put pressure on Sparta.

Cleisthenes, whose father had married the daughter of Cleisthenes of Sicyon, finding himself faced by a clubful of more conservative nobles, then 'took the people into his club' (it was probably his disgusted opponents who said it first), carrying through the Assembly a bill which made all free men of Athens, about whose citizenship there was any doubt, citizens by Act of Parliament. As there had been much immigration from Ionia, since the conquest by Persia (see below), and since no one had bothered greatly about voting-rolls under the tyrants, there were by now many among the townsfolk of Athens, the legal or marital status

of whose grandparents may have been uncertain. Solon had provided that an immigrant, who came with his family and practised a useful trade, could become a citizen; but the conservatives would have liked to eliminate as many as possible and keep the Assembly in the hands of solid Athenian countrymen who would vote with the squire. To make return impossible, Cleisthenes abolished the Ionic 'tribes' of Athens and substituted ten new ones, named after ancient Attic kings and heroes; and to consolidate the country and get rid of the local factions of Plain, Coast and Upland, he made his tribes highly artificial, each containing a group of wards or villages, called a Third, (a) from the city and environs, (b) from the coast, and (c) from inland. He did not alter most of the constitutional arrangements of Solon; but he made the voting body much larger, and much more radical. It was the Athens of Cleisthenes that fought the great Persian War.

The Persian Threat: Marathon

Assyria, exhausted by her own conquests, perished; Nineveh fell to the Medes, who had learned the art of war from Assyria herself, in 612 BC; and the empire was divided between the Medes and the Chaldaeans, a people of the Arabian desert-edge who had gained power in Babylon (Nebuchadrezzar, 605–562). But in 550 Cyrus, King of the Persians, a vassal people akin to the Medes, overthrew his overlord and made his own nation dominant. The Greeks saw little difference between them, and often called Persians Medes.

Cyrus was a man of genius. Braving a late autumn campaign in Anatolia, he conquered Croesus of Lydia in 547, and his generals soon subued Ionia; aided by disaffection within (the 'second Isaiah' hails him as the Lord's Anointed), he took Babylon in 539; he had added the whole of Iran before he was killed fighting in central Asia in 530. His son Cambyses conquered Egypt in 525, defeating an army containing many Greek mercenaries. He died in mysterious circumstances, and the whole empire flew apart in rebellion; but by 519 the young Darius, a distant cousin of Cambyses, had suppressed all revolts and rivals. Most of his long reign was spent in a fine work of imperial organization; but in 499 came an event which touched Athens nearly. Ionia rebelled against the tyrants used as city governors by Persia, and was only reduced after a severe struggle lasting for six years. Miletus was sacked, and was never again a power in the world. Sparta had refused help; but Athens, though bitterly divided over resistance or appeasement, had sent help in 498, only to withdraw it after a defeat. But Persia had been provoked; the Athenians had raided inland and sacked Sardis. A sea-borne punitive expedition crossed the Aegean in 490, winning most of the islands for Persia. It was beaten off at Marathon in one of the proudest feats of Athenian arms, directed by Miltiades, a great soldier, once lord of the Gallipoli Peninsula under Hippias. But a greater Persian effort against Greece was bound to come.

Fortunately for Greece, there was a ten-year respite. Egypt revolted (486–5); Darius died in 486; Babylon was in revolt in 482; and meanwhile Athens found a great leader, the democrat Themistocles.

Themistocles may have owed his citizenship to Cleisthenes, for, while his father came of an ancient family, his mother was a slave. He had probably already been chief archon in 493, and commanded the regiment of his tribe at Marathon. He then probably backed an important constitutional change, made in 487, by which the archons, including even the 'war-chief', were to be appointed like the Councillors, *by lot* among approved candidates. It was a radical change indeed. It meant that future archons would rarely be formidable personalities (fewer rivals for Themistocles?); that the conservative Areopagus would lose influence as the elder statesmen died off; and that the war-chief would henceforth be a puppet in the hands of his council, the ten Generals of the tribes, who continued to be directly elected, and could be re-elected, thus gaining experience. The Generals, *stratēgoi*, responsible directly to the Assembly, shortly became the General Staff of Athens.

But Themistocles' finest achievement was the creation of the great Athenian navy. Using the desirability of crushing an old enemy, Aegina, to convert the short-sighted, he persuaded the people to apply a windfall—the discovery of a rich vein in the

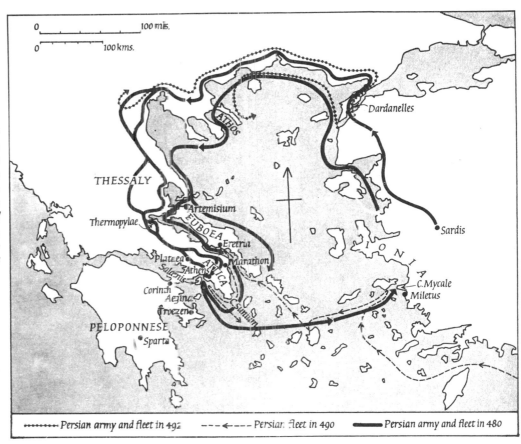

The great war with Persia. The Persians made three expeditions against Greece, the first only into the north (their fleet was battered by a storm off Athos) and the second—that of Marathon—intended merely as a punitive measure. The real invasion came in 480 under Xerxes, who gathered an immense army from all his dominions, built a bridge of boats across the Dardanelles and cut a canal through the peninsula of Athos.

········· Persian army and fleet in 492   ---◄--- Persian fleet in 490   ▬▬▬ Persian army and fleet in 480

state-owned silver-mines near Cape Sunium—to building up the fleet from 70 galleys to 200. His enemies tried to get rid of him by *ostracism* (a device of Cleisthenes, under which the people might exile for ten years, without loss of status, any man who was judged so powerful as to be a danger to the republic), but Themistocles was able to concentrate the votes of his supporters, in each 'election' against his rivals, one at a time; and one after another, they went: last to go was the 'tory democrat', Aristides the Just, who favoured defence by land; and by 480 the ships were ready, though their crews could not match the skill of the Phoenicians, who fought for Persia, on the open sea.

Ostracism was a device peculiar to Athenian democracy. The names were written upon a sherd (ostrakon), and the man whose name was found on more than 6,000 sherds was compelled to leave the city. The sherd shown here bears the name of Aristides—who was actually so banished.

Victory in the Narrow Straits

In 480 King Xerxes personally led a great and carefully organized expedition round the north Aegean. Pontoon bridges had been stretched across the Dardanelles, a canal cut through the sandy neck behind Mt Athos, where an earlier Persian fleet had come to grief in a gale. In the same summer the Carthaginians invaded Sicily, but were routed at Himera by Gelon, tyrant of Syracuse. In Greece, Athens generously and wisely conceded the chief command to Sparta, not only by land (naturally) but by sea, seeing that Sparta's allies, especially Aegina, would not consent to put their fleets under an Athenian; but Themistocles was the moving spirit in Greek strategic councils. The allied fleets took post off a temple of Artemis at the north end of Euboea, where the enemy could only come at them along the mountainous coast of Thessaly, dangerous to a large fleet for lack of anchorages; and

the Phoenician and other Levantine navies did indeed sustain serious losses there in another north-Aegean gale; losses perhaps decisive for the course of the war. Nevertheless they pressed on, to reach shelter in the straits opposite the Greek base; and after three days fighting (the very important but little publicized Battle of Artemisium), in which they inflicted further loss, the Greeks were fought to a standstill and had to withdraw.

Meanwhile Leonidas, King of Sparta, with about 7000 armoured men besides light-armed, had covered the landward flank, holding the coast road by the hot springs of Thermopylae, between cliffs and the sea; but he was left too long unreinforced, and perhaps also outgeneralled. The Persians hammered at his position regardless of losses, with the result that he kept nearly all his force on the coast road; then, experienced mountain fighters as they were, they sent their Guard division by night over hill-paths inland, with a local guide. The Greek local troops on the mountain pulled in to a peak; and the Persians ignored them and went past. Leonidas, warned by runners, sent away most of his force; he gained them time to get clear by staying himself with a sacrificed rearguard, 1100 Boeotians and his personal guard, the famous 300 Spartans. Many helots also fell fighting here.

Defeated on land and sea, the Peloponnesians had no further idea but to 'dig in' on the Isthmus of Corinth. The Athenian government withdrew to Salamis; but Themistocles persuaded the allied fleet to put in there too, first to help with the evacuation and then to defend the island, now an important military objective. The Persian fleet, weakened by its losses in storm and battle, could no longer afford to divide its forces; and Themistocles by a deceitful message to Xerxes, emphasizing the (real) divisions among the allies, induced him to order it into the Salamis strait in an all-out attack. There the Athenians enveloped the head of its column, the Phoenicians, while the Peloponnesians attacked the following divisions in flank; the Greeks are said to have destroyed or taken 200 ships, for the loss of 40; and Xerxes, probably unable to supply his large army without command of the sea, withdrew with most of it to Asia. He left a picked army of occupation in Greece under Mardonius, his chief marshal; but the Greeks (not until the Athenians had threatened to make peace if they were left unsupported) destroyed it at Plataea in Boeotia in 479. Meanwhile a Greek fleet destroyed the Persian remnants at Cape Mycale in Ionia.

On this map of the Greek World appear all the places named in the texts. The general rule has been to use the Lati...

Larissa

Sesklo· Iolcos
Dimini· Demetrias
·Gulf of Pagasae

Lesbos·
Mytilene

Artemisium

Scyros

Thermopylae

Orchomenus
Delphi· ·Gla Chalcis
Naupactus· ·Copais ·Eretria
Kirrha· Haliartos·
Chaeronea ·Thebes· ·Tanagra
Leuctra· ·
Plataea ·Eleusis Marathon
·Megara ·Athens
Sicyon· ·Piraeus ·Agios Kosmas
Corinth· ·Brauron
Gulf of ·Aegina ·Mt.Hymettos
Olympia· Mycenae· ·Midea
Argos· ·Epidaurus
Mantinea· Tiryns· ·Troezen
Bassae· ·Tegea ·Lerna
·Sellasia
Malthi·
·Mt.Ithome ·Sparta
Pylos· Eurotas
Sphacteria·

Chios

Andros

Kea
Tenos

Delos

Paros· ·Naxos

Melos

Ios

Thera

Cythera

Inset

BLACK   SEA

Olbia·

Sinope·
Heraclea· BITHYNIA PONTUS
·on

Trapezus·

ARMENIA

Halys
·Hattušaš

GALATIA
A N A T O L I A

MEDIA

A S S Y R I A

Ecbatana ◎

·Nineveh

Karatepe·

CILICIA
·Issus

Perge·
IA· ·Antioch
haselis Al Mina·
Orontes
·Mari

MESOPOTAMIA

Tigris

PERSIA

SYRIA

Euphrates

Salamis·
Citium·
Paphos·
CYPRUS

Byblos·

PHOENICIA

Sidon·
Tyre·

Babylon ◎

N

Jerusalem ◎
·Jericho
PHILISTIA
PALESTINE

·Alexandria
·Naucratis

Memphis· Nile

RED SEA

form, but Greek and modern spellings have been introduced where they were thought more suitable to the context.

41

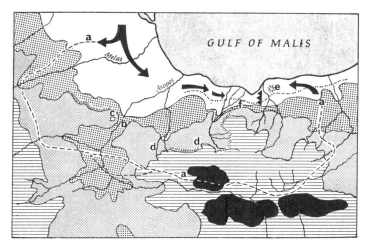

The pass of Thermophylae between the Gulf of Malis and the mountains (the shading indicates heights of 100, 400, 800 and 1200 metres). The Persian army approached from the north, crossed the plain of the Melas and Asopos rivers and marched east along the coast. The Greeks, under Leonidas, took up their position in the narrowest part of the pass, just east of the warm spring (f) which gives Thermopylae its name. Leonidas had posted guards on the cliff tops wherever the slope could be climbed (d,d) and at the citadel of the Trachinians (c) overlooking the deep narrow gorge of the Asopos (b): no ascent was possible along these routes. The Persians, however, were told of a path beginning further to the west, leading right along the ridge of the hills and descending behind the Greek lines (a,a). Part of the army was therefore able to surprise the flank-guard and take the Greeks in the rear. The last remnants of Leonidas' force retreated to a mound (e) where they were completely annihilated.

The Athenian Empire

The Greek cities of Asia were now liberated again, with support almost entirely from Athens. Sparta, hampered by internal troubles and by opposition in the Peloponnese, withdrew from assisting in the work; and it was the Athenian, Aristides the Just, who drew up the charter of a new League, with its headquarters at Delos. Athens and the liberated cities swore alliance 'for ever', for their mutual protection and to wage war on Persia. It was the opinion of many, and not least of Athens' rising soldier, Cimon the son of Miltiades, that such a war could be made to pay.

This Delian League became an Athenian Empire. From the first, Athens was accepted as 'managing director', providing the high command, choosing objectives and controlling the treasury. It was reasonable from the first that the smaller cities (there were over 200 in all), whose share of a league fleet of 100 or 200 galleys was a fraction of a ship, should commute for a money payment, while their young men served, if they chose, in Athenian ships for pay. Soon only a few preserved independent forces. Athens protected them; but on what terms became evident when some of the larger (Naxos, c. 469, Thasos, 465), feeling that liberation was now secure, tried to secede. Athens, with legal right (for the alliance was 'for ever'), coerced them. The moral rights have been debated ever since.

Soon Athens extended her power west of the Aegean; she protected Megara against Corinth, defeated Corinth's and Aegina's united navies, besieged Aegina and forced her to join the League. For ten years, 457–447 BC, she even controlled Boeotia. But her power wilted after her most ambitious eastern enterprise, supporting a new rebellion in Egypt, ended with an army and fleet being trapped in the Nile and lost (454). Athens never again willingly fought Persians and Peloponnesians simultaneously, as she had done before; and when Boeotia rebelled in 447, and Megara, with support from Sparta, in 446, she made no very determined efforts to win them back.

Meanwhile, after Cimon had died of sickness in a last and unsuccessful attempt to liberate Cyprus, Athens had made peace with Persia (449). This led to a major crisis in the empire, since the cities expected that their contributions, levied for the conduct of war, would now be suspended. But Athens was faced with the problem of converting her economy, long a war economy financed out of those contributions, to a peace footing. The solution adopted was that of a great programme of temple-building and other public works; and for this she needed the contributions and continued to levy them, arguing that, as long as she kept Persia at arm's length and policed the Aegean, she was doing what she was paid for. This was the political and economic background of the great buildings, whose artistic significance will be discussed in another chapter.

The author of this argument, of very dubious morality, as some Athenians said at the time, was Pericles, son of Xanthippus (Athens' admiral at Mycale), by a niece of Cleisthenes, and for many years Athens' leading statesman and general. He had first come to the fore in 461 as the lieutenant of Ephialtes, a fierce and austere democrat, who completed the democratization of the city, stripping the Areopagus of its power as 'guardian of the laws' —a supreme court—to interfere with legislation: a logical sequel to the reform of 487.

Pericles was the most brilliant of numerous Athenian aristocrats who served the democracy, filling many of the ten posts of general year by year, and prominent in the Assembly, though often harried there by demagogues (the word is Athenian), popular leaders, mostly of the business class, who took it upon themselves to see that the gentry did not have things all their own way. Pericles was a convinced liberal and democrat, and gained the confidence of the Assembly as no later Athenian was ever to do. But he was also a convinced imperialist. When Euboea revolted in 446 (just before Megara), he personally led the army which crushed it, after buying off a Peloponnesian invasion with a promise to negotiate, backed by a secret bribe to the Spartan king and his chief of staff; an episode which cost the young Spartan king his throne. He then made peace (445), ceding Megara and other points on the mainland, but keeping Euboea, Aegina and the rest of Athens' naval empire.

Whatever the morality of the Athenian Empire, it offered a better hope of uniting Greece politically than any other which appeared in classical times. Before the Egyptian disaster, it seemed as though Athens might actually do it—not without coercion. After 445, for fourteen years—years of brilliant artistic achievement—there was 'peaceful coexistence' between Athens, everywhere encouraging (she did not everywhere impose) democratic governments among her allies, and Sparta, favouring limited-franchise governments among hers. But there was suspicion between the two blocs, and when Corinth tried to reduce her unfilial colony of Corcyra once again and Corcyra appealed to Athens for aid, the peace broke down. The stubborn factor, preventing a compromise solution during two years of slow drift to war, was probably the mutual fear among the leaders of the two blocs, lest their enemies should be able to cut them off from the west with its economic potentialities, and lest neutrals or lukewarm allies, seeing them weaken, might incline to the other side. Archidamus, the veteran king of Sparta, worked for peace, but the ephors of 431 carried the Spartan assembly against him; and on the other side Pericles himself advised the Athenians against making any concession.

The Long War with Sparta

The war that broke out in 431 BC, a struggle between a land and a sea power neither of which could deal a deadly blow to the other, was a long-drawn series largely of indecisive operations. Its fame is due to the fact that the great Thucydides, probably a grandson of Miltiades, and himself a general though not a distinguished one, wrote the history of it, analysing with ruthless clarity the deterioration of standards of justice and political moderation under the influence of the war spirit and of fear.

The Peloponnesians could invade Attica in overwhelming force and ruin villages and farms, but could do nothing against commercial Athens, linked to the sea by impregnable 'long walls'; even less could the Athenians do anything but take useless revenge, by raiding the coasts of the Peloponnese. Pericles counted on a draw after a few campaigns, with great loss of prestige for Sparta. But in 430 Athens was struck by a frightful calamity, a plague brought by sea from Egypt; it scarcely touched the

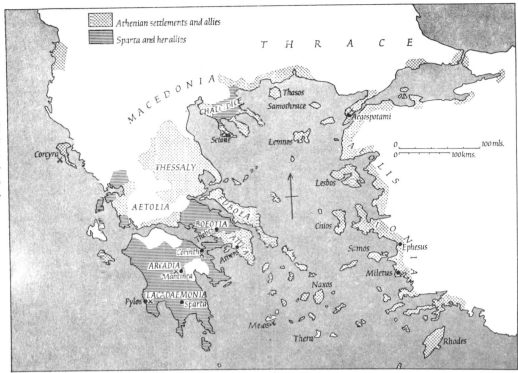

The Peloponnesian War, as the map shows, was essentially a struggle between a land-based and a sea-based power. Sparta controlled almost the whole of the Peloponnese, Athens the Aegean islands and the coastlands of Asia Minor. Thus the two sides for long never really came to grips with each other.

Peloponnese, unwittingly protected by the Athenian blockade of its east coast. It raged for three years, and about a quarter of the population of Athens died of it. Pericles himself died in 429, partly probably from its after-effects.

The war dragged on. Athens missed a good opportunity of ending it on the *status quo ante*, after capturing a battalion including 120 Spartiates, valuable hostages, on an inshore island off Pylos; Pericles was gone, and Cleon, a fiery demagogue, pressed for territorial gains. Athens was defeated with the loss of 1000 armoured men in an attempt to invade Boeotia. Brasidas, an attractive Spartan, with small forces, deprived Athens of many of her tributary cities in Chalcidice; when Athens recaptured one of them, Scione, she put all the men to death and enslaved the women and children, as, later, she did to the Dorian island of Melos, which had never belonged to her league but favoured Sparta. Peace was made at last in 421, after Cleon and Brasidas had fallen in a battle in Thrace, on the same terms which Athens could have had in 425, less Brasidas' conquests.

But many Athenians were still bellicose, and there now rose to fame a vivid and disastrous figure: Alcibiades, a young cousin of Pericles and sometime his ward, after his father had fallen in Boeotia in 447. His appearance in the pages of Plato, especially in the *Symposium*, contributes to making him, of all Athenians, one of the most intimately known. When he was a brilliant boy, Socrates, who once saved his life in battle, had tried to make something of him, but in vain. Looking to war to bring him power, wealth and the adulation which he had come to crave, he worked to involve Athens in a war between Sparta and Argos, with unhappy results; then he took up an even more 'brilliant' and dangerous project, of which some Athenians had dreamed already: that of conquering Sicily, on the pretext of 'protecting' the smaller cities against Dorian Syracuse. Thus the Peloponnese could be attacked both from east and west. When the great expedition was about to sail, he was accused by his enemies of a sacrilege, of which he was probably not guilty; but enough past cases of disrespect for religion (very shocking to the average Athenian) could be brought up against him to make a charge of 'impiety' plausible. He fled to the Spartans, frightened them with an account of Athens' far-reaching designs, and induced the Peloponnesians to send volunteers and a Spartan general to Sicily and to recommence the war at home.

The Athenian expedition was besieging Syracuse, whose citizen soldiers were at first no match for the war-hardened Athenians; but they defended themselves with doggedness and resource; in this Dorian democracy the Athenians, says Thucydides, found

opponents all too like themselves. When Syracuse was reinforced, the besiegers found their own communications cut; and finally the whole expedition, reinforced from Athens, was almost wholly lost; 175 ships and nearly 40,000 men of Athens and her allies (413 BC).

Even then Athens did not collapse. With Ionia in revolt, the Dardanelles and Bosphorus disputed, and a Spartan fortress (recommended by Alcibiades) ten miles from her walls, she built new ships and fought on for nine more years. Twice she won great naval victories, and rejected peace terms that did not restore her empire. At last, indiscipline and the cunning of the grim and able Spartan admiral, Lysander, led to her last great fleet being surprised ashore at the Aegospotami (Goat-Rivers) in the Dardanelles. Even then, she stood a siege. The war ended with Athens starving. Even her democracy was suppressed; but the group of aristocrats (some of them, also, friends of Socrates), whom Sparta installed as a provisional government, soon made themselves so unpopular (the 'Thirty Tyrants') that the people rose to restore the democracy (403); and a Spartan king had the wisdom to let it be.

The End of the Golden Age

Sparta had inherited Athens' power, and kept her own; but she failed to bring unity, more disastrously and more quickly than Athens. Her military governors proved both arrogant and full of greed of money, of which the Laws of Lycurgus deprived them at home. Sparta had gone into alliance with Persia, to finance her late naval operations; then, inheriting Athens' position in Ionia, she found herself at war with Persia; but Persia found no difficulty in using her money to finance Sparta's enemies. Within ten years of the fall of Athens, Athens herself, Thebes, Argos and Corinth were in alliance against Sparta. They were bloodily defeated before Corinth in 394; but Sparta had to recall her king and army from Asia, and in a new general peace settlement (387) she abandoned the Greeks of Asia to Persian rule. The divisions of the Greeks had undone the work of 479.

The fourth century BC is the age of late classical art, of Plato and Aristotle and of the great orators, who incidentally give many vivid pictures of Athenian life; but in political history, it reveals the moral bankruptcy of the city-state world. There is no lack of colourful personalities; one of the greatest was Dionysius, tyrant of Syracuse from 405 to his death in 367. He rose to power through faction in the Syracusan democracy, and after a Carthaginian army, reversing the verdict of 480, had sacked Himera and Selinus. Four Carthaginian wars, punctuated by wars of aggression against the Greeks of Italy, where he plundered Rhegium and Croton, left Carthage still in possession of a third of Sicily, and a trail of devastation. In the mean time Dionysius also wrote tragedies for exhibition at Athens; he fell sick and died after a feast to celebrate his being at last awarded the first prize. He was by then the most powerful man in the Greek world, and had sent troops to intervene in the wars of old Greece.

The centres of power in the Greek world were tending to move outwards. Greek civilization, like that of western Christendom after it, developed first in the relative isolation of a peninsula and its neighbouring islands, whence pressure of population had led to colonization oversea; later, as the technology and political arts of the developing civilization spread outwards, not only colonial areas but adjacent continental countries, formerly backward and thinly populated, grew in power; in the Greek world, Sicily and Chalcidice, then Macedonia and lastly Rome. In Chalcidice Olynthus formed a confederacy of cities, with which Amyntas, king of Macedonia, made alliance; for a time it even included the Macedonian city of Pella. But Sparta looked with jealousy upon this rising power and, on the pretext of defending the liberties of cities which did not wish to join, demolished the Chalcidian League in a war (382–379). While a Spartan officer with troops for this war was passing through Boeotia, a Theban political faction offered to put the citadel of Thebes into his hands. He accepted the offer, and by this act of treachery Sparta, through her friends, dominated Thebes; it was the culminating point of Sparta's power.

But a Theban band, operating from Athenian territory, liberated their city after three years; and in the war that followed it became evident that Sparta, with a disastrously falling birthrate and shrinking Spartiate aristocracy, was loth to risk the losses of a pitched battle. Thebes produced a great soldier and statesman, Epaminondas; and when at last a Spartan king gave battle in Boeotia, with superior numbers and an apparently won position, Epaminondas broke through the Spartans' own ranks with a charge by a dense column, and the Spartans' allies at once withdrew. Four hundred Spartiates, more than half those present and a third of all those between eighteen and sixty, fell with their king on this Flodden Field of the Spartan aristocracy, the Battle of Leuctra, 371.

Epaminondas invaded the Peloponnese; he liberated Messenia, encouraged the Arcadians to develop federal institutions, and broke Sparta for ever as a great power. (As a natural sequel, we then soon find Athens and Sparta allied against Thebes.) But agrarian Thebes possessed even less than Sparta the economic potential to succeed where Athens had failed; nor could she replace Epaminondas, when he fell in battle against Athenians and Spartans, with allies on both sides, at Mantinea in Arcadia (362). Within ten years, Thebes was finding herself baffled in a war even with her neighbours, the men of Phocis, who, under pressure, 'borrowed' and then more and more unblushingly spent the treasures of Delphi to hire mercenaries. The Boeotians sought for allies in their 'Sacred War' against impious Phocis. They found a very effective one in Philip, the young king of Macedonia.

The Rise of Macedon

Philip, as a boy, had been carried off to Thebes as a hostage; so far was his country from being then a world-power. In the city of Epaminondas he learned to admire Greek culture, and studied the Theban army. At twenty-two he became king (359), when his elder brother was defeated and killed by the Illyrians. Reorganizing his army and promoting in it a great general, Parmenio, he next year dealt the Illyrians a shattering blow; but he was still surrounded by enemies. He triumphed over them not only by personally leading his troops—he was repeatedly wounded—but by consummate, Machiavellian diplomacy; buying off enemies till he could deal with them one at a time, winning men by the charm of his personality, lavish of gifts to ambassadors and politicians, and of promises, which he kept no longer than suited him, to all and sundry. He made his way less by deceiving the innocent (the Greeks were no innocents) than by playing on the cupidity and ambition of men who matched him in unscrupulousness, but not in intellect.

The Lion of Chaeronea commemorates the battle (338 BC) in which the combined Theban and Athenian forces were defeated by Philip of Macedon. It was erected, according to Pausanias, by the Thebans in memory of their dead, and was restored from fragments in 1904.

Thus, he dissuaded the Athenians from helping Amphipolis, an Athenian colony, liberated long since by Brasidas, by offering secretly to trade it for Pydna, a Greek town on the Macedonian coast, which was in alliance with Athens. This very dirty deal by the Athenians was suitably paid for, when Philip's troops were admitted to Pydna by friends within, and he kept both towns. Soon after, he took Potidaea, which Athens also coveted, and presented it to Olynthus, thus ensuring that, at least for the present, Athens and Olynthus would not make common cause against him.

Athens, since 378, had been trying to reform her naval league, with safeguards against using it as an instrument of imperialism; but her allies never fully trusted her. The case of Pydna shows how right they were. In 357, for reasons unconnected with Pydna, four of the largest cities, Chios, Cos, Rhodes and Byzantium seceded; Athens failed to coerce them by force, and was left with only a few rags of her league; while Philip defeated inland tribes and secured his hold on the Pangaean gold mines, where he founded Philippi.

Philip and the Phocians first clashed in faction-ridden Thessaly, where Philip, after sustaining two defeats, drove a Phocian army into the sea near modern Volos; but the Athenians kept him out of Phocis by holding Thermopylae; Philip, ever a realist, did not attack (352). His next conquests were in Thrace; then in Chalcidice, where Athens, whipped up by the fierce oratory of Demosthenes, aided Olynthus—but too little and too late. Philip razed the city and annexed the area (348). Athens treated for peace; but the negotiations were long-drawn, and actually during them Philip marched past unguarded Thermopylae and reduced Phocis to total submission, while its leaders and their mercenaries fled abroad. He was welcomed at Delphi as a liberator and victorious crusader (346). He was master of northern Greece, and popular with the aristocracy in Thessaly. Next he completed the conquest of Thrace. He was repulsed from Perinthus, on the Sea of Marmara, and Byzantium, with help both from Persia and Athens (340); but in the same year another quarrel at Delphi gave him an excuse for intervening again in central Greece. Thebes was directly threatened. Towards Athens, Philip protested feelings of respect and a desire for friendship, probably quite sincerely; but in the name of Hellas, Demosthenes successfully urged an alliance with Thebes. In the hard-fought battle of Chaeronea, in 338, Philip beat the united armies of central Greece. His 18-year-old son, Alexander, led the decisive cavalry charge. Philip then garrisoned Thebes, but even now did not invade Attica, and gave Athens peace on easy terms.

His ambition was by no means satisfied. He was still only 43, and moreover he was not in a position to draw rein; for his armies, with a large professional or mercenary component, were so expensive that, for all his Thracian gold, he was in debt. Only the spoils of Asia could make his style of conquest pay; and Greeks had been telling each other, ever since the Ten Thousand with Xenophon had marched home from Mesopotamia, how weak Persia had become, and how easy it would be to conquer her, if Greeks could only stop fighting each other. At Corinth, where Greek general headquarters had been in Xerxes' time, Philip called a national congress; it elected him Captain-General of the Greeks for a great war of righteous revenge; and in 336 Parmenio crossed the Dardanelles to make good a bridgehead.

But it was not Philip who was to conduct that enterprise. Promiscuous in his habits, he had long been on bad terms with his queen, the fiery Olympias; and in 337 he had married the niece of one of his generals, who, at the wedding, prayed that 'a legitimate heir' might be born of the union, an open attack on Alexander's position. In 336 a son was born to him; and soon after that, Philip was murdered at a festival. The assassin, a young man with a private grievance, was killed by the guards; and who might have encouraged him remained always at least officially unknown.

Across the Known World – Alexander's Astonishing Empire

Alexander, a king at twenty, was at once faced by rebellion on all sides; but he quickly showed his astonishing quality as a general. A swift march, merely to show himself in Greece—cutting steps in the side of Ossa when the Thessalian government demurred at letting him through the Tempē gorge—averted trouble there and then; but in 335 he fought three critical campaigns. He swept through Thrace, storming the Shipka Pass and crossing the Danube, where he had an interview with fair-haired Celts on the move; across into Illyria, where he was trapped, it seemed, in the hills, and extricated himself with typical daring and cunning; and down again into Greece, where Thebes had risen and was besieging the Macedonians in the citadel. He razed the city to the ground; and Greece was cowed.

Then, in 334, he crossed into Asia, demolished the army of the local satraps after a fierce cavalry *mêlée*, and liberated Ionia; in 333 he defeated King Darius at Issus in Syria. Half the next year was occupied by a desperate siege of Tyre; necessary, because the Phoenician fleet, with Greek mercenaries and enterprising Persian commanders, was still at large, trying to raise Greece in revolt in his rear; but by the year's end, Phoenicia had fallen, and he was in Egypt. In 331 he fought his greatest battle at Gaugamela, in open country (unlike Issus) in Mesopotamia. Vastly outnumbered, he stalled off enveloping attacks with flank-guards until his infantry phalanx and heavy horse-guards could smash the enemy centre and drive King Darius once more in flight. Darius retired eastward, on Ecbatana; Alexander rested in Babylon awhile, letting rumours spread that his army was demoralized by its vices, and then marched out *south*-east, fighting his way in midwinter through mountain chains, first against tribesmen to whom Persian kings had paid blackmail, then against the home levy of Persia proper, to occupy Persepolis, the ancient capital, to destroy its palaces and, more important, to round up its young men and send them afar, to be trained by Macedonian officers as soldiers of the new king.

By this tremendous exploitation of victory, Darius was left with no army in 330, except the forces of his eastern barons; and they, in retreat from Ecbatana, put him under arrest and, when Alexander's pursuit grew hot, murdered him. But Alexander's conquest of the empire was but half done. Three years of strenuous warfare were needed to subdue the tough eastern frontier provinces, where castle after mountain castle stood a siege, and conquered provinces rose again in his rear. Unwearied still, by 326 he was conquering the Punjab; and there at last his Macedonians refused to go further. They had won a very severe battle against the Paurava rajah (the 'Porus' of western writers), who had 200 elephants; and they declined to march against the Ganges kingdoms, which were reported to have five thousand. In 325 Alexander returned to Babylon, after nearly perishing along with a column which he led to explore the desert coast of the Persian Gulf.

Alexander's character has been disputed to this day. There had been more than one conspiracy against him; one of them had been at least concealed by Philotas, son of Parmenio, general of the horse-guards, when it was reported to him—perhaps out of envy, combined with indignation that Parmenio had been left behind on base duties at Ecbatana. Philotas was put to death; and immediately thereafter Parmenio was murdered, as an inevitable preventive measure. Callisthenes, the official historian, nephew of Alexander's boyhood tutor, Aristotle, perished after a conspiracy among the royal pages, to whom Callisthenes taught history—and had talked of tyrants and tyrannicide. Alexander himself

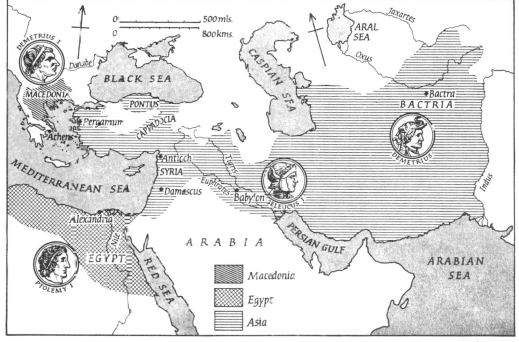

The death of Alexander in 323 BC was the signal for the break-up of his empire. At first Antigonus, the most powerful of his former generals, seized control, but was defeated in 301 by SELEUCUS I *(301–280), who, after another 20 years warfare with other claimants, became master of the whole area between the Aegean and the Indus. As time went on, however, this great kingdom was eaten into by Parthians and Gauls (Galatians). The province of Bactria became self-governing under Euthydemus and his son* DEMETRIUS *(early 2nd century BC). In Macedon* DEMETRIUS I *(294–288), the son of Antigonus, seized the throne, though he had later to relinquish it. His son, another Antigonus, however, regained Greece and his dynasty (the Antigonids) ruled until 168. Egypt was the most firmly governed part of the former empire. Here* PTOLEMY I *(died 283) seized power immediately upon Alexander's death and his descendants kept it until 30 BC. The last of the Ptolemies was Cleopatra.*

had killed, in a drinking party, his foster-brother Clitus, who had saved his life in the first cavalry battle, but who now drunkenly provoked him, complaining of his use of Persian dress and Persian despotic ways, and assumption of glory that belonged to all the army; the act cost the king an agony of remorse. Considering the strain under which he lived, these tragedies, though grim, were not numerous; but they made enemies. Certainly Alexander had a constructive side. He founded many cities; some, such as Herat and Khodjend ('Alexandria-at-the-World's-End'), were Greek re-foundations of existing towns; but the greatest, Alexandria in Egypt, was new. He set out deliberately to employ Persian officers and governors (some failed him, and had to be replaced by Macedonians) and to equalize the two master-races; a policy which his Macedonians bitterly resented. But by personally leading them in charge and escalade, repeatedly wounded, once almost to death; by sharing their hardships, by efficiency, glamour and success, he kept their loyalty, with rare outbreaks of exasperation, to the end.

On the other hand, a serious count against him is the fact that, while continually risking his life, he made no arrangement whatever for the rule of his empire or the command of the army when he should be gone. He did not even beget a son until the last year of his short life (by the Persian Roxana); though Parmenio and others begged him to leave an heir to Macedonia before plunging into Asia. Nor, though passionate in friendship, does he seem to have been homosexual. It looks indeed as though his beloved mother's comments on his father's infidelities had imbued him from childhood with an abnormal disgust with sex. All his energy poured into war and government. The theory that, had he lived, he would have renounced war, cannot be sustained. He was organizing a large new army, two-thirds Medo-Persian, one-third Macedonian, when, not yet thirty-three, he caught a fever and died (323).

'The Fetters of Greece'

So Alexander died, 'intestate'; and after years of warfare between his generals, the empire he left was divided between those who survived. Seleucus, last commander of Alexander's footguards, won most of it, in Asia. Egypt was secured by the far-sighted Ptolemy; he founded a dynasty that ended only with Cleopatra in 31 BC. It was a purely Greco-Macedonian state (its higher civilian officials Greek, its army officers mostly Greek or Macedonian), administering the hard-worked peasants through an elaborate bureaucracy; its intellectual glory was the royal 'Temple of the Muses' at Alexandria, with its great library and the salaried scholars who worked there. Cleopatra is said to have been the first of her line ever to learn Egyptian. Macedonia, after being overrun by Celts from central Europe, whom, as we saw, Alexander had met on the Danube, and who penetrated to Delphi during the years of confusion, was restored as a nation-state by Antigonus, grandson of one of the marshals, of the same name, and of Antipater, who had governed Macedonia for Alexander; his dynasty, which lasted until the Roman conquest in 168, controlled Greece through garrisons at strategic points: Demetrias, (named after Demetrius, Antigonus' father)—near modern Volos—Chalcis and Corinth; they were called 'the fetters of Greece'.

Greece, though her states were dwarfed by the new giant kingdoms, was still important as a source of trained man-power: soldiers, philosophers, poets (a royal prestige-symbol) and technicians. As in a later Europe, there was some attempt by the states to draw together; the federal Achaean League, including also part of Arcadia, and the Aetolian League in the north-west, were the two chief power-blocs, and by no means the least interesting of Greek political experiments; but unfortunately, as rivals, they were always hostile to each other. Athens, after a gallant attempt to throw off Macedonian supremacy with help from Egypt (which let her down), became more and more a 'university city'; but Sparta, strengthened under King Cleomenes III by a redistri-

bution of land and emancipation of some helots—Sparta's revolution, 300 years too late—emerged once more to alarm a world in which the rich were too rich and the poor too many; only to go down before Macedonians and Achaeans, scared into common action, in the Battle of Sellasia, six miles north of Sparta, in 221.

The Shadow of Rome

In 217, Achaeans, Aetolians and Philip V of Macedonia met in a peace-conference at Naupactus (Lepanto). Agelaus of Naupactus, welcoming them, pointed to the great struggle proceeding in the west, where Hannibal was invading Italy, and warned them that now at least it was absolutely essential that Greeks should hold together; otherwise, whichever of the giants was victor, the time would come when they could no longer call even their quarrels their own. Everyone applauded, and a peace was made; but in the following years, unwillingness to make concessions to neighbours and rivals was too much for good resolutions. The chief new feature of the next 70 years was that Greeks resorted to Rome to complain of their enemies. Greek independence ended, after a last desperate struggle by the Achaean League, with the sack of Corinth by the consul Mummius (146); and Greece became the Roman provinces of Macedonia and Achaia.

In the east, the Seleucid Empire suffered from the first from insufficient Greek and Macedonian man-power. Seleucus himself ceded the Punjab to the great Indian Chandragupta for 500 trained elephants, with which he crushed his rival, the elder Antigonus, in Asia Minor. Bactria, the north-east frontier region, with Alexander's Greek military colonies there, was soon *de facto* independent; its soldier-kings had some magnificent coins struck for them. Demetrius of Bactria ('Emetrius, lord of Ind', known to Chaucer), after 200 BC, penetrated once more far into India; one of his successors there, Menander the Just, as his coins call him, is the 'Milinda' of a famous Buddhist dialogue, recording his conversion; but meanwhile Eucratidas, perhaps originally a Seleucid general, seized Bactria behind him. Bactria was finally overrun by central Asian nomads about 140 BC, and 'Milinda's' kingdom had become fully Indianized within a century later. Meanwhile further west, where there were no garrisons, a nomad tribe settled in the old province of Parthia about 248, and formed what became, though not at once, a powerful kingdom. By 130 it had won Mesopotamia, and driven the Seleucids back into Syria.

In Asia Minor, the Celts broke in at the time of their great raids, soon after 280, founding the Asian Galatia. The Ionians drove their plundering bands back inland, led by the captains of Pergamum, who then, as kings (Eumenes I and II, Attalus I, II and III) ruled the west of the peninsula till the last Attalus ceded it to Rome in 133; the sculptures celebrating their defeat of the Gauls are famous. Native kingdoms with some Greek culture (Bithynia, Pontus) divided the Black Sea coast. Antiochus III, the last powerful Seleucid (223–187), claimed overlordship over all the kings from the Aegean to Bactria; but he was routed by the Romans, in alliance with Pergamum, in 190 and driven from Asia Minor. Rome also encouraged the revolt of the Jews under the Maccabees against his son Antiochus IV (Epiphanes). Between its foes in east and west, and with dynastic struggles within, the Seleucid Empire had perished before Pompey made Syria a Roman province in 64.

During its stormy career, however, the empire had produced in its cities some interesting sculpture and some splendid architecture, intended to impress the peoples of Asia, which it successfully did. Pontic and Bithynian kings, even Parthians, often used 'Phil-Hellene' as an additional title, and set Greek legends on their coins. Greek culture had been penetrating the Persian Empire even before Alexander; but his career brought it flooding in with the prestige of victory. His most important legacy, and that of the Seleucid Empire, was the creation of the Greek-speaking world of the New Testament.

III THE VOICE OF GREECE

The first great literature and
its living context

H.C. BALDRY

'Come, O Muse, tread a measure to the sacred choirs;

come to charm our song; come to see the waiting

crowds, assembled here in their thousands.'

ARISTOPHANES, FROGS, 674-7

The opening words of the Iliad

are the beginning of Western literature. It is a literature that pre-dates the invention of writing. The Homeric epics, composed in about the 8th century BC, were the finest fruit of a traditional form of narrative poetry, handed down by word of mouth and chanted by minstrels in the halls of kings. Later they were recited at great public festivals by professional bards, or *rhapsodes* (right). The two long poems became almost the sacred book of the Greeks, their authority being accepted for everything from the history of the gods to the boundary rights of city-states.

The central theme of the *Iliad* is a chain of incidents in the last year of the Trojan War—the anger of Achilles, greatest hero of the Achaeans, as Homer calls the Greeks. Achilles is insulted by the Greek leader Agamemnon and withdraws from the struggle; but he returns, and the climax is his fight with the Trojan hero, Hector.

Homer himself is a shadowy figure, hardly more than a name. In the earliest representation of him (*left*), on a 4th-century coin from the island of Ios, there is no sign of the blindness later ascribed to him.

Hector, the Trojan prince, is the true hero of the *Iliad. Below*: he bids farewell to his wife Andromache, who knows that he will never return. 'She set out for home shedding great tears and looking back many times.' *Bottom*: Hector's death. Three times Achilles pursued him round the city. Then he turned and faced him. 'As Hector charged, Achilles drove at him with his spear; the point went through the tender flesh. Hector came down in the dust and the great Achilles triumphed over him.'

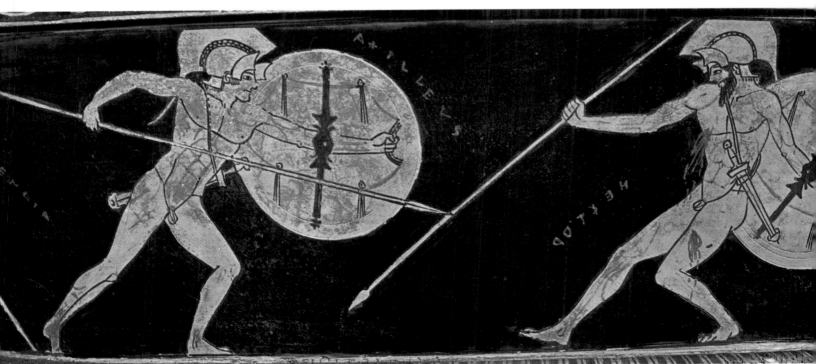

'Swift-footed Achilles', the ideal of heroic magnanimity so much admired by the Greeks, portrayed on a vase of the 5th century BC. Here he wears a leather corslet reinforced with scales and bearing (like his shield in the picture below) the symbol of the Gorgon's head, often used on armour.

The father of Hector, Priam, King of Troy, comes alone and at night to Achilles' tent to beg from him the body of his son, which lies outstretched beneath Achilles' couch.

The Orestes story, dramatized by Aeschylus, Sophocles and Euripides, tells how Agamemnon, on his return from Troy, was murdered by his wife, Clytemnestra, together with the Trojan princess, Cassandra (*above*) whom he had brought back as his captive. The cycle of blood, once begun, continued through the generations. Orestes, the son of Agamemnon and Clytemnestra, was ordered by Apollo to avenge his father. He did so, killing first his mother's lover Aegisthus (*below*) and then, aided by his sister Electra, Clytemnestra herself (she appears on the left in this vase, attempting to save Aegisthus while Orestes' friend, Pylades, holds her back). Although carried out in obedience to Apollo's command, this was a sin; Orestes was pursued and tormented by the Furies. In Aeschylus' version he found refuge in Athens.

Tragedy and comedy, represented symbolically by theatrical masks (*above*), are both Greek inventions. The plots of tragedies were usually drawn from the legends of the heroic age, already recounted in epic poetry, and the audience knew at least the main outlines of the story. The fate of the characters showed the working out of the will of the gods, who were often represented on the stage. Comedy probably originated in Dionysiac ritual, but took dramatic form by the addition of dialogue to choral song. In the hands of Aristophanes it became a brilliant mixture of poetry, pantomine, fantasy and wit, with a sharp satirical edge from which not even the most prominent citizens were exempt.

The masquerade of men on horseback (*above right*) on a 6th-century vase anticipates the chorus in Aristophanes' comedy, *The Knights*:

'Let us sing the mighty deeds
Of our illustrious noble steeds.'

Wasps, birds and frogs figure in other choruses of Aristophanes.

Burlesques of tragedy were popular throughout the Greek world. A south-Italian vase (*right*) shows a play—which has not survived—based on the ambushing of Dolon, a Trojan who was trapped at night by a stratagem of Odysseus and Diomedes. The story itself is thought to be a late interpolation into the *Iliad*.

Greek drama began as a festival held in honour of Dionysus or Bacchus, god of wine. The chorus was the oldest element; then an actor was added, then a second, then a third. The dramatic action began to dominate the choral rite, and the 'theatre' was born. At Epidaurus (*left*) the original 5th-century arrangements are still clear—the circular dancing floor (*orchestra*) on which the chorus performed, with a raised platform behind it for the actors, from which they could also step down into the circle. Later the stage was brought forward, turning the *orchestra* into a half-circle.

Masks hiding the face but vividly expressing age and character in stylized form, were worn by the actors—who were often far from their audience. In one vase picture (*above right*) a tragic actor holds his bearded mask and a dagger. Comedy often had choruses of animals or birds, foreshadowed in the bird costumes on an early vase (*below left*). The actual stage-settings (*skene*) have almost entirely disappeared (the one used at Epidaurus is modern), but here again the vase-paintings supply some indications. One fragment (*right*) shows a wooden structure with slender columns, rich entablature and roof decorations.

The whole city would attend the performance, which lasted all through the day. There would be three tragic plays followed by a farcical 'satyr-play' with a chorus led by Silenus. In the Theatre of Dionysus at Athens (*below*) the Dionysiac origins of the drama were commemorated in Roman times in a row of figures which included the god himself and Silenus (*far left*).

'The Father of History', Herodotus (*left*) is the earliest of the great prose-writers of Greece. He lived in the 5th century BC and came from Ionia. His work covers the peoples and traditions of the then known world, and is uniquely valuable as the chief source for the history of the war with Persia. He must have talked personally to many of those who took part. On this vase (*below left*) Darius is seen listening to a messenger, perhaps before setting out on the great invasion. The story of Croesus came to him from a more remote past. *Below*: 'Cyrus chained Croesus and placed him on a great pyre that he had built. And Croesus, for all his misery, remembered how Solon had declared that no man could be called happy until he was dead . . .' Exploration, too, fascinated Herodotus, and he is our sole authority for many voyages by the Greeks and their neighbours, including one of a Phoenician ship which sailed round Africa from the Red Sea to the Straits of Gibraltar. 'On their return', says Herodotus, 'they declared—I for my part do not believe them, but others perhaps may—that in sailing round Libya they had the sun upon their right hand.' The two Greek ships (*bottom*) are of the 6th century.

The first great literature and its living context

H. C. BALDRY

OF GREEK LITERATURE, as of Greek art and architecture, only a small part is known to us. Most of the remnant we now possess survives in manuscripts dispersed among the museums, monasteries and learned libraries of the world, treasured fruit of the labours of Byzantine and medieval copyists. Now and then a little more is added from papyrus finds—a few lines, occasionally a whole poem or even a play. But the total is never likely to become more than a fraction of the wealth that once existed. Of scores of epic poems, we have a mere half dozen; of thousands of plays, forty-five; of countless speeches, enough to fill a few volumes. We know the names of many authors whose works have vanished completely, while from others, by quotation or on papyrus fragments, a few precious scraps have been preserved. It is some consolation that much of what we have now was regarded in ancient times as the best.

The purpose of this chapter is to provide a brief account of these surviving documents. But there is another sense in which they are incomplete. Our manuscripts record only the words of a literature which was once far more than the written word: they give us nothing of the minstrel's song, the action in the theatre, the excited political meeting. Yet we cannot fully understand the words themselves without some conception of the vivid occasions at which they were first delivered. Hence a second aim of this section: to give some idea how far our sources of information—archaeology, statements by ancient writers, implications drawn from the documents themselves, even parallels with other peoples—enable us to illumine each branch of Greek literature by setting it against the living context from which it sprang.

Homer's Epics, the Bible of Greece

The earliest documents in Greek that can be called literature are the *Iliad* and the *Odyssey*, ascribed in antiquity, along with others, to Homer. A likely date for both is the 8th century BC.

The *Iliad*, or 'poem about Ilion (Troy)', has as its central theme a single episode in the last year of the Trojan War—Achilles' withdrawal from the struggle in anger at an insult from Agamemnon, and his eventual return to the fight and its result:

Of the wrath of the son of Peleus—of Achilles—Goddess, sing—
That ruinous wrath, that brought sorrows past numbering
Upon the host of Achaea, and to Hades cast away
The valiant souls of heroes, and flung their flesh for prey
To hounds, and all the fowls of air . . .

The incident covers only a few weeks of the ten-year siege; but the poem's name is justified, for in the course of its fifteen thousand lines, by digression and reminiscence and prophecy, we hear of the whole course and background of the war.

The *Odyssey*, four thousand lines shorter, has the less majestic but more romantic theme of Odysseus' return home to Ithaca and Penelope after the siege is over. Again the telling ranges widely—not only through all the folk-lore and fiction which make up the hero's adventures, but through other sequels to the war.

Both poems are focussed, like most Greek literature, on people: not on people in the mass, the armies or populations involved in the war and its aftermath, but on the individual actions and the utterances (often lengthy) of individual men and women, many

of whom emerge as clearly though simply defined characters as the story goes on. This is indeed 'heroic' poetry, naturally centred on a single hero and one particular chain of incidents. But its most remarkable feature for the modern reader is that other beings than men and women, though no less individual, are interwoven in the story and play the most decisive part in events—equally definite and particular gods and goddesses, superhuman in their immortality and their magical powers, but often prompted by motives and emotions that seem all too human. Homer's gods are made in the image of man.

All this is related in hexameter verse in which Matthew Arnold rightly found the qualities of plainness of thought, plainness of speech, and rapidity. It is true that digressions are frequent and sometimes, especially in the *Odyssey*, there is a leisurely piling of incident on incident and speech on speech. But Homer's way of describing a scene or an action is swift and direct. There is little metaphor in his lines to confuse or delay our understanding. Where imagery is used, it is formally set out in the simile:

As when in heaven the stars about the moon
Look beautiful, when all the winds are laid,
And every height comes out, and jutting peak
And valley, and the immeasurable heavens
Break open to their highest, and all the stars
Shine, and the shepherd gladdens in his heart:
So many a fire between the ships and stream
Of Xanthus blazed before the towers of Troy.

Dramatic or lofty moments in the poems call forth more than two hundred brief pictures of this kind, in which the story-teller often seems to go beyond his comparison and dwell lovingly on details for their own sake. In this as in other features the Homeric

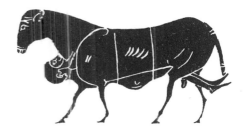

style became a model for poets of later centuries—Virgil, for example, and Milton:

> Thick as autumnal leaves that strow the brooks
> In Vallombrosa . . .

Arnold found one other principal virtue in the *Iliad* and *Odyssey*: 'nobility'. Although the word is out of fashion now, the quality is unmistakably there, and there throughout. Translators through the ages have found all Homer's qualities difficult to reproduce, but this is where they most commonly fail. His narrative is uneven in dramatic power and our interest sometimes flags: it never becomes trivial or cheap.

Who was Homer?

What is the origin of these two great epics? Who was 'Homer'? These questions have been keenly debated for centuries, and it is clear now that there is no simple answer. The poems themselves tell us nothing of their composer, and Greek tradition gave conflicting accounts of his date, his birthplace, and incidents of his life. Modern scholarship is agreed on one basic point: that the problem of authorship must be regarded as secondary, and the poems must be primarily seen as products of an evolutionary process.

In all but minor details our text of both epics goes back to the scholars of Alexandria in the 3rd and 2nd centuries BC. Before their work on it many versions must have existed, but variation was kept in check by the requirements of public performance: at festivals in a number of places, and above all at the Panathenaea held every four years at Athens, the two poems were recited to vast audiences by 'rhapsodes', who with their long staffs were familiar figures throughout Greece. For the purpose of the Panathenaic performances a stable text may have been established as early as the 6th century BC.

The rhapsode, however, is certainly not the beginning of the story. Further back still stands a more shadowy but more important figure—the *aoidos*, the singer; and it is on him and his craft, illuminated by comparison with story-tellers of today in Yugoslavia and elsewhere, that the interest of Homeric scholars has centred in recent years. Such a singer is the blind Demodocus, described in the *Odyssey* itself at the feast at the Phaeacian court:

> The crier soon came, leading that man of song
> whom the Muse cherished; by her gift he knew
> the good of life, and evil—
> for she who lent him sweetness made him blind.
> Pontonoos fixed a studded chair for him
> hard by a pillar amid the banqueters,
> hanging the taut harp from a peg above him,
> and guided up his hands upon the strings . . .
> In time, when hunger and thirst were turned away,
> the Muse brought to the minstrel's mind a song
> of heroes whose great fame rang under heaven.

When the telling of stories by such singers began, we do not know. It may well go back to Mycenaean times, though no direct evidence for this has yet come to light. But there is general agreement that the *aoidos* with his lyre is the source of the kind of verse

narration which reaches its highest achievement in the *Iliad* and *Odyssey*. The singer's art, unaided by writing, involved both improvising new material and remembering the old, and in these twin needs lies the explanation of the main features of Homeric narrative: the hexameter framework; the language, an amalgam of dialect elements and invented forms which was never used in ordinary speech, but must have been shaped by generations of singers to suit the metrical framework; the stereotyped word-groups or formulae constantly employed to fill this or that part of the hexameter line. Repetition, an essential aspect of the improviser's technique, leaves its mark everywhere in the two epics, whether a noun-plus-adjective formula ('stock epithet') is repeated, such as 'swift-footed Achilles', 'resourceful Odysseus', 'the wine-dark sea'; or a stock line recurs to describe a familiar event:

> But when early Dawn appeared, the rosy-fingered . . .

Some whole sets of lines do service more than once—a message, for example, or an account of preparations for the fight.

The Date of Homer

With the help of these means a growing body of verse stories must have been created and handed down, until recital by rhapsodes replaced the singer's chant and (not necessarily at the same time) oral composition gave way to the use of writing. Plainness of thought and speech and rapidity of movement would be their natural attributes. But at what stage in this long evolution did the *Iliad* and *Odyssey* emerge in something like their present form?

There can be no certain answer to the question. Some scholars see the beginning of festival recitations as the occasion which called such monumental poems into being; others place their creation in the time of the *aoidos*, as much as two centuries before the coming of the rhapsode. Some maintain that they cannot have been composed or handed on without the use of writing; according to others, oral composition is more credible, and a period of oral transmission may have followed. Few now suppose that epics of such magnitude, far surpassing the ordinary singer's tale in unity of theme and poetic quality, could be the product of a mere compiler of lays; but while some believe in a single 'Homer', study of the differences between the poems points rather to two poets of genius, separated perhaps by several generations, the second of whom sought to emulate the achievement of the first. Both must have incorporated in their work much narrative material handed down from the past; and some episodes—the ambushing of Dolon, for example, in the *Iliad*, and Odysseus' visit to the world of the dead—were probably added at a later date.

Amid these uncertainties one vital point is now established: both epics belong to a late stage in the evolution of such narrative verse, when the singer's art was no longer crude but polished to its highest perfection. The simile, at any rate in its elaborated form, is now thought to be an enrichment added in the final phase of the development of his technique. This lateness goes a long way towards explaining the relation of 'Homer' to history. The poems were far removed in time from the Trojan War, and it is not surprising that their representation of it is very different from the reality suggested by archaeological research, or that their picture of Mycenaean life, with its concentration on the

Penelope and her son Telemachus, from a vase of the 5th century BC. Penelope, alone on Ithaca, found herself besieged by suitors for her hand (and throne). She announced that she had first to finish a piece of tapestry on which she was employed, and then would make her choice. But in order to draw out the time until Odysseus should return, she undid at night all that she had woven during the day.

heroic individual, has little in common with the bureaucratic society revealed by the Linear B tablets. Because they combine traditional material of various periods, they reflect not one stage of social development but several; and where tradition failed, the poet's imagination must have filled the gap.

If the two epics are seen as the climax of a long evolution, other features of them are also more easily understood: their treatment, for example, of the gods. In the course of centuries the Olympian deities have been adapted to the storyteller's needs. They have been humanized and individualized until they can play their part in the narrative alongside the mortal characters, and their less reputable antics can even provide comic relief.

Equally linked with the poems' remoteness from the events of which they tell is their attitude to man. Although they are concerned with a war and its sequel, they do not take sides: Achaeans and Trojans alike are seen as subject to the common lot of mortality—a fate which the hero must undergo no less than the commoner, for all his prowess and pride. There is no mawkish sentiment in Homeric epic: its scenes of suffering and death are often too starkly realistic for the modern palate. But it does share with other great poetry the quality of compassion for the human lot. The note is struck in such scenes as the farewell of Hector to his wife and infant son, or in brief moments like the glimpse of happier days as Achilles later pursues Hector round the walls of Troy:

> There by the springs are roomy washing-troughs,
> Fine troughs of stone, where in old days of peace
> Or ever the sons of the Achaeans came,
> The ladies and fair daughters of the Trojans
> Would wash their shining robes. Thereby they ran,
> One fleeing, one pursuing.

Pity for human frailty is most strongly present in the *Iliad*, and finds its greatest expression in the tragic figure of Achilles, the mighty warrior foredoomed to an early death, whose individual drama of moral degradation and redemption is seen against the background of the larger tragedy of Troy itself.

The influence of these first masterpieces is evident in nearly all later Greek poetry. For epic they were accepted as models which all must imitate but none could equal: narrative hexameters continued to be composed in Greek until Byzantine times, but it was left to Roman Virgil, still following the same tradition, to produce a work worthy of comparison with Homer.

The *Odyssey* seems to have been soon followed by a large number of shorter poems using the same metre and technique, which centuries later were arranged into an 'Epic Cycle' covering the whole range of myth and legend. From all this only a few pages of fragments survive today. Time has been kinder to thirty-four examples of the 'Homeric Hymn'—a form which began as a brief tribute to a deity before epic recitation, but itself developed into an epic narrative relating with great charm, if not with full Homeric power, the story of Demeter and Persephone or Apollo or Hermes or Aphrodite.

The Individual Speaks

Most of these poems were associated, at any rate for a time, with the name of Homer. Others, including the still extant *Theogony*, were ascribed to Hesiod, commonly regarded by the Greeks as Homer's contemporary. But Hesiod's best-known poem, the strange 800-line medley known as the *Works and Days*, has a tone and purpose very different from epic narrative. The hexameter line, the epic language and formulae are still there, and so also is legend—the story of Pandora, and of man's degeneration from the Golden Age. The poet's object, however, is not to entertain an audience, but to advise and instruct the countryman on ways of work and lucky and unlucky days. Above all, the *Works and Days* is a *personal* poem: the author emerges clearly as a disgruntled farmer of the mainland territory of Boeotia, who rails at his brother, Perses, over the unfairness of a judgment dividing their father's farm:

> Perses, set these thoughts firmly in your heart.
> Strife that delights in mischief must not keep
> Your heart from work, as with listening ear you watch
> The court-house wrangles.

Homer's impersonal narrative has been replaced by personal feeling, the heroic past by the grim realities of Greece emerging from the Dark Age.

This aspect of the *Works and Days* is a foretaste of all the personal poetry that arose out of the conflicts and discontents of the 7th and 6th centuries BC—topical expressions of individual reaction to the events of the day which often strike a strangely modern note. Where Hesiod retained the hexameter, others turned to forms better suited to the utterance of emotion or thought: iambics, for example, nearer in rhythm and diction to ordinary speech and later to be used as the normal dialogue metre in drama; or the elegiac couplet, created by adding a shorter line to the hexameter, which subsequently became the accepted

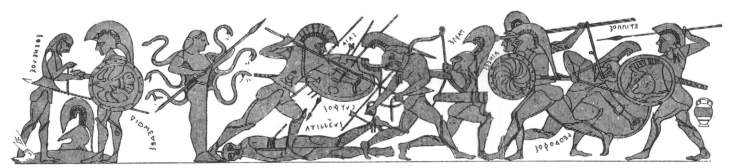

The death of Achilles does not figure in the Iliad, but was related in the later epics that gathered round the story of Troy. Achilles, it was said, fell in love with the Trojan princess Polyxena and was marrying her at the altar of Athena when he was slain by Paris, whose arrow struck him

in the only vulnerable part of his body—his heel. In this drawing from a now-destroyed Greek vase, Achilles lies dead while a struggle takes place over his corpse. Glaucus tries to drag it away by a rope, but Ajax runs him through. Paris, to the right, draws his bow.

medium for epigrams and especially for epitaphs, and so gave the word 'elegy' to European literature. Although verse of this type must have been transmitted in writing, little now survives—only brief and tantalizing glimpses, in various parts of the Greek world, of the mental and political ferment of the time.

From the island of Paros came the wanderer-poet Archilochus, son of a noble father but a slave mother, roused to bitter invective when prevented from marrying a well-born girl, driven to a mercenary soldier's life but with no illusions about the glory of war:

> A perfect shield bedecks some Thracian now;
> I had no choice: I left it in a wood.
> Ah, well, I saved my skin, so let it go!
> A new one's just as good.

Our scanty remains of Archilochus' large and varied output confirm the comment of a Roman critic: 'the greatest force of expression, a phrasing not only telling but terse and vigorous, and abundance of blood and muscle'. The loss of most of his work leaves one of the worst gaps in the literature of the ancient world.

At Athens early in the 6th century a very different figure, the statesman Solon, uses verse to declare his views and policies where a modern politician might write pamphlets in prose. He warns the citizens, for example, of the need for vigilance against dictatorship:

> As on the fiery lightning followeth the thunder,
> As from the cloudrack comes the driving hail and snow,
> From men of power comes a city's ruin; so it falls under
> A despot—by their folly its folk to bondage go.
> Once a man is exalted, hard he grows to restrain.
> Already the time is on ye to see that issue plain.

At Megara the landowner Theognis complains in bitter elegiacs that the lower orders no longer know their place, and later, dispossessed and exiled, he remembers the home he has lost:

> I heard the crane cry unto men his greeting,
> To tell them it was time to drive the plough;
> Ah, friend! he set my sorry heart a-beating,
> For others have my fertile acres now.

Dance and Lyric Song

Elegiacs and iambics, like the hexameter, lost their musical accompaniment and became poetry to be spoken or read. But there were other verse forms which always retained the character of song; for them, melody was essential, whether accompanied by the lyre (hence 'lyric' poetry) or more rarely by the flute. Some were for solo performance, and involved only words and music; in other types a third element was included—the dance. The combination of dance and song, so marked a feature of Greek poetry and Greek life, so often represented in Greek art, must go back to the earliest times. In Homer's world it is already long established, and different occasions call it forth in different forms. At a grape harvest, for example, while boys and girls carry the grapes in baskets,

> in their midst a boy
> Made lovely music with his ringing lyre,
> And sang to it the pretty Linos song
> In his clear treble, while the rest kept time
> With shouts and song, and followed up behind
> On dancing feet.

Here the lyre-player sings, the others dance. Elsewhere, usually as part of some ritual act, it is the whole dancing chorus that performs the song.

The tradition reflected in these Homeric scenes bore rich fruit in the 7th and 6th centuries BC, although its appeal to later antiquity was slight and little has survived. Today we know scarcely anything about the music of the songs, and still less about the dance. Even the text exists for the most part only in damaged and problematic remnants, but there is enough to reveal the verbal magic of some of this early poetry.

Our earliest example, already far removed from traditional folk-song, comes in the late 7th century BC from Sparta, almost the only literary evidence of the civilization that flourished there

before military austerity took its place. Recovered on papyrus in Egypt in 1855, it is part of one of the choral songs for girls for which the poet Alcman was well-known—a hymn sung by ten girls to a goddess before dawn. In spite of many difficulties of interpretation, we can still appreciate the music of Alcman's words, the liveliness, the charming quaintness of comparisons such as the chorus use of their leader,

> whose beauty seems as high and rare
> as if with brutes one should compare
> a sturdy thundering horse, a champion,
> of winged dreams the son.

From the prosperous island of Lesbos, another centre of intellectual and cultural life until it came under the domination of Persia, we possess bits and pieces of the work of two remarkable poets of the early 6th century BC. Alcaeus and Sappho composed many types of verse, but their distinctive contribution to ancient literature, perhaps developed from popular beginnings, was the simple short-stanza song for an individual singer. Alcaeus is a protagonist of the *ancien régime*: his verse is topical, vigorous, masculine, whether he utters a stream of invective against a hated politician or a call to drown such cares in wine:

> To woe the heart must not give in,
> In grief's no help. One medicine,
> My friend, alone is fit—
> Wine—and get drunk on it.

For Sappho, the one outstanding poetess of Greece, it is not power or political strife that matters but the individual—her own inward emotions, the beauty of someone she loves, whether one of the group of girls who joined her in the practice of music and song and the cult of Aphrodite, or her own daughter:

> I have a child; so fair
> As golden flowers is she,
> My Cleis, all my care.
> I'd not give her away
> For Lydia's wide sway
> Nor lands men long to see.

Our fragments of Sappho's work—we possess only one poem, a prayer to Aphrodite, complete—have a seemingly effortless craftsmanship, a radiant simplicity, a delicacy of imagery which vanish all too easily in translation. Rossetti's version of a simile describing a young bride captures something of these qualities, yet seems laboured in comparison with the original:

Like the sweet apple which reddens upon the topmost bough,
A-top on the topmost twig,—which the pluckers forgot
  somehow,—
Forgot it not, nay, but got it not, for none could get it till now.

The simplicity of these Lesbian poets, but neither Alcaeus' vigour nor Sappho's depth, reappears two generations later in the songs of Anacreon, court poet of several of the 'tyrants' of the day. A typical stanza illustrates his charming fantasy:

Anacreon—poet of wine and love—was represented on this much-damaged lekythos from Syracuse. He is playing a lyre and seems to be on his way to a party with two companions.

Once more the Lad with golden hair
His purple ball across the air
   Flings at me, true to aim;
And light her broidered slippers go,
That Lesbian lass,—my playfellow
   As Love would set the game.

Odes of Victory

In contrast with such slight and ephemeral verse stands the splendour and complexity of choral song as we find it in the early 5th century in the odes of Pindar. There were material causes for this culminating achievement. The patronage of wealthy aristocrats and 'tyrants' resulted in the emergence of professional songwriters who could pay to men the eulogies previously bestowed on the gods; and they made use of every means—the development of musical technique, for example, and the adaptation of epic legend—to further the elaboration of their art. In such a context originality, rather than tradition, was at a premium, and in spite of the division of choral song into fixed types its composers differed greatly in their handling of it: Stesichorus in the early 6th century used it for lengthy mythical narrative; Simonides, at the beginning of the 5th, brought to choral poetry the same smoothness of style and skill in the choice of words which he showed in his epigrams; his nephew Bacchylides, the last lyric poet of distinction, is consistently graceful and polished, though he rarely rises to a higher level. But most of the odes we now possess are the work of the Boeotian aristocrat Pindar, and our conception of the genre comes mainly from these.

Pindar wrote many kinds of choral song; what we now have complete is his *Epinician* or *Victory Odes*, composed for ceremonies in honour of victors at the games and divided into four groups—*Olympian, Pythian, Nemean* and *Isthmian*—corresponding to the four great athletic festivals. Praise of the victor and his family and city is only one of the threads which Pindar skilfully weaves together: with the particular occasion he combines generalization and legend, and at the same time uses the chorus as mouthpiece of his personal feelings and beliefs. Each ode has its own complex metrical pattern; and through all runs a magnificence of language and splendour of imagery which may be illustrated by the sublime description of the power of music, inspiration of the dance, at the beginning of the first *Pythian*:

O lyre of gold, Apollo's
Treasure, shared with the violet-wreathed Muses,
The light foot hears you, and the brightness begins:
Your notes compel the singer
When to lead out the dance
The prelude is sounded on your trembling strings.
You quench the warrior Thunderbolt's everlasting flame:
On God's sceptre the Eagle sleeps,
Drooping his swift wings on either side,
The King of Birds.
You have poured a cloud on his beak and head,
   and darkened his face:
His eyelids are shut with a sweet seal.
He sleeps, his lithe back heaves:
Your quivering song has conquered him.

Pindar's poetry is difficult for the modern reader to appreciate and raises baffling problems for the translator, but beyond question it is one of the greatest glories of Greek literature.

Athens' Amazing Literary Achievement

Up to this point the Greek literature known to us comes from many different places. In the 5th and 4th centuries BC, from which far more survives, it has one main source, the city of Athens; and here we can study an aspect of it which is only dimly apparent elsewhere—its relation to the society in which it was produced. In the modern world the creation and enjoyment of literature are the marginal occupation of a minority, and make little impact on the outlook or activities of the people as a whole. The secret of Athens' amazing literary achievement was its central place not only in education but in the life of the adult community, which took it for granted that literature deeply affects society and is

Chorus of youths and maidens, from an 8th- or 7th-century Attic vase. Out of early choral song and dance there later emerged the elaborate and magnificent poetry which we find in Pindar's Victory Odes, composed for performance at ceremonies in honour of successes in the games.

something with which society must be concerned. Plato's proposal to expel poets from his Utopia springs from the assumption that poetry is a force which can preserve or wreck the welfare of the state.

This does not mean that books were important at Athens. Although there is evidence of the spread of books and reading there towards the close of the 5th century BC, literature remained predominantly oral. Behind the genres that now flourished lay the part played by the spoken word in a community which enjoyed leisure as a result of slavery, used the easiest of all meeting places, the open air, and took an uninhibited delight in the gift of speech. From the assembly and the law-courts came the eloquence of the orators; from talk in the market-place, the philosophic dialogue. Most important and significant of all was the role of poetry in the great religious festivals, at which the reciters of epic or the performers of choral song competed for the judges' approval under the patronage of the whole citizen audience.

Greek bronze theatre tickets: the letter indicated in which 'wedge' of the auditorium the ticket-holder was entitled to sit. The Athenian audience was critical and sometimes noisy.

Drama: the Festival of Dionysus

Festivals in honour of Dionysus or Bacchus, god of fertility and especially of wine, provided the setting for the outstanding literary product of Athenian democracy—drama. At the Great Dionysia, the spring festival of the god, and again on a minor scale at his winter festival, the Lenaea, several days were devoted to contests in tragedy and comedy. The judges were citizens picked to give a verdict on behalf of all. The performances were financed in the same way as the provision of warships, by wealthy citizens. The Great Dionysia was a spectacular ritual occasion, at which the chief seat of honour was given to Dionysus' priest; a state holiday so general that even prisoners were released on bail to attend; a meeting point for visitors from the whole Hellenic world, to whom the city displayed the brilliance of her culture.

The requirements of the festival determined the nature of the place where it was held. As at a modern football match, there must be room for the entire public at a single performance; and this could only be achieved in daylight in the open air, on a site in or near the city suited by nature for the purpose. Structures of this kind could not easily be destroyed by either earthquakes or man, and we can still study the Theatre of Dionysus below the Acropolis at Athens as well as many others in the Greek and Roman world of which it was the prototype. But the remains at Athens share with most of the rest the defect that later alterations and additions confuse the picture; and as most of our other evidence on the subject also comes from later times, there are many doubtful points in our conception of the theatre in the days of Sophocles or Aristophanes.

The 5th century theatre was a unified whole: all those present were participants in the festival. But they were divided into three sections, to which the three parts of the theatre correspond. The use of these in tragedy must be described first.

The central feature was the *orchēstra*, the dancing-circle for the chorus. They were all men, twelve or fifteen in number, and wore masks and costumes representing their supposed sex and age and nationality and occupation. They marched on to the *orchēstra* after the opening scene of the play, and stayed until their departure brought it to an end. Their share in the performance took several forms: between the dialogue scenes they chanted choral songs to the accompaniment of a single flute; sometimes chorus and one or more actors sang in turn stanzas of lamentation or joy; their leader could intervene briefly in the dialogue; and in some plays they took part, though often an ineffective part, in the action itself. Of their movements we know little; but they certainly danced as they sang, and reacted with motions and gestures to the dialogue.

To the modern reader the utterances of the chorus often seem a tiresome interruption, and to the modern producer they present a problem. Even during the 5th century their share of the play shrank to a quarter or less. But in two ways their existence had a decisive effect on the nature of Greek tragedy. Their songs gave the action wider meaning by linking it with legend and traditional belief. Their presence, far from breaking up the play, gave it unity—not necessarily unity of time or place, which was by no means always observed, but of action: a Greek tragedy was no chronicle play, but an organic and continuous whole.

Behind the *orchēstra*, as the audience saw it, and not as yet raised above it, was the area used by the actors, although they were free to mingle with the chorus on the dancing-circle itself. At their back the *skēnē*, originally a tent for changing in, was now a movable two-storey structure of wood normally representing a palace or temple, set perhaps above one or two broad steps, and with projecting side-wings at either end. With the help of scene-painting a variety of backgrounds—even seashore or a cave—could be shown. The action took place in the open in front of the *skēnē*, events 'offstage' being reported by a messenger. Theatre devices included a crane (whereby gods could appear 'out of the machine') and a means of bringing within sight of the audience the result of violence indoors.

Late representations of the tragic actor that have come down to us portray a grotesque masked figure with exaggerated forehead, gaping mouth, and boot soles several inches thick. The 5th century, however, knew nothing of these distortions: mask and costume then were not far removed from normal life, neither

A morning in the Greek theatre ended with a satyr-play—a farcical comedy often featuring Dionysus (from whom the whole Festival originated) along with Silenus and satyrs. This detail from a 5th-century vase shows three actors holding their masks before going on to the stage. One of them has the role of an oriental king: the other two are satyrs.

probably were gesture and movement, although the balance of speech against speech and line against line in the dialogue has a ritual formality which may have been reflected in the acting. No doubt the actor's voice was the decisive factor in the competition for the prize for acting established in the middle of the century. Scarcity of men with good voices (there were no women actors) may have been the reason for using not more than three in each play, who with changes of mask and costumes shared the speaking parts between them. Silent 'extras' could be as numerous as finance allowed.

Alternation of dialogue and choral song was the fabric of each tragedy. Three from one poet were performed in succession, sometimes all on one theme, but more often as separate as three one-act plays; and they were followed by a short, boisterous and amusing piece, still by the same author, with a chorus of satyrs led by the drunken Silenus. This was the fare presented to the ten judges and the thousands of citizens, visitors, women and children, even slaves, who gathered at daybreak on the wooden seating of the *theatron* or 'watching-place', the vast natural amphitheatre from which they looked down towards the dancing-circle at its foot. Seats of honour at the front were given to officials, priests, orphans of men killed in battle, and representatives of foreign states; but the shape of the site and the clear Greek air assured that all could hear, except when hissing or applause or noisy consumption of food prevented it. Drama was a democratic occasion in the theatre at the foot of the Acropolis.

The Origins of Tragedy

On the origin of this form of drama we have only scanty and conflicting evidence, and the controversies that have resulted from it are not likely to be resolved. What seems certain is that tragedy arose out of religious ritual, and that its oldest element is the part nearest to ritual—choral song. The lyric chorus narrated legend: at some time in the 6th century BC some poet—it may have been the Athenian, Thespis, about 534—took the crucial step of introducing a *hypokrites*, an 'answerer' or 'interpreter' who could deliver speeches or converse with the leader of the chorus. Here was the first actor, bringing alive before the audience a character previously only described in narrative, adding a new dimension to that vivid presentation of individuals which pervades all Greek literature. With his advent, *drama* ('doing' the story, not merely telling it) was born; the name *tragodia*, 'goat-song', is linked in some way with the importance of the goat in the worship of the fertility god Dionysus, in whose honour drama came to be performed.

How plays became an official part of the Great Dionysia, why three tragedies were performed together, why the satyr-play was added, are questions to which there is no certain answer. The development of these beginnings into drama in the full sense was largely the achievement of Aeschylus (525–456), whose introduction of a second actor made dialogue possible independent of the chorus. From this point onwards we have extant plays by the three acknowledged masters of Attic tragedy, all presented in the 5th century though few can be given precise dates: seven by Aeschylus, including three that form a trilogy, the *Oresteia*, on a single theme; seven by Sophocles (496–406); seventeen by Euripides (485–406). To these must be added the *Rhesus*, attributed to Euripides but probably a 4th-century product, a satyr-play from Euripides, and part of one from Sophocles.

Legend on the Stage

There is enough here to show that each of these three great tragic poets had his own approach to drama, his own way of handling plot and character. Yet thanks to tradition and the nature of the occasion and place of the performance of their plays, they had much in common. They drew their themes occasionally from recent history, but normally from the rich storehouse of myth and legend already available in epic poetry—a custom which persisted even when newly invented plots had been tried: what the audience expected of tragedy was to see the heroic figures of epic and hear them speak. The handling of legend in the theatre, however, was necessarily different from its treatment in epic narrative. Most Greek tragedies presented only a climax—Agamemnon's return and death, Oedipus' discovery of the truth, Medea's revenge; and the playwright worked this climax into dramatic form by devising a series of episodes within this one phase of the story. Reference was made to earlier and later events, but they were not portrayed or even narrated until Euripides adopted the practice of opening the play with an explanatory prologue and finishing it, in many cases, with a prophetic speech from a 'god out of the machine'.

A play on this pattern leaves little room for development of character, and even elaboration in character-drawing is rare in Greek tragedy. Vigour in argument and intensity of emotion are the playwright's aim, not the psychological subtleties expected in the modern theatre. But there was great freedom and variety in depicting the figures of legend: the most familiar, Odysseus or Clytemnestra or Heracles, could be very different in different plays, even where the author was the same; and many of the lowly characters without a name—messengers, nurses, watchmen—are as distinct and memorable as their Shakespearian equivalents, although they use the same metre and practically the same language as the great.

The use of traditional material did not prevent almost equal diversity of plot. Unrestricted by religious dogma, Greek legend admitted endless variation, and the poet could select a well-known or little-known version as he chose and make his own alterations and additions. The essentials of the most familiar stories were fixed: Orestes must kill Clytemnestra, not be reconciled with her. But within these bare outlines there was always scope for originality of invention, and without wearying the audience many dramatists could ring the changes on a single theme. Their treatment of it was not limited by any narrow conception of 'tragedy' such as we derive from Aristotle: the examples that we possess include a number which have a happy ending, and their mood ranges from the horror of Sophocles' *Oedipus the King* to the romantic comedy of Euripides' *Helen*. The audience found plenty to surprise it in each poet's new handling of a traditional tale.

Three Plays of Orestes and Electra

Three of the extant plays provide an opportunity of studying a particular example of this variety and the different approaches of the three tragedians: their treatment of the revenge of Orestes, dramatized by Aeschylus in the *Libation-Bearers*, second play of the *Oresteia* trilogy, in 458 BC, and forty or more years later by Sophocles and Euripides in two plays both entitled *Electra*. The story of the murder of Agamemnon on his return from Troy by Clytemnestra and her lover, Aegisthus, and of the penalty which Orestes later exacted from them, was one of the most familiar of heroic legends. It is related briefly in the *Odyssey*, where Orestes' vengeance is represented as a righteous act of retribution against Aegisthus: the manner of Clytemnestra's death is not told. It reappeared in the 'Epic Cycle', and was the subject of a long lyric poem by Stesichorus: in his version Orestes seems to have killed both Clytemnestra and Aegisthus in obedience to Apollo, who protected him with his bow when the Furies persecuted him for the matricide. The same theme, again variously handled, is to be found in 5th-century art.

Aeschylus is said to have described his plays as 'slices from the great banquets of Homer', but his treatment of the legend in the *Oresteia* is not Homeric. Deeply concerned with its moral and religious aspect, he portrays it as a story of murder and counter-murder within the family, choosing for the three plays of his trilogy the death of Agamemnon, Orestes' revenge, and (perhaps his own invention) the end of the sequence through Orestes' trial and acquittal before an Athenian court. Like Stesichorus, he makes Apollo responsible for Orestes' act, and to suit his interpretation his emphasis naturally falls on Clytemnestra rather than Aegisthus. She is the central figure of the first play, the *Agamemnon*. In the *Libation-Bearers*, after Orestes and his friend Pylades have revealed themselves to Electra and the chorus of women and joined them in lengthy ritual at Agamemnon's tomb, the killing of Aegisthus within the palace is only a prelude to the dramatic and moral climax—the clash between Clytemnestra and her son and her pleas for mercy, rejected when Pylades reminds Orestes of Apollo's command:

Sophocles (496–406 BC) is recorded as having written 123 plays; only seven survive. Some of the greatest are products of the last years of his long life. This bronze head of the 2nd century BC is thought to represent the poet in old age.

CLYTEMNESTRA Down with your sword, my son! My own child, see this breast:
Here often your head lay, in sleep, while your soft mouth
Sucked from me the good milk that gave you life and strength.

ORESTES Pylades, what shall I do? To kill a mother is terrible,
Shall I show mercy?

PYLADES Where then are Apollo's words,
His Pythian oracles? What becomes of men's sworn oaths?
Make all men living your enemies, but not the gods.

ORESTES I uphold your judgement; your advice is good. (*To Clyt.*)
Come on;
I mean to kill you close beside him. While he lived
You preferred him to my father. Sleep with him in death.

Soon Orestes drives her into the palace. But his revenge is quickly followed by the approach of the Furies, and at the end of the play he is no righteous hero, but a hunted man. The rights and wrongs remain to be debated by Apollo and the Furies before Athena and her jurymen.

Sophocles also, as his *Antigone* shows, was far from blind to moral and religious issues. But the outstanding features of his *Electra* are his portrait of the heroine and, above all, that mastery of plot-construction in which Aristotle found him pre-eminent. His play stood by itself without prelude or sequel, and for it he constructed a version of the story close to the *Odyssey*. The recognition between brother and sister is managed with much greater skill than in the *Oresteia*, and the revenge involves a *coup de théâtre* such as Aeschylus never achieves. Orestes and Pylades gain entrance to the palace by posing as strangers bringing a report of Orestes' death and bearing his ashes. There they kill Clytemnestra. Aegisthus, away when they arrived and returning in haste at their news, is confronted with the sight of the two 'strangers' standing beside a covered body—as he supposes, the corpse of Orestes. After a moment of pretended grief he speaks to Electra, as he approaches to uncover the body:

AEGISTHUS Call Clytemnestra here,
If she is in the house.

ORESTES She is near you now,
Not far to seek.

AEGISTHUS (*lifting the covering*)
    God, what is this?

ORESTES Afraid? Of whom? Strangers?

AEGISTHUS Whose trap is this
    That I have fallen into?

ORESTES Are you so blind
    You cannot tell the living from the dead?

Not only the order of events has changed from Aeschylus' version. The dramatic emphasis has reverted to Aegisthus, and the evaluation of the story to the Homeric point of view. 'This day's work is well done', sing the chorus as they go off when Aegisthus has been taken into the palace. Of the Furies no mention is made.

In Euripides' *Electra* we are again far from Homer. Here as in many of his plays he stripped away the glamour from legend, criticized the alleged behaviour of the gods, and set the heroic characters in a new and often sordid light—realistic trends which won him little popularity in his day but made him the favourite dramatist of subsequent generations, the main link with both later tragedy and the comedy of manners. His Electra is living in poverty, married to a peasant, whose cottage forms the background to the action. The order of events is as in Aeschylus: Aegisthus is the first victim, and the climax is the killing of Clytemnestra, for which the wavering Orestes is steeled not by any reminder of Apollo's will, but by his sister's ferocious determination. The sequel to the murder is not the onslaught of the Furies, but a song in which the two describe to the chorus the horror of what they have done—the kind of scene which prompted Aristotle to call Euripides 'the most tragic of the poets':

ELECTRA She stretched her hand to my cheek,
    And there brake from her lips a moan;
    'Mercy, my child, my own!'
    Her hand clung to my cheek;
    Clung, and my arm was weak;
    And the sword fell, and was gone.

CHORUS Unhappy woman, could thine eye
    Look on the blood, and see her lie,
    Thy mother, when she turned to die?

ORESTES I lifted over mine eyes
    My mantle: blinded I smote,
    As one smiteth a sacrifice;
    And the sword found her throat . . .

This play, like others of Euripides, is ended by intervention from heaven. Clytemnestra's divine twin brothers, Castor and Pollux, appear 'out of the machine' and foretell the future, laying the blame for Orestes' act squarely on the 'unwise utterances' of Apollo. Electra is to marry Pylades, Orestes to escape the Furies by standing trial at Athens. Here Euripides echoes Aeschylus; yet five years later, in the *Orestes*, he devised an entirely different conclusion—a lurid melodrama in which brother and sister, still in Argos, go from crime to crime in their desperate efforts to escape execution by the people. Freedom in remoulding and reinterpreting legend, which has given many different versions of the Orestes story to more modern literature, was the accepted practise and one of the main attractions for the audience in the theatre of Dionysus.

The Birth of Comedy

Comedy was presented at Athens at the same festivals as tragedy. Each competing poet put on one play, approximately equal to a tragedy in length and similarly divided between a chorus (twenty-four, often split into two groups) and three male actors who performed all the speaking parts. What little evidence we have of the origins of comedy suggests that like tragedy it came into being through the addition of dialogue to choral song: acted episodes, imitated perhaps from Peloponnesian models, may have been combined in Attica with the festive singing and dancing of a *komos*, or chorus of revellers, which originated in fertility ritual and gave *komodia*, the 'song of the *komos*', its name.

To this extent the great branches of drama followed the same general pattern, but here the resemblance ends. When we turn

from tragedy to the eleven extant plays of Aristophanes—the only complete 5th-century or early 4th-century comedies that we now possess—we move from high to low: the spectator watching the comic actor play Trygaeus, the grape-farmer, or the old peasant Strepsiades, no longer had before him one of the heroic beings of legend, but a grotesque caricature of his own unheroic self—a ludicrous figure with distorted mask, padded belly and buttocks, and a large artificial phallus. In keeping with this costume the language of the dialogue was full of frank obscenity, a feature of ordinary life often reflected in vase paintings, but not normally in literature. The time represented was not the mythical past but the present: Aristophanic comedy struck a contemporary note, and its satire was always topical. Along with the Athenian equivalent of John Citizen, other actors, wearing portrait-masks, would caricature with unparalleled freedom the leading personalities of the day—Socrates, the highbrow crank, Euripides, the degenerate intellectual, Cleon, the arrogant demagogue. A fragment of Cratinus, earlier than Aristophanes, shows that even 'Olympian' Pericles was included in the rogues' gallery of the comic playwrights. The actor representing him evidently entered wearing on his head a model of the latest much-criticized addition to the Athenian building programme, the Odeum; and another exclaimed:

Here's Pericles, our own squill-headed Zeus.
Where *did* he buy that hat? With what excuse?
It's new head-cover in Odeum style—
Late storms of censure hardly left a Tile.

Topical comment could come from the chorus as well as in the dialogue. The play could be interrupted by a section in which they came forward and put directly to the audience the poet's views on current affairs. Comedy was surely the most typical literary product of democratic Athens.

In these ways comedy brought drama down to earth. But it also lifted it skywards in amazing flights of poetry and fantasy. Few things in Greek literature surpass the beauty of some of Aristophanes' choral songs; and no other author can compare with the soaring imagination of the extravaganzas which he built out of the emotional trends of the day: out of the growing desire for peace during the Peloponnesian War, the picture of farmer Dikaiopolis making a one-man truce with Sparta (*Acharnians*, 425 BC), or of Trygaeus flying to heaven in search of Peace on a dung-beetle (*Peace*, 421), or of Lysistrata leading the women in a sex strike which brings the men to their senses (*Lysistrata*, 411); out of the weariness which spread as the war dragged on, the conception of a Utopian 'Cloud-Cuckoo-Town' built by the birds in the sky (*Birds*, 414); out of the hardships of the post-war years, a burlesque of the welfare state (*Women in Parliament*, 391).

The antics and adventures of Aristophanes' 'little men' in these extraordinary situations provide most of the fun of the comedies, but he reaches the greatest heights of poetic fantasy in his handling of the chorus. Vase-paintings show that the dancing chorus masquerading as animals or birds may go back to Mycenaean times: Aristophanes uses it with spectacular effect in his *Wasps* and *Clouds* and above all in the *Birds*, where each bird has his own distinctive costume and call. Little wonder that in their address to the audience they claim that comedy is more entertaining than tragedy:

Truly to be clad in feathers is the very best of things.
Only fancy, dear spectators, had you each a brace of wings,
Never need you, tired and hungry, at a Tragic Chorus stay,
You would likely, when it bored you, spread your wings
    and fly away,
Back returning, after luncheon, to enjoy our Comic Play.

Not only his contemporaries were targets for Aristophanes' satire and fantasy. Other regular victims were the heroes of legend, tragedy, mercilessly parodied, and—by no means least—the gods. In the *Frogs*, presented in the year after the death of Sophocles and Euripides, Dionysus himself becomes a figure of fun. Disguised as Heracles he journeys to Hades, and after rowing across the Styx hurried on by a frog chorus passes through one ridiculous scrape after another before reaching the house of Pluto.

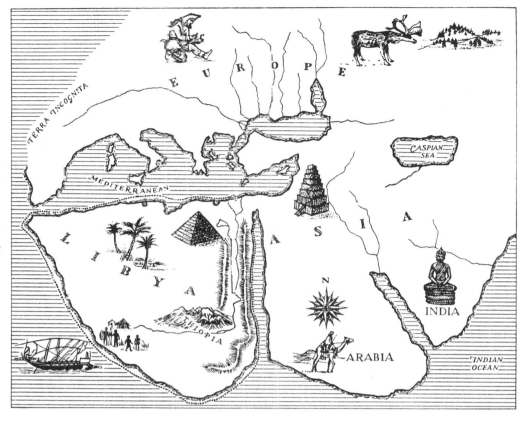

The world as it was probably conceived by Herodotus. The Mediterranean was relatively familiar, and it was known too that Africa could be circumnavigated—the route of the Phoenician sailors whose voyage Herodotus describes is shown by a dotted line. Of Ethiopia, Arabia, India and the north he had to rely on second and third hand reports, but his accuracy has been vindicated surprisingly often.

Here he is called on to decide the claim of the lately-arrived Euripides to replace Aeschylus on the throne of tragedy. With typical disregard for consistency the caricature of the god now becomes a portrait of the man-in-the-street or the man-in-the-audience, baffled by both contestants yet judging them by definite standards of morality and craftsmanship which lead him to the choice of Aeschylus. The *Frogs* is a healthy corrective to exaggerated estimates of the intellectual level of the Athenian public; but it fully confirms the existence among the great audience in the theatre of Dionysus of that lively and critical interest in drama which was the background to the brilliant achievements of the 5th century in tragedy and comedy alike.

'As it Appears to Me to Be True'

The question when prose literature first emerged in Greece is unanswerable. Even if we possessed extensive remains of early prose, we should be faced with the problem of deciding which of them, if any, deserved to be called 'literature'. But in prose, as in verse, the works now extant are products of maturity, when growing pains were past; from the many earlier writers mere scraps survive, and we can only point to trends that led up to the three main types of prose literature in the 5th and 4th centuries BC—history, oratory, and the philosophic dialogue.

Several elements contributed to the making of history: the practice in some cities, for example, of keeping local records and lists; popular non-verse telling of traditional tales. But the driving force which eventually produced Herodotus and Thucydides came less from tradition than from revolt against it. The word *historie* means inquiry or the results of inquiry—search for truth as opposed to tradition, fact as opposed to fiction; and because tradition and fiction were normally expressed in verse, the new radical spirit of *historie* which came to the fore in Ionia in the 6th century BC readily adopted prose as its medium. Inquiry might be pursued in various fields, from astronomy to medicine. Some looked for a more rational explanation of the universe, like Anaximander, who wrote one of the earliest books in prose. Others, like Hecataeus, travelled and described in prose what they had seen or heard. The opening sentences of one of Hecataeus' works happen to have reached us:

> Thus speaks Hecataeus of Miletus. What follows I write as it appears to me to be true; for the writings of the Greeks are many and in my opinion ridiculous.

In the emphasis here on truth and the assertion of individual thought against all 'the writings of the Greeks' we have the essentials of the new spirit which turned for expression to prose.

'The Father of History'

The advance from such beginnings to the creation of history was the achievement of Herodotus, the first Greek prose writer whose work we have today. Born at Halicarnassus early in the 5th century, Herodotus later lived at Athens and joined the Athenian colony of Thurii in southern Italy; but much of his life was spent in travelling still more widely over the Greek and non-Greek world. Many of the five hundred pages of his book present (along with material drawn from earlier writings) the harvest of information which he gathered on his travels: one long section takes us to Egypt, others to Thrace, Scythia, North Africa, India, Babylon. What distinguishes Herodotus from his predecessors is the inclusion of all this within a single historical framework—the narrative of the struggle between Greece and Persia, which is stated as the book's subject in its opening sentence, provides a connecting chain through two-thirds of its length, and culminates in a narrative of Persian aggression and its defeat that sweeps majestically forward almost without a break. Whether this historical pattern was in the author's mind from the first or a structure superimposed later, is a much disputed question. The result, however it came about, is a work of epic dimensions, embodying a magnificently broad conception of history. Yet for all his breadth of view Herodotus is never abstract: he is always concerned with particular places and events, particular customs and beliefs; above all, his pages are a portrait gallery of famous men and women, although the hero of his narrative as a whole is Athens itself.

Herodotus has a childlike love of marvels—Indian ants bigger than foxes, the gruesome burial ceremonies of Scythian kings—and he describes them in a story-telling style so apparently simple that its art passes unnoticed. He is too easily regarded as a mere narrator of wonders. In reality his outlook is the insatiable questioning spirit of *historie*, seeking truth and repeatedly giving voice to doubt. Of the diver who was said to have escaped from the Persians by staying beneath the surface of the sea for nearly ten miles, he writes:

> How he did reach the Greeks I cannot say with certainty, but I should be surprised if the story told is true . . . My own opinion is that he came to Artemisium in a boat.

The 'father of history', as he is rightly called, is no credulous fool. He is often sceptical, but he is not systematic in his treatment of evidence: history for him is certainly an art, not a science. For a more scientific approach, and for the first statement of principles acceptable to a modern historian, we have to turn to his younger contemporary, Thucydides.

The First Scientific Historian

Athenian born and bred, Thucydides had reached the position of general by 424 BC, when he was held responsible for a defeat and exiled. For twenty years, till he returned to Athens shortly before his death, circumstances placed him, like Herodotus, in the position of an observer. His choice was to concentrate his attention on contemporary history: his work begins with a survey of the past, but only to demonstrate 'the feebleness of antiquity' and the unprecedented size and importance of the struggle between Athens and Sparta. The rest, with few digressions, describes the course of the Peloponnesian War down to 411, where it breaks off, unfinished and unrevised.

How far the book was constructed on a single plan, we do not know; but it bears all the marks of a rational and systematic approach to the writing of history. In contrast with Herodotus' breadth of view, Thucydides restricts his theme to the military events of the war and the reasons for them. He adopts a simple summer-winter division of each year to avoid chronological confusion. He handles evidence in accordance with rules comparable with the precision of medical science at the time:

> With regard to my factual reporting of the events of the war I have made it a principle not to write down the first story that came my way, and not even to be guided by my own general impressions; either I was present myself at the events which I have described or else I heard of them from eye-witnesses whose reports I have checked with as much thoroughness as possible.

Demosthenes, greatest of Greek orators, was born early in the 4th century BC *and lived through the conquest of Greece by Macedon—a conquest which he foresaw and against which he passionately warned his countrymen, in vain. His success in oratory was due to hard application and effort: he studied the speeches of earlier orators, and stories are told of his overcoming a stammer by speaking with pebbles in his mouth and declaiming by the sea amid the thunder of the waves.*

The work of Herodotus, like Homeric epic, included speeches by leading characters in the narrative: this practice also Thucydides systematized and adapted to his own ends, putting into the mouths of the speakers the motives which prompted an action, the arguments for and against it, the policies and principles involved.

Thucydides' book, however, is more than systematic or even scientific history. It has other qualities which make it great literature. His swift narrative has a unique and paradoxical style: it breathes the spirit of contemporary rationalism yet has an old-fashioned flavour; it is concise and austere, yet forceful and impassioned. The style is typical of the man. By no means impartial, he is deeply committed to support of Pericles and his policy, deeply moved by Athens' folly (as he sees it) and its disastrous results; yet he austerely surveys the whole story as a clinical example of human behaviour under the stresses of imperialism and war. In Thucydides' account of the tragedy of Athens there is a grandeur of conception, as well as an intensity of feeling, which would have stood out even more clearly if he had been able to continue the story to the end.

Thucydides had no successor. The 4th century, mainly a century of prose, was not lacking in historians, but produced none comparable with the giants of the 5th. The only one of them whose writings are now extant is Xenophon (about 430–354), who has considerable charm but little intellectual power: his works may at any rate be a better mirror of his times than the creations of more brilliant minds. One trend reflected in them is a movement towards biography, exemplified in memoirs of Socrates and idealized accounts of Cyrus, founder of the Persian Empire, and the Spartan king Agesilaus; and much the most readable product of Xenophon's pen is autobiographical—the *Anabasis* or *March Inland*, a simple but vivid narrative of the adventures of the ten thousand or more Greeks who joined an expedition to attack Babylon in 401, and after its failure struggled back to Greece under Xenophon's leadership.

The Prose of Persuasion

Xenophon is largely free from the influence which dominated most historical writing from the 4th century onwards: the influence of rhetoric, by nature inimical to the spirit of the early historians, although Thucydides was considerably affected by it. The object of *historiē* was to discover the truth; rhetoric was concerned with *persuasion*, a process in which eloquence was all-important and truth could go to the wall. The rise of rhetoric, first in Sicily and then at Athens, in the 5th century, and its growing importance thereafter in Greek life and education and literature, are phenomena which need not surprise us in a society still far more dependent on the spoken than the written word, which now developed political forms that made oratory the highroad to success: government by mass meeting and trial by mass jury put a premium on the art of effective speech, and teachers of it—the Sophists—became familiar figures in Athens and other cities by the time of the Peloponnesian War.

The 4th century has bequeathed to us a large number of speeches by Attic orators. Many are law-court addresses, more emotional and more slanderous than those of today, and often inspired by political motives. Others are orations delivered in the Assembly, readable now only if we can recapture some of the sense of controversy or crisis which excited the original audience. A few belong to the category of public lectures, designed for great occasions such as the Olympic Games. Critics ancient and modern agree that the greatest master of eloquence, in political and law-court speeches alike, is Demosthenes (384–322), whose passionate warnings against the threat to Greek freedom have had many echoes in the modern world. There is remarkable variety of both style and matter in Demosthenes' many surviving works. As circumstances demand he can be simple in language or grandiose, address the Assembly in terms of high principle or resort to violent personal invective to entertain a jury. Two brief extracts from his famous speech *On the Crown* (330), in which he defends his own past against an attack by his political antagonist Aeschines, illustrate the wide range of his eloquence even on a single occasion. He attacks his rival's speech:

> If my calumniator had been Aeacus, or Rhadamanthus, or Minos, instead of a mere scandal-monger, a market-place loafer, a poor devil of a clerk, he could hardly have used such language, or equipped himself with such offensive expressions. Hark to his melodramatic bombast: 'Oh, Earth! Oh, Sun! Oh, Virtue', and all that vapouring; his appeals to 'intelligence and education, whereby we discriminate between things of good and evil report'—for that was the sort of rubbish you heard him spouting. Virtue! you runagate; what have you or your family to do with virtue? How do you distinguish between good and evil report? Where and how did you qualify as a moralist? Where did you get your right to talk about education?

Later he assures the jury that the policy of resistance to Macedon was in line with Athenian tradition:

> You cannot, men of Athens, you cannot have done wrongly when you accepted the risks of war for the redemption and the liberties of mankind; I swear it by our forefathers who bore the brunt of warfare at Marathon, who stood in array of battle at Plataea, who fought in the sea-fights of Salamis and Artemi-

sium, and by all the brave men who repose in our public sepulchres, buried there by a country that accounted them all to be alike worthy of the same honour—all, I say, Aeschines, not the successful and the victorious alone. So justice bids: for by all the duty of brave men was accomplished: their fortune was such as Heaven severally allotted to them.

Rhetoric was not confined to the law-courts and the Assembly but quickly spread to other fields, including some which traditionally belonged to poetry. Orations on philosophical or political topics became an alternative to drinking songs at banquets. Festivals were now occasions not only for the recitations of rhapsodes, but for exhibition speeches in the grand manner. Instruction in the technique of speaking found a place alongside memorization of Homer in the schools. Such intensive cultivation of eloquence had an inevitable effect on prose style, reshaping it into an instrument of telling argument and appeal to the emotions. Numerous teachers of the new art in the 4th century built on the foundations laid by the Sophists in the 5th: the most important of them for the future of literature was Isocrates (436–338), no great orator himself (his numerous 'speeches' are tracts or essays written for readers rather than an audience) but the chief creator of rhetoric as a distinct science and chief architect of the 'grand style' which became the model for later Greek and Latin prose. He and his pupils were largely reponsible for the extension of the influence of rhetoric not only to history and biography, but to nearly all branches of literature. From this time onwards eloquence, not truth or clarity, was the standard by which a writer was most commonly judged.

The Philosophers Speak

In contrast with this trend stand two great bodies of philosophical prose: the works of Plato (427–347) and Aristotle (384–322). Aristotle's early writings are now lost, but if we may judge by the extant fragments of them and the verdict of ancient critics, they would have given him a high place in the history of Greek literature; the treatises of his which do survive belong rather to philosophy and science, although the brief and incomplete *Poetics* has had a profound influence on the literary ideas of the modern world. Plato's works, fortunately, we possess in their entirety. Plato rightly regarded rhetoric as an art concerned with show, not with reality. On more than one occasion he exposes the shallowness of contemporary eloquence by portraying Socrates as the true orator; in the *Apology*, for example, where Socrates also defends his own past before a mass jury, he replies to his accusers' allegation that he is a clever speaker:

> I have not the slightest skill as a speaker—unless, of course, by a skilful speaker they mean one who speaks the truth. If that is what they mean, I would agree that I am an orator, though not after their pattern.

Plato's main answer to the rhetoricians, however, was the dialogue form itself. Oratory had grown out of one side of the activities of the city-state—the importance of ability to sway an audience; in the dialogue Plato crystallized another aspect of Athenian daily life—conversation between individuals in the streets or the market-place, in which lay the possibility, as Socrates had shown, of the clash of mind on mind in a joint search for truth. After Socrates' execution in 399 BC, a number of his admirers wrote conversations in which he was the central figure; Plato's achievement was the elaboration of this simple form into works which have greater literary appeal, as well as more philosophic value, than all the speeches of the orators. Some of the dialogues are dramatic masterpieces, ranging from the death-scene of Socrates in the *Phaedo* to the gentle comedy of the gathering of Sophists in the *Protagoras*. As portraiture, admiring or satiric, they are the most brilliant product of the new biographical trend in literature. They embrace an amazing variety of content and style: not only the refinements and wit of polished conversation, but parody, the subtlety of which we can only partly judge, myths that carry imaginative writing to poetic heights. In spite of his insistence on truth rather than display, or perhaps because of it, Plato is the greatest master of Greek prose.

The popularity of Menander's comedies is attested to by the number of papyrus fragments that continue to be found. In 1956 the manuscript of a whole play, the Bad-Tempered Man, was discovered, the last page of which, shown here, has the author's name and the title of the play (Dyskolos) written in capitals at the foot.

After Alexander

The centuries which followed the rise of Macedon were a time of the spread of culture. Throughout the Greek-speaking world conditions developed which the modern mind regards as favourable for the advance of literature: book production and the reading public increased; under wealthy patronage great libraries were established, festivals became more numerous and more lavish and fine buildings were erected to house them. From the large literary output of this Hellenistic Age—mostly prose, but also many types of verse—little now survives, although papyrus discoveries have added much during the past hundred years. But there is enough to show that although the production of literature grew, the great creative period had ended with the decline of the sovereign power of the city-state. Political and social change brought no radically different literary forms into being, but only modifications of the old: the new outlook on life found its chief reflection, in literature as in art, in a new concern with personal life and emotion, a new realism in the portrayal of character. The writer now sees man as an individual rather than a citizen. The little book of *Characters* by the philosopher Theophrastus sets the tone for the new age, and romantic love becomes an accepted theme.

Athens remained the home of drama, although theatres and dramatic festivals were set up throughout the eastern Mediterranean. The contests in tragedy and comedy in the Theatre of Dionysus continued, but until the last decades of the 4th century we have only brief fragments of some of the plays presented. Comedy seems to have shown the greater vitality and power of development; and when Attic drama partially emerges again from obscurity, it is comedy that we can study. Papyrus finds have given us parts of several plays by Menander (342–291), acclaimed in antiquity as the outstanding playwright of his day, and in 1956 a whole play of his, the *Dyskolos* or the *Bad-Tempered Man*, came to light. These remains, like the works of Roman playwrights based on Menander, present us with a type of drama very different from Aristophanes, and perhaps more indebted to Euripides than to early comedy. The chorus has been reduced to a mere song-and-dance interlude, indicated by a stage-direction in the text.

The language is neither fantastic nor obscene, but (although still in iambic verse) close to ordinary educated speech. There is no caricature of individuals; the characters are realistic portraits of types familiar in contemporary Athens: old men, erring sons, their womenfolk, and their dependants—servants, cooks, nurses, prostitutes, and the rest. A clever slave is often the most dynamic and amusing figure in the play. The plot is no longer farcical or extravagant, but a tale from normal life with love as its central theme and a happy ending assured. Menander's masked all-male actors in the open-air theatre would hardly have seemed realistic to a modern audience, but his realism astonished the Greeks; and through their Roman imitators he and his contemporaries gave to Europe the conception of the realistic comedy of manners.

The Scholar-Poets of Alexandria

Apart from drama and philosophy, Alexandria was the literary capital of the Hellenistic world. The patronage of the Ptolemies and the great Library which they established attracted scholars from many parts of Greece, some of whom classified and edited the literature of the past collected there and made possible its preservation into modern times. Men of such learning naturally produced many works in prose; but what we now possess from them is a slowly growing portion of their verse, remnants of a brief flowering of poetry between 290 and 240. These men were scholar-poets, highly conscious of their art and much concerned with theories of how it should be exercised. Far from the mass audience at the Panathenaea or the Great Dionysia, they wrote for a select circle of listeners or readers; and for verse forms to suit such a purpose they turned chiefly to much earlier models—the short epic, the narrative elegy, the hymn, the epigram. They found traditional but novel subject-matter in unfamiliar legend drawn from local chronicles or little-known sections of the Epic Cycle. Yet in their poetry also we find not only ingenuity and prettiness and wit, but realism, the expression of personal emotion, and other characteristic features of the time.

The most representative of the Alexandrian poets is Callimachus, a figure whose stature grows as nearly every year adds something to our remains of his verses. The six *Hymns* which survive complete combine mythology and flattery of Ptolemy in an amalgam which has little attraction for the modern reader, but as parts of his finer work have come to light they have revealed an unexpected range of content and versatility of style. Perhaps some of his epigrams have the most direct appeal today; certainly they exemplify that small-scale perfection which Callimachus made his literary ideal and championed against his critics in the prologue to his own longest work, the *Aitia* or *Beginnings*:

> Go learn, O green-eyed monster's fatal brood,
> By Art, not parasangs, to judge what's good.
> Look not to me for lofty sounding song;
> The thunder-claps to father Zeus belong.
> When first a tablet on my knees reclined,
> Apollo, lord of Lycia, spoke his mind:
> 'Give me, good bard, for sacrificial fare
> A victim fat: but let your Muse be spare.
> And listen,—when your chariot skims the road,
> Avoid the route that takes a wagon's load;
> Leave open ways and trodden tracks alone,
> And go the gate that's narrow, but your own.'
> I tuned my quill, nor let the warning pass,—
> A sweet cicala, not a raucous ass.
> Long ears and all, another bard shall bray;
> Let me go light, and flit my dainty way.

The main target of Callimachus' strictures was Apollonius, called 'the Rhodian' because he withdrew from Alexandria to live at Rhodes. Apollonius had the temerity to write a narrative poem half the length of the *Odyssey* on the adventures of the Argonauts—the first literary epic still extant. The *Argonautica* is closely modelled on Homer—metre, language, similes and all—but the story is clogged with too much learning and most of the characters, divine and human, are colourless; only the description of the young Medea's love for Jason makes the poem come alive. Callimachus seems to have been the victor in this earliest bout of

literary polemics, but the long epic survived to reappear at Rome, and Apollonius showed that he too could write an epigram:

> 'Cesspool' and 'cheat' begin with C, and so does 'crass stupidity'.
>> Who wrote *Beginnings* is the man
>> From whom the whole affair began.

The Creator of the Pastoral

The greatest of the Alexandrians is Theocritus, creator of the pastoral—the one new poetic form, if such it can be called, in Hellenistic literature. In the hexameter pieces which later became known as his *Idylls* (the Greek word means 'short poems') the familiar Alexandrian features are again present, but they rarely spoil his poetry: he is erudite, but seldom displays his learning; he flatters his patrons and inserts open or veiled allusions to his friends and fellow-poets, but usually without striking a jarring note; his constant theme is romantic love, but he tempers it with realism and humour. The collection includes a variety of forms, skilfully adapted or sometimes combined together. Some of the poems are brief narratives in epic style. Others are sophisticated versions of the 'mime', simple popular drama which had been performed by travelling players in Greece from early times, and now became a vehicle of Hellenistic realism. Even Menander does not go so far in realistic portraiture as Theocritus' Syracusan women walking with their maids through the streets of Alexandria to visit the festival of Adonis:

> GORGO Praxinoa,
>> O, look at all that crowd before the door.
>
> PRAXINOA Incredible. Here, Gorgo, take my arm,
>> and you catch hold of Eutychis there, Eunoa,
>> or you'll be separated—now let's try
>> to push in altogether. Mind, Eunoa,
>> keep hold of me—O, Gorgo, what a shame,
>> my summer cloak is torn from top to bottom.

This is a 'mime' of city life. Realism combined with romance, and with country folk-song traditions that may have included the singing-match and the refrain, to produce the pastorals, which have given us not only the idealized peasant, not only Daphnis and Lycidas and Amaryllis, but descriptions of nature hardly equalled in Greek poetry.

Under Roman Patronage

The *Idylls* were the last great achievement of Greek poetry prior to the conquest of Greece by Rome. Thereafter most of what is best in classical literature comes from Latin authors, following after their own fashion the lines of development laid down by the Greeks. But the continued abundance and variety of Greek writing even in the Roman period may be illustrated by mentioning a few of the authors whose works, in whole or in part, have survived: the historian Polybius, who under Roman patronage took Thucydides as his chief model in describing the rise of Rome to imperial power; Plutarch, whose *Parallel Lives* of Greek and Roman soldiers and statesmen are the most famous product of that biographical writing which had begun in the 4th century BC; Lucian, master of the satiric dialogue, whose lively castigations of cant and hypocrisy owed something to Aristophanes as well as to Plato; Longus, author of the romance *Daphnis and Chloe*, with its pastoral setting reminiscent of Theocritus: even the modern novel has a prototype among the Greeks. All these are prose writers; for although (as the *Palatine Anthology* of epigrams compiled in the 10th century AD bears witness) the art of verse was still practised, and sometimes to admirable effect, prose was the prevailing form of Greek literature in this later period just as poetry had dominated its earlier and more brilliant centuries.

Where an account of it should end, is a question without an answer. If by Greek literature we mean literature in Greek, its history has no ending: it is still being written today. But in a sense most of the literature of the modern world has been Greek, in that it has drawn its forms and inspiration, directly or indirectly, from the Greeks; and that is an inheritance which will last as long as the civilization which it has helped to create.

IV THE REVOLUTION IN THE MIND

Old gods and the new reason

W.K.C. GUTHRIE

'Truly the gods have not from the beginning
revealed all things to mortals, but by long seeking
mortals make progress in discovery'.

XENOPHANES OF COLOPHON, 18

The Greek 'progress in discovery'

was the beginning of the modern world of philosophy, technology and science. By sheer force of intellect, with little or no help from earlier peoples, the Greeks between 600 and 300 BC enabled mankind to rise above a reliance upon fetichism and superstition and to achieve a full, free and rational approach to the world of nature. How little, indeed, their gods had 'revealed all things', and how daring were the men who began the new approach to the mysteries of the universe, is demonstrated by the dense twilight of traditional, primitive beliefs and unreason, and the elaborate pantheon of Olympian gods and goddesses whose imagined influence permeated the whole of Greek religious and secular life.

The Greeks had no sacred book; it was the *Iliad* and the *Odyssey* which established the lasting features of the Olympians—the assembly of gods and goddesses in the image of man, with human virtues and human failings. Something of this is expressed in the sculptured relief of the Apotheosis of Homer (opposite) of about 200 BC. Homer sits enthroned in the lower left-hand corner,

holding a scroll and staff and being crowned by the World and Time. His throne is supported on one side by a figure holding a sword and personifying his *Iliad*, and on the other by *Odyssey*, holding a ship's ornament. Two mice against a roll under his footstool represent a third poem *The Battle of Frogs and Mice*, once attributed to him. A boy personifying Myth stands by the altar upon which History is sprinkling incense, while Poetry holds up two torches, and Tragedy and Comedy, wearing masks, raise their hands in salutation. Last come Nature (a child) and fair women personifying Integrity, Memory, Fidelity and Wisdom. Over the whole presides Zeus, the supreme god, with his second consort, Memory (Mnemosyne) of whom the nine Muses were born. They are below, with Apollo standing among them holding his lyre. The additional figure on the right is the man who commissioned the sculpture.

Whence did these complex conceptions come? It is not possible to disentangle the multitude of origins, but two streams of early humanity were the most important influences.

The Olympian gods ruled the world with a mixture of divine wisdom and wilful caprice. Most powerful was Zeus, originally a sky-god, cloud-gatherer, sender of rain, with voice of thunder and weapon of lightning. The bronze statue (*left*), found in the sea off Artemisium only 50 years ago, was first taken to be his brother Poseidon, ruler of the seas, but is now thought to be Zeus himself.

Zeus, aided by his grandmother, Earth, battled for supremacy against the sons of Earth, his father Cronus and the Giants. The masterly archaic sculpture on the Treasury of the Siphnians at Delphi (*below*) shows incidents in this war. Giants, in human form and the armour of Greek warriors, assail the gods with spears and swords. On the left is Dionysus in his panther skin, then Cybele in her chariot drawn by lions, one of whom is mauling a giant. Then come Apollo and Artemis shooting arrows, and a giant flees.

The orgiastic cult of Dionysus, or Bacchus, stands in sharp contrast to the clear, rational pantheon of Olympus. In origin a fertility god, the ivy-crowned Dionysus (*right*) presided over wild outbreaks of emotional frenzy which the Greeks permitted at certain times and seasons. Believing themselves possessed by the god, his votaries, chiefly women or maenads, wreathed with ivy, fir or oak and wrapped in skins, followed a young male priest up the rough path to the high plateau above Delphi, intoxicated by wine, swinging torches, dancing and leaping to the sound of pipes and drum, to reach a state of ecstasy which could culminate in tearing apart and tasting the raw flesh of animals. In their trance-like state, the dancers were insensitive to cold and pain. These outbreaks occurred in the three winter months when Apollo was believed to be absent from Delphi.

The scene *below* was painted on a vase around 435 BC to represent just such an orgiastic dance in honour of Dionysus and a goddess who may be Demeter, Artemis or Cybele. One of the performers grasps a small snake in her hand as a flute player in richly decorated garb pipes a tune. The figure holding cymbals is probably a priest.

The birth of reason, whereby men sought for the first time to explain nature by her own universal and predictable laws, occurred with astonishing suddenness amid the complex traditions of myth and mystery, of ritual and ecstasy. One group of thinkers in south Italy aimed at evolving a flawless metaphysical system, often unrelated to the real world; another, centred in Ionia, concentrated on questions which today are still the basic preoccupations of science.

Plato (*above left*) lifted the discussion on to a metaphysical plane. For him the task of philosophy was to achieve a vision of eternal and perfect entities or 'forms', in his view the true realities of the universe.

Aristotle (*above right*), after twenty years with Plato, preferred to concentrate upon a patient search for facts—an attitude which has never lost its relevance—and created formal logic in his search for the right approach.

The atomic theory was first propounded by Leucippus and by Democritus of Abdera (of whom the fine head *opposite* has been thought to be a late portrait). Matter, according to Democritus, was composed of solid, indivisible atoms, too small to be perceived by the senses, but linking in various combinations to produce the material world as we know it.

Socrates, 'the gadfly of the Athenians', drove men to exasperated reflection upon the problem of Goodness. His features are among the best known of antiquity—he was said to resemble Silenus. The statuette (*left*) is a well-known Roman copy of a 4th-century original.

Reason set the Greeks free to come to terms with nature and to improve human life, although medicine itself was still linked with religion. Patients sought cures by sleeping in temples, where, as *left*, they could dream that a god was healing them.

Plato taught in Athens around 3ε dedicated to the Greek hero Academ mosaic *opposite* probably preserves ε details (note the Acropolis, top rig seated on a semi-circular stone seat en claw legs. He holds a stick in his rig seems to be drawing a figure in the s ground, in a box, is a celestial spher stands on a column behind.

The murder of Archimedes by a Roman Sicily in 212 BC (*below*) destroyed one of t mathematicians and engineers of the an He invented hydrostatics and great' mathematics, geometry, and theoretic He invented a screw for raising water the weight-lifting efficiency of pulleys ar famous deduction on the loss of weight immersed in water.

We owe geometry as a logically deductive system entirely to the Greeks, who tended to see all mathematics in geometrical terms. Pythagoras founded a brotherhood dedicated to the idea that the universe was a 'harmony'. He was still remembered with honour in AD 230, as the coin (*above*) from Samos (his birthplace) testifies. It shows him seated, his left hand holding a sceptre, his right touching a globe on a column. The discoveries of such thinkers as Pythagoras and Archimedes were codified by the Alexandrian scholars Euclid and, later, Hero.

The papyrus fragment (*left*) comes from a book of the type of Hero's 'Geometry': the diagram at the bottom (redrawn as an inset) demonstrates the reduction of an irregular figure to simple geometrical shapes, perhaps to calculate the area.

The precision instrument of the 1st century BC (*below left*), found on an ancient wreck, startlingly reveals the amazing standard of Greek technology. Its twenty or more interlocking gear-wheels (including one mounted eccentrically on a turntable) were set in motion by an input axle (entering top right), causing pointers to move on a set of inscribed dials, indicating the positions of sun, moon, and certain planets. A reconstruction is given on p. 86.

The art of healing, with its semi-magical invocations to supernatural powers, became the science of medicine. A coin of Selinus (*below*) showing the local river-god sacrificing at the altar of Asclepius (represented by his emblem the cock) is a neat example of this ambivalence; it celebrates the ending of a malaria epidemic by Empedocles, who diverted one river to clear another which had become stagnant.

Old gods and the new reason

W. K. C. GUTHRIE

Before the Greek-speaking peoples entered the Aegean area, the dominant religion centred round a Mother-goddess. These coarsely modelled Mycenaean figurines (14th–13th centuries BC) were evidently mass-produced: over 200 of them have been found at the same site at Delphi. The union of such early cults with the sky-god religion of the Greeks is thought to lie behind the complex pantheon of the Olympian deities.

ANCIENT GREEK RELIGION was a complex phenomenon. Never crystallized, like Christianity, Judaism or Islam, in a set of sacred scriptures, it was formed gradually by the many-sided character of the Greek people and by influences from outside. From the first half of the 2nd millennium BC, waves of Greek-speaking tribes invaded the Aegean area, where the dominant religious figure was the mother-goddess. Though much in her religion seemed alien to the more masculine character of the invaders, who came as warriors rather than agriculturalists, they accepted her, and in the form of the 'Ephesian Artemis' even assimilated her to a goddess of their own whose special mark had been her pure virginity.

By the time we know them, the gods of the Greeks had already absorbed so many traits from different sources that to speak of the 'origin' of this one or that is impossible if not meaningless; but at least we know that for these invaders of Indo-European stock a masculine sky-god was supreme, Zeus the father of gods and men. The blending of the two main elements of the historical population is reflected in the many marriages or liaisons of Zeus with local forms of the Great Mother.

Gods in Man's Image

The inscribed tablets of the Mycenaean age show us the names of some of the gods of classical Greece as early as the 13th century BC, including Zeus, Hera, Poseidon, Hermes, Athena, Artemis and Dionysus. But they can tell us little about them, and for us as for the Greeks themselves, the lasting features of the Olympians were stamped on them by the Homeric poems. These present a uniquely vivid collection of deities with human form and strongly marked personalities. The poet has seized on the multitude of gods of diverse origin and with a characteristically Greek blend of visual imagination and rationalism has welded them into a compact and organized whole on the pattern of the patriarchal aristocracy remembered from Mycenaean times. Zeus is both king and father, and at the same time retains many of his functions as god of sky and weather: he is the Cloud-gatherer, sends the rain that fertilizes our mother the earth, speaks in the thunder and wields the thunderbolt. The other gods may be quarrelsome and rebellious, but they know that in the end his will must prevail.

Gods in Homer form the highest stratum of a single society organized on a strict basis of class. Their relations to men are external, not unlike those of a human king like Agamemnon to his subordinate chiefs and the common people. This in some ways brings them close to humanity. In form they embody the perfection of human beauty, and it is often difficult to decide whether a Greek statue of the *kouros* type is intended to represent a young athlete or Apollo, a female figure Aphrodite, Artemis or Hera or simply a devotee dressed like the goddess. It was the aim of men and women to reproduce in their own person the beauty of the divine.

The gods also shared human failings. By the end of the 6th century Xenophanes was already castigating Homer and Hesiod for attributing to them 'all the actions which among men bring reproach and blame—theft, adultery and deceit'. The only restraint was a feeling of *noblesse oblige*. Zeus upholds the chivalrous code

of hospitality, respect for strangers, and the sanctity of the oath, but he has his favourites and his whims. Men are betrayed by the gods and openly upbraid them, but they are helpless. Two things set the gods apart from men, their superhuman powers and above all their immortality. They even mate with mortal women, but their offspring are mortal. Here is an impassable barrier.

The Generations of the Gods

Homer depicts an established order, but from Hesiod we learn that it has not been from all time. His work, the sole survivor of a number of mythical accounts of the origin of the universe and the gods, shows traces of a composite origin, and in parts is already at a fairly advanced stage of sophistication. In the beginning Earth and Heaven were together in one mass, till a gap appeared, and in it Eros, the spirit of sexual love, and such powers as Darkness and Night, Light and Day, in pairs of male and female. From this point the world and the gods can be produced by processes of copulation and birth. In the cruder myth Earth lay with Heaven, and produced, besides geographical entities like mountains and the sea, the Titans, one of whom, Cronus, at his mother's instigation forcibly separated his parents and mutilated his father. These tales have obvious affinities with early Oriental myths. The forcible separation of Heaven and Earth occurs in the Babylonian story of Marduk, and from nearer Greece the Hittite version includes the castration motif.

Two of the Titans, Cronus and Rhea, were the parents of Zeus, with whom the hostility between father and son is repeated. Fearful of a usurper, Cronus swallowed his children, but when Zeus was born Rhea, on the advice of her mother Earth, tricked him with a stone. Zeus was born in Crete (the story of his birth in fact assimilates him to an old Cretan earth-spirit), where Earth hid him in a cave. When he grew up she continued to help and advise him as he prepared for battle first with the Titans and then with the monster Typhoeus. Her position as *eminence grise* through successive generations of gods testifies to her age-old power in the Aegean lands. Only after a tremendous struggle did Zeus secure his power. Then he was acclaimed by the other Olympians to whom he assigned duties and privileges. Of all this the aristocratic Homer seems scarcely aware, but it lives again later in the *Prometheus Bound* of Aeschylus, where to the Titan Prometheus, Zeus is an upstart ruler intoxicated with the taste of power.

The Immortals of Olympus

Each of the Homeric gods was a clearly defined character. Hera, wife of Zeus, most probably grew out of the local mother-goddess of Argos, with which city she had a constant association. Poseidon and Hades, brothers of Zeus, received the sea and the underworld respectively as their portions. Poseidon was also god states forgot their differences and a citizen of Athens, Thebes or Sparta could feel that he was part of a larger unity, the unity of the Greek-speaking world as opposed to the unintelligible *barbaroi*. Sacred and secular were happily blended. He moved among temples and statues which satisfied his aesthetic sense, sacrifice and prayer mingled with athletic and musical contests, rare feasts of meat and all the trappings of a fair. Greek enjoyment of these things, and a predominently conservative, humanistic and un-mystical outlook ensured the persistence of Homeric ideas long after the Homeric society had disappeared.

Beauty and Light, Darkness and Ecstasy

Apollo seems at first sight to typify this side of the Greek charac-ter. He represented the perfect type of physical beauty, he was god of sanity and light, of 'Know thyself' and 'Nothing too much', of the music of the lyre. He stood for law and order: no legislator would draw up a constitution without the advice of his oracle at Delphi. But within the field of law his special interest was homicide. This was because, as *Katharsios*, he held in his gift the means of purification from the pollution which followed any contact with death. When Orestes killed his mother, albeit at Apollo's own behest and to avenge the murder of his father, he was pursued by the Furies until at Delphi, under Apollo's instruc-tions, he carried out the proper sacrifices to appease the powers of the nether world.

We are used to regarding Apolline and Dionysiac as polar opposites, but at Delphi these opposites met. Plutarch, himself a Delphic priest, went so far as to say that the sanctuary belonged to Dionysus no less than to Apollo. For the three winter months Apollo was absent on a visit to the Hyperboreans in the far North, and during that time the shrine was given over to Dionysus. In the inner sanctum where the Pythia gave her responses there stood not only a golden statue of Apollo, his tripod and the navel-stone which marked earth's centre, but also the tomb of Dionysus, who as a fertility-god was of the type that dies and rises again.

In these winter months there took place the licensed *orgia* of Dionysus, god not only of the grape but of all life as typified by moisture—the juices and sap of growing plants, the blood of animals and men. Bands of Maenads officially appointed by their states surged up the rough path to the high plateau above the

Artemis (Roman Diana), twin-sister of Apollo, virgin-huntress, was—for the Greeks—goddess of the chase, of childbirth and the moon. She is shown here from a vase-painting of the early 5th century BC. *In Asia she was imagined differently: merging with the more ancient Great Mother she became (for instance at Ephe-sus) a goddess of fertility.*

of earthquakes, and had a strong and possibly original connexion with horses. Hephaestus, god of the fire and the forge, is the one ugly Olympian, short and lame, a figure of fun to the others but a craftsman of miraculous skill. Ares, brutal, blustering but cow-ardly, may have been an interloper from Thrace. Hermes, son of Zeus by Maia, is a likeable god, friendly and helpful to men, guide to wayfarers, clever and resourceful, even cunning and thievish, but without malice in the general popular belief. Zeus uses him as servant and messenger.

Athena, born motherless from the head of Zeus, is more mas-culine than feminine, goddess of disciplined war with shield and helmet, of wisdom and of technical skill. Aphrodite, of un-doubted Asiatic origin, is her antithesis, the type of soft femi-nine beauty, somewhat despised by the other gods, who allow her to be wounded by the mortal Diomedes and run weeping to Zeus for comfort. Artemis, sister of Apollo, is goddess of the wild, mistress of beasts, the virgin huntress. Yet she loves all young things and succours women in childbirth—a link with the Ae-gean mother-goddess with whom she was identified at Ephesus. Apollo and Dionysus (who plays no direct part in the Homeric narrative) will call for rather more special treatment.

With the rise of city-states in the classical period the Olympians kept their Homeric characters—the poems were, after all, the basis of a Greek child's education—but a city would have one as its especial patron, so that the Olympian religion became bound up with patriotism. This was true above all of Athens, which shared the name of its goddess. The Acropolis was her rock, where she had her sacred olive-tree, snake and owl. These mani-festations in the form of tree, snake and bird seem to take us back to Minoan times, and her cult on the Rock was certainly of venerable antiquity. The great statue of Athena the Champion dominated the citadel, and in her temple was the gold and ivory masterpiece of Phidias.

In general, thought was free and the cult was what mattered. If a man not only held, but attempted to spread, actual atheistic beliefs, then indeed in classical Athens he might be in danger of exile. Athens had her trials for impiety, but they were few. The isolated fate of Socrates has given the city a reputation for sever-ity in this respect which is probably undeserved. He could un-doubtedly have escaped execution by leaving Athens, but he re-garded that as a denial of his principles, and his lofty bearing and stubborn adherence to what he thought was right made inevitable a tragedy which was probably desired by nobody. Religion was a corporate affair, and participation was part of the duty of a loyal citizen. Yet duty is hardly the word. It was a natural response to the Greek sense of beauty and order (*cosmos*), and the recurrent sacrifices and festivals were enjoyable social occasions. This was particularly true of the festivals at the great Pan-Hellenic centres like Olympia, Delphi or Delos, where the quarrelsome Greek

The birth of Athena. Zeus is said to have swallowed his pregnant first wife, Metis, because he feared that she would bring forth a son stronger than himself. Some time later, feeling pains in his head, he ordered Hephaestus to open his skull, and Athena emerged, mature and fully-armed. In this vase-painting of about 530 BC, Zeus is seated on his throne, his sceptre in one hand and a thunderbolt in the other. On each side of him goddesses assist at the 'birth'. Beyond them, Poseidon (with trident) and Hephaestus (carrying the axe with which he has just cloven Zeus's head and holding up two fingers—a gesture of satisfaction). Athena, patron-goddess of Athens, became the Roman Minerva.

Apollo, whose oracle at Delphi was regarded as the fount of wisdom, and who presided over the arts, medicine, music, poetry and eloquence, was at the same time the bringer of sudden death. The plague, inexplicable to the early Greeks, was attributed to Apollo's arrows.

Shining Cliffs, led by a young male priest and impersonator of the god. There, intoxicated by darkness, wine, and dancing to the orgiastic sound of drum and pipe, they achieved a state of ecstasy culminating in the rending of raw animals and tasting of the raw flesh. Filled with the god, they were insensitive to cold and pain, and to their inspired eyes the mountain streams flowed with milk, wine and honey.

All this, so far removed from our ideas of classical moderation, was equally a part of Greek religion. The Greeks accepted the need for occasional outbreaks of a side of human nature which in normal social life must be suppressed, insisting only that the original wild and untamed orgies be canalized and limited to fixed times and seasons. In another aspect Dionysiac religion, to which dance, song and impersonation had always been essential, gave rise to Greek drama, and tragedy and comedy were themselves a part of the god's festivals.

Prophets and Oracles

The importance of prophecy and oracles in ancient Greece can hardly be exaggerated, and affords a good instance of the dual character of Greek religion, the contrast and interplay of the Olympian inheritance from Homer—bright, sane, classical—and the primitive nature cults with their darkness and mystery and the phenomenon of divine possession. There were two types of prophecy, sane or technical, and manic. The former was practised by individual seers who had acquired the skill of interpreting the will of the gods through signs and omens like the flight of birds or the appearance of the entrails of a sacrificial victim. Though they had special gifts, they worked by reason, not inspiration, and remained perfectly self-possessed. But at the great oracular shrine of Apollo at Delphi, the prophetess, after suitable preparatory acts calculated to put her into a receptive state, was actually possessed by the god, as Dionysus possessed his Maenads. He entered into her and she became no more than his mouthpiece, speaking in a state of trance. It is significant that at Delphi Apollo was known to have taken over what had originally been an oracle of the Earth-goddess.

The Search for Life After Death

Apollo the Purifier looked both ways, to the bright Olympians and to the darker powers of the nether world. The Greek attitude to death and its consequences is not easy to summarize. For the average man this life was everything, and he thought as little as possible about death. Homer had taught him that the *psyche* was a poor, useless thing without the body, to which it owed both strength and wits. After death it drifted away like smoke to an underworld of mouldering darkness, where it carried on a miserable, shadowy and bloodless sort of existence. Flesh and blood were everything. The pale ghosts summoned by Odysseus cannot recognize or speak to him until he has given them a draught of blood to restore a temporary semblance of life.

Yet with the disappearance of the Homeric society of lusty fighters, feasters and lovers, more normal human ideas and aspirations began to creep back. Older beliefs that the dead are powerful for good or evil underlie, for instance, the summoning of Agamemnon's spirit to aid his avenging children in the *Choephori* of Aeschylus, as they persisted among the common people. Out of this belief arose hero-cult, forerunner of the cult of many a Christian saint and often attaching the same importance to relics. The cities of classical times had their patron-heroes. When a war was

Delphi, as it was in the 4th and 3rd centuries, when Greece united in enriching it with shrines and treasuries. The entrance is bottom left. The first building on the right is the hall of the Spartans, built in celebration of their victory at Aegospotami. The Sacred Way goes forward and then bends sharp right and ascends steeply until it reaches the retaining wall (of ancient polygonal masonry) forming the substructure of the temple. Beside the path are the small treasuries of the various states—Sicyon, Siphnos, Thebes, Cnidus, Athens and Syracuse. Against the retaining wall stands the open 'portico' of the Athenians, erected after Salamis. Ascending the steps towards the temple one saw, further to the right, the huge statue of Apollo, bow in hand. The temple itself, one of the most magnificent in Greece, was built over the cleft in the earth from which the oracular power was supposed to come. Behind the temple, further up the hill, was the theatre and beyond that (not shown here) the stadium for races.

going badly for the Spartans, the Delphic oracle advised them to recover the bones of Orestes which lay in their enemies' territory, and on similar advice the Athenians after the Persian Wars brought back the bones of Theseus from Scyros. In general these figures remained 'saints', not gods. Only the mightiest of them all, Heracles, by his prowess earned himself a place among the Olympians and was given the goddess Hebe to wife.

For the ordinary man there were also the mystery-religions, especially that of Demeter the corn-goddess at Eleusis which became part of the state religion at Athens. Ancient agrarian cults like this, originally of simple peasants worshipping the Great Mother, taught a relationship between man and god utterly different from the Homeric. By analogy with the plants, which, dying, drop their seed into Earth's bosom and so renew their life, men too (who, it must be remembered, in Greek belief originally sprang out of Mother Earth as plants do) could hope for new life after death. Initiation into the mysteries of the Mother ensured a true and blessed life instead of the dismal semi-existence of the Homeric *psyche*. At Athens these rites were freely open to all; even slaves were not excluded.

More elaborate was the system of the Orphic writers and initiators. They preached a complicated dogma of the origins of gods and men, according to which men were fallen spirits who must strive to regain their divine status by a combination of ritual and the observance of certain rules in daily life designed to ensure purity. The most important was abstention from meat, for the goal lay through a series of incarnations in animal as well as human form and the body of an ox or sheep might house the soul of one's own father. These doctrines were embodied in poems ascribed to Orpheus, and were the nearest to a book-religion ever promulgated in pagan Greece. Their general influence was small, and their importance lies in the fascination they exercised over the minds of a few great thinkers like Pythagoras and Plato.

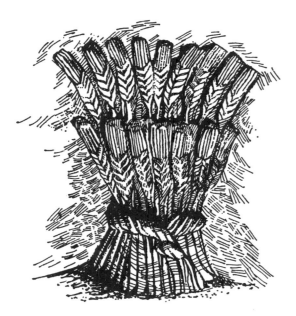

At Eleusis a mystery-religion based on the cycle of the seasons and the annual renewal of life was early established. The deity was Demeter, the corn-goddess; her symbolic wheat-sheaf (above) was part of the decoration of the Propylaea, giving access to the sanctuary. With its emphasis on salvation and its promise of an after-life, Eleusis continued as a powerful cult-centre until early Christian times.

The Birth of Reason

Early in the 6th century BC there occurred what it is fair to call the beginning of European philosophy. Certain thinkers of Miletus, a prosperous colony of Ionian Greeks on the coast of Asia Minor, felt dissatisfied with mythological explanations of the world and endeavoured to account for its origins by reason alone. Hesiod's account of the origin of the universe had already achieved a high degree of systematization, and the veil of personification

over such physical realities as earth and sky was perhaps wearing thin; but it was there, and the evolution of the cosmos was still spoken of in terms of marriage and procreation. At the same time natural events in the present world—rain, thunder and lightning, earthquakes, floods—were believed to be caused by the whim of personal deities. The Milesians swept all this away with astonishing suddenness and completeness. They sought to explain nature solely by causes *within* nature, with the corollary that universal and predictable laws took the place of unpredictable caprice.

It may still be true that the form which their speculations took was influenced by earlier beliefs. For instance, the ancient notion of the origin of the world from a primal union of earth and sky in one mass seems to be reflected in their conviction of a single basic substance from which the ordered universe was, in Anaximander's word, 'separated out'. On the other hand it is of the essence of scientific explanation to reduce the complexity of phenomena to something simpler, and a modern physicist still writes of 'the endeavour of physics to achieve a unified world-view'.

The Milesian school is represented by the names of Thales, Anaximander and Anaximenes, all of whom were active during the 6th century. Thales is said to have predicted an eclipse which must have been that of 585 BC. Little is known of him for certain, but he had the reputation of having been a practical genius both in invention and in politics, and was credited with advances in mathematics. Aristotle says he maintained that the origin of the world was from water, or the moist element, and conjectures that this was due to the connexion of moisture with life. Having discarded the personal gods of Greek polytheism, the main problem for these men was to account for movement, change and development. They did so by assuming their basic substance to contain *psyche*, life, for the main attribute of *psyche* in early Greek eyes was its power of self-motion. This may be the context of the saying attributed to Thales that 'all things are full of gods', and to that extent divinity was admitted into the new picture of the world; but from any popular notions of religion it was entirely emancipated.

Anaximander argued for a completely neutral substance, 'the indefinite', from which the 'opposites' hot, cold, wet, dry, were separated out and composed the present world. At its beginning a sphere of flame enclosed a moist mass and produced a dark vapour from it. The expanding vapour burst the sphere into rings, around which it closed, leaving only holes here and there through which the fire escaped. These are the visible heavenly bodies. Living creatures evolved from the action of hot on moist, i.e. of the sun on water or slime, and the first men were formed in the bodies of fish-like creatures. For Anaximenes, on the other hand, air was the primal substance, and the universe was formed by condensation (into water and solids) and rarefaction (into fire).

At about the same time Pythagoras of Samos, who migrated to south Italy, gave philosophy a new direction as the foundation for a way of life and a brotherhood with political as well as intellectual aims. He turned attention from matter to form, and foreshadowing modern physics, endeavoured to explain nature in mathematical terms. The world was a 'harmony', a term which reflects his discovery that the basic musical intervals could be expressed in terms of numerical proportion. He also taught the kinship of all nature and the transmigration and potential divinity of the soul.

Parmenides of Elea, who had probably been a Pythagorean, shattered the conception of the ultimate unity of the world by his ruthless logic, maintaining that what was one could never become many and that anyone believing such ideas could not possibly account for the physical world with its variety and movement. He challenged reliance upon the senses and declared them to be hallucinatory.

Heraclitus of Ephesus, known even to the ancients as the dark or enigmatic philosopher, took the opposite view. He taught that the whole world was in continuous flux and change. Rest and stability were impossible in nature, but over and above it was the *logos*, a mysterious entity which combined a law of regularity and measure in change with material embodiment in the form of fire. His obscurity detracted from his influence, whereas that of Parmenides was tremendous. He seemed to have proved that there is no transition between not-being and being. There is only 'what is'; it will not become anything else, nor can anything come to be from what is not. The attempt to evade this dilemma and allow some reality to the world of appearances led to different forms of pluralism.

Empedocles the Sicilian was a most colourful and many-sided character, rationalist and prophet, statesman, physician, exhibitionist. According to him there were four elemental substances, earth, water, air and fire. They were everlasting and changeless, but a cosmos could be produced by their mixture in different proportions. Motion was due to two separate forces named Love and Strife, part physical, part psychological and moral, for in the Italian (Pythagorean) tradition his thought had a strong religious side. It included the conception of the soul as a fallen *daimon* striving to climb back to heaven through successive incarnations which even included vegetable life.

For Anaxagoras matter consisted of an infinite number of qualitatively different 'seeds', whirling in a vortex which was started by a force that he called Mind, but apparently without any implication of a purpose behind it. What happened afterwards was, as for the atomists, a matter of chance, not design. He was followed immediately by the thorough atomism of Leucippus and Democritus. Everything was composed of aggregates of tiny indivisible particles, solid through and through, and much too small to be seen, drifting aimlessly in infinite space. They differed only in size and shape; sensible qualities—colour, sound, taste, smell—were purely subjective. The introduction of void (denied by Parmenides as 'what is not') evidently seemed to them in itself to explain the possibility of motion.

These 5th-century physical theories were seized on by the Sophists, an influential class of itinerant teachers whose main instruction was practical, to fit men for the active political life of the little city-states, above all in democratic Athens to which most of the Sophists gravitated. The most famous were Protagoras and Gorgias. The religious scepticism and the relativism of much Pre-Socratic physical thought attracted them as a basis for their advocacy of expediency in action and denial of absolute moral standards. (Protagoras was the author of the dictum 'Man is the measure of all things'.) The intellectual distinction of these men is undoubted, and it must be remembered that we see them now mainly through the eyes of a critic—Plato—whose views were diametrically opposed to theirs.

Socrates: the Gadfly of the Athenians

Into this world of thought came Socrates (469–399 BC). His active mind was early attracted by the exciting physical theories of his time, but later his passionate concern for humanity led him to abandon them as barren and devote himself to the defence of moral standards. He was convinced that 'justice' or 'courage' were realities. In any case men used the words, so they ought to be able to say what they meant. He believed moreover that a knowledge of the true nature of goodness would inevitably make men seek it. The sole cause of wrongdoing was ignorance. The activities of this 'gadfly' (for so he called himself), in stirring up the minds and consciences of the Athenians were so distasteful to them that they brought him to trial and executed him. His simple moral outlook faced his successors with some intractable philosophical problems. *Is* there such a thing as goodness *per se*, when different societies may have quite different conceptions of it? Can we know what it is? If we do, is it true that we will always seek it?

Plato: the Real and Ideal Worlds

His pupil Plato (427–347), with a more many-sided intellect, set himself to answer these questions. There is a transcendent world of 'forms' (often called 'ideas' from the Greek word *idea*, but not ideas in our sense of mere concepts in the human mind), which are eternal and perfect entities serving as models for the passing and imperfect manifestations of truth in our world. Plato had been deeply impressed by the timeless world of mathematics revealed by the Pythagoreans, and he applied its standards to the ethical and physical spheres. To the Pythagoreans also he owes his explanation of our knowledge of the 'forms'. In the other world, between incarnations, we have been face to face with

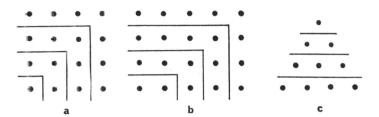

The Pythagoreans expressed numbers in the form of patterns, either square (a) or oblong (b), measured off by a shape like a set-square (Greek 'gnomon'). 'Square' numbers were 'good' because 'always the same' (i.e. the figure that results at each step remains square); 'oblong' numbers 'bad' because 'always different' (i.e. the ratio of height to length changes each time). It will be noted that 'square' numbers are odd (also 'good' to the Pythagoreans) and the oblong ones even ('bad'). By means of an elaborate table of opposites based on these and other pairs of qualities ('male/female', 'at rest/moving', 'limited/unlimited', etc.) everything was in theory given its numerological equivalent. 'They supposed the elements of numbers', says Aristotle, 'to be the elements of all things'. The number ten, 'which comprised the whole nature of number', was regarded with special veneration. It was represented as an equilateral triangle (c) showing that it consisted of $1+2+3+4$. This was called the Tetractys of the Decad, and by it the Pythagoreans swore their most binding oaths.

them, and by intellectual and moral discipline we may 'recollect' that vision.

Psychologically, he elaborated Socrates' simple 'Knowledge is virtue' by a tripartite division of the soul into appetitive, spirited or impulsive, and rational parts. According as one or other of these parts is strongest in him, the *eros* (desire, *libido*) of every man will be directed more into the channels of material gain, honour and ambition, or philosophy (knowledge and goodness). This psychology is at the root of the aristocratic and authoritarian political system expounded in the *Republic*, with its strict class-divisions; for to Plato it seemed obvious that only the philosophic type should be given the reins of government, defence should be entrusted to the spirited, and those in whom the appetitive side was strongest were the natural producers and traders of wealth.

In his later years Plato devoted more attention to problems of logic and the theory of knowledge, and his work in these fields attracts much attention today when these problems are in the forefront of philosophers' interests. But though he saw the difficulties in the doctrine of 'forms', he never abandoned it, and in the *Timaeus* he constructed an imaginative world-picture, including the origin of the universe and living beings, and a detailed consideration of the bodily as well as psychical functions of mankind, which was entirely based on his two-world theory. Nor must one forget the poetry of the great myths about the adventures of the soul in the other world with which several of his dialogues close. The dialogues defy classification. They are a unique and inimitable blend of philosophical discussion, religious feeling, poetry and dramatic characterization.

Aristotle: the Spirit of Research

Aristotle (384–322) was for twenty years a member of Plato's Academy, and this left an indelible impression on his mind; but his philosophical temperament was very different from Plato's. Born at Stagira in the north of Greece, he was brought up in the semi-Greek court of Philip of Macedon, to whom his father was court physician. The medical schools of Greece were closely linked with the philosophy and science of their time, but introduced into them a valuable note of empiricism. They distrusted vague generalizations and broad intellectual constructions, preferring to base their conclusions (as a doctor must) on the meticulous observation of individual cases. Of this the great Hippocratic Corpus, a still extant collection of medical writings from the 5th century onwards, is ample witness. The craft was handed on from father to son, so we may be certain that for Aristotle this approach to science was in his early upbringing as well as his ancestry. His own patient collection of scientific data, notably in zoology, is proof that he found it congenial, and much in his philosophy is explicable by the conflict between this empirical instinct and his Platonic training.

He retained the conception of form, as opposed to matter, as the determinative factor or 'essence' of things, but decisively abandoned belief in its existence beyond our world. Forms exist only in the sensible objects. Everything in nature, animal or plant, has an urge (*dynamis*) to realize its proper form, exemplified for it in its parent, so far as the limitations of matter allow. This impulse is activated by the one existing pure form, which is not, like a Platonic 'idea', the form *of* anything else, but God. God is perfect, and therefore does not move or change in any way. He is unadulterated intellect, spending his life in eternal self-contemplation. At the same time he is the Unmoved Mover or ultimate cause of all development in the natural world, for the mere existence of his perfection fills all nature with the desire to emulate it. (He did not *create* the world, for Aristotle believed it to have existed from all time.)

By his division of existence into potential and actual Aristotle gave the final answer to the dilemma of Parmenides. There is such a thing as becoming, or change from one state to another, although as Parmenides said, it cannot proceed from not-being to being. What is not *x* is not non-existent, but simply at the moment not *x*, and may have the *dynamis* of becoming *x*. In all this Aristotle was greatly indebted to the analysis of the different senses of being which had been carried out by Plato.

In his writings on ethics and politics Aristotle was nearer to the Sophists than to Plato. There is no single 'good' over and above all other goods; what is good differs for different people or circumstances. Conduct is taken out of the sphere of philosophical knowledge, whose subject-matter must conform to permanent laws, and confined to the contingent. Its regulation becomes a matter of practical good sense, almost of knack or flair. On this basis Aristotle worked out his doctrine of each separate virtue as a mean between two extremes. As to the exact point on the scale between, say, foolhardiness and cowardice at which true courage lay, he could only say it is 'where the man of practical wisdom would put it'. Conformably with his scientific outlook, his writings on political theory were based on a collection of descriptions of no less than 158 different Greek constitutions amassed by himself and his pupils. This invaluable collection of historical material was entirely lost until the *Constitution of Athens*, written by Aristotle himself, turned up on a papyrus in the sands of Egypt in 1890.

By the introduction of symbols Aristotle was the first to evolve a system of purely formal logic. This was based entirely on the syllogism, the varieties of which he classified exhaustively. (At its simplest a syllogism states a general rule—the major premise—, specifies a particular case as coming under that rule—the minor premise—, and draws the conclusion: e.g. 'All animals are mortal; men are animals; therefore men are mortal'). All logic in its formal aspect, even induction (the argument from particular cases to general laws), was reduced to syllogistic form. The system had immense influence through the Middle Ages, and it is only in the present century that the 'traditional logic' based on Aristotle has been substantially modified.

The Age of Disillusion

The world of Plato's *Republic* and Aristotle's *Politics* hardly outlasted their lifetime. After the Asiatic conquests of Aristotle's pupil Alexander the Great, Hellenic culture spread all over the Middle East, and large kingdoms replaced the autonomous city-states, whose importance became municipal rather than political. With their eclipse, something was lost to the Greek mind, not only in political thought but in a fading of the spirit of bold speculation and all-embracing theories of reality and the cosmos. Learning, science and technology flourished, especially at the court of the Ptolemies at Alexandria, but the emphasis was on research and the patient accumulation of facts. In religion, the disturbing changes in the social order led to an upsurge of mystery-religions of oriental type, of Isis or Cybele, which promised some form of 'salvation' to the individual. In philosophy the chief schools were the Stoic and Epicurean, both of which were con-

tent to take over and adapt earlier cosmological schemes as a basis for ethical theories aimed at securing peace of mind.

Epicurus (341–270 BC) saw the root of spiritual malaise in religion, which put men at the mercy of capricious gods and fears of torment after death. He banished divine agency from the world and taught that death brings annihilation, and so is no more to be feared than a dreamless sleep. The aim of life was *ataraxia* (freedom from worry) or 'pleasure', by which he meant in fact the negative ideal of freedom from pain. Indulgence in sensual pleasures was discouraged as inimical to physical and mental peace. What mattered was the state of mind, and Epicurus himself bore with unruffled calm the extremely painful illness from which he died. There is something very attractive about his philosophy, in which a high place was assigned to friendship, and the community of the Garden, presided over by his gentle spirit, must have been a delightful one; but the emphasis was on negation and passivity. The responsibilities of public life were rejected for the cares that they would inevitably bring. The physical basis for this philosophy was Democritean atomism, which demanded none but blind mechanical causes for the origin and present working of the natural world.

Zeno from Citium in Cyprus (332–262 BC) revived the *logos*-fire of Heraclitus, and taught that the divine mind which produced the universe is itself present in every part of it. In its highest form it is pure reason, and man too, by his possession of reason, shares in the divine nature, though in him it is contaminated with lower, animal elements. The Sage (the Stoic ideal of man) knows that our duty is to live according to the highest that is in us. If all is well with the inner self, man is completely self-sufficient and will be 'happy on the rack'. Strictly speaking all external circumstances are indifferent, though as a concession to our animal nature and position in the world, the Stoics allowed that some might be preferred to others. In its strictest form Stoicism allowed no degrees of wisdom or folly, virtue or vice. One was either a Sage or a fool, just as a man is drowned whether his head is several fathoms or only six inches below the surface. In practice this impossibly severe doctrine was modified, especially as it became the favoured philosophy of the Roman ruling class. The Stoic Panaetius in the 2nd century BC became the friend of Scipio Aemilianus and elaborated the application of his philosophy to practical affairs. This tradition was carried on by Seneca, and in the 2nd century AD the Emperor Marcus Aurelius was himself the leading Stoic philosopher.

The best side of Stoicism is seen in its teaching that, since wisdom and virtue were all that mattered, there should be no distinction between rich and poor, slave and free, or between different races or states. Epictetus, who had himself been a slave, taught that all men alike are kinsmen by nature, children of God. In commending the Gospel to a Greek audience, St Paul could remind them that the brotherhood of man was already a Stoic ideal.

Stoicism in one form or another pervaded the intellectual life of the Graeco-Roman world, and the other schools existed under its shadow. The Academy founded by Plato took a sceptical turn, and Aristotle's school, the Peripatos, after his immediate successors Theophrastus and Strato, confined itself to detailed research of a rather trivial kind. Cicero, himself a Roman, did valuable service to philosophy by preserving and interpreting Greek thought in Roman dress. His dialogues show intellectual Romans enthusiastically arguing the rival claims of Stoics, Epicureans and Academics, with many references to Plato, Aristotle and earlier thinkers.

The Challenge of Christianity

In the 3rd century of the Christian era Plotinus, one of the greatest of all religious philosophers, an Egyptian by birth who taught at Rome, started the movement known as Neo-Platonism. The Good or the One, the highest form of being in Plato's philosophy, he identified with God. The other Platonic forms are thoughts in the mind of God, and all lower modes of being form a descending series of radiations or emanations from his own. Mystical union with God is the highest possible experience for man. This last great flowering of pagan thought found itself opposed by the rising star of Christianity. Many of the Neo-Platonic writers were its conscious adversaries, and sought to discredit it as an irrational superstition. They were formidable rivals, and though the Church was victorious, the struggle compelled it to set its own teaching on a more philosophical basis. As a result the Christian community produced its own notable Platonic, and later Aristotelian, philosophers. Their genius has achieved a noble synthesis between Christian theology and the best in non-Christian Greek thought, which in the first place owed much to the stimulus of the Neo-Platonists.

Reaching Towards Science

Of the Greek scientific achievement only the most general characteristics and a few random examples can be given here. In Pre-Socratic days there was obviously no hard and fast line between science and philosophy, and much scientific thought took the form of speculation about the origin and structure of the universe. It must be remembered however that much of our information on this period comes through Aristotle and his successors who were themselves imbued with the ideal of knowledge for its own sake and metaphysics as the highest type of knowledge. Their reports are selective, and the early thinkers may have been more interested in the practical applications of science than our main sources would suggest. Thales concerned himself with calculating the height of the pyramids and the distances of ships at sea, and with the navigational uses of mathematics and astronomy. Anaximander designed a map of the world. Mathematics and astronomy were leading interests. The Ionians had plenty of contact with Egypt and Mesopotamia, to which the Greeks always acknowledged a debt in these two sciences.

In earlier ages these older civilizations will also have had much to teach in technological fields such as pottery, spinning and weaving, and metal-working. The Greeks were eager learners. Their great contribution to thought was that whereas with other peoples practical considerations were paramount, and they were content if a process worked, the insatiable curiosity of the Greek always prompted him to ask 'Why?' In this search for causes he added theory to practice, dealt easily in universal concepts, and sought out general laws.

Technical interests come out most strongly in Empedocles. He founded the Sicilian medical school, and himself freed the city of Selinus from malaria by diverting one of its two rivers to flow into the other which had become stagnant. In his writings he liked to illustrate physical theories by analogies from the crafts. The four elements mix like pigments on a palette, the action of heat on moist matter to produce life is compared to what happens in baking or pottery. He notes that two soft metals can together form a harder alloy. To account for hot springs, he mentions a water-heater which must have had much in common with its modern counterparts, a system of coiled pipes to ensure that the water passes through the same fire often enough to heat it, so that it goes in cold and comes out hot. In his explanation of breathing he demonstrates that air is a material substance by reference to the clepsydra, a device for lifting wine or water from a shallow vessel. It was funnel-shaped, with a strainer full of holes covering the broad base. This was dipped into the liquid, and the orifice at the top covered with the thumb before lifting it out, so that the liquid was retained in the vessel and released when the thumb was removed. These illustrations are often called experiments, but as compared with modern experimental technique they are rather to be described as acute inferences from familiar experience. It is in the Hippocratic medical writings that we occasionally find something more like the true experimental method.

The tremendous influence of Plato and Aristotle was not conducive to the practical application of natural science. They would have approved the words of their contemporary Xenophon that 'what are called the mechanical arts carry a social stigma and are rightly dishonoured in our cities'. The main sciences encouraged in the Academy were mathematics and astronomy, in which Plato himself and his associate Eudoxus made considerable advances. Aristotle's consuming desire for a deeper knowledge of nature was not concerned, like modern science, with obtaining power over her. Less of a mathematician than Plato, he excelled mainly

The Universe according to Ptolemy. The idea that the sun and not the earth lay at the centre had been put forward (c. 270 BC) by Aristarchus of Samos, but Aristotle had given his authority to the geocentric system and it was this which, elaborated and codified by Ptolemy, was accepted as true throughout the Middle Ages. This diagram of 1528, with the 'spheres' of earth, air, fire, the moon, the sun, five planets and the fixed stars, shows how it persisted up to the time of Copernicus.

in the fields of biology and zoology. Here his work shows an astonishing range of observation, a gift for rational classification, and a reluctance to generalize on insufficient evidence which have made him a model for all later generations. The botanical treatises of his pupil Theophrastus continue this work. In astronomy Aristotle took the results of Eudoxus and Callippus and further developed the system of concentric planetary spheres revolving in different directions which, on the assumption that the earth occupies the centre of the universe, seemed necessary to account for the apparently irregular motions of the heavenly bodies. That their paths were circular, and the irregularities only apparent, was an unquestioned assumption based on metaphysical and theological preconceptions. This is the system which found its culmination in the epicyclic model of Ptolemy in the 2nd century AD, according to which the planets were imagined as revolving in small circles whose centres were all fixed on the circumference of a great circle revolving round the earth.

It will be clear from what has been said that the Greeks had a particular bent for mathematics. With their naturally visual approach to the world, their main achievements were in geometry. They saw numbers as shapes (whence we still call them 'figures' and speak of square and cubical numbers), and solved arithmetical problems by geometrical means. The 'theorem of Pythagoras', if not actually due to him, was at least familiar in the 5th century BC, and much of the content of Euclid's *Elements*, written about 300 and still the basis of elementary instruction in our schools, was a compilation of results discovered during the previous two centuries. The early application of mathematics to practical problems is seen in the extraordinarily complex structure of a building like the Parthenon at Athens, with its inspired use of curvature and asymmetrical spacing to correct optical illusion and give the effect of straightness and symmetry. Advances continued to be made in the Roman period, notably by Archimedes, Apollonius of Perga and Ptolemy. The engineering triumphs of the Romans themselves, notably in their roads, bridges and aqueducts, are of course well known and in many places still visible today. Vitruvius, who lived under the Emperor Augustus, wrote a book on architecture and engineering (both civil and military) which has survived and tells us much about their methods.

Medicine also was eagerly pursued from the classical age through the later Greek and Roman periods. Although linked with religion in the worship of Asclepius, god of healing, it reached in the Hippocratic writings a remarkable degree of rationalism and experiment. Dissection was practised by Alcmaeon

Jet-propulsion in Hellenistic Alexandria—a machine reconstructed from a description by Hero. A hollow globe is suspended on two pipes over a closed-in cauldron. Steam from inside the cauldron passes up one of the pipes and into the globe; from here it escapes through two outlets pointing forwards and backwards, and in doing so exerts a pressure in the opposite directions. The globe then revolves on its axis.

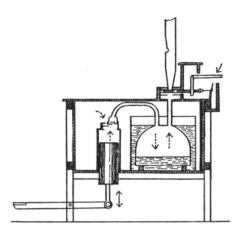

Ctesibius's water-organ: the problem here was to maintain a constant air-pressure to the organ-pipes when the pump available provided only intermittent pressure. Air is sucked through a valve into the chamber on the left by means of a foot pump, and forced out again through a second valve into a hollow vessel surrounded by and partially filled with water. Since the water inside is trying to find its own outside level, the air now exerts a steady pressure upwards through a third valve (worked, on a slot mechanism, by the musician) to the organ-pipes themselves.

in the early 5th century, and later by Aristotle and others. It is also worth noting that the city-states of classical Greece already possessed public health services, with doctors paid by the state and free treatment for the patients. The Hippocratic writings were succeeded by a number of different schools, which were summed up and consummated in the work of Galen in the 2nd century AD. His own intellect and achievements were impressive, but the tremendous influence which he exercised over later centuries was not altogether to the advantage of science. As a follower of Stoicism he believed firmly in an inevitable purpose underlying all mundane events, and this outlook, when inherited by lesser minds and combined with a sense of his absolute authority, had an inhibiting effect on the development of free and unbiassed research.

Jet Propulsion and Engines of War

The Alexandrian age, in addition to the collection of scholarly and scientific data, saw considerable developments in mechanical devices, though their use was often confined to the production of 'miracles' in the temples or amusing toys. In these the principles of the siphon and of the expansion of heated air played a large part. One such device described by Hero of Alexandria employs the principle of jet propulsion. Ctesibius constructed pumps (including fire-engines), waterclocks, and a hydraulic organ. Much ingenuity also went into the production of engines of war. Archimedes was justly celebrated both as mathematician and as engineer. He built a planetary model or orrery which claimed to re-

produce all the movements of the heavenly bodies, invented a screw for raising water, lifted huge weights by a system of pulleys and devised various defence-works when Syracuse was besieged by the Romans. Unfortunately they were unavailing, and his genius was brutally snuffed out by a Roman soldier when the city was captured in 212 BC.

In geography Eratosthenes made a scientific calculation of the diameter of the earth which on the most likely hypothesis (there is some doubt about the length of the 'stade' which was his unit of measurement) gave a result only fifty miles short of the true polar diameter. Astronomy flourished, and Aristarchus in the 3rd century BC was the first man to put forward the heliocentric hypothesis. It received no support from his contemporaries, but Copernicus was aware that Aristarchus had the credit of having forestalled him.

These few illustrations will suffice to indicate the ferment of scientific activity that went on in the Hellenistic world, and to qualify the widespread belief that the Greeks as a whole were not interested in technology. A final example may bring the point home even more strikingly. Only fairly recently has the expert cleaning of an object recovered from an ancient wreck off an island in the Dodecanese proceeded sufficiently for its purpose to be understood. There is no doubt that it belongs to the 1st century BC, and it turns out to be an elaborate astronomical calculator using a complex system of gears mounted eccentrically and probably working on an epicyclic system. At least twenty gearwheels have been preserved. The gears worked a system of pointers on graduated dials, some with a smaller subsidiary dial like the seconds dial on a watch. They show such things as the annual motion of the sun in the zodiac, the risings and settings of stars and constellations throughout the year, and the phases, risings and settings of the moon. Besides the figures and lettering on the dials, other areas of the instrument are covered with Greek inscriptions (now badly damaged) explaining its use. The main axle may have been turned either by hand or by some automatic device like a water-clock. Mounted in a box, with hinged doors to protect the dials, it is said to have resembled a well-made eighteenth-century clock. It is not surprising that its investigator finds it 'a bit frightening that the ancient Greeks had come so close to our age, not only in their thought, but also in their scientific technology'.

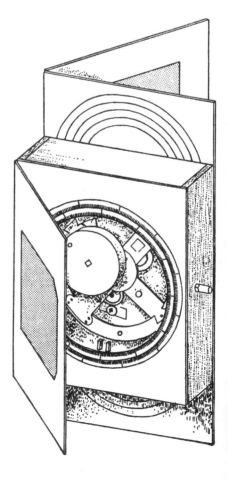

The precision instrument shown on p. 78 is here reconstructed with its wooden case. The input axle projects on the right. Inside can be seen the turn-table with another wheel mounted on it eccentrically. Round the circumference are the graduated dials from which, when the axle was turned and the pointers moved, it was possible to read off parallel information on the astronomical cycles known to the Greeks – the sun, the moon, the fixed stars and certain of the planets.

V THE SUBLIME ACHIEVEMENT

The art and architecture of ancient Greece

JOHN BOARDMAN

*'Our love of what is beautiful does not lead to extravagance;
our love of things of the mind does not make us soft'.*

THUCYDIDES, BOOK II

Aphrodite, daughter of Zeus,

goddess of love, incarnation of beauty, rose (said the Greek legend) motherless from the waves of the sea, perfect in every feature. To later historians it has sometimes seemed as if Greek culture itself sprang out of nothingness in much the same way—a classical perfection, absolute for all time and all men, and consistent throughout its history to one standard and one law. That traditional view has had to go. To us, in the twentieth century, the miracle is not so much the standard itself (which we recognize as only one of many valid standards) as the historical fact of its development at a particular time and place; not so much its homogeneity as its variety and range. 'Greek art' is not one style, one single achievement: it is the record of a thousand years of hard discipline and unceasing experiment, of changing techniques and purposes, of exotic influences from abroad and of sharp revolutions in taste and sensibility.

A miracle, however, it remains. The birth of Aphrodite is a fitting symbol of something that was new in human experience, and the sculptor of the 'Ludovisi throne' (detail, right) has caught the wonder of that awakening moment. The goddess rises from the water while two women on either side reach down to draw her up, her damp clothes and hair clinging to her body. The relief was carved about 460 BC in one of the Greek colonies of south Italy or Sicily.

The dawning Greek art of about 1100 to 700 BC marks the beginning of a new tradition, owing little to the arts of the Mycenaean palaces that had been destroyed in about 1200 BC. Pottery returns to a stage of primitive simplicity and then takes an entirely new path. The vase on the *left* is one of several magnificent funeral craters found in Athens at the Dipylon Cemetery. It is over 4 feet in height and $2\frac{1}{2}$ feet across the rim. In the lower row is a procession of two-horse chariots driven by warriors with helmets and heroic shields. Above them is a funeral: the dead man lies on a bier which stands on a hearse drawn by two horses. A man holds the horses by a rope and mourners lament.

From the East came the idea and the basic shape of the square stamp-seal (*below left*), but the decoration is already Greek. The gold ear-ring (*centre*), decorated with minute precision in the new technique of granulation, also from the East, was probably found in a grave of the 8th century; the centre was inlaid, perhaps with amber.

Stylized figures, which might have stepped from the vase paintings, characterize bronze and terracotta work of the period. *Below*: man grappling with a centaur, the man-horse monster invented by the Greeks and for long a popular figure with their artists.

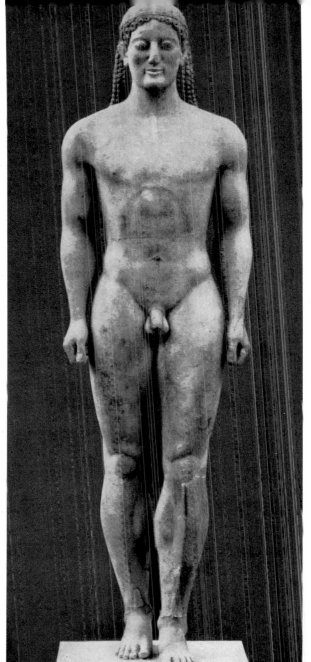

The human form was the subject in which Greek sculptural mastery was most clearly demonstrated. In the early figurine from Auxerre (*above*), the long wig and 'mother-goddess' gesture associated with the Phoenician Astarte are preserved. The male figure (*centre*), over 6 feet high, is one of the *kouroi* (youths) which became so characteristic of the Greek Archaic period. *Far right*: girl wearing a light and heavy dress (*chiton* and *peplos*), *c.* 530 BC.

Scenes in relief gave greater scope for naturalism. *Right*: Olympian gods discuss the news from Troy. Aphrodite and Artemis lean forward eagerly while Apollo turns round to speak to them.

Growing freedom from the rigid conventions of Geometric marks the beginning of the Archaic period. The 7th-century griffin jug from Aegina (*below left*) uses drawing in outline rather than silhouette. But at Corinth the 'Chigi Vase' (*above*) shows the finest 'black-figure' technique with lavish colour, for a battle scene. This technique soon dominates, as in the Spartan cup (*below*) with King Arcesilas of Cyrene supervising the weighing of wool, bales of which are being stored in the cellar.

The culmination of black-figure came when the technique was adopted by the Athenian vase-painters, who more often now sign their work. The inside of an Athenian lip-cup (*right*) includes a border of seventeen dancing maidens, probably the Nereids, and in the centre Heracles wrestling with Triton. Heracles is astride the sea-monster and clasps it round the waist. In the famous amphora by Execias (*below*) an unparalleled delicacy of detail is reached. Achilles, on the left, and Ajax are playing a game. Note the lion's head on Achilles' shoulder guard, the tiny differences between the two beards and hairstyles, the crest of Achilles' helmet (Ajax has taken his off) and the two richly embroidered cloaks.

Oriental inspiration is seen more clearly in the smaller bronze-work than in large-scale stone sculpture. Features such as the fierce griffin-heads (*above*) on the handles of cauldrons look towards Eastern craftsmanship.

A human figure as the handle of a mirror is an idea that comes from Egypt, but the Greeks made it into something expressive and charming. Griffin-heads appear again on the gold ear-rings (*above*) from Melos. There would have been a separate hoop, with pointed ends, which pierced the ear and from which the pendants hung.

Some of the finest work of the early Archaic period is in ivory, an expensive material that tempted the best craftsmen. The kneeling youth from Samos (*right*) is perhaps their masterpiece, a perfect union of Eastern technique with Greek feeling for pattern.

Articles of daily use are often those on which the liveliest imagination has been lavished. Perfume-flasks and small objects of this kind gave opportunities for lightness and humour. Clay figure vases were given human or animal shapes. These (*above* and *below*) are from East Greece. The grotesque Gorgon (*above right*) supports the rim of the famous Vix crater (a huge mixing bowl for wine), found in the grave of a Celtic princess in France. The arts of the engraver were practised on stone—for gems and seals—and on metal—for the dies used in minting coins. Impressions of seals from the islands (*below*, top left and centre) show the popular animals; the later gem with a satyr is in the developed style of the 6th century. The two silver coins on the right of the photograph are from Athens (Gorgon's head) and Acanthus in north Greece (lion tearing a bull).

A new age began for the Greeks after their triumph over Persia at Salamis and Plataea (480–79 BC). 'As the buildings rose, imposing in size and unsurpassed in grace of proportion', wrote Plutarch of the rebuilding of the Acropolis, 'the artists vied with each other in making them finer and more beautiful.'

In sculpture, a point of balance had been reached between the discipline of pattern that had marked Geometric and Archaic art and the realism to which it had all the time been striving. The votive relief of Athena (*left*) carved between 470 and 450 BC, shows the goddess standing with bowed head before a stone, perhaps a decree. The weight of the body rests on the right leg and the staff in the left hand. She wears the Attic *peplos*, fastened at the shoulders by clasps, and falling below the waist in simple parallel folds.

The high rock of the Acropolis dominated—and still dominates—the city at its foot; and the complex of buildings that the Athenians built upon it in the second half of the 5th century BC, after the earlier temples had been totally destroyed by the Persians, expressed in monumental terms both their devotion to the goddess and their new-found national pride. The mature Doric style is represented pre-eminently by the Parthenon, Athena's own temple. Here (*opposite*) we are looking along the south peristyle, the crisp flutes of the columns taking the sunlight like the folds of drapery in figure-sculpture.

The nude becomes a subject of intense interest to Greek sculptors, and is treated now with complete mastery. Most of the key-works exist only in Roman copies (*right*: the Discus-thrower of Myron and, *far right*, Cnidian Venus by Praxiteles) but the late classical bronze girl *below* (*c.* 400 BC) sums up the advances that had been made: the relaxed pose, the weight entirely on one leg, the trunk bent and turned in a simple, natural movement.

A rhythmic, lyrical life now seems to animate the drapery patterns, while at the same time revealing the form and pose of the body beneath.

The photograph *below* should be compared with that on p. 91. It is part of the Parthenon frieze, showing girls in the procession to Athena.

Emotion is still conveyed by the gesture and pose of the figure rather than by facial expression. On Athenian grave reliefs the grief of parting is expressed with poignant calm and serene dignity. The monument of Hegeso (*left*) shows the dead woman taking a necklace out of a jewel-case held by a maidservant. It belongs to the last years of the 5th century.

The flying drapery of the figure on the right (*below*), forming both an aesthetically satisfying pattern in itself and a vivid indication of swift movement, looks forward to the more violent sculptural language of Hellenistic art. The relief is from the shrine of Artemis at Brauron, showing Zeus, Leto, Apollo and Artemis.

Major Greek painting has been almost entirely lost, but many of its conventions, such as the indication of depth by different ground lines, were taken over by the vase-painters. The *dramatis personae* of this rocky landscape (*left*) is not entirely clear. Heracles stands in the centre, to the left a warrior and behind him Athena. In the foreground, lying on the ground, is a warrior holding two spears and above him another sitting on his cloak and holding his knee in his hand. These two figures almost certainly derive from a wall-painting. It is known that in a picture by Polygnotus at Delphi, Hector was shown sitting clasping his knee in just this posture.

A window on life is provided by the exquisite painting on Greek pots and vases. *Right*: a boy being sick is comforted by his girl-friend. The painting is inside a wine-cup and would be under the eyes of the drinker. *Opposite left*: a widow receiving her husband's helmet, a delicate drawing on a funeral wine-jar (*lekythos*). *Below right*: vase by the Cleophon painter showing a warrior taking leave of his wife, the attitudes of the two figures subtly expressive of their emotions.

For a less sophisticated public, the vase-painters of south Italy went to acrobats, clowns and scenes from comedies.

The most exquisite works of Greek art are often found on gems and coins, and can easily be overlooked. *Above*: a cast from a metal belt-buckle showing Odysseus mourning; and two engraved gems by Dexamenus, a flying heron in chalcedony and a portrait in jasper.

Heavy gold bracelets with terminals in the form of animals' heads (these are rams) are a sign of influence from the east. Gold was in general use, silver rather more rare.

The ivory Apollo (*right*) is a miniature copy of Praxiteles' Apollo that stood in Aristotle's Lyceum. The god was holding a silver bow in his left hand, after shooting the arrows of the plague. Found recently in the Athenian Agora, this small statuette has been reconstructed from over 200 fragments.

Masterpieces of draughtsmanship, like the famous Aphrodite with Eros playing five-stones with Pan (*below*), were incised on the hinged lids of small mirrors. This type of mirror had no handle, but in another variety, fashionable somewhat earlier, the polished disc stood on a support in the shape of a woman (*left*); animals and birds chase one another round the rim and there are flying Erotes each side of the girl. *Bottom*: a silver tetradrachm from Naxos in Sicily, about 460 BC—a seated Silenus about to drink from a wine-cup.

The graceful arabesque patterns seen in metalwork appear also in Hellenistic ceramics. The little vase (*left*), of the type known as 'West Slope' because some were found on the slopes of the Athenian Acropolis, has a black gloss paint with tendril reliefs in a creamy colour.

The charm of the commonplace was now exploited for the first time. Little painted terracotta figures like the boy sitting on a rock (*above*) from Tanagra, 3rd century BC, became popular all over the Eastern Mediterranean.

Mosaics of natural pebbles survive at Alexander's capital at Pella. In the detail (*left*) from a lion-hunt, the figure is outlined with bronze strips.

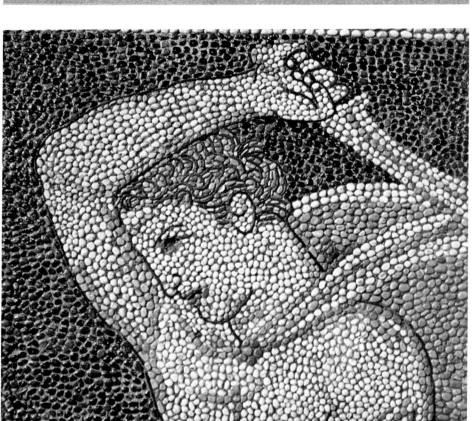

The Hellenistic Age is the name given to the last great period of Greek culture, from the late 4th century to the time when it was swallowed up by Rome. Alexander's sudden brilliant empire had turned the art of classical Greece into an 'international style', current from the Danube to the Indus. Although the old centres like Athens gradually lost their intellectual leadership, much that was sensitive and precious still found expression. The central portion of a gold diadem (*above*) comes from south Italy. Its intertwining tendrils, palmettes and buds, partly worked in granulation, are typically Hellenistic.

Translucent glass was a new achievement. The large amphora (*right*) from Olbia, south Russia, *c.* 200 BC, is not of blown glass but is made up of two pieces of cut glass riveted together in the middle by a strip of gilded bronze. The knob on the lid, the ends of the two handles (the lower ends are masks) and the spout at the bottom, in the form of a satyr with wine-jar, are also of gilded bronze.

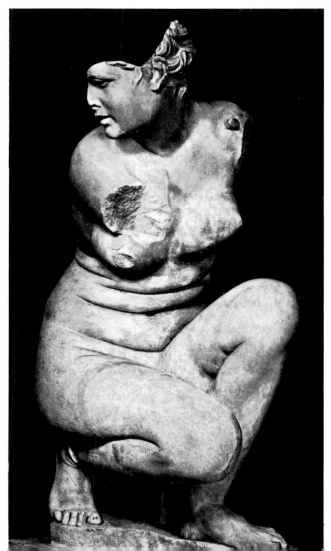

Wings outstretched and drapery swirling in the wind, the goddess of Victory alights on the prow of a ship (*left*). The statue by Pythocritus stood overlooking a fountain on the island of Samothrace. 'In the whole range of Hellenistic art', it has been said, 'Pythocritus alone dares comparison with the Parthenon master and Michelangelo.'

Anguish and fear replace classical repose. The emotional tensions and the suffering which had previously been idealized were now conveyed directly through agitated gestures, facial expression, and muscular strain. The Pergamum Altar (detail, *opposite above left*) was erected in about 180 BC to celebrate the victory of the Pergamenes over the Gauls. The frieze transposes the struggle into mythological terms as the war of the gods against the giants. Athena has seized the winged Alcyoneus by the hair.

The female nude was also treated with greater naturalism and a more frankly sensuous charm. Venus, the goddess of Love (a concept which itself was changing since the days of Pericles), was a favourite subject. She was portrayed crouching at her bath by Doedalsus of Bithynia (a Roman copy exists, *opposite far left*), the head turned in one direction, legs and lower part of the body in another.

The boxer with flattened nose and cauliflower ears (*opposite centre*) is typical of the new range of subject-matter opened up by the sculptors of the Hellenistic age.

Under Roman rule the huge Temple of Olympian Zeus at Athens was completed, after being laid out 600 years earlier on the model of the Artemisium at Ephesus. The finished building, though in a colossal Corinthian order, is still Greek in style.

The art and architecture of ancient Greece

JOHN BOARDMAN

A shipwreck, from an Attic Geometric jug. Narrative scenes such as this mark a departure from the purely formal decoration used hitherto and point to the more developed naturalism of the Orientalizing and Archaic periods. The ship has capsized; one man sits astride the keel, the others swim (or drown) among the fish. It may illustrate an episode from the Odyssey.

THE ART AND ARCHITECTURE of ancient Greece have set the standards for western art for more than 2000 years The influence has been so strong that successive generations have come to regard 'Classical' art as being both the highest and indeed the only art of civilized man. This is patently wrong, and the artists and teachers of this century have done right to try to correct the balance and to establish new standards which a new age might respect as its own. If they fail it is likely to be through the lack of that sort of discipline which has sustained the arts in all the major civilizations of antiquity.

It has been easy enough to acknowledge this debt to the past, to build our churches with the façades of pagan temples, to make Ionic columns of cast iron, even, like Le Corbusier, to try to generalize the feeling for proportion shown by Greeks, Romans, Egyptians, moderns. But how very mixed in fact are our 'Classical' standards: the architecture more Roman than Greek, and that translated for us by the Italian Renaissance; the sculptural beauty that of the late blowsy Venuses which appealed to Roman and Italian taste. We are at the mercy of our translators—of the Romans, of the Renaissance, of the Romantics and neo-Classicists, and the popular conception of 'Classical' art is as far from the truth as the popular conception of the grave, philosophical and beautiful life of the ordinary Greek of antiquity. As though there was no bad Greek art; as though the Greeks were so unlike most of the agricultural-merchant peoples of the Levant today.

So our preconceptions must go. Pericles would have been shocked to the marrow by the Venus de Milo. A bare century ago the finest products of Greek Geometric art could be dismissed as Phoenician or Egyptian because they looked so unlike the Elgin marbles. To understand Greek art we must watch it grow and see each work in its setting: the Geometric vase as the product of a people to whom representational art was almost unknown: the Elgin marbles as ambitious examples of what was, in the 5th century BC, a revolutionary new style: the Venus de Milo as the end-product of years of experiment in the representation of anatomy and emotion in cold marble, and not just another pretty girl, proper because divine, and so a suitable subject for Victorian mantelpieces. That is why, in this chapter, the art and architecture of Greece are presented as a historical development, with no special emphasis given to any one period, style or genre; for in its way the story of the growth of Greek art—as indeed of the rest of the Greek achievement—is more impressive than Greek art itself. Two hundred years before the Elgin marbles they had not even learnt to cut marble; two hundred years before Sappho they could not even write.

After the Dark Age: a New Beginning

When the palaces fell and the Mycenaean empire dissolved, about 1200 BC, they took with them also the last examples of a great artistic tradition. But it was a tradition, which was already exhausted and a tradition in which we search almost in vain for traces of what the Greeks were to achieve in later centuries. Only at a very low level was there continuity, in the familiar shapes of objects used and the familiar simple patterns with which they were decorated.

Two places claim our attention because there the continuity was strongest. One is Athens, which survived the invaders from the north who overwhelmed the other Mycenaean capitals, and survived in some measure too the conditions which wrought such dire depopulation in Greece—for it is hard to attribute this all to the sword, and one thinks also of the more terrible effects of natural disasters like plague and repeated droughts. The other place is Cnossus, in Crete, once the seat of the Minoan empire and never wholly abandoned. It was Athens which was to be the home of the first awakenings of the new Greece, but in a way which her Mycenaean past could never have led us to expect. The slate was wiped clean and we start afresh.

It is inevitable that we learn most about comparatively primitive societies from their pottery—it is the only material which always survives, and usually survives in some quantity. It is from the pottery of Athens in the Protogeometric Period—about 1000 to 900 BC, that the period takes its name. It represents the beginning of a new tradition. Certainly some of the old shapes are used and the old patterns can be recognized but there is a new discipline and sense of balance which introduce an art of a sort hitherto unknown in the Aegean world. The patterns are few, but meticulously executed—groups of concentric circles and semicircles drawn, not freehand now, but carefully with the compass, and simple geometric patterns like triangles, zigzags and chequers. The vases are made with a new attention to the preparation of the clay and paint, a new eye for proportion, and above all a sense of how the decoration can best be suited to the shape. If Greek vases of later periods command our attention for their more accomplished technique or the skilful drawing upon them, still for sheer simplicity and effect Athens' Protogeometric vases are hard to match.

The style spread over the Greek world and was widely imitated. Only Crete succeeded in introducing, or rather in maintaining, some measure of independence in pottery design. We know the Protogeometric period almost wholly by its pottery and a few weapons in the new metal—iron. No settlements or temples have been excavated but for a Cretan hilltop town; there is no jewellery; there are no bronze or clay figures, except again for some grotesques in Crete or potters' fantasies. But in Athens this new art represents the first chapter in a continuous story of development through the classical arts of Greece and Rome to the later achievements of the west.

An increase in population, prosperity and demand, a growing repertoire of shapes and patterns, these occasion and characterize the full Geometric period of the 9th and 8th centuries. Again we follow it best on vases. The new patterns—maeander, swastika and all variety of forms that ruler can devise—are deployed more generously now by the painter, and they spread over the whole vase. Eventually figure decoration is introduced—an important moment—but even so the rows of goats or horses are often treated more as a geometric frieze than as studies from life. And with his human figures too the Geometric artist stylized limbs and torsos into stiff silhouette shapes which appealed to his sense of pattern rather than to a sense of realism. His convention demanded that he showed all that he knew to be there. In a side view of a four-horse chariot we are not denied the full tally of sixteen legs, four necks and four heads. Once admitted, these figures are ambitiously used. Crowded scenes of mourners at the laying-out of the dead, processions and ship-fights decorate the massive vases which served as grave markers in Athens' cemetery. On the smaller vases are scenes of the dance, of battle, of sport; and—for this is the age of Homer—even scenes of myth. With the Geometric Heracles slaying the lion or a shipwrecked Odysseus we observe the very beginnings of narrative art, as the west understands it, just as in the Iliad and Odyssey we see the beginnings of western literature.

This Geometric art of Greece is a native product, evolved from the discipline of Protogeometric, barely reminiscent of anything Greece had produced before and in no way influenced by the art forms of other countries. This is, then, a moment to dwell upon, for the later course of Greek art is in some ways conditioned by the impact of the arts of the Near East and Egypt, and to appreciate what the native Greek contribution was we have especially to remember the meticulous technique and the strong sense of pattern shown by the Geometric artist. These remain the characteristics of Greek art long after the conventions of figure drawing had relaxed to admit far greater realism.

Not only in his vases can we observe the artist at work in this important formative period. The small bronze animals, made for dedication in sanctuaries—as that of Zeus at Olympia—reveal the same sense of form and pattern. Here too scenes of myth and action may be admitted—a hero grapples with a centaur, a hunter strikes down a lion. But these belong to the end of our period, and in the mere presence of the lion—not a creature met in Greece in those days—we are given warning of the new 'orientalizing' phase which is going to supplant, though not wholly suppress, the traditions of Geometric Greece. Within the Geometric period itself these intimations are still slight, and the eastern forms are geometricized. This applies to the figure drawing or modelling—as of the lions, and to the decoration and shapes of new classes of work in clay, metal (like the impressed gold bands and diadems found on the heads of corpses, and jewellery) and even the occasional seal-stone, where the conception and shape are foreign, the decoration Geometric Greek.

ARCHAIC GREECE c. 700–480 BC
Quickening Breath from Egypt and the East
By about 800 the Greek islanders, notably the Euboeans, had established a trading post on the coast of North Syria, at the mouth of the River Orontes. The arts of the east were again revealed to Greek eyes and in the 8th century exotic and unfamiliar objects appear beside the Geometric dedications in Greek temples and tombs. The effect of these new art forms was not immediate, but they slowly worked a revolution in Greek art. They introduced new motifs—monsters, flowers, curvilinear patterns to replace the old geometry; and new techniques—hammered bronze work, the jeweller's craft, ivory carving. Nor were these innovations introduced simply by imports, for it seems certain that Near-Eastern craftsmen too came west and taught the Greeks.

The Greeks were quick to learn but they never merely copied. They chose and adapted the motifs and forms which attracted them, and translated them soon into styles which no easterner would have recognized, and which can be taken as wholly Greek. The extent of Greece's debt to the east in this period is becoming more generally realized now, but it would be wrong to think that the example of the east did more than give new direction to an already flourishing and individual art. In the east the arts had over the centuries become conventionalized, almost sterile. In a very short while the east was to learn again from Greece new ways with the old forms, which the east had itself first inspired.

After the middle of the 7th century the Greeks repeated their overseas experiment with a trading post established in Egypt, at Naucratis, near one of the mouths of the Nile. The arts of Egypt, notably her monumental stone sculpture and architecture, had their effects on the visitors and were the immediate inspiration for Greece's first essays in these fields.

The influence of the Near East and Egypt conditioned the development of Greek art in the 7th and 6th centuries, and the story of Greek art in this, the 'Archaic' period, is the story of the way Greek artists reconciled their native sense for pattern and for the monumental with their foreign models. In a way this is the most crucial period in the history of western art.

Changing Conceptions of the Human Form
The stone sculpture of the Near East was mainly architectural and did very little to influence the development of sculpture in Greece. The Geometric tradition of making small figures, freely modelled in clay or cast in bronze, continued, and the source of the new 'orientalizing' spirit is perhaps a rather unexpected one. Clay plaques showing the naked goddess Astarte facing the front, with her hands at her breasts and loins, were common objects in Syria and Palestine. They were made in moulds and so could be easily mass-produced. The goddess was identified by the Greeks as their Aphrodite, and they soon clothed her and forgot her indelicate gestures. But in making these and other figures and plaques of clay they learned the use of the mould. This led to mass-production and to significant stereotyping of proportions and features which are broadly based on the oriental models, but are generally more angular—more 'geometric'.

We call these figures 'Dedalic' after the probably mythical sculptor Daedalus, to whom the Greeks attributed many early works. The characteristics are a facing head, triangular in outline, with a flat top and row of forehead curls, and a version of the oriental wig for the hair which fell in broad masses onto the shoulders. In a way this was a retrograde move after the freer modelling of the Geometric figures, but it set a new fashion and projected, as it were, a new conception of the human form for Greek eyes. In the 7th century the Dedalic style is represented in clay, and in statuettes carved in soft limestone which could be cut with but little more difficulty than wood (which must have been the most common material, but has not survived). The statues stood as dedications in sanctuaries, or they decorated temples—the two most common purposes for statuary at all periods in Greece.

Dedalic art was a form without a future and although the limestone figures, boldly cut and tricked out in bright colours, introduced the Greeks to stone statuary, they offered nothing to catch the imagination. New direction was given by the example of Egyptian statuary. In the country of the Nile there had been a long tradition of carving statues in hard stone at more than life size. These are the two new features—material and size—which the Greeks adopted. To a lesser degree they were influenced too by the forms of Egyptian sculpture, by the set canon of proportions used in Egypt and by the appearance of the statues of standing men. But the Egyptian male figures were stiff, hieratic statues, their weight thrown back onto one leg, the other foot advanced to steady the mass. The Greeks were already used to similar but better balanced figures in their small bronzes, and from the beginning their statues—we call them by the Greek word for youths, *kouroi*—have more immanent life than the Egyptian.

The hard stone was readily found—fine white marble which could be quarried with no difficulty in the Greek islands, especially Naxos; and it seems likely that the islands saw the first of the colossal marble *kouroi* of the new style in the last quarter of the 7th century. In the early statues the artist is still wrestling with the difficulties of his material. The block-like shape of the quarried stone decisively influences the form of the statues which the viewer is invited to look at from front, back, or sides, but never obliquely. Features and anatomical detail too were subjected to the Greek sense of pattern and seem to be applied to the figures rather than become an integral part of them. Growing mastery of the material and observation of anatomy lead us to the

last of the *kouroi*, at the end of the Archaic period, and with them we find the same conventional pose treated with a much fuller understanding of the parts of the body yet with the sense of pattern still the overriding feature.

These naked *kouroi*—only the earliest of them wear a belt—stood as grave monuments or dedications (they were long known as Apollos) in all parts of the Greek world. We can detect the styles of local schools but are more impressed by the uniformity of style and development. The *kouroi* are the dominant type for Archaic sculpture, but of course not the only type. After the naked Astarte-Aphrodite figures the Greeks preferred their statues of women fully clothed. The early ones—of Dedalic type—have flat, formless bodies. The same conventions were observed for the earliest executed at life size or more in white marble. During the first half of the 6th century the sculptors came to appreciate the opportunities for pattern offered by the folds of drapery, and these were exploited in the series of maidens—the *korai*—which also served as dedications in sanctuaries.

This surface patterning of drapery seems to have been practised first by East-Greek artists, of Chios and Samos, but soon spread to other centres, and it is in Athens that we can observe it best. This is largely due to the accidents of discovery. In 480 the Persians sacked Athens, burnt its Acropolis and overthrew the statues upon it. When the Athenians returned they buried the broken dedications which have thus survived the robbing and the threatening lime-kilns of later centuries. Excavated and mended, the statues can now give us a vivid picture of the fine works which had adorned Athena's sanctuary rock in the 6th century.

Works in relief and in the round also decorated the 6th-century temples. In the development of the drapery and forms of the figures on them they keep step with the development of the *kouroi* and *korai*. The triangular gables of the temples offered an awkward field for the sculptor which he filled with set pieces or with animal groups. The rectangular metopes over the columns of Doric buildings afforded panels for simpler groups in relief. And in the long friezes which decorated Ionic buildings there was the opportunity to exercise in sculpture that feeling for narrative which we can probably observe more vividly in the vase-painting of the same years.

The First 'Storied Urns'

It is fortunate for us that Greek artists of the Archaic and Classical periods were so interested in pottery decoration. We have already seen how it is that pottery, being indestructible, can be a valuable source of information about the art and culture of any period,

and is generally available in quantity. When that pottery also attracted elaborately painted decoration, both figured and abstract, and often by artists of the first rank, we are offered an unrivalled opportunity to observe development in fashions and change in artistic taste. Thus it is that the 'orientalizing' phase of Archaic Greek art is best documented in the decoration of clay vases, although eastern vase-decoration (which was comparatively unimportant) was never the source of inspiration.

We find that the harsh Geometric conventions for figure drawing are relaxed, and that the animals or parts of the human body are represented in something approaching their natural form, in imitation of the eastern conventions, instead of being stylized as geometric patterns. On the vases themselves there were two ways of doing this. One clung still very much to the Geometric tradition for proportion of figures, and even in the size of the great grave-marking vases which were being made. The figures are drawn more in outline than in silhouette, the details being rendered in a simple linear manner. Pattern is still all-important: ears, for example, are often stylized as little scrolls with palmettes growing in them. The technique of vase-painting did not allow of much variety in colour, but in this style we do find some broad masses of colours—red or brown—laid on areas of dress or body. This is the style which was favoured most in Athens—which had been the home of the Geometric style—and in the Greek islands.

The other style, more go-ahead and ultimately more successful, was invented in Corinth. This is what is called the 'black-figure' technique. The figures were drawn in silhouette still, but with plumper, more natural masses, and the details on them were represented by scratching lines on the black paint so that the pale clay of the vase showed through. Added red paint could be used for some details. The technique may have been inspired by the incised decoration on eastern ivories and metalwork. The fine incised lines suited smaller figures than those which appear on the big Athenian and island vases, and the best examples of black-figure are on small perfume flasks from Corinth decorated in a true miniaturist style.

As well as this new treatment of figure drawing and the new repertoire of figures, monsters and narrative scenes, the subsidiary ornament of the vases was also changed. Floral and curvilinear patterns replace the angular geometry. Chains of lotus and palmettes ring vases where once the maeander ran, and the backgrounds to the figure scenes are filled, like a tapestry, with rosettes and hooks, spirals and flowers, instead of simply zigzags and stars.

The two styles—black-figure and outline drawing—flourished through the 7th century. Besides the orientalizing animals we find more and more scenes from myth and the Homeric poems. Corinth's vases were the most popular and are found all over the Greek world, and far beyond it, wherever Greek colonists or traders carried the outward trappings of the Greek way of life. Popularity was to spell the end to the Corinthian potters' success, for it led to mass-production and a lowering of standards. But more important was the acceptance of the black-figure technique by Athenian artists at the end of the 7th century. They married the new technique of precision and detail to their developed sense for the monumental and narrative, and produced a series of black-figure vases which by the mid-6th century had driven the decorated Corinthian vases from the markets of the Greek world.

Athenian black-figure vases are as characteristic of the Archaic period as, in sculpture, were the *kouroi* and *korai*. The lithe figures, with their delicately incised features and dress, acted out a variety of scenes from myth or everyday life, on vases which are as remarkable for the excellence of their potting or their paint as for the quality of the draughtsmanship practised upon them. For this is drawing rather than painting, and colour, but for details of white and red, plays little part. The background and subsidiary decoration too dwindles or disappears so that the artist could give full and immediate expression to what was always, for a Greek, of prime importance, the representation of human bodies. Landscape, and even the background details of trees or scenery were generally ignored. Even the friezes of animals and monsters are relegated to relatively obscure positions in the course of time.

Proud of their achievements the artists—painters and potters—sometimes signed their work. We are able to distinguish clearly the individuality and mannerisms of the painters, whether we call them by their own names—as Execias—or by a name we invent for them—like the Andocides Painter, or the Antimenes Painter, called after their potters or after youths honoured in mottoes inscribed on their vases.

Athens and Corinth were not the only vase-producing centres in Archaic Greece. In the 7th century the islands and East Greece. produced attractive and distinctive vases, comparable in varying degrees to those of the big cities of mainland Greece. And in the 6th century there are notable schools of black-figure in East Greece, Sparta and in one of the western colonial cities of south Italy where the so-called Chalcidian vases were made. These other wares are often close to the Athenian but never so prolific and rarely of such high quality.

Even so, the black-figure technique which Athens had learned from Corinth and then mastered to Corinth's discomfiture, was not to be the last word in vase decoration. About 530 BC a new technique was introduced which, within a generation, was to supplant black-figure. This is known as red-figure, and is the reverse, or, as it were, the negative of the older technique. The figures, instead of being painted black and with details incised on them, are now reserved in the red clay ground of the vase while the background is painted black. The inner detail is painted on and not incised. In effect this means that outline drawing has again replaced silhouette, the brush replaced the graver. The new style allowed greater freedom to the painter, but was more uncompromisingly black-and-white. The early examples, still of the Archaic period, express all the precision in observation of anatomical detail and drapery patterns which can be seen in the latest of the marble *kouroi* and *korai*.

New Techniques in Bronze and Gold

It is in objects of bronze that we can most easily identify the sort of oriental products which so influenced the Greeks in the 8th and 7th centuries BC. The Geometric Greeks had made bronze statuettes, and bronze cauldrons on tripod legs with big ring handles. Eastern craftsmen introduced new hammered techniques for bronze decoration which in Greece are practised on a variety of objects which betray other signs of oriental inspiration. Notable among these are the big shields with animal-head bosses made in Crete, and the griffin-heads which were made to decorate the newer, orientalizing cauldrons. These vessels might otherwise carry cast decoration—sirens or animals—some of which are imported from the east, others copied by Greeks and given the pert angular features which the Greeks preferred to the rather flabby oriental ones.

Later on the small cast statuettes became more common and they mirror in miniature the works of major sculpture in stone. They can be used too for the decoration of implements or objects of toilet and furniture. The Egyptian fashion of having a bronze figure as the handle for a mirror was copied and several exquisite Greek versions of the 6th century are preserved. On bronze vases the body of a youth or animal might serve as handle, and the attachments of the cast handles were regularly fashioned as palmettes or animal heads. The thinner sheet bronze of the vessels themselves is often not preserved and we know many only from their handles and other decorated attachments. Some of the finest big bronze vases of the Archaic period—craters for mixing wine—have been found far from Greece: the crater from the tomb of a Celtic princess at Vix, little over 100 miles from Paris, and others of similar style from barbarian Illyria (Yugoslavia) and south Russia.

On bronze armour again we find decoration—on helmets, greaves and corselets; incised or in relief. The most elaborate are the strips of bronze which were fastened to the inside of shields and decorated in low relief with panels showing mythological scenes. This sort of delicate bronze relief work, sometimes worked by hammering over a mould, was also used as sheath decoration on furniture.

For their gold jewellery the Greeks had re-learned from the east the techniques of granulation—powdering with tiny globules of gold, and filigree. Rhodes and the islands specialized in elaborate ear-ring pendants on which the figure of a goddess or an animal is impressed in the sheet gold and the whole elaborated with wire and granule detail. Spiral ear-rings have their terminals shaped as griffin-heads. Rosette discs carry on their golden petals superb miniature heads of animals, or flies and bees worked in gold. The earliest of the jewellery in these forms copies the Dedalic conventions of larger works, but the island workshops did not continue in production long into the 6th century. We can, however, find some later pieces in the same tradition in the gold work made by the East Greeks in the Black Sea area for their neighbours the Scythians, in which Greek orientalizing motifs are wedded to the Scythians' 'animal style' and appear on objects of native type.

Carving in Miniature: Ivory, Seals and Coins

Ivory-carving—like the material itself—was one of the novelties introduced from the east in the orientalizing period. Already in the 8th century, it seems, an eastern craftsman had taught his trade in Athens, and in a grave there we find ivory figures of women which are inspired by the eastern Astarte figures. These, however, are slim mortals with lively, angular features which only a Greek, used to the Geometric tradition, could have given them.

In the 7th century various new schools of ivory-workers are found in Greece. In Corinth or some other centre of the Peloponnese disc seals were carved with intricate animal patterns. More important are the little statuettes. These generally copy the style and proportions of larger works but the expensive material invited the attention of the best craftsmen, and some of our finest examples of Dedalic art are ivory miniatures. Relief-work too appears, as for comb-backs or little decorative plaques. In East Greece the schools retain more of the oriental qualities of modelling, with the rounder features and fuller limbs, as in the fine statuettes from Ephesus and Smyrna, and a god with his lion, which was taken west to Delphi. But the very finest of the eastern ivories—the slim kneeling youth from Samos, perhaps from a lyre—shows none of these features, and he expresses more fully the precision and feeling for pattern which characterize the main stream of Greek art.

Statuettes and plaques of clay we have noted already in discussing the early stages of stone sculpture. The potter too turned his hand to the production of clay figure vases (ambiguously called 'plastic vases') in the form of animals or heads, usually for use as perfume flasks.

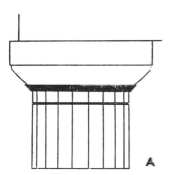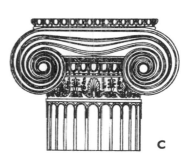

The classical 'orders' survived longer than any other feature of Greek architecture. They are distinguished from each other in a number of ways, some of great subtlety, but are most easily recognized by their capitals. The Doric (A), originating on the mainland of Greece, is the simplest. The Ionic (C) developed from an earlier version known as Aeolic (B)—shown in a restored capital from Neandria: the characteristic volutes were diminished and linked in a scroll across the top of the column. The capital of the last order, the Corinthian (D) is a further modification, the volutes being combined with acanthus foliage. The orders also differed systematically in their proportions and details of their entablature.

The arts of the seal-engraver had received a great impetus from the example of the east, and not only in the matter of ivory seals, but also of stone. The softer stones were used at first, with devices which are very close to the figures on contemporary vases—generally animal with a few simple compositions with humans. Before the middle of the 7th century artists in the islands—notably Melos—were inspired by the fine prehistoric gems which they found in old tombs, to copy the old shapes and some of the old patterns. The products of this extraordinary throw-back to Bronze Age models can be traced for about a hundred years, to the mid-6th century. Then, however, the engravers were introduced to the harder, semi-precious stones, especially carnelian, and copied more often the scarab-beetle shape of seal which had been popular in Egypt for centuries. Their fine engraving has given us some of the masterpieces of Archaic art, comparing in the delicacy of detail and skill of composition with the finest contemporary drawing and sculpture.

The men who cut gems were probably the ones who cut the dies for coins. The Greeks learned to mint coins from the Lydians at the end of the 7th century. By the end of the Archaic period their mastery of the difficult technique was such that the finest coins, of mainland Greece as of the western colonies in Italy and Sicily, can match closely the best extant gems. And many coins could, of course, be struck from a single die, could circulate and be admired, instruct and please. Still, though, the conventions and motifs are the same, and an essential unity of treatment can be observed whatever the material, size or purpose of the object may be.

The earliest temples (before 600) were primitive structures of wood, brick, or, more rarely, stone, sometimes with a porch on two pillars in front of the entrance. Pottery models, like this from the Heraeum of Argos, have survived and show their general appearance. A large window occupied most of the gable; the roof was probably thatched.

Houses for Gods and Men

The Greeks were slow to evolve the monumental styles of architecture by which we best know them, slower than in their acceptance of the idea of monumental sculpture, which we have already discussed. For the earliest period all we know about is their domestic architecture. In the Geometric period there are one-roomed houses, rectangular or apsidal, sometimes with a shallow porch which has two columns in it, and only one door; the roof either flat, of mud, or pitched, with thatch. The construction of the walls depended rather on materials available and it was not often that the walls were of stone to their tops. Not until near 600 BC were rectangular blocks (ashlars) cut for walls, but the less regular stones were often most carefully fitted together in what is known as the 'polygonal' style—a difficult and most attractive masonry. More often the walls are of mud-brick above a low socle of stone; the columns of the porch or roof-supports being of wood. By the end of the 7th century large flat clay roof tiles were being made.

Temples—houses for the gods—were built in the same way and with the same plans, but they were naturally often much larger and were the first buildings to attract elaboration in the way of colonnades or sculpture. Rows of columns might be introduced along the centre of the main room (cella), across the porch or along the sides, until the basic plan of the classical temple was evolved. Now too there may be a back door and room to serve as a treasury for the god. His cult image stood inside his temple. The altar—generally no more than a simple rectangular structure—stood before the door, which was normally at the east.

The conception of monumental architecture, as of monumental sculpture, was picked up by the Greeks from the great buildings of Egypt. The result was the evolution of 'orders' of stone architecture in which the forms of columns, bases, capitals and upperworks became canonized and within which any further development was closely circumscribed. Two main traditions developed—the Ionic and the Doric. The Ionic was born in East Greece. There, already by about 600, all-stone temples were being planned. The accepted 'Ionic' features do not appear at first, nor at any time do we in this tradition meet much which reflects Egypt beyond the simple idea of all-stone orders for buildings. The first capitals, for instance, are bell-shaped with oriental leaves or florals carved on them. The other oriental forms, best known on furniture, are copied in stone—capitals with two curling volutes springing from the shaft (so-called Aeolic) and finally the usual Ionic form of a flat cushion with volutes at each end and a row of leaves—later the egg and dart—beneath. The Ionians were ambitious builders and within about fifty years we have three colossal buildings planned (two, successively, at Samos; one at Ephesus) which rival in size anything the Greeks were to attempt for centuries to come. The first Temple of Artemis at Ephesus, with its forest of columns, many with sculptured bases, was a deliberate challenge to the palaces and temples of the east and Egypt; almost a deliberate impertinence on the part of a people to whom these arts were so new.

The Doric order was evolved on the Greek mainland, and the earliest examples which we know are at Corinth, at Olympia and on Corfu (the Corinthian colony of Corcyra). The capitals are more austere, like broad plain bowls, and far closer to forms met in Egypt. Egyptian too are some of the minor decorative mouldings. The upperworks are much more a decorative translation into stone of the elaborate timbering which must have been a feature of earlier temple building. And even with the Doric order of stone columns wooden upperworks were often to be found.

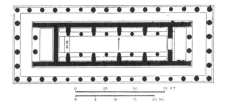

The Temple of Hera at Olympia dates from the end of the 7th century BC *and stands at the very beginning of the Doric style, but already the familiar plan has been evolved—the cella (here subdivided by spur walls) with porches at each end, the whole surrounded by a colonnade. The original wooden columns were gradually replaced by stone ones.*

These might be encased in elaborately decorated clay revetments with richly painted floral and abstract patterns, which both protected the timber and lent a touch of colour to the building.

Architecture and sculpture in Greece went hand in hand and we have already remarked how sculpture in the round and in relief might be fitted to both Ionic and Doric temples. Temples were not of course the only major architectural undertakings in the Archaic period, but their form, their colonnades and even sometimes their plans deeply influenced the few other public buildings of which we know something.

CLASSICAL GREECE 480–323 BC
The Climax which Inspired the West

The turning point between Archaic and Classical in the history of Greek art is generally set at the time of the Persian Wars and Greece's successful assertion of her independence of the new empire of the east. It is not convenience only that equates this momentous political and military victory with a new period of art, but there is no connection between the two, unless we wish to see in Classical art Greece's final rejection of further inspiration from the east, which would be far short of the truth. But in these years, and just before, we can readily pick out significant new trends in the senior of the arts—sculpture, and the fact remains that the recovery of Greek prosperity after the Wars became the occasion for a number of major public works which gave the opportunity for the fullest expression of the artists' powers.

But what is Classical art? Should we say that it represents the artist's final victory in the representation of the human form in two or three dimensions? Or that it is the art of pride and empire, fostered by a rich and sometimes tyrannical Athens? Or that in it the artist strikes the neatest and ideal balance between the rule of pattern and the rule of realism? None of these explanations is wholly true, and taken all together they still do not explain much. Now more than in any other period of Greece's history its art can be fully understood only in terms of the rest of the Greek achievement—literature, thought, political aspirations, science—the matters discussed in other chapters of this book.

The art-historian finds it particularly difficult to account for the character of a period by a single idea or expression. Greek art developed steadily through the 5th and 4th centuries. It advanced from the new confidence won when the archaic conventions were abandoned, to a degree of sophistication which, in another hundred years, was to reach a point where it might be said that there was nothing more to learn about representational art. Within this range what is the true Classical? The sculptures of Olympia which still express something of the Archaic; the Parthenon marbles with their mingled idealism and impressionism; or the subtler graces of a Praxiteles? It is not a monument or a single artist or school, rather is it the growth and maturing of a tradition which had its roots in Geometric Greece, and whose achievement is probably best measured by the way in which succeeding generations looked to it as an inspiration, as a sort of Golden Age of the arts. It was a period in which even a plain cooking pot shared something of the grace and elegance of proportions of the major works; an age in which, one might say, as much care for proportion and finish would have been devoted to the building of a public lavatory (if there had been such things) as to the building of a temple.

The Sculptor Set Free

The archaic *kouros* stood four-square, facing the front. Split him from crown to groin and each half mirrors the other. This rigid symmetry and frontality remained the rule until the point was reached at which the artist's command in the accurate representation of details of anatomy led him to experiment with more realistic poses for the whole figure. Now, instead of standing with his weight equally carried by each foot, the figure relaxes, one leg straight to bear the weight, the other flexed lightly with the hip lowered, the trunk lightly bent. A simple and natural movement, but by showing it, and showing it successfully, the artist broke with the conventions of Archaism. This is to be the new type for standing figures, naked or clothed, male or female—a relaxed natural pose with limbs and drapery naturally composed, blending the native sense for pattern and proportion with a new realism. Gone now too is the fussy prettiness of the drapery of the archaic *korai*. The light *chiton* with its massed folds which invited the patterned zigzags of hem and cloak, is replaced by the heavy *peplos*, falling straight from the shoulders, revealing subtly yet distinctly the form and pose of the body beneath. From this moment on the development of Greek sculpture can be described in terms of a growing command of realism in both pose and detail, of a concern with the expression of new factors—emotion, pathos, divinity, and of a variety of experiments in the rendering of drapery which anticipate everything which the later history of western sculpture can offer.

Our evidence for the Classical period is twofold. First, the original works which have survived and are generally architectural sculpture, from the temples at Olympia, Athens, Bassae etc. Secondly, the evidence for works by famous sculptors afforded by copies executed in later periods. These may take us some removes from the original masterpieces, but details of pose and style can often be understood, and many copies were obviously exact works lacking only the master's finishing touch and the subtleties of expression which can mean so much.

Here too it may be remarked that Archaic and Classical statuary was regularly painted—hair, eyes, lips, drapery—in colours (usually now lost) which lent life to the blind pallid figures, and which would have mellowed the glare of the brilliant sun beneath which they were displayed. The bright bronzes too had inlaid eyes, lips, fingernails.

The sculpture from the temple of Zeus at Olympia typifies the new freedom of pose; the composed group of one gable contrasting strongly with the vigorous, struggling figures of the other. Of these years, before the mid-5th century, we hear of the sculptor Myron, and copies of his works show his concern with new problems of pose—like the famous Discus-thrower—and with narrative groups—like Athena and the satyr Marsyas. But still emotion is expressed not by the features, which are set, classical, ideal, and rarely broken by expression of feeling, but by the gestures and pose of the whole figures. We soon recognize the conventional signs for mourning, despair, passion, surprise.

The sculptures rescued from the temple of Athena—the Parthenon—on the Acropolis at Athens by Lord Elgin express for most of us the high point of Classical art. The greatest subtlety of composition is combined with a new treatment of drapery, deeply cut so that with the play of light and shade it has a mass, almost a life of its own, and yet does nothing to hide the bodies and gestures of the figures. The classic, set features lend especial dignity to the great frieze which encircled the building within the colonnade, and showed the burghers of Athens in procession to do honour to their goddess. The same dignity and serenity characterize the grave reliefs of this period, showing poignant but calm scenes of farewell, or the dead woman at home with her jewels and servants.

The name of Phidias is associated with the Parthenon, and the same master wrought the colossal gold and ivory cult figures which stood in the temples at Olympia and Athens, but have not survived to our day. A near contemporary of his was Polyclitus of Argos, who revived the old tradition of the *kouros* with a new canon of proportions, and set a standard for the stocky athlete figures of the later 5th century.

We approach now an age of experiments, each of which can be

The two pediments of the Temple of Zeus at Olympia (finished in 456 BC) illustrate the sculptor's growing mastery over form and movement, the composed grouping of the east pediment (top) contrasting with the struggling figures of the west (bottom). The subject of the east pediment is the preparation for the chariot-race between Oenomaus and Pelops, the legendary origin of that at Olympia. Zeus stands in the centre, with Pelops and Hippodameia on his left, Oenomaus and Sterope on his right, their two teams of horses behind them. The west pediment depicts the combat of the Lapiths and the Centaurs. Here the central figure is Apollo, bringing victory to the Lapiths.

With the sculpture of the Parthenon the climax of the Classical style is reached. The reliefs of the frieze and metopes and the free-standing figures of the pediments are the work of several sculptors, under the supervision of Phidias. The west pediment (reconstructed above) portrayed the struggle between Athena and Poseidon for the land of Attica. To left and right their teams of horses rear up, reined in by Nike and Amphitrite.

associated either with a known sculptor's work or with some surviving original group or figure. Around 400 comes an interest in representing drapery wind-blown tight against the figure, which shows clearly through as though the stuff were transparent. At the same time more attention is paid to the sympathetic and accurate representation of the naked female figure—a subject in which the Greek sculptor had been frankly uninterested hitherto, but which, with the new drapery styles in sculpture, offered boundless new possibilities. The best examples of the new style are the Nikai (Victories) on the balustrade around the temple of Athena Nike on the Acropolis, of before 400 BC.

With the name of the sculptor Scopas, who worked in the first half of the 4th century, we associate new methods of treating the human features, letting the brow overhang deep-sunk eyes in a way which lends an intensity of expression appropriate to scenes of emotion or aggression. For the first time the features are regularly carved in a way to suggest emotion, while hitherto this effect was sought mainly by pose and gesture.

Praxiteles excelled in the expression of subtler emotions and was best known for his statues of divinities. His Hermes at Olympia is still extant, although many argue that the statue is a late copy. It gives a good idea of his style, supple, almost languorous in the representation of the body, rather ethereal in the features. He also first popularized the representation of goddesses naked—especially, of course, Aphrodite. His statue of the goddess for Cnidus won great fame in antiquity and served as model for a host of later and poorer works. He is said to have modelled from life.

By far the most important of the 4th-century sculptors was Lysippus. He introduced a new canon of proportions for male figures—broad-shouldered, with small heads—but his most significant contribution to the development of Greek sculpture was in the matter of pose. Hitherto virtually all free-standing statues had been designed to be seen from one viewpoint only, the front, although there were generally several satisfactory subsidiary views. Lysippus' figures do not invite the spectator to stand in any one position but to move around them. This is done by contrasting the apparent direction of motion by the direction in which the head is looking, or by subtle refinements of swirling drapery. It represents a new freedom for the sculptor, which was to be exploited to the full in the succeeding period.

We are told that Alexander the Great would allow only Lysippus to carve portraits of him, and it is with Lysippus' name that we should perhaps associate the true beginnings of Greek portraiture. In general, however, 4th-century portraits are of men long dead—the poets, philosophers and politicians of the 5th century—and although some details of their features may have been recorded, and even copied on gem-stones or clay figures, it is clear that the portrait heads are strongly idealized to express the appropriate character of the subject. Greek portraits were always to some degree idealized, but after Lysippus they are also living and real likenesses.

The advent of Alexander marked the end of the age of the city-state and of the sort of public and private patronage which had sponsored the artists' work. At this time too a decree against luxurious burials in Athens put an end to the great series of grave reliefs from Athens' cemeteries. So in many ways this political turning-point marks also an important stage in the history of Greek sculpture.

The Lost Masterpieces of Greek Painting

No Greek wall-paintings are preserved from the Archaic period, and our only intimations of what might have been executed must be got from vases, or from works in Etruria and Phrygia which are inspired and sometimes made by Greek artists. But, so far as we can judge, the conventions and compositions were much as those of the vase-painter. With the 5th century we begin to find record in ancient authors of painters whose work was held in especially high esteem by their contemporaries and by later generations. This is particularly important when we recall that the names of vase-painters were forgotten once their art was no longer practised, and that we know them only from their signatures on vases.

But again, of the major painters' work we have no originals surviving, only their names—Polygnotus, Mikon, and others—and vivid descriptions of the great compositions, on wooden panels or fresco, with which they decorated the public buildings and temples of the major towns of Greece.

It seems that they worked generally on a white background, and could of course use a great variety of colours. Depth was shown by putting figures at different levels. The effect of these features on vase-painters we shall remark in a moment. On a wall or panel there would of course have been far better opportunities for shading, highlights, for representing figures in the round and in depth, and we soon hear of real 'trompe l'oeil' works—like the painted curtain which the spectator instinctively wishes to draw back. The few paintings on marble which have survived, generally tombstones, give us a very poor idea of an art which in antiquity was clearly rated far above the vase-painter's, which is all that survives for us to admire.

Greek vases assumed a variety of shapes, determined by the function they were intended to fulfil (none were simply ornamental). Those shown above are: wine-jars—column crater (a), volute crater (b), and calyx crater (c)—an oil-jar (lekythos) (d), a wine-jug (oenochoe) (e), a drinking-bowl (kylix) (f) and a bell-shaped crater (g). These drawings are not to a common scale.

The Supremacy of the Athenian Potters

In the Classical period the history of Greek vases is wholly that of Athenian vase-painting. Athens' vases had, by their excellence and especially with their new red-figure technique, swept all other wares from the markets of the Greek world. Here and there imitations are to be found, but virtually all the finely decorated vases in Greece in the 5th and 4th centuries were made in Athens. Emigrants from Athens started workshops in the Greek colonies of south Italy, and these too in time produced a considerable number of dull imitative works. Some of their more ambitious and extravagant products in the 4th century we shall have occasion to mention later, but the fountain head of all these local styles was Athens.

The old black-figure technique barely survived the Persian Wars. The red-figure, with its emphasis on brushwork and linear detail, offered the artist more opportunities in the representation of the human body, but also to a very large extent circumscribed his art. The uncompromising black background imposed the necessity for a bold outline. It made compositions with several overlapping figures a difficult matter, and it meant that the figures had, as it were, to act their parts on a narrow stage in front of a black curtain, since any real expression of depth was impossible. In time the artist found means of suggesting figures in the round, but they were seldom effective in such a purely linear, 'black-and-white' style. Shading appears rarely, and more often the contour is suggested by the lines of the drapery folds drawn over plump limbs. Composition in depth could only be shown by overlapping, hardly ever by even rudimentary attempts at perspective. The convention of major painting, to show figures standing on different ground lines up and down the field of the painting, was copied occasionally in the 5th century, and regularly in the 4th, but the black background spoiled the effect. Moreover, only few of the finest artists successfully related their drawing to the shape of the vase they were decorating, and many fine figures are best appreciated in trick photographs or drawn copies, because on the curved surface of the vase their full height cannot be seen in proper proportions.

The painters' growing command of anatomical form and pose can be followed in much the same terms as the sculptor's. The proper profile view of the eye, and representation of the body in three-quarter view, came quite early. The elaborate zigzag patterns of Archaic drapery are abandoned, as were those of the *korai*, for simpler lines. Broken lines within the main folds correspond with the drapery of the Parthenon sculptures, and the transparent drapery of the end of the 5th century is shown by drawing the naked figure in outline first, then adding the drapery, emphasizing the fulness of the forms by the lines of the folds. In the 4th century the quality of the drawing rarely matches the supple command of anatomy and pose shown by sculptors. By this time the vase-painter was over-conscious of the works of major painting which were being executed, and attempted unsuccessfully to copy them. But the black background of his vases too effectively broke up massed compositions, and the application of white paint and gilding simply produced an effect of cheap gaudiness. In this the south-Italian painters were the worst offenders.

One special class, of the mid-5th century and after, abandoned the black background and offers us some of the finest examples of Greek vase-painting. These are the white-ground *lekythoi*, cylindrical oil-vases regularly left as offerings in Athenian tombs. The outlines of the figures, many of them strongly reminiscent of those on classical grave reliefs, are painted in bold outline on the fine white background, and the drapery and details added in broad masses of colour such as could not be admitted on red-figure vases. Unfortunately the white ground is fugitive and all too few of the vases have survived with their colouring intact.

Of the red-figure vases most of the more popular shapes are intimately connected with the pleasures of the table. Craters, or mixing bowls, of various forms, are big open-mouthed vessels in which the wine was mixed with water. One-handled jugs or dippers were used to take out the wine. The cups themselves were generally very broad and shallow, more of the proportions of a modern soup-plate than a wine-glass, and the most elegant of them stood on slender high stems. Out of use they hung on the wall and the near-disc surface they offered served as two broad fields—between the handles—for the painter to decorate. In use, the toper would see in the base of the cup a disc with the scene of a satyr and maenad, of dancers, of lovers, sometimes a warning of the awful after-effects of too much wine!

The content of the scenes on the vases is in most cases their greatest value to us. Mythological scenes remain very common, and conventions were adopted for showing certain scenes and figures much in the way that conventional scenes are copied time and again in Byzantine and Renaissance painting. Many of the subjects now, though, are inspired by contemporary plays, others by the new major wall-paintings appearing in the temples and public buildings of Athens. There are many scenes of athletes practising, and the gymnasium and palaestra were the obvious places for an artist to go to sketch from life. Of the scenes from everyday life those associated with the ultimate use of the vase are prominent—drinking parties, dancers, or the wild rout of satyrs and maenads attending the god of wine, Dionysus. Religious scenes are uncommon except on vases made specifically for certain ceremonies, as those in which the water for the bride's bath was fetched from the local spring and then kept warm.

In the 4th century the Athenian vases concentrate more on a limited repertoire of mythological scenes or everyday life—the boudoir especially, while the south-Italian vases offer gross tableaux inspired by stage plays. By the end of the 4th century the vase-painter had to admit that his technique could offer no more of value to this genre, and abandoned his attempts to ape major painting. Fine, plain black pottery was being valued no doubt for its very lack of pretentious or vulgar decoration.

Bronze, Silver and Gold

Major bronze sculptures were executed by the same artists as the marbles, and so far as we can judge the different techniques made little difference to the result, although some features are obviously better suited to one than the other. But few major bronzes have survived—the best, oddly enough, from the wrecks of Roman treasure ships. Minor works in bronze are, however, more plentiful, and the finest of them mirror all the best qualities of the larger statuary, while some show an instinct for miniature statuary as an art in its own right.

A great many of the bronze figures in the round which are pre-served are still, as in the Archaic period, to be found as attach-ments to vessels or other objects. The women serving as mirror supports are still to be seen, fashioned in the new style of the 5th century. Other figures serve as handles or decorative attachments to bowls and jugs. A special class of water jars *(hydriae)* have a siren with spread wings at the base of the handle, and often, at the top of the handle, we find a head looking into the vessel or across its top.

Far more elaborate repoussée work is now attempted, some of the figures being worked in what seems impossibly high relief. This sort of decoration is found on a great variety of objects—on the cheek-pieces of helmets, on belts, on attachments to furniture, and especially decorating the backs of the folding lids of circular mirrors. Another, and rarer way of decorating a mirror back was to incise a scene upon it.

When we look at ancient bronzes today it is as well to remember that we generally do not see them with anything like their original colour, which would have been bright and golden or slightly coppery. We see instead the greenish or blue patina of age, or, if they have been cleaned, a brownish chocolate surface. This is deceptive, because fine detail, especially incision, is lost in it unless brought out by skilful lighting or, for the incision, by a powder filling. But then the effect is the reverse of true for we see white lines on a dull surface, instead of dark lines etched on a brilliant surface. With the bronzes, as with the marble figures which have lost their original colours, we have to make a conscious effort of the imagination to visualize their original condition and appear-ance.

In the working of precious metals it is of course the miniaturist who excels. Granulation and filigree, all the jeweller's techniques, are combined to produce the most intricate compositions for necklaces, ear-rings and pendants. But some of the most impressive work is simpler, like the heavy bracelets with terminals worked as animal heads—a form especially popular with the Persians and eastern peoples, and one which the Greeks were not slow to copy. Gold remains in general use; silver is rather more rare (or, at least, less often preserved); and on occasion we find inlay decoration, of enamel or glass.

The Flourishing Minor Arts

Clay figurines and plaques are common finds in Greek temples and tombs, where they are found as offerings, and they must have been very common in the houses too, where they served as deco-ration. They could be mass-produced from moulds but the origi-nal, from which the moulds were cast, was often a work of art in its own right, and the many copies of it may mirror its quality in every detail. Since they are found even more often than the small bronzes we have in them a fuller record in miniature of contem-porary styles in statuary. The subjects too may be more varied and instructive—cooks in their kitchens, actors in their costumes with masks. Some were children's dolls with jointed legs; others seem almost portraits with lifelike and individual features. Another popular form of decoration was the clay plaque, either cut-outs like the series made in Melos in the 5th century, or the rectangular plaques with cult scenes on them, made in south Italy at Locri. Some of this sort of relief work in clay reminds us so strongly of metal reliefs that it seems likely that the moulds could sometimes have been taken from metalwork.

Ivory was still worked, for statuettes and jewellery, but less is preserved than of the Archaic period, and we hear more of its use for flesh parts of the colossal gold and ivory cult statues.

The cutting of gem-stones flourished. This is an art to which all too little attention is paid, for some of the masterpieces of Classical art are to be looked for on the tiny engraved stones. At the end of the Archaic period the favourite shape was the Egyp-tian scarab, which was often set on a ring so that it could be worn on the finger. In the 5th and 4th centuries the 'scaraboid' is commoner—an oval stone about an inch long, with a low domed back and flat engraved face. The material was most often chalce-dony. These too might be mounted on finger-rings but could also be worn as pendants on a necklace or at the wrist. Now too we find finger-rings of solid gold, silver or bronze, with the metal

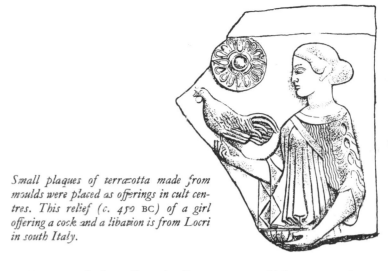

Small plaques of terracotta made from moulds were placed as offerings in cult cen-tres. This relief (c. 450 BC) of a girl offering a cock and a libation is from Locri in south Italy.

itself engraved. As well as the figure scenes, which correspond closely with contemporary work on vases and in sculpture, there are two other classes of decoration on gems which deserve note. The first is of animals—subjects which we often think the Greeks to have avoided, but which on gems and coins are represented with loving care and a shrewd eye for accurate detail. The second class is of heads, some of which, even as early as the 5th century, must be portraits. Occasionally the artists sign their names, and one, Dexamenus of Chios, has left us some of the finest animal studies of water-birds as well as the earliest of the portrait heads.

The art of the engraver of dies for coins is close to that of the gem-engraver, but his subjects are usually different. Occasionally we think we can detect the hand of the same artist in the two media. Coins invited more often head studies, of deities and eventually of living rulers. But there are many genre scenes still in the tradition of the Archaic period, and a number of superb animal studies—like Zeus' eagle at Olympia. On the whole the nature of the coin-engraver's task demanded a greater conserva-tism of motif and treatment, and, except for the superb portrait heads, the coins of the later periods tend to monotony and lack the originality we see in the 6th and 5th centuries.

The Perfect Buildings of a Troubled Age

In the Classical period the Doric and Ionic orders find expression in the finest temple buildings of any period of Greek art, and, fortunately, in some of the best preserved. We think first of the Acropolis at Athens. The Parthenon is a classic Doric temple, unorthodox only in the frieze which ran along the top of the wall within the outer colonnade. The exquisite carving of the smallest detail in the clear white marble, and the subtlety of the curves which, though barely perceptible, lighten the rectangular mass of the structure, exemplify the highest standards of technique and design—although not of engineering, since in such buildings the Greeks played extra-safe piling stone on stone. The Ionic and Doric orders stood side by side in the monumental entrance way (Propylaea) to the Acropolis. The strange and beautiful Erechtheum opposite the Parthenon, with its Maiden-porch where Caryatids stood as sculpture columns, is in the Ionic order, as is the small temple of Athena Nike, beside the entrance way. Down in the town, above the market place, is another well-preserved Doric temple, that of the god Hephaestus. All these buildings belong to the middle and second half of the 5th century—the years of Athens' empire and pride, even to the years of her bitterest struggles with Sparta.

In these years too a third order was invented, differing from the Ionic only essentially in the form of its capital which is like a basket out of which grow broad leaves of acanthus, topped at the corners by volutes. Indeed, the basket and shrub story was told in antiquity as the way this new 'Corinthian' order was in-spired. It was to become one of the most popular types of capital, lending itself to a greater variety of treatment than the canonic Doric and Ionic.

The achievements of Classical architecture were by no means confined to temples. Theatres had once been simple dancing floors at the foot of a slope which gave a sort of grandstand for

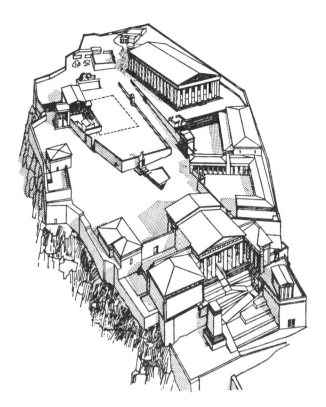

The Athenian Acropolis, a flat-topped rock falling away steeply on all sides except the west, was the site of the first settlements in remote prehistory, and in Mycenaean times was surrounded by a fortification wall which in part survives. In the Archaic period it became a site for the temples and altars of the city—the famous kouroi and korai were made for them. During the Persian war the enemy occupied Athens and the Acropolis and all the buildings were razed to the ground. Under Pericles new ones were built, the masterpieces of the Classical Age whose ruins can still be seen. Entering up the steep flight of steps from the west, the visitor found the Temple of Athena Nike on the bastion to his right. The elaborate entrance (Propylaea) led into an open space dominated by the large statue of Athena Promachus by Phidias. Beyond this lay the Erechtheum and the Parthenon, the largest temple on the Acropolis, dedicated to Athena the Virgin.

spectators. New deep cuttings are made into the hill side for the seats and at the back now are stage buildings. These theatres are impressive for their elaborately planned seating and fine acoustics rather than architectural decoration, although this was not lacking. Roofed buildings for assemblies are square in form with tiers of seats on three or four sides, the roof supported in series of inner columns. Such was the Music Hall (Odeum) at Athens, the Hall of the Mysteries at Eleusis, and Council-houses at Athens and other cities. Assemblies of the whole citizen body were held in theatres or theatre-like auditoria, like the Pnyx in Athens.

A new type of building is the stoa, which was long, open at one side with a continuous colonnade, and often two-storied. The rooms at the back might be for shops or civic offices, but the stoas could also serve as law-courts, and the covered colonnade could both shelter gatherings and act as grandstands for ceremonies in the market place. The Agora, or market place, at Athens gives us a very good idea of civic architecture: flanked by stoas, some for law-courts, others for commerce, others again for government officials; a meeting hall for the Council, a strange circular building (tholos) which served as a sort of official reception and banquet hall. The stoas and other buildings looked onto the square where there were altars, dedicatory statues and official notice boards, and through the square ran the Panathenaic Way along which the processions passed up to the Acropolis to honour the city's goddess. The usual Doric and Ionic orders are used for all these civic buildings as for the temples.

Town plans were generally irregular—the result of gradual growth, but as early as 700 BC it was found possible to impose a rough grid plan where a town had to be re-built after a disaster—

as at Smyrna. To Hippodamus of Miletus was attributed grid systems of town plans in new cities, like Athens' colony at Thurii in south Italy. Where fortification walls were needed they ran along convenient heights and, before the age of missiles at least, need not be more substantial than to withstand the battering ram. Towers, or jogs in the wall line, ensured that all parts could be covered by the defenders' fire, and gateways were specially strengthened. If there was an acropolis or citadel-refuge, this would be more substantially defended, but the Greeks were quite ready to throw up long lines of fortifications across country to link a town with its port—as Athens and Piraeus—or block a pass like that between the Athens and Eleusis plains.

The house plans are a great deal more sophisticated than the simple one-roomed Archaic dwellings, but there are no palaces as we understand the word. The approach to a typical 5th-century town house would be through a narrow passage from the street, with shops or workrooms at either side. It leads to an open courtyard flanked by colonnades—Doric or Ionic—along one or more sides, and possibly with a mosaic floor in the centre over the house's cistern. The other rooms open off the colonnades, and at the back of the house there may be two stories. We know most about Classical Greek houses from the discoveries at Olynthus, Priene and on Delos. At the last two sites named we can trace the development on into the succeeding period in the more luxurious Hellenistic houses, but the general type and plan was established already, it seems, in the 5th century.

In Asia Minor the Carian dynast, Mausolus, had built for him, by his wife, a magnificent tomb building, colonnaded, set on a high base and lavishly decorated with sculpture, which has given its name to all such monuments—'mausolea'. Greek tombs were generally marked by no more than a carved gravestone, but the fashion for something grander was now established.

HELLENISTIC GREECE 323–30 BC
Under Royal Patronage: a Rich Extravagance

Alexander died in 323 BC and the great empire he had established, from Egypt to the borders of Pakistan, broke up into smaller but still powerful kingdoms. The heyday of the Greek democracies and city-states was gone. Artists were more naturally attracted to the courts of Alexander's successors for employment and found there commissions for works on a scale considered suitable to the dignity of a king. The natural tendency was for local schools to spring up—in Pergamum, Antioch and Alexandria—and it is possible to distinguish some of the characteristics of each in different fields. More important is the ambitious scale of the new works. Colossal temples, massive statuary groups, lavish painting and jewellery, the sort of thing which the city-states of the past were rarely able to compass or afford. This access and show of wealth in itself did little to help Greek art, except to develop its capacity for the extravagant and the showy. But the mastery of techniques and natural skill in composition can still impress and move us. And this was the art which the Romans found, encouraged, copied, and handed on to be the heritage of the Renaissance and western art as we know it today. So it deserves our attention. Some measure of the growing impoverishment in invention, or perhaps simply dissatisfaction with the new trends, can be seen in the schools which consciously imitated the great works of the Classical period.

The Romans sacked Corinth in 146 BC, but under the Republic, Roman taste (already thoroughly hellenized) and demand did little or nothing to affect the development of Greek art, and so we take our 'Hellenistic' period down to the foundation of the Principate.

Realism and Emotion in Sculpture

In earlier centuries the problems of anatomy, of pose, of the expression of emotion and, to some degree, of portraiture, had been worked out. In the Hellenistic period all these skills were exercised to the full by artists whose imagination had not yet been dulled by the weight of tradition. There is a new boldness in composition. Features of body and face may be subtly distorted to express forceful emotion or energy. Tricks of drapery carving suggest even folds beneath folds. Only in portraiture is full realism tempered still by a measure of idealism; while elsewhere the fullest realism is exercised in other subjects sympathetically treated for the first time—old people, cripples, children.

The works of individual schools or even artists are difficult to distinguish. But the vigour and almost brutal realism of works made for the rulers of Pergamum can be readily picked out. It is best shown in the relief of gods fighting giants carved for the Great Altar at Pergamum, and in the two groups of vanquished Gauls which Pergamene monarchs dedicated at home and in Athens—among them the famous 'dying Gaul' known to us from the copy in Rome which was for long wrongly known as the 'dying Gladiator'.

Athens, as we might expect, is thought to have clung rather to the Classical tradition, probably best represented by the fine series of portrait statues of statesmen and philosophers or commemorative statues in poses and styles strongly reminiscent still of Lysippus.

To Alexandria, seat of the Ptolemies, is attributed a softer style of carving, less dramatic, more appealing. But to a very large extent we are forced to appreciate Hellenistic sculpture in terms of the individual works which are preserved, in original or copy, and which we are often seriously at a loss to date at all accurately. Most of these are very familiar to us because they were liked and copied in the Roman period.

The Venus de Milo is perhaps the best known Greek statue—a Hellenistic work of a type which had already been long popular, since the days of Praxiteles. There are many other Aphrodites of the Hellenistic period, partly dressed or naked, holding attributes or wringing out their hair. They were much copied in the Roman period and our galleries and museums are well stocked with them. The Venus de Milo is a rare and fine original. Other popular Aphrodite figures show the goddess crouching, at her bath. The poses and drapery are copied time and again in Renaissance and later classicizing work.

Next best known, perhaps, is the Laocoon group, of the priest and his sons wrestling with the serpents sent by Apollo. The anguish and desperate tension are expressed by the features and by the heavy knotted muscles of the central figure.

Dramatic treatment of drapery added to the effect which the artist could win from realistic anatomy and features. The windswept drapery of the great Victory of Samothrace both reveals the strong and sensuous forms of the young goddess and heightens the vivid impression that she has just landed on the prow of a ship. In other statues of women, of the later Hellenistic period, we can detect also a taste for proportions rather different from the classic of Praxiteles: taller figures now, with slight shoulders and breasts and full hips, leaning languidly against small columns or busy at their toilet.

The principle of being able, indeed obliged, to view a figure from more than one aspect had been established by Lysippus. In the Hellenistic period it is applied to groups (not, though, the Laocoon) like Dirce being tied to a bull by Zethus and Amphion. But such groups seem, fortunately, rare and vulgar *tours de force*.

The realism of portraiture was applied not only in heads or statues of contemporaries but in genre studies, of athletes, boxers with cauliflower ears, cripples and the deformities of old age: subjects which earlier sculptors would have idealized if they had admitted them at all.

The later Hellenistic period is characterized by new compositions which deliberately reflect the style, pose and features of Classical statuary, and by the beginning of the regular mechanical copying of earlier works. This was done by the pointing process, essentially that still used in studios today, by which a wholly accurate copy of a figure in the round can be taken at the same size or reduced. Famous works of artists like Phidias, Praxiteles and Lysippus were copied, and these helped to popularize other works in a classicizing style which sometimes only lightly adapted their models. The patronage of Rome was the main reason for this spate of copying, but this new market had not yet made any serious and apparent effect on the character of Greek artists' work. Later, under the Empire, the artists are still usually Greeks but the character of their work is firmly dictated by and moulded to Roman taste.

The last phase of Greek pottery, in Hellenistic times, is characterized by vases decorated not by painting but by figures or patterns in relief, made in moulds. This 'Homeric bowl' probably shows an incident from the Iliad.

Clay Vases Patterned in Relief

Although painted figure decoration is no longer generally admitted, the Hellenistic clay vases are still elaborately fashioned. They are often left in their fine lustrous black paint, and if there is any painted decoration at all, it is of florals and other patterns in white, yellow and gold. More often we find relief patterns, inspired by metalwork and often closely copying metal vases. This may take the form of relief figures or groups applied to the surface of the vase, or simply metallic details and patterns, like fluting. Ordinary drinking cups of clay are either rather like tea-cups, but with two handles and a foot, or are hemispherical and covered with patterns in relief. The latter are made in moulds and are most characteristic of the period. The patterns are sometimes taken from fine metalwork, but more often remind us of trivial stucco relief work on country-house ceilings. There is, indeed, a connection. For these Hellenistic moulded bowls are the immediate forerunners of Roman *terra sigillata*. The Romans preferred a red paint, and many of the later Hellenistic bowls are in fact fired brown or red. The Roman bowls carried similar patterns, were prized and collected in Renaissance Italy, and partly inspired encrusted relief work on walls, ceilings—and vases—then and later. Remotely, a Wedgwood tea-pot is descended from Hellenistic relief vases.

At Alexandria the old Egyptian techniques of real glazing were employed on vases of clay or faience (a sandy composition) which are Greek in shape and carry Greek decoration. Some of the finest are decorated with relief figures of the Ptolemaic queens as priestesses.

Murals, Mosaics and Roman Copies

In this, probably the greatest age of Greek painting, we are again deprived of all but the poorest examples of the art. Painted tombstones, even a few painted figures on vases from Sicily, give us no idea of the style and subjects of the wall paintings. As with so much of the sculpture we have again to rely on copies of the Roman period, but these are far more difficult to identify and attribute to the masters of their originals. A great many of the fine wall-paintings from the houses of Pompeii and Herculaneum, which were overwhelmed by the eruption of Vesuvius in AD 79, show scenes which must derive directly from 4th-century or Hellenistic Greek originals. Often the same scene is copied more than once, the later artist sometimes adding details or figures of his own choice. As we would expect, the best are of mythological scenes or groups in which studies of human figures are prominent, treated with full command in representing the third dimension by shading and even with a rudimentary idea of perspective. But as well as these set scenes it seems likely that the Hellenistic period also saw the birth of a real interest in landscape—at least for the setting of myth—and of the mock-architectural wall-painting which is such a feature of the Pompeian houses.

The wall paintings were executed on plaster. On the floors are mosaics which often carry figure scenes, themselves derived from famous paintings, or original compositions. The range of colour and detail is of course more limited, but the effect can still be most impressive. Some of the earliest mosaics, from Macedonian palaces of the 4th century, are made of coloured pebbles with different areas sometimes set off by metal strips. In the Hellenistic period the more usual 'tesserae' are used—little cubes of coloured stone or glass. Some fine and original mosaics survive in Greece, notably on Delos. Others, in Italy, reflect Hellenistic or earlier designs, like the famous mosaic in Naples from Pompeii showing Alexander the Great at the battle of Issus, which certainly derives from a wall painting, and possibly one painted in the lifetime of Alexander himself.

Rich Work in Metal

There is an infinite new richness and variety in the metalwork of the Hellenistic period, the result of the renewed access to the riches of the east, opened up by Alexander's conquests. The old forms, of decorative mirrors and vases, are embellished, and we meet now more often precious metals inlaid in bronze to lend colour and detail to figures and patterns. Now too there is a touch of the grotesque in the use of figures or animals as decorative attachments or handles for vases. Work in beaten relief is again most popular and was copied by the potters. The sculptural forms and poses of course match contemporary styles of sculpture and relief work in stone. Some of the finest chased silver vases found in Roman hoards must be derived directly from Hellenistic metal-work. A particularly popular form, for gold or silver, is the animal-head cup with relief decoration around the rim—an eastern form which had already been popular in Greece in the Archaic period.

Jewellery becomes yet more ornate and more often we find decorative or semi-precious stones used as inlays or beads. Ear-ring pendants often take the form of tiny figures of Eros below a big rosette, or else the whole ear-ring is an open hoop with one pointed end and at the other an animal head. Diadems are lightly embossed and bracelets with animal-head terminals long remain popular. Wreaths—as prizes, for festive occasions or, indeed, for the dead—copy closely the natural leaves of laurel, ivy or oak. Necklaces may take the form of strings of golden berries or nuts or flowers. All this extravagant jewellery was naturally most in demand at the courts of the Hellenistic princes, and much that has survived comes from the centres of their kingdoms, in north Greece and Egypt, rather than the older cities of Athens or Corinth.

Engravers' Arts and a New Craft: Glass

The engraved gems of earlier periods were usually bulky stones which were set on a swivel and worn as pendants or finger-rings. In the Hellenistic period they are more often cut to be set actually into a metal ring, in the modern manner. A far greater variety of stones, some semi-precious, was used, but besides these there was a brisk production of cheap insets for finger-rings, made of glass or a paste composition. Since several of these could be made from one mould their value as personal signets was slight, but it is likely throughout Classical antiquity that these stones were as much in demand for their decorative value as they were as seals.

Now too the engraver turned to a new class of gem—the cameo. For this the stone was cut in relief, not hollowed out as a seal to be impressed in clay or wax. Banded stones were used for cameos, like sardonyx in which layers of brown and white alternated, so that according to the height of the relief-carving different parts of the visible surface were picked out in different colours.

With Alexander and his successors the 'cult of personality' was particularly cherished. This led to a lively interest in portrait sculpture, which is reflected also in the superb heads of Hellenistic rulers which appear on coins of this period. Devices other than these portrait heads are often over-elaborate now, or treated in a comparatively summary fashion.

Clay plaques and figurines remain very popular. Best known are the 'Tanagra statuettes'—so-called from the place where many were found but representing a type common to all parts of the Greek world. A favourite motif is of a standing woman, elaborately dressed and coiffed, holding a fan or mirror. These are elegant, stylish figures, which so warmed Victorian hearts that copies and forgeries of them abound in collections today.

Finer and more valuable works in clay, generally from the cities of Asia Minor, represent current statuary types in miniature. Detail of modelling is exquisitely worked, and the whole is often gilded over, an enhancement which has generally, and fortunately, not survived. As well as these elaborate works there is a host of smaller decorative or votive figures. From Alexandria, for instance, we find series of grotesque figures, hunchbacks and cripples, the sort of realistic subjects which had also attracted the sculptors.

Vessels were generally still of clay, the better ones of bronze, but a new material was becoming widely used—glass. In the later Archaic and Classical periods the small glass flasks were wholly opaque and multi-coloured. By the end of the Hellenistic period more elaborate works of cut or moulded glass are found, and at last the techniques of glass blowing were discovered. But the full exploitation of this new craft, which served both for common vessels and for works of art, was to lie in the hands of the Romans.

The Lighthouse of Alexandria has completely disappeared, but some authentic features, such as the figures of the gods on the top, are preserved in this stylized picture from an Alexandrian medallion.

Temples, Palaces and Citadels

The main developments in the architecture of the Hellenistic period are in the design of public buildings and in the scale of the works undertaken. The idiom remains the same and the same orders—Doric, Ionic and the new Corinthian—still provide the standard forms for columns and upperworks, and dictate the appearance of the buildings.

At several places Alexander and his successors took the opportunity to perpetuate their names by founding new cities or radically re-shaping the old ones. A proper grid system of roads could be laid out, and public buildings suitable to such extravagant new foundations were designed. Most of these are to be found outside the world of old Greece, which was in this period less rich and where there were fewer opportunities for radical new plans. Thus, Alexandria had its new lighthouse, some 440 feet high and reckoned one of the Seven Wonders of the World. The new temples rival the ambitious dimensions of the earliest Ionic temples at Ephesus and Samos. The 'Temple of Diana of the Ephesians' had been rebuilt already, after a fire, in the 4th century. At Didyma, near Miletus, the new temple of Apollo, with its forest of columns, had an open central court in which a smaller shrine stood. Its ruins still dwarf the Turkish village by its walls. Several of these grandiose plans took long to complete. A classic example is the Temple of Olympian Zeus in Athens which was laid out in the 6th century but only completed under the Roman Emperor Hadrian, and then in the Corinthian order. The great Ionian stepped altars were surpassed by the Great Altar of Zeus and Athena at Pergamum, whose sculptures we have already mentioned.

Older buildings, such as theatres, cult places like the Hall of Mysteries at Eleusis, and even temples were re-modelled in the spirit of the new age. The new or re-planned cities of Asia Minor had assembly- or council-halls. Gymnasia or palaestrae were erected for athletic training. These were generally large open courts with colonnaded sides and changing rooms or baths attached.

Private houses are somewhat more elegant variants on what had been current before. The main courtyard in the finer houses has colonnades on all sides now, and there is very often also a second court or small garden at the back. Hotels, which were built for visitors to the principal sanctuaries, also take the form of a courtyard, or several courtyards, with rows of rooms around them behind shadowy colonnades. There is no good reason to believe that the Greeks indulged in anything like the sort of landscaping which attends every major building project today, but they had as good an eye for the spacing and siting of buildings in relation

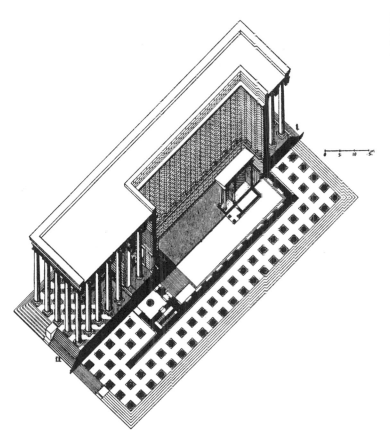

The Temple of Apollo at Didyma: one of the largest buildings of the Hellenistic Age. It was surrounded by a double colonnade, but after passing through the porch and along a narrow tunnel, the worshipper emerged not into a dim naos but out again into the open air of an inner court. Inside this open court, originally planted with bay trees, stood a small Ionic temple housing the Archaic bronze statue of Apollo.

to each other as they had for the proportions of individual structures, even in their details.

The construction of fortification walls depended upon the weapons to be used from or against them. In the 4th century we find tall strong towers to carry catapults. Heavier missiles thrown against the walls and skilled sapping meant that they had to be built more stoutly and with more involved defence works outside the main line—ditches and forward batteries, like pill-boxes. These are typical of the Hellenistic cities, but possibly the best example is seen at Syracuse in Sicily.

A BRIDGE TO ROME: THE ETRUSCANS

The art of Etruria is important and interesting for various reasons. In the first place it shows what the impact of Greek life and art could be on comparatively unsophisticated peoples outside the Greek world. Next, beside orientalizing Greek art, it shows us how the same sort of stimulus, from the east, acted upon peoples of quite different temperament. Finally, the strongly hellenized art of Etruria was to play an important part in the make-up of Roman art.

The centre of Etruria lay in the hilly, but fertile and well-wooded country north of Rome and west of the Apennines. We do not know exactly where the Etruscans came from or when, but they are clearly not natives of Italy, and the tradition that they came from the east, probably from Asia Minor and the area of Lydia, some time in the Greek early Iron Age, is quite likely to be correct. They settled in separate fortified towns and assimilated much of the native culture of Italy (still a Bronze Age culture). Their remains offer little enough to illustrate their eastern origins.

In the 8th century Greeks from Euboea established colonies almost on their doorstep, on the island of Ischia and at Cumae. They must have been placed there at least partly with a view to fostering the trade with Etruria. The Greeks, it seems, sought metal. In return they carried objects from the eastern markets which they had already been exploiting, and their own artefacts. The effects of this sudden arrival of oriental and of Greek Geometric art upon a virtually artless people were electrifying. Very soon Greeks were making versions of their Geometric vases for the Etruscans, and teaching the Etruscans to paint vases for themselves. The oriental objects introduced new patterns and techniques, and once native Etruscan schools of artists were established we can see in their products an exotic blend of what attracted them most in either Greek or oriental. It was not always the best, but it was generally the most spectacular and their work is nothing if not lavish. Oriental forms were copied indiscriminately, never properly assimilated as they were by the Greeks who could impose their own discipline and artistic tradition, well founded in the Geometric period.

By about 600 BC Greek influence was paramount and although by now many of the artists were no doubt Etruscans, superficially their art is Greek. But it is very provincial, and native Etruscan taste inspired new patterns, and their workshops invented new forms, so that we can soon distinguish individual Etruscan schools for sculpture, bronzes and clay vases. Their battles with the Greeks, who by the 5th century controlled most of south Italy and Sicily, made no difference to the way Etruscan art developed as a parallel though somewhat aberrant branch of Greek art. The burghers of Rome, although not Etruscans, lived in a very similar artistic climate, and when they grew powerful and rich, able even to absorb Etruria, their art was as Etruscan in appearance as it could be. But their attitude to the Greeks and to Greek art was quite different.

The Sculptors Learn a New Technique

Sculptural technique is very largely determined by available materials. Greece had the fine white marble to match the hard stones of Egypt. Etruria had not, so that when monumental sculpture was attempted soft limestone was used, or clay. There is literary evidence for the arrival of Greek craftsmen in Etruria who taught the techniques of making big statues in clay. They were produced too in Greece, but less often since finer materials were available. But in Etruria many of the earliest statues, even life size and more, are of clay. Best known perhaps are the great figures which strode along the roof of the temple of Apollo at Veii. These carry all the outward trappings of Archaic Greek art—pert, lively features, elaborate drapery patterns—but also a gross strength which is foreign to Greek art and a wayward treatment of details which seems over-involved. Many such works betray clearly the influence of East-Greek art, a trait which can be observed in other fields, and which may be the result of the arrival of Ionian artists in Etruria, chased from their eastern homes by the Persians in the mid-6th century. The same influence is discernible in the low relief decoration of the stone cinerary boxes from Chiusi.

The earlier Archaic works reveal more of the oriental influence, although much of this was no doubt carried by Greeks. In stone there are fine funerary lions and sphinxes from Vulci. The major works are closely copied in the small bronzes, in many of which freshness and elegance are achieved in a completely un-Greek manner. In a country rich in metals bronze sculpture was likely to be popular, but the difficulties of the technique discouraged major works until later periods, from which there are such masterpieces as the Arezzo chimaera.

Statuary in clay and soft stone we have in plenty from the Classical period. There is laggard copying of Greek styles, but beside the wholly graecizing works, there is more and more which is unmistakably Etruscan in conception, form and execution. The idealizing tendencies of Greek art meant nothing to Etruria, which may explain why the Archaic conventions died hard there. We find, for instance, the sort of characterization of heads which heralds true portraiture. This was encouraged by the practice of making heads or whole figures for grave monuments. The Romans shared this custom, and this explains the subtly different approach to portraiture shown by them, after the Greeks.

Greek Models for the Vase Painter

The Etruscan vases which reflect most clearly the native tradition are in bucchero—fine black all through with impressed or moulded, not painted, decoration. The best are handsome workmanlike vessels, but most are very coarse. These are made both in native shapes, and in shapes copied straight from the Greek, and they were in production in the 7th and 6th centuries, at a time when Greek painted vases were being imported in considerable numbers and being imitated locally. Some enterprising Greek potters even copied native shapes deliberately for the export trade to Etruria.

All Etruscan painted pottery derives in varying degrees from Greek. The Geometric copies the more banal Corinthian and Euboean patterns. In the 7th and early 6th centuries 'Italo-Corinthian' vases ape the animal friezes of Corinthian black-figure, rendering parts of the bodies as fantastic patterns and occasionally adding oriental motifs which the Greeks had not generally admitted on their vases. In the 6th century more Athenian vases were imported but they were not the only or even the main source of inspiration for Etruscan vase-painters. East-Greek immigrants set up shop in Etruria in the second half of the 6th century, and the earliest Etruscan vases in a developed black-figure style are more influenced by East-Greek styles and conventions than by Athenian ones.

Later Etruscan black-figure vases offer the same bizarre patterns as the sculpture. Greek mythological scenes may be copied, but we find also some odd native variants or misunderstandings, as well as some native demons or stories. The style is sometimes lively and bold but too mannered to hold our interest.

Later still the red-figured Athenian vases were imitated, at first by painting in red on black, and then with the proper reserved technique. But the Etruscan adaptation or copies of Greek styles in vase-painting in this, as in other periods, offers less of what we might hope to pick out as native Etruscan art and taste than do the other arts.

The Etruscan Reflection of Greek Wall Painting

The finest Etruscan tombs are in the form of chambers cut in the rock, or stone-built and covered with a mound of earth. The tomb chambers often have painted walls and have been found with the colours of their decoration still remarkably well preserved. The figure decoration in these tombs—of the 6th century on—is, like all else in Etruscan art, derived from the Greek. But in Greece there are no structures like these tombs in which early examples of wall-painting could have survived, and what we know of Greek painting has in some measure to be learnt from what they executed for the Etruscans, or inspired the Etruscan artists to paint for themselves.

Among the earliest are big clay plaques which were fixed to the wall to form a frieze. These, and contemporary wall-paintings, closely reflect the style of the figure decoration on Greek vases and its conventions. There is, of course, much more colour, but the style is very like ordinary line drawing with fill-in colours, as in a child's painting book. Some paintings are so close in style to the vases painted in Etruria by Greeks, which have already been mentioned, that it has been thought that the same artists may have been at work.

In the Classical and Hellenistic periods technique improves immensely and the uses of shading are eventually appreciated. But the paintings are pale reflections of what we know or can deduce about contemporary works in Greece.

Many of the subjects of the early paintings are taken from Greek mythology, or the sort of scenes of everyday life found on Greek vases, but Etruscan beliefs about the underworld also lent subjects, like their sinister demons. Another feature, and one which, so far as we can judge, is more characteristic of Egyptian than of Greek painting, is the interest in landscape and the readiness to subordinate human figures to their setting. The Greeks were always reluctant to let nature dwarf man.

The Native Genius in Other Arts

In the 7th century Etruscan art acknowledges the character of the orientalizing influences to which it was subjected more directly than does Greek art. This is especially well shown in crafts other than those like vase-painting in which the Greeks, and so Greek influence, excelled. Ivories carved in the round or in relief are closer to eastern models than their Greek orientalizing counterparts. More specifically Phoenician influence can be detected elsewhere—in the jewellery, with the accomplished use of the most difficult techniques of filigree and granulation, in the shapes of bronze jugs, in the engraved decoration of silver vessels. At all times Etruscan jewellery was extravagant and vulgar, better admired for its excellent detail than its overall effect.

From the 6th century onwards Greek influence is dominant and the stranger oriental conceits are abandoned. Important schools of bronze-workers were established, producing distinctive Etruscan works—elaborate candelabra, for example, crowned by exquisite statuettes of single figures or groups, hammered reliefs for the decoration of furniture and chariots, and some individual variations on Greek types of plastic attachments to metal vases. In the 5th century begins an important series of bronze mirrors with their backs carrying incised figure scenes. This is a practice seldom met in Greece, and some of the Etruscan mirrors are unusually finely drawn, although the late ones are very dull and repetitive. Similar incised decoration is met on cistae—cylindrical boxes, with statuettes as handles on their lids.

Ionian artists introduced a type of gold ring, with a long oval bezel incised with animals or mythological scenes. In the later 6th century the local production of sealstones begins, generally scarabs of cornelian. The quality of the finest early pieces matches the best Greek, but the style and technique coarsens rapidly and the same scarab form is retained into the Hellenistic period, long after it had been abandoned by the Greeks.

For clay work, we do not find the mass of statuettes which are so common on Greek sites, but the material was used for major statuary, as we have seen, and also for the elaborate clay revetments which sheathed the wooden parts of buildings. These are painted or moulded in relief.

Etruscan architecture is generally simple although in the later periods they soon mastered important building techniques which were to be further developed by the Romans. Several details too of their architecture were retained by the Romans, notably the temples on a high platform and with three rooms side by side.

Greece Meets Rome

In the Archaic period Rome had been dominated by Etruria. After winning independence she waxed strong and in the 3rd century BC it was Etruria which owed allegiance to the Roman state. All this meant that Roman life and art was thoroughly conditioned by contact with Etruria, and that in this way she had absorbed all those mixed Greek traditions which informed Etruscan art. At the same time Roman expansion was overwhelming the Greek cities of the west, in the south of Italy and Sicily where the arts of the Greek homeland had flourished in an extravagant, though somewhat provincial manner, and gradually Rome was stretching out her hand to the riches of Greece herself. In these three ways Greek art acted on Roman taste—through the hellenized barbarians of Etruria, through the Greek colonies, through direct contact with Greece. This was the background only and Greeks were still to play an active part.

In Greece itself the coming of the Romans brought diminished prosperity, new allegiances, new markets and patrons for artists. In many respects—for example in portraiture—the arts in Greece remained little affected by Rome. What of the Classical past was not pillaged by Romans remained to instruct and set a standard which the Romans too were ready to admire and respect, and no little of the art of the Christian East is moulded in the same Classical form. The course of these twin streams of the Greek tradition, in east and west, into later periods of Western Civilization, will be mapped in other chapters.

VI THE ANCIENT LIFE

The Greece and Rome of everyday

F.R. COWELL

'Those who had found it easy to bear hardship and dangers,

anxiety and adversity found leisure and wealth,

desirable under other circumstances, a burden and a curse.

Hence the lust for power first, then for money, grew upon them.'

SALLUST, CATILINE, 10

The burden of daily life

pressed more heavily upon the common people of Greece and Rome than it does upon most peoples of the West today, who have had over two thousand years in which to improve upon their heritage. Existence was narrowly secured at the price of unremitting toil; many were slaves without human rights; those who were free—farmers, fishermen, artisans and traders—were lucky if they won much more than a bare subsistence for themselves and their families. But for the poor of republican Rome, the squalor and dirt of pest-ridden Athens was giving way to water-supply, sewers and street-paving, the flat-topped hovels to large, barrack-like apartment houses, divided by narrow streets into blocks or *insulae*. Some impression of these living conditions is given by the Roman relief (right) found in Lake Nemi. It shows part of a small town, with houses two and three storeys high huddled within a defensive wall. One building at the back is unmistakably a basilica or town hall. The four-wheeled carriage that has been superimposed outside the wall is from a relief found at Vaison in Gaul. The elaboration of the horses' collars, the two men sitting in such dignified attitudes on top and the heads decorating the sides make it likely that this is a ceremonial coach, used for civic occasions.

One solution for poverty, tried by all at some time in the ancient world, was to rob one's neighbours, and none succeeded better than the Romans. Their vast empire, won by Roman legionaries, was gradually pacified and organized, to a large extent under the rule of law and for long under a tolerably efficient form of public administration. From such a foundation, wealth flowed rapidly into the hands of traders and those in imperial favour. Rich Etruscans and, especially, rich Greeks had shown the Romans an example of sophisticated living—an example which was raised, in their long imperial peace and from their greater material resources, to a standard of elegance and luxury that was not seen again in Europe until modern times. Eventually the people benefited also, from gardens, public squares, public recreation centres and a constant food supply and ample water which brought freedom from famine and a degree of ease and comfort.

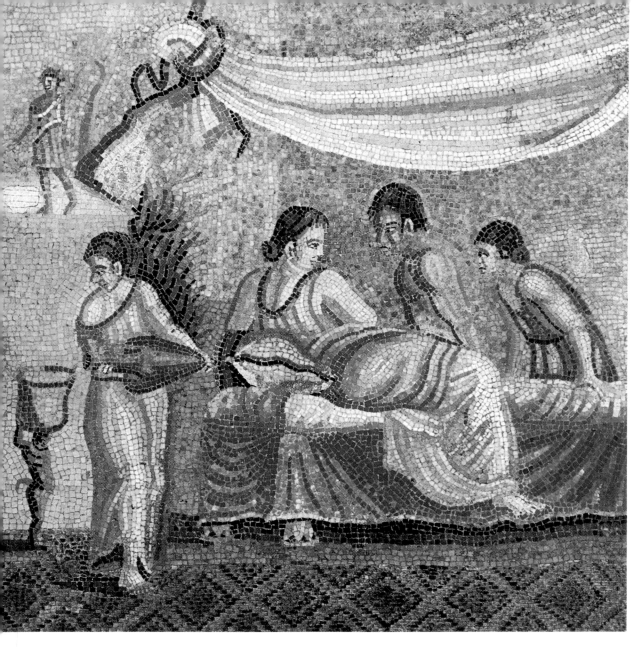

Furniture was sparse by modern standards, but often remarkable for the richness of its materials—cedarwood, ivory, gold, ebony—and the high quality of its workmanship. A couch or bed was the main item in most houses, being used both for sleeping on at night and for reclining on at meals. The small Roman mosaic of a love-scene (*left*) shows such a couch covered by a heavy cloth and a mattress. There would also be chairs, but no tables as we know them.

Wild birds such as the thrushes (*left*) and hen's eggs must have been welcome additions—even luxuries—to the monotonous diet of the poorer Romans. The staple food was wheat or barley in some form or other—either boiled into a thick porridge or made into flour and baked. The simple but elegant jug and beaker would have been owned by a middle-class household.

A moulded glass goblet and bird ornament such as would be owned only by the rich (*right*). Fine glass was rare and often fetched fabulous prices.

A chair with a back was for the Romans long a symbol of dignity or respect, reserved for high officials or women of rank (the modern ceremonial use of thrones is a vestige of this tradition). In the fresco *right*, from a villa near Pompeii, a noblewoman plays on the *cithara*. Her chair is of bronze and has low arms and ornamented legs. Actual furniture in this style has been recovered from Pompeii.

The necessities of daily life, such as food, drink, clothing, tools and equipment, were provided by a host of small traders and craftsmen, many of them slaves. *Left* and *right*: two scenes from Greek life illustrated on vases. One shows a fishmonger slicing a tuna-fish with a huge knife, while the customer (somewhat caricatured) stands watching. In the other a boy is being measured for new shoes. The cobbler cuts round his foot on a piece of leather.

Roman shops were mostly one-room booths opening directly on to the street. *Left*: a cutler at his workshop. One man holds an iron bar and works the bellows for the fire at the back, while another hammers on an anvil. Various tools, including pincers, hang above. *Right*: a cutler's shop; behind the shopkeeper and his customer a fine array of cutlery is displayed including sickles and several sorts of knife.

Two customers of rank (*right*) sit in a draper's shop while assistants hold up a large piece of cloth for their inspection. Their own two slaves stand on either side.

More small watercourses than are in use today served to transport merchandise in the Roman Empire. In the relief *left* a small barge carrying two barrels of wine is being pulled along a stream in Gaul. Two men tug at the ropes (there must have been three originally) and another steers with an oar. *Right*: a large flour-mill worked by a horse. Slaves and prisoners also were used to turn the huge grindstones.

Produce of the countryside was brought in huge quantities to the Roman markets during the night—Julius Caesar having prohibited carts during the daytime. *Left*: a small greengrocer behind a trestle table calls out the price of his wares (he is saying 'Three!'). Vegetables that can be identified are cabbage, kale, garlic, leeks and onions. *Right*: a butcher at work on a pig's head. Behind him hang another pig's head, a ham, pigs' udders, a side of bacon and a lung. The relief comes from the tomb of a butcher, and someone with small respect for the dead has carved, ungrammatically, 'To Marcius always drunk'.

MARCIO SEMPER EBI

A wedding was usually the occasion for the greatest ceremony that most ordinary men and women had in their lives. In the scene from an Archaic Greek vase (*above*), the bearded bridegroom is setting off with his bride. She lifts her mantle with one hand and holds on to the chariot with the other. Among the women are figures connected with the cult of Kore (Persephone) and Demeter; most wedding scenes of this date (570–560 BC) contain characters from mythology.

Banquets and drinking parties enlivened existence for the rich, and on special occasions for the poor too. A fresco at Pompeii (*below*) shows a Roman banquet. No effort was spared to make the guests comfortable. One slave removes the shoes of a newcomer (often a necessary precaution in view of the state of the streets), while another proffers him a cup of wine. The man at the back is attended by a Negro slave.

Gods and humans mingle in the famous 'Aldobrandini Wedding', depicted on the wall of a mansion in Rome. The bride, dressed in white and wearing her veil, is being consoled by the goddess Aphrodite; in Athens and early Rome women had no choice, being compelled to marry as their guardian decided. In the centre a young woman—perhaps one of the Graces—leans on a short column and pours out scented oil. To the left, an older woman, possibly the bride's mother, dips her hand into a basin as if to test the temperature of the water. Soon the bridegroom will enter, to the singing of the nuptial song.

Preparing for the party: a wealthy lady (*right*) is seated in a round-backed wicker chair with her feet on a footstool. She is not in a beauty-parlour, for none existed, but at home. Her four neat slave-girls are busy around her: one holds a perfume flask, a second poses a mirror, a third waits with a small pitcher, and arranging her hair is the *ornatrix*—an important member of the slave household who also saw to the rouge, lipstick and eye-shadow.

The innate brutality of the Roman mob demanded fiercer excitement than the athletic contests of the Greeks. They never tired of witnessing men and animals being done to death. Lurid scenes such as those shown *above* were staged day after day in the huge Colosseum at Rome. On its sanded, bloodstained floor gladiators hacked each other to death or fought lions and panthers. On the rack in the middle are seven eggs, one of which was removed after each event; the raised box on the left is that of the patron of the games. Criminals or defenceless prisoners were torn to pieces by savage beasts. The Libyan prisoner (*below*) is about to be killed by a panther as he stands bound in chariot.

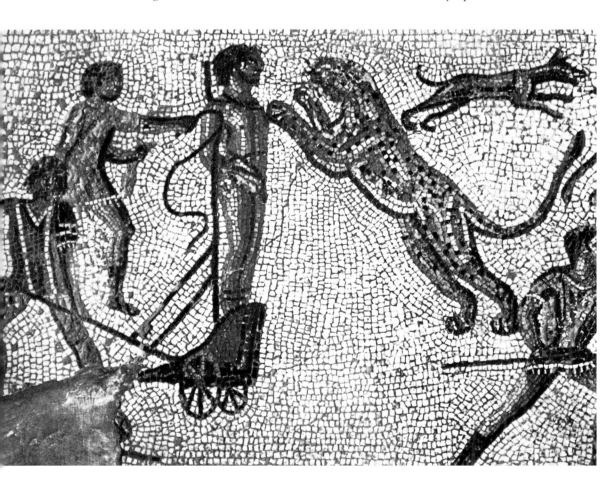

Animal was pitted against animal—elephant against lion, bull against elephant (*above*)—in hideous death struggles. By comparison the four-horse chariot races in the great circuses (*below*) were almost peaceful, although charioteers and horses, urged to crazy speed by the huge, frenzied, yelling mob, often had disastrous spills, when the driver's only hope of survival lay in his ability instantaneously to sever the reins tied round his waist, with a sharp knife carried at the belt. The oblong course went round a wall of masonry—the backbone (*spina*) of the circus—marked on the relief (*below*) by double obelisks at each end and a single obelisk in the middle. The ranks of spectators are only sketchily indicated.

The boys and girls of ancient Greece and Rome seem to have enjoyed themselves very much as children do today, though they were surrounded by more serious dangers. The pathetically short life of a little Roman boy is depicted on his tomb (*above*). We see him as a baby at his mother's breast; next being admired by his father who has him in his arms. Before beginning his lessons and reciting to his father in the final scene he is happily driving a little carriage pulled by a donkey. The Roman school (*below*) is in Gaul and both teacher and pupils wear heavy clothes and leather shoes. Two of the boys are already seated in comfortable chairs; a third has arrived late and begins to apologize. Greek education tended to be more broadly cultural than Roman, where the emphasis was upon the practical and the useful. In one scene (*right*) a boy is taught to play the lyre, while another is reciting Homer's *Iliad* (the scroll held by the master is not true to life: not only are the letters much too big, but the lines should run in 'pages' parallel with the sides). A Greek child's toys (*below right*) were put with him into the grave. There is a rattle in the shape of a pig, a clay top, a doll with jointed limbs, a toy jug and a goose with a man on its back.

'Slavery is worse than any calamity,' said a slave in the 2nd century BC, and most Greeks and Romans must have felt the same. Cruel punishments, like the pillory (*above*) or even death, were inflicted for the most trivial offences. Many slaves, however, achieved their freedom and became employees of their former owners. The portraits (*right*) are of Demetrius and Philonicus (probably his son), freedman of Publius Licinius. Surrounding them are the tools of their trade.

'We lead a life of freedom, not only in our politics but in our mutual tolerance of private conduct' was the boast attributed to Pericles in his speech to the Athenians in 431 BC. Even when Philip of Macedon defeated them in 338, he guaranteed their democratic constitution. In 336 BC they passed the 'Law against Tyranny', inscribed on a *stele* of which the crowning relief is shown here: 'Should anyone, in an attempt at absolute power, rise up against the people or try to overthrow the democracy of Athens—whoever kills him shall be blameless.'

Election manifestos written on the wall of a private house in Pompeii (*right*) announce gladiatorial combats—the best way of winning popularity—paid for by Lucretius Satrus, and invite electors to support Q(uintus) Postumus, among others. Under the emperors, political competition was limited to local affairs.

The Greece and Rome of everyday

F. R. COWELL

LIKE ALL OTHER peoples of antiquity, the early Greeks and Romans were strictly conditioned in their daily lives by the use they were able to make of their by no means very favourable natural surroundings. Theirs was the Mediterranean climate, the zone of the vine and the olive. They were able to survive their often sharp but relatively short periods of severe cold in winter without great difficulty and to live more or less out-of-doors for most of the year. So hot is the Mediterranean sun however that shade is as necessary in summer as their braziers of red-hot charcoal could be in winter. Sun shelters were therefore a part of all better houses and large shelters were built in the open market-places in which, from very early times, Greek and Roman men had been in the habit of meeting together. In the stoas around the public open space or Agora of Athens and in the basilicas of the Roman Forum they were able to fortify their sense of community, to sustain one another, to learn news and rumours and above all to talk. Theirs was the talk, as this volume shows, which was to create a framework for the civilization we know.

Magnificence and Squalor

The entire State of Athens at the height of its glory in the 5th century BC probably had a population of rather less than 300,000, considerably less than that of any large European or American city today. Rome, on the other hand, at the beginning of our era already had about a million in and around the city with another thirteen millions or so in the rest of Italy. At least four millions were slaves.

Command over the wealth of the known world enabled rich Romans to live in town and country houses of an elegance in design, in their layout of courtyards and gardens, in the lavishness of their materials, construction and decoration that no Athenian could match; nor indeed were they equalled or surpassed again until modern times.

The poor lived in a squalor that they had probably always known, but they fared worse in Athens than in Rome. There, from late Republican times, had sprung up huge barrack-like apartment houses covering like an island whole city blocks, and known as *insulae* in consequence. By the 4th century AD there were over 44,000 of these *insulae* against less than 2,000 private houses. Some of the apartment houses of Rome contained elegant homes of a rich middle-class but the majority housed ordinary folk on very small incomes. The Athenians at their most flourishing period, seven or eight hundred years earlier, had nothing on this scale. 'Most of the houses were mean, only a few good', said a Greek about Athens of that time. Another Greek, Strabo, who had seen Augustan Rome, later contrasted Greek priorities of 'beauty, fortification and harbours' with Roman care for 'water-supply, sewers and street-paving'.

The living quarters of Athens, compared with those of Rome, were such as would disgrace any small, dirty, slum-town. The narrow alleys between small flat-topped hovels were filthy with house refuse and excrement rarely carted away. A by no means uncommon sight down to the 4th and 3rd centuries BC would be the tiny naked bodies of unwanted new-born babies, mostly girls, left at the crossroads for the slave traders or famished dogs. Down such alleys, muddy in wet weather, deep in dust in summer

heat, swarming with flies and vermin, an unbelievably foul hazard to health and decency, the Athenians were content to trudge barefoot or in sandals.

At night, as in Rome, the inhabitants, if they were out at all, groped their way by the flickering light of their resinous torch or small lantern, for there were no street lamps and any windows from which house lamps might cast their shafts of light were shuttered. Rich folk always had their slaves to escort them and in Rome especially, in imperial times, they were borne along by six or eight slaves in luxurious litters which in former times had been reserved for women. Such was the press of traffic in Rome's streets that they were early paved and drained with underground sewers to carry into the Tiber filth and refuse that in Athens filled the streets. Moreover continual rebuilding made life in Imperial Rome very much more convenient than it had ever been in Athens.

The furniture and equipment of a Greek house can to some extent be visualized from vase paintings while those of the Romans are much better known from actual remains found in the buried cities of Pompeii and Herculaneum. By our standards both Greek and Roman houses were sparsely furnished, rather on the lines of the traditional Japanese interiors.

A small altar stood in the entrance court of a Greek house on which pious heads of the household performed ritual sacrifices on sacred occasions and from which they sprinkled visitors with the ceremonial water of purification. There would be little to see in the small rooms round the central courtyard apart from the couches and a few small tripod tables in the dining room and a bed or two in other rooms. The poor slept on palliasses or on a few piled up skins or old bits of cloth, all often verminous and dirty. Chairs with backs and arm rests were less common than simple stools. Beyond a wooden chest to hold the household woollens and linen there would be some earthenware vases, jars, basins and cups in niches hung along the wall or ranged along the floor. Good clay was abundant while metal was scarce and difficult to work because the Greeks and Romans did not know how to increase the temperature of a fire by a blast furnace and they had no coal. So poor Greeks not only had pots and pans, but braziers, small portable ovens and cooking ladles all of earthenware. They soon got dirty of course and there was no soap or good detergent with which to clean them, but they were cheap and, except for the very poor, expendable. By the 3rd century BC, richer Greeks were using bronze for wine ladles and some other utensils.

The Romans, with their greater resources, did better although they also used earthenware fairly generally in earlier times and poor Romans were always dependent on it. What has been unearthed at Pompeii and elsewhere indicates that iron, steel, copper and bronze had become much more common by the 1st century AD. Wealthy Romans of imperial times far outstripped the Greeks, not so much in the number of their belongings as in their superior quality and workmanship. Costly materials were used for furnishing such as cedar, silks, ivory, tortoise-shell, gold, porcelain from the East; and there was a great luxury in silver-ware, among which choice antique pieces made by a Greek master-craftsman of olden times would be given pride of place.

Roman rooms moreover were larger, more lofty and lavishly decorated with wall-paintings, floor mosaics, rich tapestries and carpets as wall hangings when the walls were not adorned with paintings. They varied from simple colouring sometimes in imitation of the marble facings of the very rich houses up to architectural designs and later to scenes of dramatic quality. Even the slick commercial artwork of ornamental borders or of little cupids engaged on human tasks have a freshness and charm that few modern wall-papers can rival. The Greeks began this use of wall-space for decorative purposes and rich Athenians such as Alcibiades were already commissioning paintings before the end of the 5th century BC, but no Greek equivalent of Pompeii or Herculaneum has been discovered, and all Greek painting has perished.

Floors are more durable, and we are better able to trace the development of those decorated pavements with which wealthier Greeks first covered the bare dirt floors of their ancestors. The use of varied coloured small marble stones set in patterns developed into a geometric and pictorial art of no mean quality. The Romans carried the practice to much greater lengths. The heat of Roman summers and the dirty and downright disgusting table-manners of many Romans made a stone floor necessary and carpets impossible as floor-coverings. So skilled slaves and freedmen were set to work to devise patterns and pictures in multi-coloured stone that remain today wherever imperial Romans trod, to astonish visitors to museums and the sites of Roman villas.

Roman furniture shows very little marked difference in design and style from what record we have of that of the Greeks. There was more of it in the larger Roman homes; it was perhaps more solidly built and certainly often of rarer materials and workmanship. Yet the choicest pieces created by the famous craftsmen of Greece became collectors' treasures for which high prices were paid. Tables of rare cedarwood, antique lamps of splendid design, gilt couches, rare cups and so forth could cost a fortune in Rome of the early imperial period, yet the houses of rich Greeks and Romans would have seemed almost bare in comparison with middle-class homes of today.

Heat, Light, Water and Waste

Heating and lighting a Greek or Roman home was a serious difficulty and the poor were often without either. 'The lamp is not an ancient invention' wrote Athenaeus in the 3rd century AD, 'for the ancients used the light of torches and other things made of wood.' The poor grudged the pint of oil needed to provide a small flame in the average little earthenware lamp for about 40 or 50 hours. When, in Roman times, candles were made of tallow solidified around a long twisted wick, they also were used sparingly by the poor, because fat, like oil, could be eaten. Unless many lamps or candles were lit at once, the light indoors at night would be dim, so none but the well-to-do could do much work after dusk. This was a far bigger handicap than we can imagine because there were no spectacles or artificial aids to better vision. Very much more reading and writing had to be done by trusted slaves as their masters and mistresses began to suffer from the declining vision of middle-age. Eye-troubles are often referred to and they may have been brought on by eyestrain as much as by the infection from the dust and dirt of the filthy streets of Athens or Rome, which is usually blamed. Eye-salve was a staple article in great demand by Greeks and Romans.

In an exceptionally cold spell, all except the well-off might suffer miserably. Lavish supplies of charcoal and a good deal of slave labour were necessary to keep a few braziers constantly glowing. Wood could not be burned on them because of its choking smoke which had no outlet since there were no chimneys in the average house. In imperial times wood was burned in large quantities in furnaces under the floors of expensive houses. The hot air so produced circulated round the walls of rooms which

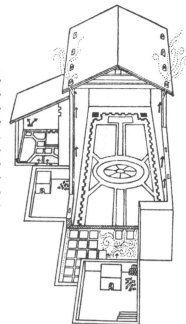

A typical Roman hypocaust system. The furnace, burning wood, is in the foreground in a cellar. Behind it the hot fumes pass between the square piers supporting the floor and then up flues in the wall, escaping eventually through holes in the roof. The smaller room on the left is heated by a charcoal fire; this produced hot air relatively free from fumes, which could pass directly into the room through openings near the floor.

were specially built with a sufficient air-space for the purpose. These were the celebrated Roman hypocausts, first used for heating baths. Without them, it has been said, Graeco-Roman civilization would never have spread northwards in those early times. It is doubtful whether they were very efficient and they could not have been economical, but then, neither were the braziers.

To get a flame to start a fire or light a lamp might be a long job. It was impossible unless there was a supply of dry touchwood or leaves and a steel and flint from which a spark could be struck. Pliny's recipe in the 1st century AD was to 'rub ivy wood with bay'. Usually city dwellers took a short cut by borrowing a flame from a neighbour's hearth or lamp if by mischance theirs had gone out.

Water was a more precious commodity in Athens than in Rome. It was not that the Greeks lacked supplies, but that they were heavy to fetch home from the few public fountains. Water-carrying was a woman's job, slave or free. So it was in Rome, but there massive aqueducts channelled mountain streams across the city to feed not merely fountains and baths but to provide piped supplies to the ground floors of the houses of those rich enough to pay for the lead pipes and the annual charge made for the water. The Romans not merely had ample water for drinking, washing, bathing and gardens, but, what was vitally important in a city of a million or so inhabitants, for public latrines and sewage disposal through a system of sewers running into the Tiber. The Romans, like the Greeks before them, had primitive washing facilities until the 1st century BC. The few public baths in Athens mentioned by Aristophanes at the end of the 5th century were a foretaste of what the Romans were to provide on a truly magnificent scale. The Greeks never had anything so good. Although many of them strove as hard as any people to keep fit through exercise and moderate living, they suffered terribly from sickness and plague due to inadequate hygiene. But then they knew nothing about germs or the causes of disease. Neither did the Romans, whose medical knowledge was borrowed from the Greeks and not improved in the borrowing. Believing that all human ills were inflicted by supernatural spirits, the Romans sought to placate them and to ensure recovery by religious rites.

The Food and Drink of Daily Life

'Bread and a relish' sums up the staple food situation for the average Greek and Roman, just as it would for the average poor European until quite modern times. 'Bread' here stands for wheat or barley, either boiled into a thick porridge or ground into flour and baked on a hot hearth in the form of circular, flat dough-cakes. Leavened bread is not mentioned before the 4th century. More barley than wheat was eaten in Attica but the Romans preferred wheat and could more easily get it.

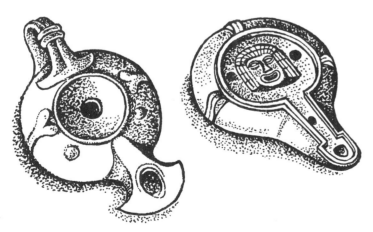

Household lamps were dim and smoky and the olive-oil used in them was expensive. The small Greek and Roman lamps shown here (left, Greek, late 2nd century BC; right, Roman, 1st century AD) both work on the same principle. The oil was poured into the hole in the centre and a wick of flax fibres or papyrus would have hung down out of the spout.

Grinding was a job for slaves. Everybody hated it. Where there were no slaves the women of the household had to spread grain out on a flat stone and rub it with a small round one. This traditional manner of getting flour, rough as it usually was, lasted long into Roman times when more use was made of a pestle and mortar, and a small rotary hand-mill or quern had been invented. By that time most city dwellers bought their bread from commercial bakeries. Bakers are first recorded in business in Athens in the 5th century BC and in Rome not before 172 BC. Then much larger grinding mills were brought into use. More and more Romans during the 2nd century BC were glad to be relieved of the daily need to grind corn and of the bother of kneading flour and baking bread. Bakers ground out flour on a large scale, sometimes in cellars which were also slave-prisons. There are grisly stories of free Romans being kidnapped on the streets and flung into such places to spend the rest of their life, driven by the lash to work themselves to death at the heavy task of turning the huge stone mills. Donkeys and mules were often harnessed to the mills, with equal brutality, if the horrifying story of the *Golden Ass* by Apuleius (2nd century AD) is typical. Water power never completely replaced human and animal energy, although at the end of the imperial era there seem to have been a dozen or so water mills along the Tiber. Some Roman bakers made fortunes, to judge from the lavish tomb of M. Vergilius Eurysaces of the Augustan era.

The 'relish' with the bread depended on what was easily obtainable. In Homeric times barley meal, 'the marrow of men', roast beef and wine made a feast. The 'fishy Hellespont' must have been a great stand-by and perhaps because it was so common, not much is said in Homer in praise of fish. The same is true of game and vegetables. Sheep's milk and goats' milk were drunk but not cows' milk. Cheese was made but there is no mention of eggs nor of cocks and hens until the 6th century BC, although as geese are mentioned it seems likely that their eggs were eaten in some form or other. A 'black pudding' or haggis made by filling goats' intestines with blood and fat and toasting it in front of a fire seems also a common dish in these early times. Food habits endure and some old-time dishes never quite died out. The great difficulty in classical and Hellenistic times was to get sufficient beef. It became so scarce and expensive that the Greeks were forced to eat far more fish than their ancestors would have relished. By then soups of beans, peas or lentils relieved the monotony and olives and olive oil, used not as a food but as an embrocation in Homeric times, were eaten. The only sweetening was wild honey until the art of bee-keeping was developed after Homeric times.

Although European vegetables such as leeks, shallots, carrots, beet, parsnip, skirret, endive, chicory, sorrel, mountain asparagus, lovage, cabbage, lettuce, artichokes, cress, and orach can all be grown in Greece, none seems to have been raised in that large quantity that the Romans produced much later. The Greeks had less fertile land and above all they were short of water. Constant warfare also interrupted cultivation. So the relishes with their bread did not include so much greenstuff and roots as the Romans were able to enjoy. Many flavouring herbs grew wild on the mountain slopes of Greece and some could be cultivated in small pots at home, such as rue, sage, thyme, sesame, parsley, cumin, or caraway, pennyroyal and marjoram. For stronger flavours, favoured by less fastidious folk, there were onions, horse-radish, mustard, radishes and above all, garlic. As civilization developed, garlic in any quantity was left, because of its strong odour, to the poor and uncouth. One greatly-prized flavouring came from a plant grown to perfection in Cyrene called silphium; *silphion* in Greek, *laserpitium* in Latin. It became extinct, but a Persian version of it is said to be akin to asafoetida.

To this basic diet of cereals and vegetables, Greeks and Romans added, according to their means, cheese, eggs, olives, meat, fish and other delicacies such as eels, poultry, hares, wild birds, shell fish, mushrooms, wild boar, fruit and nuts. Rich Romans of imperial times could command a greater bill of fare than the Greeks were ever able to enjoy, for new and exotic foods were introduced such as peacocks, peaches, nectarines and, contrary to what has generally been believed, oranges and lemons. Such delights were not for everybody. The problem for most Greeks and Romans was not so much to gratify their palates with new dishes

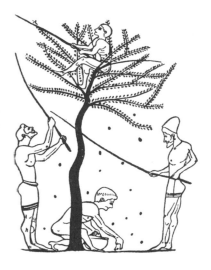

Olives were part of the diet of Greeks and Romans, and the oil from them had many uses. This drawing from an Attic black-figure vase shows them being picked. Two men knock them down with sticks; another reaches the high ones by climbing the tree, while a fourth picks them up and puts them in a basket.

and fresh flavours, but to get enough sheer bulk of food to fend off hunger. Lurid Roman stories of lavish banquets, of hundreds of larks' tongues, stuffed dormice, boars' heads, capons and roast geese, and of lavish extravagance in the search for new gastronomic sensations belong to the late Republic and early Empire and then to a small, limited circle of the very rich. Moderation was the rule in Greece as it was also in Republican Rome before the 1st century BC.

Both in Greece and Rome, religious feeling long remained associated with food and its preparation. For centuries, pious Roman families paid reverence to the spirits who were supposed to preside over the store-cupboards, food and the fire. A waist-high hearth was the centre of early Roman homes and on it lay an accumulation of ashes ready to be blown up into a flame when food had to be cooked. In Greece, cooking facilities seem to have been more primitive, for there was not generally a separate kitchen before the 4th century BC. Small portable terracotta stoves served for boiling and frying. Bread was baked by raking red-hot ashes on one side of the hearth-stone, putting the dough on the hot spot and covering it with a lid. The ordinary house had no oven.

While most Greeks and Romans drank vast quantities of water, of which the Greeks especially were connoisseurs, everyone also expected to be able to drink some sort of wine. In Homeric times already, the Greeks knew that wine improves with age. To entertain Telemachus, Nestor calls for wine that has been eleven years in its jar. Some favoured spots, such as the island of Chios, became renowned for the excellent quality of their wine and right down to the days of Julius Caesar, Greek wine was thought far superior to Roman wine. Then Roman wines, notably the Falernian, Setinian, and Caecuban began to be highly prized and the Romans ended by achieving a high standard of taste in producing and maturing fine wines.

Greeks and Romans alike would not drink wine undiluted with water, a habit which persists to this day in some European lands. It has been explained by saying that their wines were stronger than ours. Certainly, all manner of strange substances used to be added, such as ashes and lime to neutralize excessive acid, as well as salt, almonds, goats' milk and red-hot iron to aid the process of maturing and to give the wine a flavour. Resin was among them because it seems that the Greeks used to line their porous earthenware wine jars with pitch to prevent them leaking and so they got used to the flavour. To this day, some Greek wine is so flavoured. Wooden barrels were left to barbaric northerners who alone knew beer. Spirits also were unknown in ancient times because the process of distillation had not been discovered.

Eating and Feasting

Breakfast for most Greeks and Romans, when they had any, was usually a simple affair of a piece of bread dipped in diluted wine, just as in Latin countries today it is often a roll dipped in coffee. Midday lunch also was little more than a snack. The real meal of the day was dinner. Both in Greece and Rome the hour of dinner got later and later as time went on, so that it ceased to be eaten at

The wine for a Greek banquet was kept in pitch-lined amphoras which could be placed inside larger vessels filled with water. It was then ladled into drinking cups.

midday as it was in heroic times and became the main event of the evening. In imperial Rome the hour of dining got put back because people went to the Great Baths as they would to a social club in the afternoon.

Greeks in early and classical times ate all their meals either at home or in a friend's home. The one exception might be the midday snack which could either be taken along or bought from itinerant sellers in and around the Agora. Greek inns were very primitive, uncomfortable and verminous but travellers needing a meal could buy food for the woman innkeeper to cook.

While in the vast majority of simple Greek and Roman homes dinner was an ordinary enough affair, those who could afford to entertain found in the leisure, comfort and conviviality of the evening meal with friends both relaxation, stimulus and entertainment. We have stories of a dinner with Socrates where the talk was on an exalted philosophical level and the food and drink of no importance and, five hundred years later, the long story of the tremendously ostentatious gourmandizing of the rich Roman ex-slave Trimalchio told in all its succession of fruity scenes, by Petronius. More than a century later still, evidence that the old Greek traditions survived, and indeed spread, is provided by the long, rambling, gossipy 'Banquet of Learned Men', the *Deipnosophists* of Athenaeus, an Egyptian.

By classical times, Greek men had copied the oriental practice of reclining on a couch for their meals, propping themselves up on their left elbow. Roman men copied the Greeks. Neither thought it proper to include women in dinner parties until relatively late in their history, although the Etruscans, Rome's first exemplars of refined living, never shut their women away as the Greeks did, in separate living quarters. When women began to join in the feasts, they were provided with chairs on which to sit upright, but before long, in some free and easy households, they too reclined with the men.

When the guests arrived, slaves would bring them bowls of water for their hands, remove their sandals and wash their feet, for they had trudged through the filthy alleys of Athens. Then they were crowned with a garland of leaves or wild flowers because, as Sappho sang:

> offerings of flowers
> Do please the Graces, who hate all those
> Who come before them with uncrowned heads.

Food was served on little tables from which the guests helped themselves with their fingers. Until late Roman times bread did duty as a spoon. The small Roman spoons had thin stems with which shell fish could be extracted. The pieces of bread which the Greeks and Romans used in order to convey the eggs, salted fish, sausage, black pudding, grilled beef, mutton, pork, goat, wild birds, and especially in Greece, fish and so forth to the mouth were thrown on the floor for the dogs, cats and, in the country, even for the chickens of the household. Slaves swept up the rest. Then followed the second course or dessert of figs, grapes, pears, apples, honey-cakes and nuts. The real business of the evening then began, which was to drink wine, to be entertained and to talk. A master of the feast was chosen haphazard by lot to say what amount of water should be added to the wine and in what

order the drinking should go on. The Greeks usually called for three ceremonial libations, the first to Zeus, supreme god, the next to the Greek heroes, ending with one to the domestic deity, Zeus, Protector of the home. A pious chant to the accompaniment of a flute was often a part of this ceremony.

While the feast and the drinking was still going on, there would be entertainments and amusements of various kinds. In earlier times the guests provided it by taking turns to sing or by joining in round games and games of chance. A favourite Greek diversion, the *cottabus*, was a competition in skill in flicking the wine remaining in the cup so that in either struck an object at a distance or fell with a satisfying plop into a receptacle serving as a target. It had many refinements as it became more complicated and competitive.

Later in both Greece and Rome, entertainments at dinners became more lavish and costly in rich households. Professional talent was hired if the domestic resources did not suffice, just as those without a good cook were easily able to hire one for any occasion from those standing around in the Agora or Forum, waiting for a client. Music became more popular in the 4th century in Greece and it was provided by slave girls, naked or very sketchily clothed. They could be hired at any time from the brothel keepers whose trading enterprise became as much a part of economic life as that of the bakers or fishmongers.

Pompeii and Herculaneum show something of the retail food trade of a Roman town. The oven in one bakery in Pompeii was so well preserved that eighty-one round loaves weighing just over two pounds each were discovered intact, just as they had been left on the fatal evening of 23 November AD 79. There also and in Ostia, the remains have been found of some of those little street-corner booths, snack-bars and taverns which abounded in Roman cities in imperial times. There were eventually many grades of them, but at first, as in Athens, it was a disgrace for an honest citizen to be found in one, for they were the haunts of slaves, grimy labourers and prostitutes. Decorated on the outside with striking signboards and displays of their wares, they gave some of the streets of Rome the appearance of a vast tavern. Many had a busy trade and on the walls at Pompeii some large written advertisements announce that a tavern is for sale with an elegant dining room. Another refers to a dining room of three couches with all conveniences.

So popular were these resorts that some Roman emperors viewed them with suspicion, as they did all popular assemblies. Tiberius, Claudius and Nero all tried to curtail their activities, but as Vespasian later also decreed against them, it is evident that imperial prohibitions were not very successful.

The great attention and energy devoted to food and feeding by the rich, led to many cookery books and dictionaries of cooking but none has survived except part of one put together around the end of the 4th century AD and bearing the name of Apicius. A vivid pen-picture of the monotonous simple fare of the country small-holder is given in a short poem, long attributed to Virgil, *Moretum* or *The Salad*.

Greek children playing with their toy carts and a bunch of grapes. This drawing comes from a jug that is itself a toy—a tiny red-figure vase about two inches high.

Playing Games and Watching Sport

Life for most ordinary Greeks and Romans in town and country had always been mainly 'bed and work'. Their children however, when not at school, were often at a loose end, so they played the sort of games that children have always played with balls, hoops, tops, knuckle-bones, marbles, pitch and toss. They played with

Roman gladiators specialized in peculiar forms of fighting—the 'retiarius' with net, trident and dagger, the 'secutor' with helmet, sword and shield, the 'andabatae', who charged each other blindly on horseback, wearing vizored helmets without eye-holes, and others. This little bronze statuette is of a 'Samnis' who fought in traditional Samnite armour: a shield (on the ground), a sleeve of leather or metal with a shoulder piece on the right arm, a belt, greaves on the legs, a vizored helmet with crest and plume, and a short sword.

each other at leap-frog, hide-and-seek, pick-a-back, seesaws and some had little model animals like those of the Noah's Arks of more modern times. Girls had dolls and boys played at soldiers. Pet animals and cage birds enlivened many a modest dwelling. All childish enjoyments were given up when the threshold of adult life was reached and toys and childish belongings were solemnly laid aside with a little religious ceremony. There was no cult of ephemeral, pseudo-values of 'teenagers' for commercial profit. Young Greeks and Romans soon had to take their place in a man's world and train hard at gymnastic exercises. The girls, who were married sometimes in their early teens, soon had to begin housekeeping.

Adult diversions in the heroic ages were found in the many religious festivals and processions such as the great Panathenaea every four years in Athens and the Latin Games in Rome. Athletic contests and combats were the essence of the immensely popular national 'Games' accompanying such festivals, and so also in time were the serious dramatic shows from which the tragic theatre developed. Later the Greeks invented the comedy which became enormous fun. When Greek comedies came to Rome in the 2nd century BC in the translations and adaptations of Plautus and Terence they were very popular. As entertainment for the masses however, they did not survive, but were replaced by slapstick pantomime and worse. The urge for stronger sensational stuff and the need to satisfy the mob steadily replaced wit by grossness and lasciviousness.

When, during the early Empire, economic and political conditions led to a vast increase in out-of-work Roman citizens, many flocked to the great city of Rome for the free corn and water, the Baths, the shows and the endless excitements of city life. The urge for stronger stimulation than the tame theatre could provide was partly met in Rome by the tremendous thrill of the chariot races. Like the theatre, they also had their origin in some religious rites, probably connected with the harvest festival.

By the 2nd century AD there were five or six circuses in Rome, of which the Circus Maximus was the greatest. Accommodating about a quarter of a million spectators, it exceeded in size any similar stadium ever yet built. The passions aroused by the varying fortunes of the four competing teams, the reds, the whites, the greens and the blues, were more intense than anything we can now imagine.

Passions of a lower and more brutal kind were aroused and kept going by the bloody death struggles of men and beasts in the great Roman arenas, and they seem to have become a bigger draw than even the chariot races. The Greeks were too civilized

to endure such sights, but nothing could rival their popularity in Rome. Humane characters like Cicero might say they were distasteful but he was oddly singular, and even he had to take his young daughter to them. 'Bread and circus shows' were all that the Roman mob demanded from life according to the stern moralist Juvenal.

Public baths in Athens were not, as in Rome, for everybody. Athens had neither the water, sufficient space, heating facilities nor cash to provide such a great luxury for such vast numbers as those who got the public-bath habit in Rome. There, the *thermae* attained their fullest development in the 3rd century AD. Those built by Caracalla and Diocletian were on a colossal scale covering as much or more ground as the British Houses of Parliament or the British Museum and being far more magnificent in design, materials and construction. These Roman *thermae* were much more than mere bathing establishments. They were social centres, serving as people's clubs, for both sexes, with every facility for physical exercise and recreation, having gardens, library and itinerant sellers of snacks and drink. The Greek and Roman tradition of striving for physical fitness through exercise and sport as an essential condition of victory in the national games as well as on the field of battle may have led to the development of these great *thermae* as its culminating point, but they also encouraged and satisfied the vast horde of lazy loungers of imperial Rome. Copied on a smaller scale throughout the Roman Empire, they at least provided the possibility of a constructive use of leisure to off-set the horrible brutalities of the arenas.

Spinning was done at home by the women of the house, unless they had slaves to do the work for them. This Greek red-figure painting shows the housewife dressed in peplos and chiton, drawing thread from a distaff held in her left hand.

Dignity and Distinction in Clothes

'She worked with wool'. Many a Roman's last tribute to his dead wife on her tombstone included, among the catalogue of her virtues, this evidence of her true Roman nature. It was a tradition that the Greeks did not emphasize as much as the Romans. When Augustus sought to revive the tarnished virtues of old Rome, he made a point of wearing tunics and togas made at home by his wife Livia, aided no doubt by her slave women. Most Roman ladies by that time rarely had a spindle in their hands, nor did they spend much time standing at the loom. Like Greek ladies centuries earlier they either left such jobs to their slave girls or bought woollen and linen tunics, togas, *stolae*, and mantles from the fullers or the drapers. The great change in this direction began with the sudden influx of wealth and slaves into Rome during the 2nd century BC. New materials too, cotton, silk and dye-stuffs came upon the Roman scene.

Alexander the Great and his troops are supposed to have first encountered oriental silk on his great raid into India. The ingenious Greeks had however discovered a substitute for themselves by using the cocoon of the *bombyx*, a grub found on oaks and ash trees in the island of Cos. Then Coan silk met competition from the looms of other Greeks who succeeded in making true silk from the mulberry silkworm, but the result was never as good as the fabric made of Chinese silk, the *vestis serica*, because, unlike the Chinese, the Greeks had never discovered how to unwind the cocoon. Silk always remained a great luxury and as late as the 3rd century AD. Diocletian in his desperate effort to fix prices of everything allowed as much as three pounds weight of gold to be paid for one pound of silk.

The Greek chiton, worn by both men and women (though the men's version was shorter), consisted of a single oblong piece of cloth. One arm went through a hole and the two top corners were fastened together by a clasp at the shoulder (see the girl on the left, who is in fact wearing a double chiton). The open side was normally sewn together below the hips, and the garment was gathered at the waist by a girdle. The girl on the right holds part of the dress in her mouth while she ties this up. Other distinctive Greek garments such as the peplos and himation were worn over the chiton.

To distinguish between a Greek and a Roman by his or her clothes isn't easy to the casual eye of a museum visitor looking at ancient marble statues. Yet to the people of antiquity the difference was at once apparent. Both Greeks and Romans had to spin raw wool or flax into thread and then to weave it into cloth. Having made a length of cloth web they just draped it round the body and fastened it, if at all, by large metal fibulae, or safety pins. In this way were made the Greek chiton and Roman one-piece tunic, the Greek peplos and himation, and the Roman stola and toga. Simple as they seem, himations and togas required a lot of raw material, all patiently spun and woven by hand, and they were by no means cheap. A good himation would cost more than the wages of a working man for a month.

The basic garment was the chiton or tunic, tied round the waist with a belt. Greeks had no other underclothes but some Romans had a loin cloth and Roman women had a bust support, sometimes of soft leather. Children and slaves went about in tunics although little boys and girls of good families may have had smaller versions of the himation or toga and stola of their parents for special occasions. These longer, vaster outer garments were the distinctive national dress of the Greek and Roman people. Clumsy as they were, togas had to be worn by all free Roman citizens in the City. They were glad to shed them when they got home or were in the country.

Ladies were allowed freedom in the use of colour, as time went on, but men's togas in Rome were uniformly white, for colour early had a religious significance, especially the scarlet and purple bands on the togas of priests and magistrates and on those of young boys, a pleasant reminder of the Roman ideal that young boys must be treated with the greatest respect.

In cold weather extra tunics might be worn. Augustus suffered so much from the cold that he sometimes wore four at once. Heavier capes of various styles and sizes and of a thicker weave were also used in bad weather. Soldiers on a campaign would use theirs also as a blanket at night. None of these articles of clothing was waterproof unless much more of the natural grease was left on the wool by cleaning methods available to the fullers than we use today. Successive visits to the fullers would in time soon remove any such protection, so shelter in heavy rain was much more of an imperious necessity in the ancient world than it need be now.

The fullers' business throve in ancient Rome, for it was a badge of poverty to go about in a dirty toga or stola. Cleaning methods without soap were primitive by our standards, but they seem to have done the job. Potash, nitre, and fuller's earth, an alkaline clay, were the main materials, supplemented, it is said, with human urine from the public lavatories. Clothes were then rinsed in water and exposed to burning sulphur to bleach them. The fuller's job, treading out the wash barefoot in such liquid mixtures and exposed to poisonous sulphur fumes was not one for the squeamish.

Clumsy and awkward as first attempts can be to don and wear either himation or toga with grace and ease of movement, they undoubtedly achieved an elegance that has hardly since been equalled. Artists and sculptors down to quite recent times long sought to lend to some of their sitters the dignity and distinction of the timeless garb of classical Greece and Rome.

Most accounts of Greek and Roman weaving stop short of giving some account of the rich and lavish wall-hangings, curtains, pictorial ceremonial robes and the humble but essential tents and ships' sails. All have perished, but occasional references in ancient writings testify to the excellence they sometimes attained.

Splendid draperies were woven for the statues of goddesses which were painted in bright colours and lavishly clothed in the way that images often are in Roman Catholic churches today. Those annually provided at a solemn festival for the glorious gold and ivory figure of Athena in the Parthenon at Athens, the creation of the famous artist Phidias, were exceptionally fine and famous. So were the curtains and hangings in that wonderful temple. In heroic days time, energy, industry and wealth were lavished upon cult objects of this sort rather than upon human beings, however distinguished they may have been in public life.

Those Greeks who could afford shoes or boots in the country had them made to measure. For centuries the custom of walking barefoot, especially indoors, persisted. Socrates kept up the habit but by the 4th century he was already somewhat singular and shoemakers began to prosper and to create, especially in the Hellenistic period, attractive alternatives to the simple sandals with their cork or wooden soles that still sufficed for the great majority.

Romans are usually depicted with sandals of very various types or with more elaborate leather footwear. From early times, social distinction was indicated in Rome by the style and colouring of shoes; patricians for example, wore small half-moons on theirs to distinguish themselves from plebeians while the scarlet shoes of the two Consuls marked them off from everyone else. Scores of small cobblers' booths were to be found in the City, working half in the street, and they specialized, to be able to turn out heavy country boots, elegant town shoes, simple sandals or slippers. The guild of Rome's slipper-makers alone had 300 members.

A fuller at work in Roman Gaul. His job was to clean the cloth after it had been woven and remove the natural grease still remaining in it. He supports himself on the rails of a square tank and treads the cloth with his bare feet in a mixture of water and fuller's earth, an alkaline clay. Behind him, on a beam supported on brackets, another piece of material is drying.

In Search of Elegance

Clothing was by no means the only badge of wealth and elegance in the later history of Greek and Roman everyday life. Scent, jewellery and elaborate hairdressing were others. In the Iliad, Homer makes Venus sprinkle rose-scented oil on the dead body of Hector, but if there had been any religious motives of this sort for using scent, they were soon overlaid by its mundane employment. Much scent came from the East where the Persians had learnt the art of making it from the Indians. Alexander the Great was said to have been the first to bring oriental perfumes to Greece when he captured a great store of them in the baggage train of the Persian king Darius.

Having no alcohol, the Greeks and Romans made scent from various oils such as calamus, balsam and olives with which they compounded flowers, notably roses, violets, marjoram, iris, narcissus. In vain, efforts were made to restrain the trade. In 189 BC the Censors in Rome forbad the sale of 'exotics', as perfumes were called. Enthusiasm for every kind of gratification of the senses made a dead letter of such a rule and the trade soon grew to great proportions. Pliny in the 1st century AD records that large sums were paid for imported perfumes, notably from the Persians who were able to use sub-tropical blooms. According to Pliny, they 'quite soak themselves in perfume and by this borrowed recommendation, disguise their own bad smell'. Vast numbers of Greeks and Romans in their lack of soap must have had cause to approve such a practice by many of their own countrymen. So no Roman banquet could begin before slaves had anointed the guests with perfumes after washing their feet and crowning them with garlands. Men as well as women soaked themselves, although Socrates had indignantly asked in the 5th century 'how can women want perfume for their husbands when they themselves are redolent of it?'

Many Roman men also emulated the women in wearing rings or amulets set with precious stones, but feminine adornment had, almost from the beginning of time, provided the main motive for the jeweller's craft. We may still admire the exquisite creations of master-hands in Greece, Etruria and Rome, although it is difficult to know how much of the splendid treasures of the Romans were created by Greeks. Nobody has excelled the skill of the Greek master-craftsmen in engraving precious and semi-precious stones. Among the many which Pliny lists are emeralds, beryls, opals, sardonyx, onyx, sapphires, amethysts, rubies, jasper and crystal. Diamonds rather defeated them because they were so hard to cut.

The vagaries in hairdressing in Greece and Rome would be a long story, best perhaps told in pictures. In early times most men were bearded. Alexander the Great is credited with having set the fashion for being clean-shaven in Greece, which was not copied in Rome until another great general, the Scipio called Africanus from his victory in the mighty struggle with Carthage, had led the way. Beards then mostly disappeared until, in Cicero's time, they were revived by young fops who sought to attract notice by appearing different. It was not until the first quarter of the 2rd century AD that beards again came in fairly generally, following the example of the Emperor Hadrian who wished to conceal a blemish on his face. Roman men had good reason to prefer beards because there were no really good steel razors and it was difficult or impossible to make a good job of shaving oneself. The barbers' shops were many, for they were centres of gossip rivalling the Baths and the small snack-bars and taverns.

Elegant ladies in Greece and Rome had all the time they wished for the hairdressers, who were usually their own slave-girls, and many and striking were the creations they achieved over the centuries. Whether with all the artifice and eager search for novelty, they or their multitudinous successors today ever surpassed the simple Grecian style is a matter upon which everyone will have a private opinion.

There are few tricks in the matter of make-up that sophisticated Roman ladies had not at their command. They powdered and painted, shaded their eyes with charcoal or saffron, cared for their fingernails and spent hours in front of the mirror.

All brief outlines of Greek and Roman life inevitably pick out the highlights in the daily round of well-to-do town folk, simply

A cobbler cuts his leather, two pairs of finished boots on the cupboard behind him. Such industries were mostly carried out in small one-man shops, though in Rome at least a certain degree of specialization had been reached. Some concentrated on heavy boots with nails, others on women's shoes and others on slippers.

because it is of them only that much record remains and because they tended to set the tone and the standards of behaviour of their times. Yet all the time there were the vaster numbers of humble folk in town and country somehow surviving on a very sparse diet of flavoured barley or wheat, drinking river water, rarely washing and sharing their cramped quarters with their domestic animals, if they owned any. Theirs was the energy and hard work whether slave or free or semi-enslaved, as they became towards the end of the Roman Empire, which kept the whole social fabric intact as a going concern.

The Heroic Life Dissolves in Luxury

During the 5th century BC the Greeks became less and less able to resist the lure of luxury. Contact with the Persians is usually blamed for this indulgence, just as the far greater indulgence of the Romans after the middle of the 2nd century BC is also blamed on Rome's first massive contact with the Near East and with Greece. A better explanation is probably increasing wealth, the natural distaste of human beings for hardship and discomfort, the lure of pleasurable sensations and that urge for human society which makes men ready to take trouble to give their friends a good time. Nor must the urge to learn be forgotten. Samuel Johnson thought that 'every human being ... would give all that he had to get knowledge' and the eating and drinking together, the symposia of the Greeks and Romans, could, amongst oceans of triviality, serve to spread opinions, including much error, and so help to generate truer ideas.

Before long self-indulgence went too far. After the 4th century in Athens it was a far cry to the simplicity, restraint and vegetarian diet prescribed by Plato for his ideal Republic. When, instead, the rule became 'drink up or get up and go' everything else was to match, including the music which had a gayer more frivolous sound than any that Plato would have approved. He was already reacting against sensual, hedonistic tendencies threatening to get out of hand.

'By our men becoming perverted to a passion for show and money and the pleasures of an idle life, and either not marrying at all, or if they did marry, refusing to rear the children that were born, or at most one or two out of a great number, for the sake of leaving them well off or bringing them up in extravagant luxury' ... with these words, Polybius, an intelligent Greek who had lived long as an exile in Rome, explained, in the middle of the 2nd century BC, the decay of his own countrymen.

At the same time he saw unmistakable signs that the Romans were afflicted with the same disease. 'Dissoluteness had, as it were, burst into a flame at this period', he wrote of the Romans. They had just conquered Macedonia when he wrote these words and he speaks of 'the immense difference made, both in public and private wealth and splendour, by the importation of the riches of Macedonia into Rome'.

When Rome finally took over Greece as a dependent province, the primitive heroic simplicity of the Fathers of the Republic was already something of a joke. Romans inherited the whole stupendous achievement of Greece in art, letters, music, theatre, philosophy and everyday life. They did not see it, as we painfully strive to do, through the fragments which survive. They had it entire. Quickly Roman social and cultural life followed the longer, slower evolution through which it had been developed in Greece. With far greater resources in money, slaves, trade, industry, travel possibilities and with far greater inherited and stolen stores of material possessions, the Romans were able to push self-indulgence to lengths of which few Greeks could have dreamed. Eating and drinking, with other sensual pleasures, became ends in themselves until the disgusted Seneca who had witnessed the wild excesses of Roman society in the days of Nero, could say that his countrymen 'ate to vomit and vomited to eat'. It has been suggested that one reason for this truly nauseating habit was that it helped to stave off that helpless intoxication with which only too many Roman dinner parties concluded. Belated revellers then staggered home, supported and guided by their slaves, or carried silently home behind the drawn curtains of their luxurious litters.

Romans were becoming a different breed of men by the 1st century AD. The continuity of history is but one aspect of the study of the past, for history is a study of change in human affairs. In their everyday life we see clearer than in their military and even political life, how greatly Romans were changing, how different their whole scheme of values had become since the heroic days of the earlier Republic. By the beginning of our era, political troubles had eliminated many of the outstanding men of the leading old Roman families, and had deprived what few survivors there were of sufficient social influence to be able to make a stand against the prevailing trends, even if they had thought it worth while doing so. To act the puritan in the court of Nero was tantamount to suicide as even so favoured and skilful an operator as the philosopher Seneca discovered. The newly-rich, many of them descendants of slaves and freedmen, had no such ambitions.

Julius Caesar, of all people, had tried to enforce moderation in his very brief period as dictator of Rome, by forbidding purple-coloured clothes, pearls, lavish banquets and litters. Augustus did not do more than to try by his own personal example to recommend a modest way of life, but he did renew Caesar's law against heavy expense on meals although he had to double the upper limit of expense. Still the complaints about luxury and the disregard of such laws went on. His successor, Tiberius, to whom an obsequious senate referred the matter for decision, replied testily by asking the senators 'What am I to begin by prohibiting or restraining to old time standards?—huge country mansions?—hordes of slaves from every country?—masses of silver and gold?—marvels in bronze and painting?—splendour in clothes that makes men's dress look like women's?—or that luxury by which our women drain our treasure away to pay foreign, even hostile countries for their jewels?' All-powerful as the Roman emperors were, this was a task clearly beyond them. Horace had already pointed the moral 'of what avail are laws if we lack principle?'

So the urge to grow wealthy drove the great majority of Romans in their yearning for the pleasure of the senses. The comprehensive catalogue drawn up by Tiberius sufficiently indicates the main objects on which all the money went, but he left out some things such as the colossal expenditure on food and drink, on flowers and perfumes.

Waste of wealth is not the whole story, nor did the whole of Roman society suddenly slide into a life of voluptuous indulgence. The world's work had to go on, which it did, in growing prosperity but too many leaders of society were infected by the new lax ways. Some rich men remembered the poor. The old Greek tradition which allowed any poor man to seek admission to a dinner party was not observed in Rome where the huge, stout doors of Roman houses guarded by slaves and savage dogs, made short work of any misguided gate-crasher. The poor 'clients' of the rich, a special dependent class in Rome among which were many freed slaves, might line up outside every morning to receive any scraps of food and a few coins which the charity of the master of the house or of his minions might be ready to bestow. A few wealthy patrons, notably Maecenas, patron of Virgil and

Horace, endowed literary men with a generosity that has immortalized his own name, and a natural human benevolence to the poor and helpless was not unknown before it was recommended by the Stoics and before it was preached as the later, Christian doctrine of charity.

Many wealthy people thought, with Aristotle, that to give money to the poor, 'is like water poured into a leaky jar' because 'the poor are always receiving and always wanting more'. In Rome most poor householders were provided with free bread by the Emperor. Together with some occasional charity of patrons to their poor clients, free water and free entertainment, this corn dole was the Roman's only approach to that Welfare State, the bare idea of which was only born yesterday.

On a Greek red-figure vase two women fold a richly embroidered cloth for a wedding. The trousseau is doubtless to be kept in the chest beside them, and a mirror hangs on the wall behind. Weddings were among the few exciting events to enliven the monotonous routine of women in ancient Greece.

'We Women are Nothing'

Roman fathers had absolute power over their families and this was something peculiar to Rome. As long as the father of a family was alive, his word was law. When he died, his eldest son succeeded to all his authority. If there was no son, the women of the household had to come under the guardianship and tutelage of the nearest male relation. No member of the family owned any private property, even a son's army pay belonged legally to his father, until Augustus altered the law. The father owned the dowry which his daughter-in-law brought with her. All such drastic limitations upon personal liberty seem quite outrageous, but they were nothing compared to a father's right to put any member of the family to death. Far fewer Roman children were thrown out at birth to perish on rubbish heaps than were Greek infants, although in common with other peoples of antiquity, Roman parents were able to exercise the right if they chose. But they had to get five neighbours to agree to the death sentence at which public opinion did not easily connive. Slowly such primitive unconcern for what we regard as elementary human rights were brought under some control, at first that of custom and public opinion and later, to some extent, of law.

If sons were treated in this way, the position of daughters was very much more hazardous. Sons were traditionally cherished because national survival as much as family survival depended upon manpower in the fields and in battle, but except in Sparta daughters were of small account. Their place in the home was easily taken by slaves, their ability to earn a living in any honest way was practically non-existent. Marriage was their only destiny and it meant passing from the control of one's own family to that of the husband's.

In early times in both Greece and Rome, much was made of betrothal and more of the actual ceremony. Everybody likes the excitement of a wedding especially in the dull routine of life on the land or in a small city alley. Both marriage customs and the

Hairstyles in the ancient world show a bewildering variety, though Greek women were far more traditional than Roman. Left: a Greek terracotta from S. Italy, showing the so-called 'melon-style' The hair is pulled back in plaits, tied with two ribbons and made into a chignon at the top. Right: three styles from imperial Rome—mid 1st century AD (left), later 1st century AD (centre) and 2nd century (right). Fashions changed so quickly that one sculptor made a portrait head with detachable scalp, so that he could keep the hairstyle always up to date.

laws concerning marriage had a long history and they showed many forms, some of which can be plausibly traced back to very early times. In Athens, the position and the customary rights of women worsened after Homeric times, and by the middle of 5th century, except always in Sparta, they were in a miserable state of dependence. 'We women are nothing,' says a character in a play of Sophocles, 'happy enough in childhood, without a care, but when we arrive at maidenhood, driven away from our homes, sold as merchandise, compelled to marry and to say "All's well".' What was worse, a woman had no claim on her husband's property and if he died she was turned out of her home. Then a man of her own family, her guardian, who retained powers over her even during her husband's lifetime, was responsible for finding her another husband. Her dowry, which gained in importance after Homeric times, when it was unknown, did not belong to her or to her husband but to her guardian. Her grown-up son would be her guardian if she had none of her own family.

Gay as the wedding ceremonies might be with garlands of flowers, torch processions, festal costumes, flute-players and the marriage feast all preceded by a ceremonial bath in the cool water of the Callirrhoe fountain in Athens, it was all but a prelude to what, to our way of thinking, would be little better than a life of servitude. Athenian women were expected to remain indoors except for occasional visits to the theatre or to take part in religious festivals. The poorest class of women fared better to the extent that, lacking slaves, they were compelled to go out shopping, while some had stalls in the market. Country women also had more freedom. Legally an Athenian woman was virtually without rights, neither did the death of the husband to whom she had been bound without her consent, set her free. If he had also become her guardian he could give her in marriage to another man during his lifetime and even direct in his will whom she should marry after his death.

In Rome, a woman's situation was at first little better, but as time went on, it improved instead of worsened, as had the lot of the Athenian woman. There were two traditional forms of Roman marriage, one relatively simple which had developed from the primitive practice of bride-purchase, and the other, characteristic of the patrician families, a religious ceremony involving, among other rites, the exchange of wheaten wafers, *confarreatio*, and the taking of auspices. Otherwise the public demonstrations, the giving away of the bride, the procession to her husband's home and her reception there was rather like a formal Athenian wedding. To annul such a marriage was difficult, and in olden times impossible. For this and other reasons these ceremonial marriages declined steadily. Among the other reasons was that they put the woman and all her property legally in her husband's hands. To escape such control, a simpler form of union which did not involve such legal surrender was devised. Already in the 4th century BC the law of the Twelve Tables had allowed a woman to escape complete subjection if she spent three nights a year away from her husband. By taking advantage of this and by the development of the dowry which a husband had to repay if the marriage broke up, Roman women were able to secure a degree of independence which in comparison with the fate of Athenian women, was truly remarkable.

Such is the traditional view of the wrongs of womanhood in ancient Greece and Rome and there can be no doubt but that they were often grievous and heavy, as indeed the hard fate of countless women has been ever since and yet remains in many parts of the world in our own day. Perhaps, however, this traditional picture is drawn too darkly and that in the ancient world as in the 19th century, when women were without many of their present-day liberties, their homes and families were after all firmly held together by human affection and their own sheer strength of character so that the vast majority of Greek and Roman women were able to lead a reasonably satisfactory life even if its framework was not of their own devising.

At the Mercy of Men: the Slaves

The slaves, men, women and children, who occupied so large a place in the everyday life of Greece and Rome were not even inferior citizens like the clients in Rome. Destitute of civic rights, they were mere additions to the stock of domestic animals, liable to be worked as they could be worked, unremittingly and to the point of exhaustion for little or no reward except their bare subsistence. Upon their hard relentless toil the whole of Greek and Roman society very largely depended. Too much of life in ancient times was an almost constant war to the death with neighbouring peoples. A settled order of society endured as long as its menfolk were able to beat off the armed assailants who came to kill them, steal their land and cattle and to lead all their women and children capable of work away as captives to spend the rest of their lives as slaves of their conquerors. Any vanquished warriors whose lives might be spared would also be driven off to be sold and bought along with the oxen and asses and other booty. The families of the defeated were broken up and husbands, wives and children parted for ever. Warfare was not the only source of slaves. Some were kidnapped, others captured by pirates, many were children of slaves and a few were picked up from the infants exposed to perish and reared for slavery.

All slaves were completely at the mercy of their owners by whom they could be cruelly punished, chained or killed with impunity. How little concern was felt for their feelings is evident in many stories of sickening brutality. As a matter of course, any slave required to give evidence in a lawsuit was tortured in the belief that only then would he or she speak the truth. Thousands died in frightful agony as a result. Then they were thrown into a common grave and denied the rites and ceremonies both Greeks and Romans thought it essential to lavish upon deceased members of their own families.

As the wealth and power of the State grew, slavery became of much greater importance in daily life than it had been in the heroic days of either Greece or Rome. In the age of Pericles, around 450 BC, nearly half the population of Attica, or about 115,000 out of 315,000 and of Athens, or about 70,000 out of about 155,000 were slaves. In Rome, although again the figures are mere estimates, the proportion of slaves to free was probably higher than in Greece, while absolutely, the number of slaves was much greater. Slaves from non-Italian peoples were much more numerous in Rome than the non-Greek slaves in Greece because Rome's world empire greatly increased the area of

A Roman teacher sits on a high chair with a cushion, while his little pupil attends to the lesson. Roman schools were not regarded as very inspiring places—
'*Where smoky vapours Virgil's pages soil
And Horace looks one blot, all soot and oil.*'

recruitment. In Rome it has been guessed that there were between 200,000 and 300,000 slaves and half a million or three-quarters of a million free.

Slowly in the later history of both Greece and Rome, the earlier harsh treatment of slaves seems to have become somewhat milder. In Rome especially the practice of manumission or of freeing slaves, led to a special class of 'freedmen' who joined the clients of their former master but whose sons became full Roman citizens. Through hard work and skill, some Roman freedmen grew very rich and in the early days of the Empire, one or two freedmen of the Emperor became politically very influential to the intense disgust of Romans of the old school. So great were the numbers of slaves and freedmen and their descendants in imperial Rome that it has been plausibly argued that to them was due that marked change in the whole character and style of Roman life which facilitated the oriental despotism of the later Caesars. It would have been intolerable to Romans of the heroic age, but no novelty to the ancestors of many of the slaves.

It is as difficult to generalize about the treatment of slaves in the ancient world as it is about the treatment of animals in different countries today. All depended upon the kindliness and humanity, or lack of it, of the slave's master and mistress. Four casual lines from a satire of the highly civilized Horace show what that could mean: 'If a slave girl or boy is handy when your lust is hot, surely you won't forego relief? Not me, I like a cheap and ready love'. To be completely stripped of every vestige of personal dignity and security would be no mean hazard in any state of society, for human brutes are bred in every generation whom nothing but the law and police protection can restrain. Slaves were utterly without either until later in imperial times when a beginning was made, under the influence of Stoic teaching, somewhat to lessen their miserable dependence. Economic factors, contrary to what might be imagined, aided this process, because it became more and more evident that if slaves were to compete successfully with free men, they had to be treated no worse than free men. Despite any such improvements, there was no question, even among the early Christians, of giving all slaves their freedom.

'Youth is for an Hour'

The Athenians invented education. Spartans and Romans were interested only in training. Like all generalizations, so sweeping a statement is an over-simplification, but it spotlights our enormous debt to the Greeks for making the vital distinction between education as the full development of the human mind and mere training as a way to fit the young for special tasks.

Just as it is a difference that is often overlooked today in our technological society, so many Greeks were probably also not very clearly aware of it either. In heroic, Homeric times what mattered above all else was that children should be trained for survival, particularly for victory in sieges and battles. The ancient world did not need to be told as we still do, that 'defence is much more important than opulence', so the young Greeks had to become taut and hardy, able to bend the bow and hurl the spear with deadly effect. The Spartans concentrated their energies so intensely on this supreme task that for them education meant little else.

Military might was essential to the Athenians also, but, alone, it was not enough. Over and above their careful and thorough physical and military preparedness, they valued the life of the mind. They had no wish to limit education in Spartan fashion to intense military training and to live all their lives in barrack rooms and on parade grounds. Such a life, Aristotle said, produced not men but wolves.

Just what it means to become a civilized member of society was what the Greeks wanted to know, and their philosophers helped them to find the answer. For they were perpetually trying to decide what was the highest good for man, what it is that most reflective people prize above all else. A sure instinct seems to have led them aright.

The Greeks from early times tried to inspire boys with a love of poetry and literature; they tried to endow them with a lively sense of verbal and musical rhythms, including some ability to make music themselves upon a lyre; they put them continually through gymnastics carefully designed not only to improve physique and physical fitness, but to impart grace of movement and bodily control. Such were but the beginnings of a self-education supposed to go on in deepening awareness and increasing creative power throughout life.

When schools were first set up, no doubt most Greeks sent their boys to them in the hope that by gymnastic training, by learning to read and write, they would better be able to take their place in the world. It was the philosophers who saw that schooling should provide foundations upon which a true humanistic education of the whole man could be built. It was probably their greatest, most rewarding discovery, for it has turned out to be a revelation of all that which can give meaning and value to life.

'Meaning and Value'—these vague and seemingly nebulous words sum up the Greek discovery that the nature and destiny of man is more than life upon the animal or merely biological level of eating, drinking, sexual excitement, and lounging in the sun; more than ploughing, sowing, harvesting, fishing, building, manufacturing, trading and getting rich. Yet they still sought their kingdom in this world and they found it in the harmonious development of three separate supreme human interests. They are the interests which drive men irresistibly to search for knowledge, or truth; for delight of eye, ear and mind, or beauty; for friendly, orderly and socially worthy conduct, or for moral worth or goodness. The discovery of these three main ways of adding meaning and values to life was momentous. It is still one from which humanity many continually profit, for it points the way to an all-round culture which not teachers alone, but all individuals in their private lives, all corporate bodies and governments in their public policies, should regard as their supreme and overriding aim.

Greek education consisted largely of private lessons. Here the teacher (who was likely to be a slave) sits with his stick behind him; his writing tablet is open on his lap and he holds a stylus.

'What about trade, manufacturing and technology?' may well be the hard-headed comment upon this Greek emphasis upon truth, beauty and moral goodness. It is true that the best Greek thought did not worry so much about the material side of life as we do. 'Economics' for them was a matter of good-housekeeping, as indeed it was generally also until nearly the end of the 18th century. The Greeks rather despised the pursuit of wealth for its own sake. Aristotle, who wrote, 'great is the good fortune of a state whose citizens have a moderate, sufficient property', did not glorify work or even commend it as a way to get rich, because for him 'the first principle of all action is leisure', and leisure was necessary in order to lead a good life. The poets might sing that 'God oweth glory to him that toileth' or that 'virtue comes through toil' but in the main the Greek idea was 'Six hours are enough for work, the next say to men *Live*.' So they did, for the command in Greek, 'live', was the letters which served also for the numbers 7, 8, 9, 10—ζηθι.

Slaves and workmen could be relied upon for the material needs, and they of course had to be trained. Builders and carpenters, potters, weavers, fullers, farmers, fishermen, barbers, shopkeepers and suchlike learned their jobs by following in the footsteps of either their fathers or of some other craftsman. Content to perpetuate traditional crafts by traditional methods, the Greeks gave little thought to lightening the burden of human toil, or to increasing the comfort and convenience of life by inventing machines and harnessing power to make them work. It was an attitude of mind that the Romans were very ready to share, so technology and mechanical invention, apart from building, made little progress in the ancient world.

The Schools of Athens

Before the 5th century BC most Greek children got what education they could pick up at home. When schools became more common it is by no means likely that most children were sent to them. Those that went were accompanied by a slave, *paedagogos*, as chaperone, servant and tutor, who was also supposed to teach the child good manners and morals. The aim was to turn out good citizens able to maintain the state, so the time was divided between physical training and literary learning. Reading and writing were taught with a minimum of equipment, the pupils sat on little stools and rested their tablets on their knees. The love of literature was implanted early by making boys learn passages from the poets by heart. Some could recite both Homer's *Iliad* and *Odyssey* from memory, a feat not unknown among some 19th century English schoolboys. Many poems would be sung to notes on the lyre which was the favourite musical instrument.

Before this simple and elementary form of schooling had developed into the more complicated and formal system of later Greek history, to include arithmetic, geometry and painting, the great cultural pioneers of Greece, Sophocles, Pindar, Herodotus, Aeschylus, Euripides, Thucydides, Phidias, Praxiteles, Socrates, Plato and Aristotle, were already dead. That such genius can flower in the absence of universal education and carefully devised syllabuses, that it should fail to reappear in spite of the earnest labours of generations of school-masters, that, instead of progress, there should be a serious decline in public spirit and above all in private standards of conduct, is a fact sufficiently startling to sober the enthusiasm of advocates of educational systems as the one cure for the world's ills.

Inadequacies in Greek schooling can no doubt be found in the limited outlook and attainments of teachers, in the lack of cultural interests in the home and in human laziness and stupidity in general. All such failures were but a part of the general decline as materialistic interests more and more swamped the cultural values of earlier times. Just as humanity could not be forced to live down to the parade-ground discipline of Sparta, so it proved unable to keep steadily in view the highest standards of truth, beauty and moral worth and so to live up to the civilizing education of Athens.

Beyond the existence of the papyrus rolls of which Greek and Roman books were made, we know nothing about the private libraries or book-collections of the Greeks before Roman times. If the writings of Homer were regarded by the Greeks as The

Libraries, both public and private, were numerous throughout the later Roman Empire—Rome in the 2nd century AD had over twenty-five public libraries. This relief comes from the northern capital of Trier. The books, mass-copied by rooms-full of scribes writing to dictation, were stored in the form of rolls, with the title written on a label at the end. A normal roll could take only a book the length of one of the Gospels—a longer work would require many rolls. They were cumbersome to consult and difficult to read, because there was rarely any space between the words or punctuation.

Book, rather in the way the Bible has been in Western Europe and America, it seems likely that some Greek homes would possess something of the *Iliad* or the *Odyssey*, although each required about 150 feet of rolled papyrus. Many a Greek mother may have needed them to help her sons with their task of learning them and she would herself learn much in the process. But how the book trade was run, what books cost, how many an average middle-class Greek family owned, how often they read them, we cannot say.

In Roman times we know from Cicero's letters, for he was a great book-collector, that there was an active trade and that precious volumes were sought for eagerly in Rome and Athens to add to the often elegant libraries of wealthy collectors. Sulla is said to have looted Aristotle's library which he brought to Rome. A considerable trade in books was made possible by dictating the text of a book to a room full of slaves, and it is probable that the Greeks were the first with this modest example of mass-production in the ancient world.

It was not until the heyday of the Roman Empire that parchment sheets, fastened together in pages to form the codex, began to rival the papyrus roll and to foreshadow the shape of books to come.

The Practical Schooling of the Romans

The Romans, tough, dour peasants that they were, followed their traditional way of life for some centuries before they seem to have considered it necessary to look for anyone to help them in the task of training their children to live the lives they themselves learned from their own parents. In this way Roman boys were taught to cultivate the family plot, to manage the domestic animals, and to prepare to fight in Rome's constant wars. A girl had to learn to carry water from the well or fountain, to turn raw wool into clothing, to cook and keep house. Both boys and girls were early imbued with reverence for the guardian spirits of the Roman home, the *di penates*, Vesta, the goddess of the family hearth, and the *lar familiaris*, the deity of the farmland and later of the house as well. Like the Spartans, the early Romans who wanted farmers and fighters, did not consider it their duty to rear sickly or weak children, or many daughters, but they became much more humane in this matter of child slaughter than the Spartans or Greeks could afford to be. Boys probably had a better life when they got all their training from their fathers as they did until well into the historic period, than when they began to depend upon school-masters for their education.

According to Plutarch, the first Roman known to have divorced his wife was also the first to set up as a school-master teaching for fees. This was around 230 BC soon after the first Punic War, and roughly at the first faint beginnings of Roman literature. The pupils were boys, for it is doubtful whether the Romans took any more trouble about educating girls than the Greeks had done. Yet a few Roman girls contrived to get some education, as some girls generally seem to have done before they were sent to schools in the nineteenth century.

Sketchy and inadequate as the learning passed on from father to son may have been, it stood comparison with anything that the average school-master could provide, and as an introduction to the problems of life, it was far better. The *litterator* who provided elementary instruction in reading, writing and arithmetic, was, it seems, generally both brutal and a poor teacher. The relatively few boys whose parents could afford to prolong their education by sending them to a *grammaticus*, the next stage in education, arrived at best with little more than the rudiments of ability in reading and calculating, with some skill in taking dictation and some ability to repeat a string of copy-book maxims and the text of the Twelve Tables containing the fundamental laws of Rome, an extremely poor substitute for the verses of Homer's *Iliad*. Roman boys had a rough Latin version of Homer's *Odyssey* which Livius Andronicus translated after about 270 BC.

On this modest foundation the *grammaticus* endeavoured to build. His task was to teach boys to speak well and to write with clarity and if possible, with distinction. Some close study of literature, particularly of the poets came next and the better *grammaticus* was able to add music and geometry to the extent that either were likely to improve the lad's chances of making a mark in the world. Young men of leading families aspiring to a public career as lawyers or magistrates who, up to Cicero's time in the early 1st century BC, learned their skill by attending as a 'junior' some distinguished public figure, were often sent on during the Empire, from the *grammaticus* to a *rhetor* or professional teacher of public speaking. Cicero as a young man had gone to Greece to study there and ever afterwards he spoke of Athens as his spiritual home. He sent his own son there, for in the 1st century BC following the traditions of Plato and Aristotle, Athens had become a kind of university or centre for higher education for the Roman world.

Greek learning had then become as fashionable an accomplishment of Roman gentlemen as French was to become for educated Englishmen in the 18th century. It had been a slow process, for the first beginnings can be detected before the middle of the 2nd century BC in the so-called 'Scipionic Circle' of admirers of Greek culture. Within a couple of generations the contagion had spread widely. Cicero, who shared the contempt most Romans felt for the Greeks of his own time, made no secret of his tremendous respect for Greek thought. Lucretius spoke of mankind wallowing in dark night before 'First a man from Greece' bade them look at the light. A generation later, Horace told how Greece, overcome by Rome, 'captured her savage conqueror and brought her culture into clownish Latium'. Great as was the impact of the Greeks, however, it did not alter the fundamental nature and purpose of Roman schooling which remained severely practical. It was not technological, for the Romans shared all the prejudice of the Greeks against soiling their hands at any kind of craft. Very many more Romans than Greeks were able to rely on an unending supply of slave labour to take all burdens off their backs and all tools from their hands. Many of Rome's slaves came from Greece and the Near East and they were often far more skilled and intelligent than their employers.

Reflective Romans were outspoken in condemning the deficiencies of Roman education. Quintilian, writing in the second half of the 1st century AD, gives the impression that little or no progress had been made in schooling the young despite all Rome's enormous advantages as a rich, imperial state. More than schooling was required to produce men such as Cicero, Catullus, Varro, Virgil, Lucretius, Livy and Horace. When, during the Roman Empire, schools abounded both in Italy and in the provinces such as Gaul, when Emperors started to take pains about their number and quality, cultural life seemed unable to rise above a dull, repetitive, uncreative level. In the absence of political liberty, school education alone of the type then provided proved powerless to stimulate the inhabitants of the Roman Empire to

rise to the height of the demands which changing conditions of life were making upon them. A similar absence of great creative, humanistic achievement characterizes Hellenistic Alexandria, despite its schools and men of learning. Undisturbed by serious wars, beautified by successive generations after its foundation by Alexander the Great in 332 BC, it survived despite civic commotions, for a thousand years to astound its Arab conquerors who were dazzled by its marble magnificence. Long the University of Egypt and the resort of scholars, its famous library, botanical gardens and zoological gardens served the study of poetry, mathematics, astronomy and medicine. Euclid, Aratus and Callimachus were among its famous sons, but in spite of all its many advantages, it can hardly be said to have contributed to the advancement of civilization and culture on a scale commensurate with that of Athens where Socrates, Plato and their companions with next-to-no such material resources, first set mankind on the path to knowledge.

The rise of Christianity did not, for a long while, involve a break with the old classical curriculum, as the effort by the pagan Emperor Julian (361–363) to shut Christians out of the schools clearly shows. When, at the end of the 4th century, Christianity became Rome's sole official religion, the writings of men such as St Jerome (AD 340–420) and St Augustine (AD 354–430) testify to the vigour with which Greek and Latin classics were still studied in Roman schools. They testify also to the narrow, illiberal ideas which such pious Christian leaders entertained about cultural values, many of which they sought to destroy in a blind fanaticism which recalls some of the worst features of Spartan and later totalitarianism.

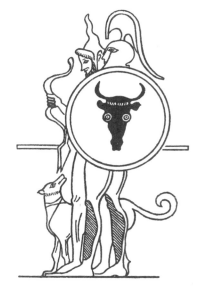

A Scythian archer (behind) and a Greek hoplite, from a black figure vase of the time of the tyrants. Under the democracy these Scythians, public slaves, were used as 'police' to keep order at meetings and carry out arrests on the orders of officers of state, and it has been plausibly suggested that this continues a practice introduced by the tyrants—who would try to avoid using citizens who might develop political views of their own.

Justice for the People

Not for slaves alone was life in the ancient world for long periods horribly insecure. Apart from ever-present fears of disease, plague and famine, and the constant threats of war and enslavement from without, there was also the danger of oppression from the high-handed arbitrary behaviour of the rich and powerful within the city community. For at first in Greece and Rome there was no guarantee of justice between man and man. The relatively poor and weak could not count on fair play. They could be and often were victimized by the strong, even to the point of losing their liberty by becoming slaves to their oppressors. There were no

Roman keys were heavy but ingenious. As in a modern model, the mechanism would only turn when the complicated pattern in the key engaged with the same pattern in the lock. The prongs in this example then fitted between three rods which withdrew the bolt.

QVASINOVAMISTAMREMINTRODVCIEXHORRESCATISSEDILLA
POTIVSCOGITETISQVAMMVLTAINHACCIVITATENOVATASINT · ET
QVIDEMSTATIMABORICINEVRBISNOSTRAEINQVODFORMAS
STATVSQVERESPNOSTRADIDVCTASIT

'[Do not] react with alarm, as though what I bring before you were something new, but think rather how much has been changed in this city and through how many forms and constitutions our state has passed from its beginning.' Part of a speech by the Emperor Claudius to the senate of Rome in AD 48, as a result of which the senators passed a decree allowing the citizens of Gaul to become candidates for high office in the state and members of the senate—a step disliked by some of the conservative senators. A copy of the Emperor's speech recommending the new privileges and answering the objections raised by the senate was engraved on a bronze tablet in the fine monumental script of imperial Rome, and set up by the grateful Gauls near Lyons. A large fragment of it was rediscovered in 1528.

police in Athens until slaves from Scythia were given the job in 470 BC. In Rome, despite atrocious street brawls, murders and robberies, it was not until AD 6 that Augustus enrolled 7,000 men as police and firemen in a not very successful effort to make life in Rome less hazardous.

It was in grappling with such evils that the Greeks and the Romans won their greatest triumphs and in doing so created a respect for law and standards of civilized life in a community which have been models ever since. The Spartans led the way when at the end of the 7th century BC they remoulded their way of life by very strict laws attributed to a mysterious figure, Lycurgus. They were harsh and narrow rules and in the end they had to go, but not before many generations of Spartans had conformed obediently to them. The Athenians also looked to laws to inspire their way of life. Unlike the unphilosophical Romans, they regarded the law as more than a mere body of rules by which everyday disputes, crimes and misdemeanours might be regulated.

Athenian law had been revised and restated by their great lawgiver, Solon after about 594 BC. By then they had distinguished between public law enforced by penalties and fines due to the state, and private law through which wronged and aggrieved folk sought compensation for themselves. Elaborate rules of procedure had to be observed in both sorts of actions. In private suits about such matters as property rights, buying and selling, contracts, leases, loans, the first step was to appeal to the Forty who referred the case to an arbitrator, who could be any Greek citizen of 60 years, in the hope that he could find a solution which both parties would accept. If he failed, the case went before a court of judges, not less than 201, and in serious cases perhaps as many as 2,500 chosen by lot by the archons from the full panel of 6,000 judges. Pericles began the payment of 2 obols for each day's service as a judge soon after 461, Cleon increased the fee to 3 obols a day in 425/4 BC. The decision of these judges was final, and there was no appeal. The proceedings were complicated and thorough, based upon the written records produced by the arbitrator after his full enquiry and supplemented by the oral statement of their case by each party to the dispute. The large number of judges was to prevent them being bribed or intimidated.

Greek legal procedure was evidence of Greek trust in the good moral common sense of the average citizen and his ability to make just decisions. Its defects however were serious. Because judges were not in constant session and because skilled advocates were not allowed in court, there could be no legal profession. The Greeks were unable to build up a case-law or a system of jurisprudence resting firmly upon precedents, because each court, as a committee of the sovereign people, was a law to itself, although in giving its decisions it was of course bound to respect the laws of Athens which all young soldiers had to learn in their first two years military training. The decisions of one court could not bind another. The verdicts they gave were too liable to be swayed by passionate appeals to the prejudices and emotions of the judges. Such faults in procedure must not however obscure genuine Greek loyalty to the fundamental principle that justice must prevail. Their courts were a standing testimony to their faith in their laws as a guide to life and in the moral sense of their democratic citizens. Through the enforcement of laws and respect for justice they strove to find reasonable working arrangements to manage human relations in village, town and city and so created the study they called politics, the affairs of the *polis* or city-state.

The great discovery of the Greeks was The Rule of Law. So momentous is this phrase that it deserves to be printed in golden capitals over every law-court and every parliament building in the world. For we are still far from realizing in our own lives what the Greeks learned over two thousand years ago. 'The people should fight for the Law as if for their city-wall', said Heraclitus around the beginning of the 5th century BC.

'As a city we are the School of Hellas', Pericles told the Athenians in his great speech after the first year's fighting in the deadly Peloponnesian War in 431 BC, because, as he explained, 'we are called a democracy, for the administration is in the hands of the many and not of the few'. The men of Athens were all able to discuss public matters and to plan future action. Anyone who did not take part as 'a fair judge of public matters' was looked upon 'not as unambitious, but as useless'. They made citizens participate in public affairs so completely that every man during a normal lifetime was not only compelled to serve at need as soldier or sailor in the wars but also as one of the 200 to 500 or more judges in each of the ten courts of Athens, and as a member of the Assembly voting on laws and public business. He was also quite likely to become a member of the Council of 500, preparing laws, when he would have to serve on one or more of its committees. Men were chosen quite arbitrarily, by lot, for these duties and so they were also for actual administrative jobs on public boards dealing with the state's revenue and expenditure, leasing public contracts, inspecting weights, measures, public markets, ports and harbours. About one in six Athenian citizens at any one time were probably serving as Civil Servants and being paid for their work. They were the Government. In such active cooperation in public business, ability in leadership soon wins recognition, so the Athenians had good opportunities to select the ten best men when they had to elect their chief executive and military body, the Board of Ten Generals, who carried the responsibility, for a year, of the higher command.

There was nothing about public business that an intelligent active Athenian did not learn after a lifetime so spent. This was something very new in human history. Professor Sterling Dow of Harvard describes it as 'government of the people and for the people and also by the people to a far greater extent than is possible in the large representative democracies of the present'.

We may lament that Athens remained so tiny a community, for if there had been ten times the number of Athenians, they might well have invented representative government, and the world need not have waited two thousand years for the English parliament.

Yet there was much more to Athenian politics than such direct personal involvement implies, far-reaching in its effects as it was. Pericles summed it up for all time—'we are prevented from doing wrong by respect for the authorities and for the laws'.

A hundred years later, in his book *The Politics*, Aristotle, who had painstakingly studied the political and constitutional history of over 140 city-states, summed up the essence of political wisdom and denounced the dangers from demagogues, and the folly of listening to the strange delusion that human envy, greed and cupidity could be stifled and removed by preventing people having more wealth than their neighbours. He also restated the necessity for the Rule of Law, saying 'he who bids the law rule may be deemed to bid God and Reason alone rule, but he who bids man rule, adds an element of the beast, for desire is a wild beast, and passion perverts the mind of rulers, even when they are the best of men'. (Yet he accepted slavery as a matter of course.)

Roman Law: A Living Tradition

It was the Romans rather than the Greeks who created a practical legal tradition in Europe that is by no means dead and they were able to do so by creating a legal profession and by making legal decisions depend not merely upon laws but also upon the interpretation and application of the laws in particular special instances as each arose. By making legal judgments a matter of record and by learning from precedents, they allowed law and the forms of legal action to change and evolve almost continuously during the thousand years of their history. That is why Roman law still merits study quite apart from its specific laws and legal decisions, illuminating as many still are to those who seek to analyse and understand the complex nature of human motives and actions in a settled society today.

At first the Romans needed no other guide than ancestral custom which they tenaciously preserved with deep religious feeling so that law was a matter for the priests on the rare occasions when a higher authority than that of the heads of households was required to make decisions. Not until these old customary ways began to change with the struggle of the Orders did Roman law begin. It was a natural growth beginning with the famous Laws of the Twelve Tables of about 450 BC, drawn up, it was said, after a commission of enquiry had spent three years study in Greece. The fragments that alone remain of the Tables bear a pronounced Roman stamp, in which it is difficult to discern much Greek influence. At best the Twelve Tables did little more than state general rules. The duty of applying them was what mattered. Undertaken at first by the consuls, it was made the special task of a new official, a *praetor urbanus* after about 366 BC. The judgments given by these praetors in their 'edicts' year after year became of immense importance because many were recorded. Although there was a newly elected praetor each year and although he was not bound by what his predeccesors had done, nevertheless he was undoubtedly influenced, so that slowly a system of case law was built up which pushed the Twelve Tables into the background. By Cicero's day Roman boys no longer had to learn them by heart, as he said he had in his youth. About 242 BC a second praetor 'peregrinus' was annually elected to decide disputes in which foreigners were involved.

This Roman development of case-law made the administration of the law more flexible and kept it more in line with public opinion although it did not, as in Athens, decide disputes by a sort of public opinion poll. The praetor, and not a committee of the people or a set of jurors, gave rulings and the praetor was always a senator.

The second marked difference between Athenian and Roman legal practice was that a well-defined class of expert interpreters of the law grew up in Rome, the *juris consulti*, of whom men like Cicero and Hortensius were the most famous. They also were a natural development, for in olden times priests and senators were available to give legal advice. Professional advocates were not allowed to accept fees but their grateful clients found ways of rewarding them and the more successful earned handsome fortunes. Their weight of knowledge and experience influenced the praetors and the public on legal questions.

In civil lawsuits about such matters as guardianship, marriage, wills and succession, property, obligations and contracts the contending parties first appeared before a magistrate, usually the praetor. If he agreed that the case should be tried, he stated the law applicable to it and directed the parties to agree upon a judge chosen from the panel of senators, and later of knights (*equites*), and to abide by his verdict. If the issue was of great importance it might come before the large panel of 105 popularly elected

judges, three from each of the thirty-five tribes, the *centumviri*. There was no appeal from either of these courts until later in the Empire.

Criminal law covering more serious matters such as accusations of murder, poisoning, serious injuries, sacrilege, adultery, bribery and forgery was the province, after 149 BC, of special courts consisting of jurors selected by both parties from a panel of senators until 123 BC, thereafter, until Sulla, of knights only, and after 70 BC from both orders of society. Their number varied, 51 and 75 are not unusual. They were few enough to be bribed, as Cicero lamented when Clodius was found not guilty of his notorious sacrilege of 62 BC.

Soundly rooted in public esteem and broadly and securely based on a tremendous tradition, Roman law survived the fall of the Republic to reach its greatest development in the 2nd century AD. Its administration however began to change for the worse until, towards the end of the Empire, all judges were the Emperor's creatures just as laws all required his approval in accordance with the pernicious doctrine 'the Emperor's decisions shall have the force of law'. Roman law had come full circle since the earliest days of customary, tribal law, although such was the weight of traditional wisdom by which it had been enriched during the centuries of its free development that not even the worst and most arbitrary imperial tyrant could abolish it all. Rome's greatest living legacy to subsequent generations of men remains.

To this day, in many lands, every would-be lawyer still has to study the law of Rome. For it has fortunately been preserved in its essential outline. The *Institutes* of Gaius (around AD 161) and to some extent a fragment of the work of Ulpian (early 3rd century AD) already indicated its nature. Not long before the fall of the Roman Empire in the West, the Emperor Theodosius II, ruling the world from Constantinople, had a great compilation made of the laws and imperial decrees from the reign of Constantine in AD 313 to 438. To this Theodosian Code succeeded a supplement of New Constitutions down to 468 AD and then, after the fall of the Western Empire, a different and vaster enterprise was set on foot by the Emperor Justinian (AD 527–565). In a series of compilations, of which his *Digest* or *Pandects* was the foundation, he sought to collect and state the law, eliminating everything that was obsolete, inconsistent or repetitious. At the same time, 30 December AD 533, he issued a more elementary work for students. It was, he said, for 'young men desirous of the law' that 'we have ordered the composition in four books of these Institutes, destined to contain the elements of the whole science of law'.

This renowned work looked back to the unwritten laws of Sparta, to the written laws of Athens and to the whole series of laws and legal decisions transmitted down the centuries since the earliest political and legal activity of the Roman Republic, a continuous legal tradition of over one thousand years.

Justinian's *Digest*, his *Institutes*, a later *Code* and his supplementary decrees or *Novels* together formed that *Corpus Juris Civilis* upon which the study of law in Europe was subsequently based. From the 7th century the *Digest* was virtually lost to Western Europe until in the 11th century it was revived at the law-school of Bologna. Thereafter it steadily grew in influence, indeed it is said that no other book except the Bible has given rise to so much literature. Edited, re-edited, explained and commented upon, Justinian's record of the work of Roman judges and lawyers ensured that the authentic voice of Rome shaped and guided vast numbers of mankind in their daily relationships in business, family and neighbourly affairs. New generations of students arriving at the law-schools in Britain, France, Germany, Italy, the United States and elsewhere are still required to learn the rules of so large a part of civilized living first written in the language of Cicero. They do but follow in the footsteps of thousands of their famous predecessors, Erasmus, Bacon, Selden, Grotius, Marshall, Eldon and others. There can hardly be a better testimony to the idea that some cultural achievements of Greece and Rome, some elements of the everyday life of those ancient times, never die but survive as enduring values to guide and to illuminate mankind.

VII 'A CITY OF THE SCATTERED EARTH'

From Tiber's seven hills to world dominion

R.A.G. CARSON

'You brought the nations one great fatherland,
You raised the savage with your taming hand,
Broke him, but gave him laws to be his aid.
A City of the scattered Earth you made.'

RUTILIUS NAMATIANUS, 63–66

The world has never ceased to marvel

at the story of the rise and fall of Rome. In comparison with the best of the Greeks, for whom the life of the mind was the only life, the Romans, with their massive achievements in conquest, administration and law have made a more tangible impact on the West for over two thousand years.

Yet there was nothing about the few thousand farmers centred upon the seven small hills by the Tiber to warrant belief in their future greatness. They were well placed for defence—and for commerce on the route to the sea and the lowest north-south crossing of the river—and recent research suggests that by the beginning of the 5th century BC they were united into a township, to be consolidated under a century or more of Etruscan rule. But they were surrounded by enemies and invaded by Gauls from the north, and their survival was in doubt through a further two hundred and fifty years of bitter struggle.

They emerged victorious. By 250 BC they dominated the whole of Italy from the Po valley to the Straits of Messina, and such was their social cohesion, their 'piety' or devotion to hearth, home and national gods, so well had they organized and reorganized their army, that within another hundred years they had the whole of the Mediterranean world firmly within their power. But men and morals changed. Unscrupulous men struggled for personal position, prestige and security, and Rome's republican constitution went down to ruin.

The empire that replaced it was consolidated by the Julio-Claudian emperors, and after the turmoil of civil war in AD 61–69 was again solidly established by the Flavian line of emperors. It reached its widest extent by the middle of the 2nd century AD under the emperor Trajan. Then followed a time of troubles: plague, constant warfare, and feeble, vicious or incompetent emperors, as frontiers to the north and east burst into flames. Such was the tremendous dynamism of Rome that amazing recoveries rewarded the energy with which the legionaries, now recruited largely from provincials, fought back under the more resolute emperors.

At length the irresistible tide of internal change and invasion from without submerged all. But the idea of Empire lived on. Men still travelled along the countless roads that led to Rome, as they have done ever since, spellbound by magnetic memories of its mighty past.

'Of all the birds with which we are acquainted', said Pliny, 'the eagle is the most noble and most remarkable for its strength.' Fittingly therefore the eagle became an emblem of the might of Rome, after Marius in 104 BC surmounted the standards of the Roman legions with silver eagles. The loss of such a standard was regarded as a disaster so grave that it sometimes led to the disbandment of the legion. The onyx eagle opposite was engraved around AD 40, its setting much later.

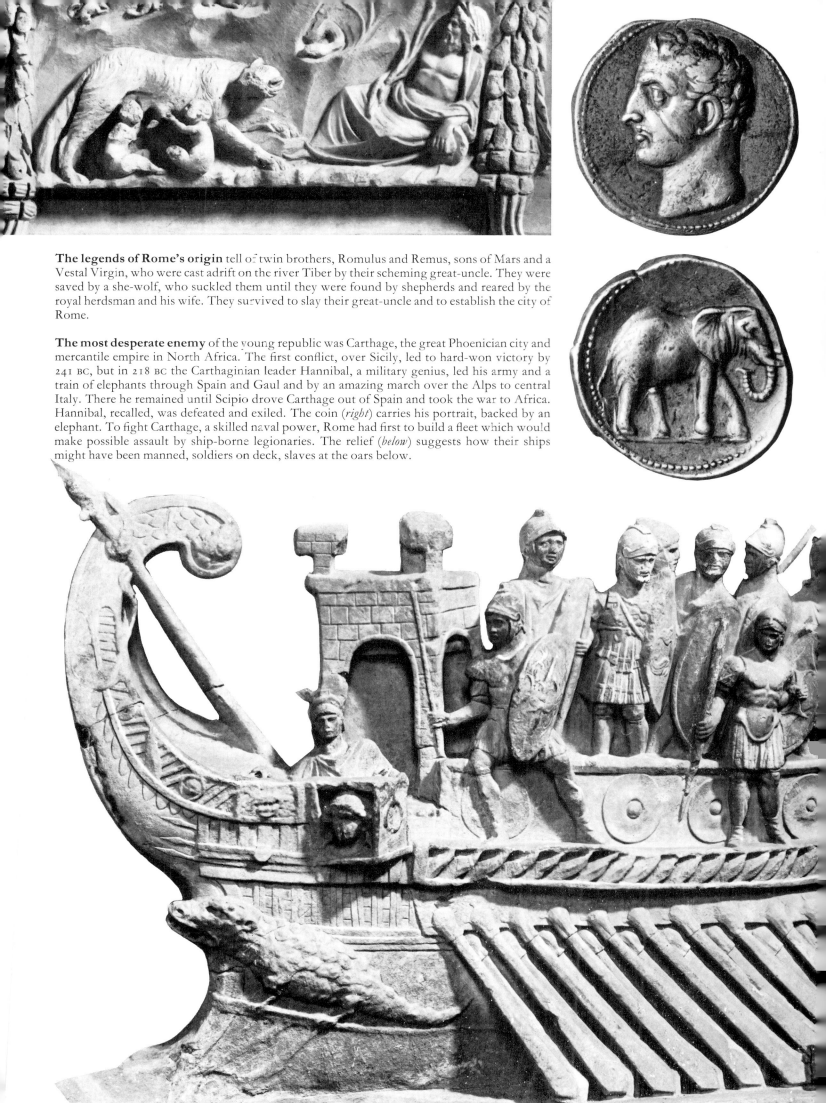

The legends of Rome's origin tell of twin brothers, Romulus and Remus, sons of Mars and a Vestal Virgin, who were cast adrift on the river Tiber by their scheming great-uncle. They were saved by a she-wolf, who suckled them until they were found by shepherds and reared by the royal herdsman and his wife. They survived to slay their great-uncle and to establish the city of Rome.

The most desperate enemy of the young republic was Carthage, the great Phoenician city and mercantile empire in North Africa. The first conflict, over Sicily, led to hard-won victory by 241 BC, but in 218 BC the Carthaginian leader Hannibal, a military genius, led his army and a train of elephants through Spain and Gaul and by an amazing march over the Alps to central Italy. There he remained until Scipio drove Carthage out of Spain and took the war to Africa. Hannibal, recalled, was defeated and exiled. The coin (*right*) carries his portrait, backed by an elephant. To fight Carthage, a skilled naval power, Rome had first to build a fleet which would make possible assault by ship-borne legionaries. The relief (*below*) suggests how their ships might have been manned, soldiers on deck, slaves at the oars below.

Ambitious men extended Rome's empire but threatened her liberty. **Marius** (*above left*), elected by the people, re-organized the army and defeated the Celts who threatened the north. **Sulla** (*centre*), an aristocrat, defeated Mithridates in the East, and, after a reign of terror at home, made himself effective dictator (*c. 86 BC*). **Pompey** (*below left*) subdued Spain after a long and bitter campaign, while Spartacus and his army of slaves and peasants lost their lives in rebellion and crucifixion at home. Put in control of Rome's might in the East, Pompey destroyed Mithridates and conquered Syria and Jerusalem. His army returned laden with the treasure of the East. Meanwhile, in the West a new and powerful figure had arisen: **Julius Caesar** (*above*). After striking a bargain with Pompey and Crassus for supreme power he was allotted Gaul, and from 58 to 51 BC he fought, invading Britain and defeating the Gallic leader Vercingetorix. Rivalry with Pompey, and the enmity of the conservative Senate, led to his return across the Rubicon and victory over Pompey in Greece. Whether Caesar intended to seize dictatorial power and abolish the Republic will never be known, for twenty-three senators conspired to assassinate him on the Ides of March, 44 BC. They were led by Brutus, on whose coin the cap of liberty and daggers summarize the purpose and the weapons of the conspirators (*below*).

Augustus was Caesar's great-nephew. His defeat of the conspirators at Philippi and of Antony at Actium in 31 BC began the one-man rule of the Roman world. Honoured in 27 BC with the title Augustus, he was given supreme command of all Roman armies—a steel fist beneath a velvet glove of civic dignity. **Tiberius** (*above right*) consolidated the empire—this coin records his help to cities of Asia Minor, destroyed by earthquake. Intrigue in his later years provoked a reign of terror. Died AD 37. **Gaius**, called 'Caligula' (little-boots), stepped up tyranny and campaigned on the Rhine, but his cruelties and probable insanity provoked the Praetorian Guard. Assassinated AD 41. **Claudius**, made emperor, despite the Senate, by the Praetorian Guard (the coin *below left* shows him in their camp) invaded Britain and brought Gauls into the Senate. Poisoned by his wife, AD 54. **Nero**, a spendthrift despotic playboy, murdered his mother, wife and many leading Romans, but considered himself an artist and sought a reputation as performer. His crimes provoked rebellion and his suicide, AD 68.

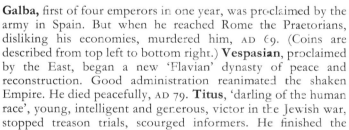

Galba, first of four emperors in one year, was proclaimed by the army in Spain. But when he reached Rome the Praetorians, disliking his economies, murdered him, AD 69. (Coins are described from top left to bottom right.) Vespasian, proclaimed by the East, began a new 'Flavian' dynasty of peace and reconstruction. Good administration reanimated the shaken Empire. He died peacefully, AD 79. Titus, 'darling of the human race', young, intelligent and generous, victor in the Jewish war, stopped treason trials, scourged informers. He finished the

Colosseum; died in AD 81. Domitian is shown distributing fruits at the Saecular Games of AD 88. But he was autocratic and cruel and renewed the treason trials. Assassinated AD 96. Nerva reformed the economy. The mules at grass commemorate his abolition of the tax which paid for the imperial post service, now to be a state charge. Died AD 98. Trajan, a military genius and statesman of Spanish descent, added a new province by the conquest of Dacia—victories recorded on the great column which still stands. Died AD 117.

The emperor Hadrian, subject of this magnificent portrait in stone (*right*), toured the outer fringes of the provincial empire, inspecting and consolidating the defences. In Britain in AD 121 or 122 he began a triple line of defence from the Tyne to the Solway (*above*). Forty-five miles of the eastern end was a stone wall, 10 feet thick and 15 feet high; 31 miles of the western end was of turf, later replaced by stone.

The price of empire was continual vigilance against the inroads of barbarians, who fought savagely and bravely. The incident in the Dacian wars (*below*, from the relief on Trajan's column) shows a Roman attack on a barbarian camp. Behind the heavy-wheeled wagons are their women and children, part of the victors' booty.

The **barbarian threat** continued to grow. In the relief *above*, the army of Marcus Aurelius is seen repelling the Marcomanni, invaders from across the Danube. The danger from the East is revealed by the Sassanian relief (*right*) in honour of the victories of King Sapor I. Beneath his horse's feet lies the young Gordian III. Kneeling in supplication is Philip the Arabian, while held by the wrist is Valerian.

The chaos of civil war followed Valerian's capture. Postumus, shown below on a fine coin from Gaul, established a separate empire reaching from Britain to Spain.

Rome was not yet to fall, for out of the chaos emerged Diocletian, whose reign was one of the last great milestones. He established the Tetrarchy, himself as Augustus of the East with Galerius as his Caesar, Maximian as Augustus of the West with Constantius Chlorus as Caesar. It was Constantius who destroyed the power of the independent empire of Britain and North Gaul, set up by Carausius—a victory celebrated by the medallion (*left*) on which he receives the surrender of London. Constantius also campaigned on the Rhine, Maximian in North Africa, Diocletian in Egypt, while the Persians' triumph over the Romans was reversed when their great general Narses was beaten by Galerius (AD 298). The Arch of Galerius at Salonica was built in his honour: reliefs on it (*below*) show him in battle cn a prancing horse, watched by Jupiter's eagle, and Diocletian and Maximian seated above the river gods of the Tigris and Euphrates. The reforming hand of Diocletian enabled the West to survive for two more centuries, and the East for another millennium.

From Tiber's seven hills
to world dominion

R. A. G. CARSON

THE WESTERN WORLD, aware that much of its civilization, culture, institutions and even its language are a direct heritage from Rome, pictures her as the all powerful mistress of the whole Mediterranean basin and controller of her great empire in the Near East and in Europe. This image of her greatness colours the general concept of the earlier history and perpetuates the belief that the mark of greatness has been on Rome from the very earliest times.

Until quite recently, practically the only account of early Roman history was that provided by Rome's own historians and poets. In this traditional account two strands are woven together. One is the legend of Romulus and Remus, twin-brothers who were cast into the Tiber by their wicked great-uncle, but who survived to be suckled by a she-wolf. Rome, according to this story, was founded by Romulus on 21 April 753 BC and was ruled by kings until the late 6th century BC, when they were driven out and the Republic established.

The other strand is the legend of Aeneas the son of Anchises and Venus, who after fleeing from Troy had settled in Italy, and married Lavinia, the daughter of King Latinus. Aeneas' entry into the story is of relatively late date. Terracotta statuettes of Aeneas and his father Anchises, dated to the 6th century from finds in Etruria, show that the story was known in this part of Italy, but the theme of a hero arriving from overseas, marrying the daughter of the native king and fighting his battles, can be paralleled elsewhere in Italy. The story in some form had become associated with Rome long before it was taken up and immortalized by Virgil in the Aeneid.

Archaeological investigation, however, presents a much less picturesque account of Rome's origins. The choice of the hills of Rome as a site for settlement was natural for a number of geographic considerations. The hills beside the Tiber are steep-sided and in the different climatic conditions then prevailing were well-wooded and were made even more defensible by the marshy land between them. The settlements, once made, lay on the route west to east from the sea and at the lowest point on the Tiber where the route from north to south could cross; all these advantages were to play an important part throughout the whole of Rome's history.

Excavations date the earliest settlement on the Palatine to the Early Iron Age about the middle of the 8th century BC. Wattle and daub of primitive huts have been found and their post-hole pattern suggests a shape akin to that reproduced by the cinerary hut urns found in tombs in various parts of Latium. The Esquiline and Quirinal seem also to have received settlers about the same time, probably Sabines, who buried their dead. These Oscan-speaking people from north of the river Anio had been driven by the more powerful Aequi to migrate into Roman territory. Gradually the villages on the seven hills created some kind of union, with which was connected the religious festival known as the Septimontium. The next stage in the 7th century is probably represented by the area enclosed by the Republican *pomerium* or ritual furrow. The most recent archaeological research suggests that the various villages were united into a township, *urbs*, with the Forum as its centre and with earthwork protection about 575 BC.

To return to legend. After Romulus came seven kings. The first united the Romans with the Sabines. The second organized the priestly colleges, adopted the twelve month calendar and founded the *regia* or palace. The third destroyed Alba Longa and built the *curia* where the senate met and the fourth extended Rome's sway as far as the mouth of the Tiber.

The last three kings, much more substantial historical figures, represent a new phase of Rome's history. However much late Roman nationalism has tried to disguise the fact, it is clear that Rome for a time came under the political and cultural domination of Etruria. Tradition dates the beginning of Etruscan rule to 616 under Tarquinius Priscus. He was succeeded by Servius Tullius, whom one account represents as a Latin, and to whom succeeded in turn the last Etruscan king, Tarquinius Superbus, who was expelled in 509. Recent research suggests that the period of Etruscan domination may have been considerably shorter and somewhat later, namely from 550 to about 475 BC. The city was then opened to Mediterranean commerce and was surrounded by a protective wall more than six miles long. This is not the so-called Servian wall, of which portions survive and which in fact dates from after the capture of Rome by the Gauls in 390. To this Etruscan period, too, belong the construction of great drainage works of which the Cloaca Maxima formed part and the buildings of the temple of Jupiter, or rather the triad of Jupiter, Juno and Minerva, on the Capitol. King Servius Tullius according to tradition organized an army of 20,000 men.

The Gods of Rome

Primitive Italian and Roman religion involved the worship and propitiation of the *numina* or spirits which presided over natural localities such as springs and groves, as well as over men's actions. Roman religion contained little of a real spiritual character; it did not set out to improve man morally but to avert danger and to protect from evil. The basis of religion was the family. The doorway of the house was in the charge of Janus, the supply cupboard of the Penates and the hearth fire of Vesta. The state religion was, in essence, the family religion writ large. In the temple of Vesta in the Forum burned the sacred fire of the state, tended by the Vestal Virgins, while the position of the head of the family was held initially in the state religion by the *rex*. The king's body of advisers were known as a college of *pontifices*, and after the expulsion of the kings this college and its chief, the *pontifex maximus*, gained in importance. For advice the *pontifices* had recourse to a college of augurs skilled in portents and divination.

The Roman pantheon consisted of quite a small number of native gods to whom many others were added from outside. Vesta has already been mentioned and parallel to the Janus of the family was Janus in the sacred gate of the Forum. Jupiter, king of the sky and god of lightning, widely worshipped in Italy, had a cult centre on Mons Latiaris in the Alban hills, dominating the whole Latin region. Under the Etruscan kingship Rome became important as a cult centre, and a temple to Jupiter was founded on the Capitol by Tarquinius Superbus. Some cults proper to other cities of Latium were shared in by Rome, such as that of Juno Sospita, whose original cult centre was at Lanuvium. Mars, too, the warlike deity, has, from the beginning, connections with Rome and takes his place as the mythical progenitor of Rome's founders. Under Servius Tullius the worship of Diana was transferred from Aricia in Latium to a temple on the Aventine, and Minerva, imported from Falerii in Etruria, formed, with Jupiter and Juno, a triad on the Capitol.

Of Greek gods, Apollo made the transfer to Rome without change of name as, in effect, did Hercules, but Demeter suffered a change to Ceres. The anthropomorphism of Greek religion was alien to the Latins, but in the course of the early centuries of the Republic the representation of the deities in human form became common, and the temples housing them numerous. Other gods were added by the peculiar custom of *evocatio* or summoning out. The gods of a besieged town were summoned by an incantatory formula to go over to Rome on the promise of more worthy temples and worship: it was probably in this way that Rome called Castor and Pollux at the battle of Lake Regillus against the Latins in 496 BC; it was certainly thus that Juno Regina of Veii was received in Rome in 386. Though the Forum had become the centre of cults derived from the original constituent villages on the hills, some of the ceremonies and feasts continued to be celebrated on the sites connected with the events whose memory they preserved, for instance the Palatine rituals of the Lupercalia on 15 February, and the Paulia on 21 April celebrating the traditional foundation of the city.

THE REPUBLIC
The Republic is Born
Rome's economic prosperity under the Etruscan kings had resulted in the creation of a two-class system—the rich and the poor, the patricians and the plebs. The patricians probably organized the revolution that led to the expulsion of the kings; in their place they elected two annual magistrates known as consuls, and the senate, consisting entirely of patricians, came to play an increasingly dominant rôle. The plebs, deprived of royal protection, were at first powerless. But since it was they who supplied the manpower and formed the army, they were gradually able to assert their rights—first the recognition of their own officers (the tribunes), then the publication of the Twelve Tables of the law and finally (in the 4th century) the right to stand for the consulship itself.

The newly independent Rome was surrounded by enemies. Other Etruscan cities made war against her including Clusium (Chiusi)—witness the story of Horatius and Lars Porsenna. But about 493 BC she negotiated an alliance with the other towns of Latium, and in time became the leader of the League. In the early 4th century Etruscan power was beset by Celtic invasions in the north; Rome seized the opportunity to capture Veii in 396. But a few years later the Romans were defeated by the Gauls at the Allia; the city itself was plundered and burned, but the Capitol, though besieged for some eight months, succeeded in holding out.

The Gallic invaders were said to have been bribed to depart. Rome's expansion in south Etruria and the Tiber valley then began anew. Colonies were set up at Sutrium and Nepete, and, after the Aequi and Volsci had been successfully subdued, at Sutricum and Setia. In 343 BC Capua and other Campanian towns appealed to her for aid against the Samnites. Rome won the war for them, but her control was now extended and strengthened. The result was a widespread rebellion by her former allies and dependencies, but she proved equal to that challenge too. Of the defeated allies some were incorporated into the Roman state while others were enrolled as allies again, but on a different footing. It was at this time that the Romans hit upon the principle of alliance in isolation which they later developed into an imperial system. Marriage and trade between the communities was prohibited: each had to co-operate independently with Rome alone. Some of

the newer dependencies were transformed into colonies such as Antium whose fleet was destroyed, the prows of the galleys, the *rostra*, being brought to Rome and set up on the speakers' platforms in the Forum.

The pacification and resettlement of the rebellious allies was completed by 328, and none too soon, for in the next year Rome was again at war with the tough highland Samnites. This was a much sterner and more protracted struggle which brought one severe Roman defeat and humiliation at the Caudine Forks in 321, but it ended with Rome's final victory in 290.

Roman control in Italy had still to meet one more challenge—that of the Greeks of Magna Graecia. By 280 BC Roman interests were beginning to clash with Greek. War broke out, and for the first time Rome was faced with trained forces the equal of her own. She was defeated at Heraclea and again at Asculum. But once again her resilience saved her. The army was re-created, the campaign renewed and soon after 275 Tarentum and the other Greek cities were forced to submit.

Masters of Italy
By about 269 Rome's rule ran from a line from the Arno to the Rubicon in the north to the toe of Italy. In two and a half centuries Rome had advanced from being only one small city state among many to a position of mastery of virtually the whole peninsula. By making the towns of many of their allies into Roman cities, by establishing a network of colonies of citizens, and by securing other allies by rights of *connubium* and *commercium* the Romans won over more and more citizens who looked to Rome as their centre and whose loyalty to Rome was to stand the test of Hannibal's invasion of Italy towards the end of the century.

Roman dominion was maintained by successful political expedients but it was the Roman army that gained mastery of Italy and later of a much wider realm. Tradition has it that the original Roman army consisted of three regiments, each of a thousand men and commanded each by its *tribunus militum*. Under the reorganization attributed to Servius Tullus five classes of citizens, assessed on a property qualification, supplied each so many centuries of soldiers, the wealthiest supplying most on the principle that they could best equip and maintain themselves. Four legions were thus formed, the principal formation in action being a phalanx, six ranks of five hundred. The richest class provided the centuries of cavalry.

Rome's territorial expansion brought changes in organization, armament and deployment. The legion with a nominal strength of 4,200 comprised 1,200 *velites*—light armed troops—1,200 *hastati* and 1,200 *principes* armed with *pila* or javelins for throwing and a sword for close-quarter fighting, and finally the *triarii* armed with *hasta* or thrusting spear. The legion was divided into smaller, more manoeuvreable units called maniples. To each legion was attached ten squadrons of cavalry, each of 30 men. By the late 5th century help towards the equipment of the soldier was being supplied but the basis of Roman military power continued to be the citizen soldier right down to the 1st century. By that time the situation of a small class of wealthy citizens legally bound to serve but reluctant to do so, and a large body of men anxious to serve but excluded by the property qualification made a change in the basis of recruitment necessary.

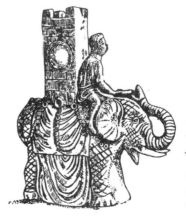

Terracotta model of a war-elephant. African elephants were in ancient times to be found in the Atlas mountains and were trained for battle by the Carthaginians. When Hannibal set out for Italy he is said to have had 37 elephants in his train. Several of them were lost in the passage of the Alps.

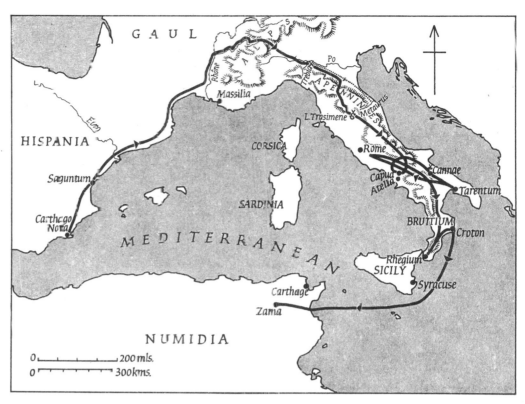

Hannibal's route during the Second Punic War. He set out from Carthago Nova in the summer of 218 BC, avoided a Roman force that had landed at Massilia, and crossed the Alps by a route that is still a matter of controversy. The first clash with the Romans, in which Hannibal cleverly ambushed his enemy, took place on the Trebia; during the next two years he inflicted two more crushing defeats at Lake Trasimene and Cannae. But lacking resources for a siege he failed to take Rome, and although a few cities came over to his side the general rising of Rome's allies for which he hoped did not materialize. In 207 a relief force under his brother Hasdrubal was annihilated at the river Metaurus. In 204 Scipio carried the war to Carthage and Hannibal had to leave Italy to defend his own home. The final battle was fought at Zama in 202 BC; it was Hannibal's first and last defeat.

The Duel with Carthage: Hannibal

The geographical configuration of Italy made it natural for the Romans to look westwards rather than eastwards, but the west of the Mediterranean basin was still firmly under the control of Carthage, the rich Phoenician city in North Africa which in the past three centuries had built up a great mercantile empire. Rome's expansion had brought her in south Italy to the Straits of Messina which alone now separated her from the nearest areas of Carthaginian influence in Sicily. In the centuries-old struggle the Greek cities in Sicily had succeeded in keeping Carthage out of eastern Sicily but in 265 BC the Mamertines, Campanian mercenaries, who had been used by Pyrrhus and had subsequently occupied Messina, when attacked by Hiero II of Syracuse allowed Carthage to install a garrison. The Mamertines also appealed to Rome for alliance and help, and Rome, answering the appeal with the despatch of a force of two legions, began that enmity which was to last for over a century and to give her control of the Western Mediterranean.

Rome, though her legions were more than a match for the Carthaginian mercenary armies in Sicily, had now to adapt herself to naval warfare. By building up a fleet and introducing new tactics involving the use of the *corvus* or 'crow', a kind of grapnel boarding-bridge which made assault by the ship-borne legionaries possible, the Romans gained an initial success at Mylae in 260 BC. But good fortune at sea did not continue to follow them; an attempted invasion of Africa ended in disaster, and several fleets were destroyed by storms, while on land in Sicily Carthaginian resistance under Hamilcar Barca prolonged the struggle. When both sides were nearing exhaustion, Rome, in a last effort, equipped a new fleet and defeated Carthage at the Aegates Islands in 241. This finally secured command of the seas and the war was ended with the cession of Sicily to Rome. In 239 Rome, invited by Carthaginian mercenaries, also took Sardinia and Corsica. Hiero II of Syracuse who had become Rome's ally in the course of war was left in control of western Sicily. In 227 the Romans elected two extra praetors who, next to the consuls, had more power than any other magistrate, one to take charge of eastern Sicily, the other of Sardinia and Corsica.

Under the energetic leadership successively of Hamilcar, Hasdrubal and finally Hannibal, Hamilcar's son, whom he taught to vow eternal hatred of Rome, the new Carthaginian empire was extended up the eastern coast of Spain. Prompted by her old ally, Massilia, anxious at the prospect of closer Carthaginian competition, Rome in 226 made an alliance with Saguntum, and an agreement was reached fixing the river Ebro as the limit of Carthaginian expansion. Saguntum, though lying south of the Ebro, refused to submit to Carthaginian control when attacked by Hannibal in 219 BC, and its capture provided a pretext, perhaps not unwelcome to Rome and obviously sought by Hannibal, for a new war.

In 218, before the Romans were able to launch attacks on Spain and Africa by sea, Hannibal seized the initiative. His amazing march with his train of elephants through south Gaul and over the Alps by a route still much disputed is an epic story that has always seized mankind's historical imagination. He carried the war to the enemy with great effect, overcoming the Romans defending the Trebia river defence line and annihilating another Roman army at Lake Trasimene in the same year. Fabius, now in command of the Romans, earned the title *Cunctator* by his famous delaying tactics which bought time for reorganization, but not a sufficiency of time, as the next disastrous defeat of Rome at Cannae in 216 proved. Hannibal moved south; but although he

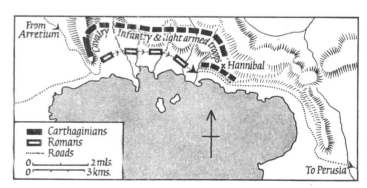

The battle of Lake Trasimene was fought where the road from Cortona to Perusia (Perugia) skirts the edge of the lake. The Roman army, under Flaminius, was following Hannibal, who was marching south towards Rome. During the night Hannibal drew his troops off the road and stationed them on the semi-circle of hills overlooking the lake. In the morning, as the mist lay thick in the lowlands, but the hills were clear enough for Hannibal's soldiers to signal to each other, Flaminius walked into the trap. As soon as the whole army—30,000 men—had entered the valley the Carthaginians attacked. There was no time to form into order of battle, nor was the issue in doubt. Flaminius himself and half the Roman force were either slaughtered on the spot or driven into the lake and drowned.

seemed to have shattered Roman defences, their Latin allies and most of the Greek cities remained loyal, though some cities, such as Capua and Atella, went over to him, as did Syracuse. Syracuse was retaken in 212, and the Roman siege of Capua was not abandoned despite Hannibal's dramatic but fruitless march on Rome. The Romans, hanging on grimly, refused to despair and in 207 BC at the Metaurus river managed to defeat Hasdrubal, Hannibal's brother, bringing reinforcements from Spain.

It was the turning point of the war. In Spain itself Publius Cornelius Scipio captured Carthago Nova and in 206 drove the Carthaginians completely out of Spain. In the next year he assembled an invasion force in Sicily and in 204 he carried the war to Africa. With assistance from Masinissa, the King of Numidia, Scipio twice defeated Carthaginian forces, and Hannibal was at last recalled from Italy, where, in Bruttium, he had stood at bay while Rome recovered her control of the peninsula. At Zama in 202 Scipio was victorious. It was the final battle. Carthage retained her territory but was disarmed and agreed to pay a vast indemnity of 10,000 talents.

Hannibal was expelled in 195 and, still trying to organize opposition to Rome, died in Bithynia (Asia Minor) in 183; but Rome's suspicions of Carthage were not laid to rest. Romans of the old school, such as the vigorous old Censor Cato, could not forget or forgive. He ended all his many speeches shouting the slogan *Carthago est delenda*—Carthage must be destroyed. Carthage endured for long the encroachments of Rome's ally, Masinissa, but in desperation at last in 151 took up arms against him although it involved a breach of the peace treaty with Rome. The Romans had the pretext for war many of them wanted. This third war was relatively short. Siege was laid to Carthage in 149 but it was not till 146, after enduring incredible sufferings, that the Carthaginians were finally overcome by assault, when the walls of Carthage were pulled down and their city was razed to the ground.

Rome was the ultimate victor in a struggle which had begun over a century earlier, and the lands which Carthage had possessed were formed into the Roman province of Africa. Roman dominion in the West was now beginning to take shape: after the second Punic War the whole of Sicily had been united into one province and from 197 BC Spain was organized into the two provinces of Hispania Ulterior and Hispania Citerior—Further and Nearer Spain. Many years were required for the final pacification of Spain and it was not until the capture of Numantia in 133 BC that the country was finally settled by Scipio Africanus the younger.

The Kingdoms in the East

From the empire of Alexander the Great had emerged the three great Hellenistic kingdoms of Egypt, Syria and Macedon. Shortly after the Romans had come forward as a Mediterranean power by successfully resisting Pyrrhus, the Roman senate had concluded commercial arrangements with Egypt and maintained friendly relations. With the other two great powers Rome's relations were to follow a different pattern. During the second Punic War, Philip V of Macedon's alliance with Hannibal and his threatened invasion of Italy brought him into war with Rome, allied with other Greek cities. In 197, after Zama, Philip was routed by Flamininus at Cynoscephalae (South Thessaly in Greece) and forced to submit.

His defeat was the signal for his eastern neighbour, Antiochus of Syria, to step in. When the Roman troops withdrew from Greece in 194 the Syrians attempted to take their place, but the Romans returned and under Acilius Glabrio beat them at Thermopylae in 191. Pressing their advantage and aided by Rhodes and Pergamum, the Romans crossed the Dardanelles in 190, defeated Antiochus at Magnesia (in Lydia) and established a general protectorate in Asia Minor. In 148, after further unrest, Macedonia became a Roman province. No separate province of Greece was set up but a general control over the whole country was exercised by the governor of Macedonia.

In Asia, also, no formal provincial organization was carried out immediately, but by the middle of the century the kings of Syria were kings by permission of Rome, and Rome's suzerainty was acknowledged by Egypt. Rome saw her way also in the course of the century to depressing the status of her powerful allies, Rhodes and Pergamum, and finally in 133 BC Attalus III on his death bequeathed his kingdom of Pergamum to the Roman people. It was then that the Roman province of 'Asia' was formed.

Crisis at Home: the Gracchan Revolution

In very little more than a century Rome had advanced from the position of mistress of Italy to that of controller of practically the whole of the Mediterranean basin, and success came much too quickly for the health of the Roman and Italian economy, or for that of the newly won provinces. The taxation exacted by Rome was perhaps no heavier than that levied by the former rulers, but now much of this revenue found its way to Rome and not back into the local economy as it used to do. In Italy native industry and agriculture were dislocated as a result of the sudden inflow of booty, slaves and imports from the provinces: the wealthy—officials, contractors or tax-farmers—who were able to batten on Rome's new subjects invested their winnings in land in Italy, often buying out the small farmers, many of whom were returned soldiers with small skill and less interest in farming. The agricultural economy of small peasant-owned farms began to give way to great estates cultivated by slave labour: the displaced peasantry flocked to Rome and other cities to form a growing urban proletariat for which no adequate urban industry or other means of support could be found.

The old struggle between patricians and plebeians had been over the question of who made laws and ruled the Republic, and it ended when the magistracies, especially the consulship, had been thrown open to all citizens. In time a new upper class developed, for the old patrician families were joined by others, formerly plebeians who had held the consulship, and their descendants. Together they became an oligarchy from whose ranks the senate and the magistrates were chosen. Throughout most of the period of Rome's expansion overseas it was the senate which exercised control and to the senate the magistrates were subservient. There was, however, no constitutional basis for this arrangement, and by the middle of the 2nd century the senate's power began to be eroded. The magistrates in Rome could be controlled and influenced by the senate but the proconsuls abroad—the generals and governors with armies loyal in the first place to them—were much more independent. In the changed economic circumstances, in which the upper class grew steadily more wealthy while poverty increased amongst a now largely landless proletariat, the people were less and less ready to accept senatorial government without questioning.

In 133, the year which saw the creation of the latest and greatest province in the East, Asia, the first attempt to rebuild the class of free citizen smallholders was begun by Tiberius Gracchus, a tribune of the plebs. To find land for them required the resumption of control by the state of common land, much of which was now included in the large estates of wealthy landowners, and its redistribution. When the senate, the organ of the wealthy, opposed his policy, Tiberius, remembering that the people in their popular assembly were supposed to be sovereign although it was a long while since they had been able to prove it, appealed to them over the heads of the senators. They readily agreed to his proposals. The exasperated landowners whose estates were being reduced by the Land Commission which Tiberius created to divide up her surplus acres for the benefit of the landless Romans broke out in violent rioting in which Tiberius was murdered.

Ten years afterwards his brother Gaius who was elected a tribune in 123 took up the cause. More determined than his mild mannered brother, Gaius had more thorough-going plans for reform. He continued his brother's scheme for 'sharing the wealth' in land. He tackled unemployment by settling colonies both in Italy and overseas. To keep the cost of living as low and as steady as possible, he began state-trading in wheat so as to sell it at a low cost price to the really needy. His land-owning opponents grew more vicious and they seized their opportunity when Gaius Gracchus took the very just but unpopular step of proposing to extend the franchise to Rome's Latin allies. It proved fatal to his chances of being re-elected to the tribunate. No longer protected by his inviolable position in the state it was easy for his enemies to attack him. Faced by an armed mob, Gracchus fled and committed suicide.

So ended the Gracchan Revolution; it had done something but not enough to help the landless poor who were every year more numerous and more discontented. The attempted agrarian reforms of the Gracchi achieved little of real worth, but the dissension between *optimates*, the conservative senatorial party and *populares*, the party of those eager for reforms which would break the senatorial monopoly of political power, had become more acute and the political means to be used by the latter to attack the senate had been made plain.

Much else had suffered a change besides things economic and political. Roman conservatism had for long preserved the strict moral discipline maintained by the *pater familias*, but in the centuries which transformed Rome from a city-state to a world power the standards of private morals and public religion altered. Under the influence of slaves and descendants of slaves, daily more numerous, native cults and gods were steadily replaced by cults imported from abroad. The close contact with Greece in the second century intensified the hellenizing of religion seen in the spread of anthropomorphic cult statues, of Greek-style temples and the continued import of foreign cults. Thus it was that the cults of Cybele, the great Mother Goddess from Asia Minor, of the Egyptian goddess Isis and of Dionysus flourished and grew.

Violence and Terror: the Struggle for Power Continues

The blood bath which had extinguished Gaius Gracchus and some three thousand of his supporters cowed the popular party. It was some ten years before anyone again tried conclusions with the senatorial ascendancy. In North Africa corrupt and inefficient commanders sent by the senate had failed dismally against Jugurtha of Numidia who had risen in revolt and had achieved more by bribing his opponents than by fighting them. In 109 the popular party, despite senatorial opposition, elected Gaius Marius as consul and commander. He was an experienced officer, but a 'new man' without distinguished or noble ancestors. In 104 Marius returned victorious to Rome bringing Jugurtha to be strangled after parading him through the streets and Forum. He next had to set out on a more formidable task. The Cimbri and Teutones, whose ancestors had sacked and burned Rome, were threatening north Italy. Before taking the field, he first reorganized the Roman army. Old divisions based upon wealth and class were abolished. The legions were streamlined, given uniform equipment at state expense, and paid. Conscription was given up and recruits were attracted to the army as a career by the pay and prospects of booty. With his new model army Marius faced and annihilated the Teutones in 102 BC and the Cimbri in 101 BC.

Rome could breathe again and in 100 BC Marius was for the sixth time triumphantly and gratefully re-elected consul. Then things went wrong. Two would-be reformers, Saturninus and Glaucia with whom Marius was first allied, provoked riots which Marius had to suppress. He thus became unpopular with both sides.

In 90 BC the cause of reform was again taken up by Drusus, another aristocratic tribune of the plebs. Like Gaius Gracchus, he advocated, as well as an agrarian and law reform, the extension of the Roman franchise to Rome's Italian allies, who because they had to fight and die for Rome, resolved to win the privileges of Roman citizens. The assassination of Drusus, which seemed once again to doom their cause, was the signal for the outbreak of the disastrous Social War, the war between Rome and her allies. After severe defeats and very heavy losses Rome managed to survive the bitterly fought campaign only by conceding the grant of citizenship to all Italians who would give up the fight.

Meantime in the East the denial of justice and fair treatment by Roman governors and business men had roused such bitter hatred that when Mithridates VI (the Great) of Pontus invaded Asia, after a fierce massacre of Italians and Romans, a determined effort was made to shake off the yoke of Roman tyranny.

Amongst the generals in the Social War, Lucius Cornelius Sulla, an aristocrat, had specially distinguished himself. As consul for the year, the task of defeating Mithridates was legally assigned to him by the senate. The popular party, by a demagogic manoeuvre,

A high-priest of Cybele in full vestments, with medallion-studded wreath and a scapular banging round his neck in the form of a tiny shrine with an image of Attis. In his right hand he holds the pomegranate (symbol of life), in his left a dish of fruit and phallic pine-cone (symbol of fertility). Beside him are the magic rattle, drum, flute, cymbals and whip for self-flagellation.

then got a vote from the people to give the command to Marius. Sulla, deserted by his officers, at once marched his legions on Rome. For the first time a Roman consul heading his legions entered Rome as though he had conquered the city. Marius barely escaped, and Sulla after quickly trying to improvise a government likely to support him hurried off to deal with Mithridates (87 BC).

Marius promptly returned. The Consul Cinna broke his oath to Sulla, allowing Marius and his gang to start massacring very many of Sulla's supporters. Early in 86 BC Marius fortunately died. At Rome Cinna and the Marian party tried to consolidate their command of the Republic. In the East, Sulla, though disowned by the government in Rome, defeated Mithridates, concluded a peace with him and celebrated a triumph in Athens in 84 BC. Backed by his enthusiastic troops who were laden with loot, he crossed to Italy in the following year when, utterly ruthless, he cut the Marians and their allies to pieces under the very walls of Rome.

There followed another, even worse, reign of terror and proscriptions. Sulla made himself dictator, an emergency but constitutional office placing power in the hands of one man. He then reshaped the government on completely conservative lines depriving tribunes of much of their power to impede senatorial action and he reduced the consuls to the position of servants of the senate. While he lived everyone was too scared to oppose his one man rule. He resigned the dictatorship and retired in 79. His death in 78 released once more the political ambitions and disorder which he had so violently restrained.

In all the years of turmoil since Tiberius Gracchus began his agitation in 133 very little of any consequence had been done to remedy the evils that had driven him to martyrdom. New evils had developed. The executive power of the consuls may have been curtailed, but Rome's subject peoples were bled white in the absence of any effective check on the rapacity of the provincial commanders and governors, and, what was worse, upon the business men who collected provincial taxes. A yet more sinister and fatal change resulted from the replacement of a citizen army by a regular army. The soldiery began to give their loyalty to their general to whom they looked for easy wars and great booty instead of to the state as of old. No other single thing did more to bedevil the history of the Republic and much of that of the Empire.

The whole area of this map, except for Europe north of the Danube, was at one time part of the Roman Empire. All place names mentioned

Inset

Brescia · Verona · Treviso · Aquileia
Patavium
Mantua
Ferrara · Pola
Mutina
Bologna
Marzabotto · *Rubicon* · Ravenna
Luca · Pistoria
TUSCANY · Sarsina · Pisaurum · Fano
UMBRIA
Metaurus · Split
ETRURIA
L. Trasimene · Asisium
Clusium · Hispellum
Asculum
Cosa · Reate · Interamna
Fescennium · Amiternum
Sutrium · Falerii
Veii · Nepete · Sulmo
Tiber · *Anio*
Rome · Tivoli · Tusculum
Ostia · Alba Longa · Monte
Lavinium · LATIUM · Cassino
Aricia · Setia · SAMNIUM
Antium · Arpinium
Lanuvium · Aquinum · Caudine
Terracina · Formiae · CAMPANIA · Forks · Cannae
Suessa · Capua · Venusia
Aurunca · Naples · Nola
Cumae · Puteoli · Misenum · Salerno
Herculaneum · Pompeii · Paestum
Atella · LUCANIA · Heraclea
Thurii

Olbia
Panticapaeum
TAURIS

DACIA
Tomi
Danube · Abrittus · BLACK SEA · PONTUS
Nish
MOESIA
Golden Horn
Bosphorus
Adrianople
THRACE
Philippi · Constantinople
EDONIA · Chalcedon BITHYNIA
Salonica · Sea of Marmara · ARMENIA
Olynthus · Mt. Athos · Nicaea
THESSALY · Portus · Ankara · CAPPADOCIA · COMMAGENE · Selinus
Dardanelles · Hellespont · GALATIA · ASSYRIA · PERSIA
Cynoscephalae · Troy · Edessa
Pharsalus · Mytilene · Pergamum · Carrhae
Thermopylae · LYDIA · MESOPOTAMIA
Chios · Smyrna · *Maeander* · PARTHIA
Eleusis · IONIA · Tralles · CILICIA
Corinth · Athens · Ephesus · Magnesia · Alahan · Tarsus · Antioch · *Euphrates* · Dura Europus
Bassae · Priene · Miletus · PAMPHYLIA · Ctesiphon
Delos · Aspendus · Side · ISAURIA · *Tigris*
Naxos · Perge
Cos
Rhodes · Emesa · Palmyra
Pyla
Crete · Cyprus
SYRIA
LEBANON · Baalbek
Damascus
A · N
PHOENICIA
PALESTINE · Jerusalem
Jordan · Bethlehem
Cyrene
Alexandria
Nile

n the texts are included; Latin spellings are used in general, but Greek and modern forms are introduced where suitable to the context.

Roman skills in government and administration were no longer what they had been in the old heroic days. From the death of Sulla in 78 until the establishment of the principate by Augustus in 31, a succession of ambitious men shamelessly exploited the miserable subject peoples in the Empire which Republican armies had won.

Powerful and Ambitious Men: Pompey and Caesar

In 77 Cnaeus Pompey, who for his defeat of the Marians in Africa had been greeted by Sulla with the title Magnus—the Great—and accorded a triumph, was despatched to Spain with proconsular authority against Sertorius, who was still holding Spain for the Marian party. A long-drawn-out, difficult and bitter campaign was required to subdue Spain, and even after the murder of Sertorius in 73 Pompey spent a further two years in pacifying the province. Italy itself endured nameless horrors when Spartacus, a slave who had escaped from a gladiators' school, gathered round him an army of runaway slaves and dispossessed peasants. With the fierce courage of desperation, for two years they roamed over the country looting and burning and slaughtering the Roman legions sent against them until they were finally defeated by Crassus. Spartacus and thousands of his followers were fortunate in meeting death on the battlefield instead of by the slow agony of crucifixion to which all the six thousand survivors were subjected.

Pompey and Crassus, two victorious and rival commanders, with their troops, then encamped outside the walls of Rome. They had no difficulty in being illegally elected consuls for the year 70, and they used their position to curry popular favour. The privileges and prerogatives of the tribunes were restored, and censors were appointed to remove from the lists Sulla's partisans who packed the senate. The conservative brakes which Sulla had tried to fasten on the Republic were removed. Pompey's reward, however, did not materialize immediately. It was not until 67 that he was given command against the Cilician pirates who had virtually destroyed all sea trade in the eastern Mediterranean, even raiding Rome's own sea port at Ostia. For all-out war against them, Pompey was given complete authority for three years over all Roman officials in the provinces. In 66 Lucullus was told to hand over to him the command in the war against Mithridates. Pompey was therefore in supreme control of the whole of Rome's might in the East. It did not take him long to finish off the pirates. Their ships were captured, and their strongholds, dockyards and arsenals in Cilicia were destroyed. Mithridates retreated before Pompey, but was brought to battle in Lesser Armenia and defeated. Pompey did not pursue Mithridates but turned his forces against Tigranes of Armenia who had made himself also king of Syria. Tigranes surrendered Syria which became a Roman province and Pompey advanced southward besieging and capturing Jerusalem. Mithridates, surrounded in Panticapaeum, committed suicide in 63 BC, and Pompey, accepting the submission of Mithridates' son Pharnaces, began his triumphant return to Rome. He and his army had looted the treasures of the East and they brought back fabulous wealth, most of which they kept.

Pompey's absence left a vacuum of political power at Rome and made ambitious men very uneasy. Julius Caesar, as the nephew of Marius and son-in-law of Cinna, possessed a ready-made claim to the leadership of the popular party. By his agitation against the creators of the Sullan terror and on behalf of the victims of the proscriptions, as well as by the lavish games which he gave when he held the office of aedile, he worked hard to acquire popularity. Crassus, the only obvious rival to Pompey, could not rest until he too had achieved a position in the Republic as splendid as that which had been granted to Pompey. He used his vast wealth to win likely supporters and Caesar was one of them. The conspiracy of Catiline, a bankrupt noble, who had twice failed in the consular elections, and now attempted to harness to the cause of a new revolution all the discontented elements—the Sullan veterans, the dispossessed peasants and runaway slaves—brought discredit on the popular party which was automatically identified with any radical movement. Crassus and Caesar seemed implicated because Catiline had been one of their nominees for the consulship in 63. Cicero beat him in the election.

A warrior of Gaul, with his characteristic large shield. It was oval or hexagonal and made of wood with a big central boss of metal—the 'umbo'. This figure, probably of a chief, dates from about 40 years after Caesar's time. He wears a coat of mail and a torque (perhaps of gold) round his neck.

It was in the crisis of Catiline's conspiracy that Cicero, already famous as orator and advocate, reached his greatest heights of popularity and honour as a statesman. His prompt and energetic action unmasked the conspirators and in the following year a Roman army crushed Catiline's forces. Cicero thought that he could cure Rome's political problems if he could only persuade the senatorial nobles of Rome and the equestrian order, representing the great middle-class of Italy, to agree to work together. He was all for the senate as the governing body, but a senate representative not of one small privileged class, but of the whole community. The realization of Cicero's political ideal of a *concordia ordinum* had little chance of success in a world which contained such powerful and ambitious men as Pompey and Caesar.

When Pompey returned from the East in 62 he dismissed his army, confidently expecting grateful approval for all that he had done and arranged in Asia, and also allotments of land for his troops. The senatorial party foolishly made difficulties about both. Pompey, now powerless, was very disgruntled. When Caesar in 60 returned from Spain, where he had held a propraetorship, he was a candidate for the consulship. He struck a bargain with Pompey and Crassus, for their support. This was the celebrated First Triumvirate, the rule of Rome by three men determined to get their own way. Elected consul for 59 BC Caesar saw to it that Pompey got satisfaction.

Caesar secured the military command for five years of Cisalpine and Transalpine Gaul, as well as Illyricum, and for ten years after 59 BC he was up to his neck in difficulties endeavouring to subdue the Gauls. At last he succeeded in bringing the whole of Gaul under Roman rule. Caesar led the first Roman crossing of the Rhine and the first Roman reconnaissance in force of Britain. As soon as he had left Rome in 58, the tribune Clodius, who was in his pay, had a law made that anyone guilty of putting a Roman citizen to death without trial by the people should be outlawed. This was Caesar's way of teaching Cicero not to resist him, for Cicero had executed some of Catiline's supporters without a trial, so he was forced into exile. The riots and disorders caused by Clodius brought a reaction and Cicero was allowed to return in 57. His renewed attempts to build up a middle party ran counter to the ambitions of the coalition or Triumvirate which met again at Luca in 56, and he was powerless to restore the old political freedom of action.

In the next year Caesar's command in Gaul was renewed for five years, while Spain was assigned to Pompey and Syria to Crassus. Pompey preferred to remain in Rome and to send lieutenants to Spain. Crassus went to his death in Persia where mounted archers shot his army to pieces at the battle of Carrhae (53 BC), when several legionary standards were captured by the Parthians. The rivalry between Pompey and Caesar then became more pronounced. As the man upon whom the stability of Rome depended, Pompey found his position more and more identified with that of the conservative senatorial party which was anxious to end Caesar's command. They tried to insist that Caesar could not stand for election to the consulship without appearing in person in Rome, that is, without his army. Caesar would agree only if Pompey likewise resigned his command. Negotiations to obtain a compromise were fruitless, and when Caesar was required by the senate to disband his legions, he immediately crossed the Rubicon, the frontier between his province and metropolitan Italy, and marched on Rome with only one legion. Pompey, who had not made proper preparations to meet him, managed to escape to Greece, in the hope of calling on the resources of the East, where his triumphs had been obtained.

Caesar first mastered Italy, secured the control of Pompey's provinces of Spain and then crossed to Greece in 48. At Pharsalia he defeated Pompey who fled to Egypt where he was murdered. Pursuing him there, Caesar was delayed in 47 BC by his affair with Cleopatra VII, a ravishingly beautiful girl of 19 of the royal house of the Ptolemies. Caesar was 53. Africa, still held for the senatorial party by Cato, was next gained by Caesar's victory at Thapsus in 46, and the final battle of the Civil War was fought at Munda in Spain where Pompey's sons had raised a fresh army, only to suffer defeat. Caesar had been appointed dictator for life and in early 44 he was granted the right to have his portrait on Roman coins, the first occasion that this privilege had been accorded to a living Roman.

Although master of Italy, Caesar had little time to work out a new deal for Rome. The problems were appalling in the chaos of long drawn out political uncertainty and of bitter Civil War. He had first to consolidate his grip over the Republic and its Empire. All authority was centred in him; the military commanders and provincial governors were his legates. Yet the façade of the old constitution of senate and magistrates was still maintained. At the festival of the Lupercalia on 15 February 44 BC, Caesar ostentatiously refused the kingly diadem offered by Mark Antony but he was a king in all but name, as Cicero was calling him in private letters to his friends. Whatever plans he may have had for the reorganization of the Roman state, they will never be known, for twenty three senators led by Brutus and Cassius conspired together secretly and assassinated him on the Ides of March of 44 BC.

Antony, Cleopatra and Octavian

In the alarm and confusion which followed Caesar's death Cicero made a last attempt to harness the goodwill of all parties to achieve a restoration of republican government, but the animosities and the jealousy about filling the position left vacant by Caesar doomed his efforts. Initially the most powerful contender was Mark Antony, who had the support of Caesar's veterans but he met unexpected opposition from Octavian, Caesar's greatnephew and heir. The third contender was Lepidus, Caesar's master of horse, who had succeeded to the office of *pontifex maximus* or high priest left vacant by Caesar's death. Lepidus took over the provinces of Spain and Gaul, but when Antony attempted to take over Cisalpine Gaul, assigned to him by the senate, he was resisted by Decimus Brutus, ringleader of Caesar's assassins. The senate now declared Antony a public enemy and gave the command against him to Octavian who defeated Antony at Mutina in 43. The Republic seemed likely to survive, but later in the year, when Antony, in alliance with Lepidus, re-entered Italy, Octavian came to terms with them, to form a triumvirate *republicae constituendae*—ostensibly to reorganize the state, but in reality to inherit Caesar's power. The most notable of the many victims to meet his death in the brutal proscriptions which this trio decreed was Cicero. In the following year Antony and Octavian crossed to Greece and at Philippi defeated Brutus and Cassius.

The last hope of saving Republican political liberties and the old Roman political way of life then disappeared. The only question was who was to be supreme. Fulvia, wife of Antony, and Antony's brother Lucius opposed Octavian on his return to Italy, and were besieged in Perugia which Octavian captured in 40. The death of Fulvia opened the way to a reconciliation between Antony and Octavian, signalled by Antony's marriage to Octavia, the sister of Octavian, and formulated by the Treaty of Brundisium. In this division of the Roman world Antony took as his portion the East, where he fell under the influence of Cleopatra, while Octavian claimed Italy and the West, with the exception of Africa which was left to Lepidus. Octavian with the help of his

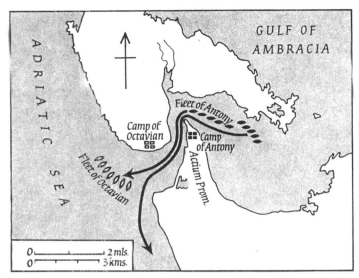

The battle of Actium took place on September 2nd 31 BC, after the armies of Antony and Octavian had faced each other for several weeks across the entrance to the Gulf of Ambracia, in Greece. Against the opinion of his advisers, Antony decided to offer battle at sea. His fleet, more numerous than Octavian's but not so well manned, engaged the enemy off the promontory of Actium. He might well have prevailed had not Cleopatra, whose squadron sailed in the rear, fled in the heat of the battle; Antony turned and followed her and the battle was lost. His entire army and fleet were taken prisoner by Octavian.

able lieutenants, Maecenas and Agrippa, consolidated his position in the West. In 36 Sextus Pompey who, since his defeat at Munda in 45, had exercised a piratical control over the Western Mediterranean with his base in Sicily, was defeated. Lepidus, summoned to help Octavian, tried to take Sicily for himself but was stripped of his honours, except that of *pontifex maximus*. Octavian and Antony now divided the Roman world between them. In the East, Antony's fortune was more uneven. He obtained a victory over the Parthians through his lieutenant, Ventidius, in 39, but a second campaign in 36 ended in disastrous retreat. His campaign against Armenia in 34 ended with the capture of the Armenian king Artavasdes.

The inevitable trial of strength between Antony and Octavian was hastened by Antony's action in divorcing Octavia in favour of Cleopatra. The senate, at Octavian's behest, deposed Antony from his command and declared war on Cleopatra. The decisive battle, fought at sea off the promontory of Actium on the Ambracian Gulf on 2 September 31, was gained for Octavian by Agrippa's tactical skill. Antony and Cleopatra escaped to Egypt but, when Alexandria was invaded by Octavian, they both committed suicide. The remaining eastern provinces were taken over in the course of 29 and for the first time for sixteen years the Roman world was at peace. Peace reigned only because, once more, one man had successfully flouted Roman law and the Roman constitution, and, in complete disregard of political principles, had by the illegal and cunning use of force succeeded in making himself unquestionable master of the Roman world.

THE EMPIRE

Rome Ruled by One Man

On 13 January 27 BC Octavian staged a spectacular, sham resignation of offices which he had held since 43 BC and formally restored the Republic. In exchange the senate bestowed on him the title Augustus and also granted him for the next ten years an *imperium*, a military command over all the armed forces, and thus over all the provinces in which there were armies. Augustus, as he is now to be styled, also held the consulship for several years, but this proved an unsatisfactory basis for power, as it was annual, collegial and more civil than military. In 23 BC he gave up the consulship and received instead the *imperium proconsulare*, the function by which great military and provincial posts were formerly held and one which did not produce any suspension of the constitution, as an extraordinary power such as that of dictator would have done.

The imperium of Augustus was declared to be *maius*, that is, superior to that of other magistrates. The tribunician power, the weapon which the plebeians had used against the patricians in the early Republic, was also assumed by Augustus as a further means of controlling the senate and as something which made him the representative of the people and his person sacrosanct.

The senate was retained because it gave prestige to the new régime and was used by Augustus as the instrument of his policy, and as a source of administrative officials. The composition of the senate was controlled by Augustus. As commander-in-chief he had in his grant the appointment of military tribunes, the necessary preliminary to a senatorial magistracy; he could exercise his commendation at elections; as censor he could remove senators and by his special power of *allectio* he could appoint direct to the senate. The public assembly was left with scarcely any part to play in the new constitution and almost its sole function in the empire was formally to accept imperial decisions and formally to recognize a new emperor. Such were the main features of the great Roman revolution. The old Republican constitution to which all the temporary elected magistrates had, for almost half a millennium, been subservient was no more. Henceforth, however disguised, Rome was ruled by one man, the *imperator* or emperor.

'I found Rome of brick, I leave it of marble', said Augustus. This detail from a tomb relief shows one of the large cranes used in the extensive building programme that now began to transform the city. Stones are raised on the thick ropes attached to pulleys at the top. The driving force is supplied by a treadwheel worked by slaves.

After two generations of chaos, civil war and ruin, Rome needed a fresh start. Augustus set about giving it. He overhauled and improved the administration of the empire. In Rome itself departments for the city services were set up—police, fire-brigade, drainage, conservation of the Tiber banks, and, most important, the provision of the corn dole. In Italy the road system was improved, new colonies were planted to revive rural life and the responsibility for routine local administration was entrusted to municipalities. Augustus restored a sound money system and the confidence he created enabled economic welfare to make a great stride forward. Building on a new scale of magnificence began to transform the city.

Only those provinces in the interior of the empire which were at peace and did not require a permanent legionary establishment were entrusted to a governor and other officials appointed by the senate. All the provinces in which there were armed forces, chiefly the frontier provinces and Egypt, were governed by an imperial legate and to imperial legates was also given the command of the legions.

Throughout the reign of Augustus the consolidation of the imperial frontiers continued. The defeat of Crassus by the Parthians in 53 BC and the loss of the legionary standards had left a scar on Roman pride, but Augustus was too shrewd to embark on a war with Parthia, the then other imperial power. Instead he sent Tiberius, his step-son and eventual successor, to negotiate for the return of the captured standards, thus providing at least a propaganda triumph. The Eastern frontier was secured by the establishment of protectorates over Armenia, Commagene and Cappadocia, while Galatia was annexed in 25 BC.

In the south, the frontier in Egypt was maintained with no difficulty at the First Cataract, after initial dispute with the Ethiopians, but the southern frontier of the province of Africa continued to be subjected to sporadic raids by the nomadic desert tribes. Mauretania was held as a client kingdom by Juba of Numidia until his death in AD 40. In the west Spain was finally pacified in 19 BC, and Augustus was content to leave Rome's frontier at the Channel and not repeat Caesar's crossing to Britain.

The northern frontier was a much greater problem. With the annexation of Moesia, Pannonia and Noricum the line was carried up to the Danube but only in AD 9, after a series of hard-fought campaigns and repeated uprisings, was the frontier firmly held. The original intention to advance north from the Danube and east from the Rhine to a new frontier along the Elbe was abandoned after the disaster of the Teutoburg Forest when the general Varus and legions XVII, XVIII and XIX were destroyed by the Germans, an unforgettable military disaster. The frontier, thereafter, was fixed on the Rhine and Danube. Germany remained outside the civilizing power of Rome.

The Imperial Army, Instrument of Policy

After the battle of Actium, the combined armies (the defeated legions of Antony and Octavian's own) numbered sixty legions, a force at once too great for the economy to maintain, and too powerful and dangerous. By a policy of demobilization, settlement and pensioning-off of veterans, Augustus reduced the army to twenty-eight legions, though later there was a slow rise in the number. Since a legion consisted only of some 5,500 men, divided into one cohort of 1,000 and nine of 500, the whole imperial army seems, to modern eyes, inadequately small for the tasks which it had to discharge.

The military policy of Augustus and his successors in the first two centuries of empire was based on two cardinal principles—the maintenance of the army at the lowest point consistent with meeting its commitments but yet avoiding undue strain on the economy, and the avoidance of the danger of a central army concentration. The purpose of the Roman army was principally to defend the frontiers of the empire, with, as a subsidiary rôle, the maintenance of peace in the provinces. It was only occasionally that the imperial army took the offensive with a view to conquest, as distinct from a local offensive for defensive reasons. Under Claudius the legions extended the empire to Britain, and, under Trajan, Dacia was conquered and Arabia incorporated into the empire.

The legion, each now with a number and a distinctive title as well, e.g. Legio III Parthica, was commanded by a *legatus* and officered by *tribuni*, all posts of senatorial rank, but the backbone of the service was provided by the continuing professional element, the centurions, of whom there were sixty in a legion. The army under Augustus was still a permanent professional body, recruited by voluntary enlistment. The legionaries were still Roman citizens, but few of them of Italian stock.

The attraction of the army must have lain in the certainty of the conditions, for the terms of service themselves were not very enticing. The period of service was fixed at twenty years, and the pay at 10 *asses* per day, some 225 *denarii* per year. The soldier had to pay for his own food, clothing and arms. The legionary was equipped with tunic, coat and boots, the *caligae*, from the diminutive of which, *caligula*, the emperor Gaius gained his name for his boyhood was spent in camps with his father Germanicus. The soldier wore a breastplate, helmet and greaves, and was armed with shield, sword, javelin and dagger.

Where the frontiers of the empire did not coincide with natural boundaries, such as rivers or deserts, or where these were not adequate, reinforced defence works were built. Strung out along the frontiers were the army's permanent camps, the great legionary

Roman soldiers of the 1st century BC are demobilized: a detail from a relief on the temple of Neptune, Rome. On the left a scribe enters the names in a book. The man next to him—now in civilian dress—holds in his left hand his 'tabula missionis', or certificate of discharge. Two others wait and talk. To provide home and work for these retired veterans a system of new towns, 'coloniae', was established in parts of the Empire that needed development.

fortresses. The continuous service of a legion in such a centre created a kind of local patriotism which was to be the source of rebellion and separatism in the later empire. Round the fortresses grew up civilian settlements (*canabae*), housing the shops supplying the soldiers' wants and also the soldiers' concubines, for marriage on active service was not permitted until the time of Septimius Severus. The children of such unions usually enlisted in the legion, the only way in which they could gain Roman citizenship.

The legions of the army, however, were supplemented by the auxiliary forces, almost equal in number to the legions. These troops were recruited from the less-civilized, more war-like peoples within the empire, and provided not only the bulk of the cavalry but also the special arms, such as archers or slingers. Originally these auxiliary forces served in the area from which they were recruited and were commanded by their own officers. When the civil wars of AD 68–9 revealed the danger of revolt stemming from local nationalism, auxiliaries raised in one area were posted for service elsewhere in the empire and were commanded by Roman officers.

In the early empire the only troops stationed in Italy itself were the corps of imperial guards, the praetorian cohorts each of 1,000 men, recruited from Italy or from the Romanized provinces. Under Augustus three cohorts were stationed in Rome, the remainder in other parts of Italy, but from the reign of Tiberius all nine were concentrated in one camp at the Colline gate of Rome. As the only body of troops at the centre of affairs they played a critical rôle in the politics of the early empire whenever an appeal to force was made.

The aim of Augustus and his successors had been to maintain the army as an instrument of policy and not to allow it to shape events. The main force, the legions, was dispersed on the frontiers, and when not actively engaged was often used for the construction of roads and canals, as well as military works such as the great defensive northern wall in Britain between Tyne and Solway built under Hadrian. Under the Julio-Claudian emperors the army as a whole had been successfully excluded from politics, though it was the action of the Praetorian guard at Rome in AD 41 that gave the succession to Claudius. The civil war of AD 68–9 after the revolt against Nero revealed the dangerous secret that emperors could be made elsewhere than at Rome, for then in turn Galba was proclaimed Emperor by his legions in Spain, Vitellius in Germany and the ultimate victor, Vespasian, in Syria.

The reshaping of Roman life by Augustus had not been confined to practical matters of political constitution and military reorganization but was extended to the field of religion as well. He wanted to revive the antique Roman virtues and to improve personal and family morals, so he tried to reanimate the old formal religion. Virgil and Horace are supposed to have written some of

their poetry to help him. Throughout the centuries of the Republic, the old gods of Rome had been increasingly swamped by new deities from Italy and Greece, with their new rituals and new temples. By the time of Augustus many old Roman deities, with their rites and institutions, were practically forgotten despite the continuing appointment of the *pontifices*, the priests of the several cults, the augurs, the interpreters of signs and portents, and the Vestal Virgins, all dignitaries of the official religion. Augustus restored more than eighty temples in or near Rome itself, revived such sacrificial priesthoods as the *Flamen Dialis* and the *Fratres Arvales*, as well as the ancient colleges such as the Salii and the Luperci connected with the celebration and commemoration of the events of Rome's foundation. In 12 BC on the death of Lepidus, who had held the post of *pontifex maximus* (chief priest), Augustus succeeded to the title which was thereafter held by every reigning emperor.

Fresh impetus was given to some cults by the erection of new temples. A new shrine was built on the Palatine to Apollo, for Apollo of Actium was said to have favoured the cause of Augustus. In the new Forum a temple to Mars Ultor, the avenger of Caesar's murder was erected, as well as a new temple of Vesta, closely associated with the palace of Augustus on the Palatine. In Rome and Italy Augustus did not sanction emperor worship: the idea of a divine ruler was a concept familiar from the history of the great Hellenistic kingdoms but was as yet too much for senatorial conservatism to accept. However a representation of the Genius of Augustus was added to the *Lares Compitales* at the street crossings in Rome. No such political caution was necessary in the provinces, where the cult of Rome and Augustus was accepted as natural, and flourished accordingly.

Peace in the Empire, Terror at the Top

On his death in AD 14 Augustus had been master of the Roman world for just under half a century. Using the old republican institution as a façade he had craftily created a new system which had brought to the Roman world external security and internal peace and prosperity. Despite the outward republican trappings and however much Augustus' insistence that he was nothing more than *Princeps*—first citizen—in practice all real authority had come to reside in one man and, though technically on his death the old Republic could be restored, it was clear that his system had somehow to be perpetuated. In his lifetime Augustus had sought to find a successor from his own Julian family—first his nephew Marcellus, then Agrippa, the faithful lieutenant to whom Augustus' success owed so much, and now married to Augustus' daughter, Julia. Later, the two young sons of this marriage were adopted by Augustus as his heirs, but the untimely deaths of Lucius in AD 2 and Gaius in AD 4 left Augustus at last with no option but to designate as his heir, not one of his own Julian family but his step-son Tiberius, of the Claudian family.

Tiberius, despite his abilities and experience both as general and administrator, had earlier been used by Augustus as at best a

Under Augustus and Tiberius the Italian countryside achieved prosperity and peace after the bitter ravages of the previous century. This relief of about AD 50 shows a peasant on his way to market with animals and produce—a cow, a pig, two lambs and basket of fruit.

potential stop-gap regent for the young Julian princes, and in 6 BC he retired from public life to self-imposed exile in Rhodes, perhaps because of disappointed political ambitions and personal resentment at being compelled to marry the profligate Julia, now widow of Agrippa. Now in AD 4 Augustus adopted Tiberius as his heir and as a colleague sharing both in the *imperium* and the tribunician power. These powers Tiberius was still holding in AD 14 when Augustus died, and there was no possible rival. Despite the professed reluctance of Tiberius, the senate immediately proclaimed him emperor and invested him with the *imperium* and the tribunician power for life.

The essentially conservative reign of Tiberius served to consolidate the imperial system of Augustus and brought about considerable improvement in the administration of the provinces. The emperor's care for the provinces is instanced by his generous assistance to the twelve cities of Asia Minor destroyed in the earthquake of AD 17, a generosity well publicized on a coinage issue of AD 22–23. The boundaries of the empire were little changed: the campaigns of Germanicus, the nephew and heir of Tiberius, beyond the Rhine frontier in AD 14 and 16 achieved nothing, while the rebellion of Florus and Sacrovir in Gaul in 21, and the raids of Tacfarinas in Africa caused only local and temporary upset. In the East, the frontier was consolidated by the annexation of Cappadocia and Commagene and the incorporation of Cilicia into the province of Syria, but the drama of the Crucifixion in Jerusalem passed unnoticed by the world of Tiberius.

The felicity enjoyed by the empire at large did not extend to the sphere of relations between Tiberius and the senate and Tiberius and the imperial family. Augustus, before his death, had made Tiberius adopt as his heir, not his own son, Drusus, but his nephew, Germanicus, who was at least partially a Julian. The sudden death of Germanicus in Syria in 19 and the allegation of poisoning involved Tiberius in the suspicion of clearing the way for his own son Drusus. If this indeed were so, retribution was not long delayed, for Drusus died in 23 and a few years later Tiberius retired to Capri. The story that Tiberius there abandoned himself to all manner of vices reflects little more than the anti-imperialist bias of ancient sources, but for some years Tiberius left affairs more and more in the hands of his prefect of the Praetorian guard at Rome, Sejanus. His supreme influence at this time made it possible for Sejanus to secure by intrigue the banishment of Agrippina, widow of Germanicus, and of her son Nero, as well as the imprisonment of her second son, Drusus, now the immediate heirs to Tiberius. At last in 31 the dangers of Sejanus' ambition became apparent to Tiberius; Sejanus was arrested and executed the same day. As a consequence, suspicion of treason and plots darkened the last years of the reign, and charges of *maiestas* or high treason, readily levelled against all whom the emperor suspected, sent many innocent victims to a premature death. The succession now also presented its problems, for the deaths of both Nero and Drusus left as possible heirs their younger brother, Gaius, nicknamed Caligula, and Tiberius' own grandson, Gemellus. Because of the latter's extreme youth, Tiberius appointed both Caligula and Gemellus as his heirs, though not without misgivings as to the instability of Gaius' character. In 37 Tiberius left Capri but died at Misenum on his way to Rome.

Caligula, because he happened to accompany Tiberius on his last journey, has been suspected of expediting his end. He had already been named Tiberius' heir and was immediately proclaimed by the senate. The careful economies of Tiberius had ensured a full treasury which enabled the new emperor to bribe the troops and the dregs of the populace with lavish largesse and to mount elaborate games for their delectation. The statecraft of Augustus and Tiberius had maintained at least an outward semblance of traditional government, but now the devil-may-care attitude and questionable sanity of Caligula revealed the autocracy which in reality ruled the Roman world. The treason trials and confiscations of Tiberius' reign were resumed; Gemellus, originally declared his heir, was executed and even members of his own family on whom he had at first heaped honours were fortunate to escape with the penalty of banishment. Caligula, setting off in 38 to organize an expedition to Britain, reached the Rhine in time to scotch a revolt, but it was not until early 40 that the situation was

sufficiently in hand to permit an invasion of Britain—when threatened mutiny by the troops caused Caligula to cancel his plans and return to Rome. By 41 Caligula's initial popularity had vanished and his alienation of some of the officers of his Praetorian guard led to a conspiracy and his assassination.

On the death of Caligula there was no declared heir to the principate, and in the senate there was even vague talk of restoring the Republic. The Praetorian guard, however, seized the initiative, for on discovering Claudius, uncle of Caligula, concealed in the palace they acclaimed him as emperor and escorted him to their camp. Thereupon the senate meekly confirmed the choice of the soldiers whom the new emperor promptly rewarded with a lavish donative. Ancient sources were content to represent Claudius as something of a buffoon, while more modern historians, recognizing the solid achievements of his reign, explain the ancient reports as merely the façade by which Claudius had succeeded in avoiding the dangerous attention of earlier emperors. Unorthodox as was the manner in which Claudius was proclaimed emperor, he was in fact a fairly obvious choice, for Caligula before the onset of his paranoia clearly regarded Claudius as a potential regent for the now deceased Gemellus.

The invasion of Britain planned by Caligula was effected by Claudius. In 43 a force of legions and auxiliaries landed with little opposition, halted its advance at the Thames, until it was joined by the emperor himself for the victorious crossing and assault of Colchester. Before the end of the reign, the frontier had advanced to the line of the Fosseway from Exeter to Lincoln, and Colchester obtained the status of a *colonia*, a settlement whose inhabitants possessed Roman citizenship, at much the same time as did Cologne and Trier. The gap between Italy and the provinces was further narrowed when for the first time Gallic nobles were recommended by Claudius for admission to the senate. Departments dealing with various aspects of imperial policy were set up by Claudius and their administration entrusted to freedmen. Claudius was perhaps too open to influence by these freedmen and by his wives, first Messalina and then Agrippina the Younger. Certainly Agrippina prevailed upon him to recognize Nero, her son by an earlier marriage, as his heir, though he had a son of his own, Britannicus. Agrippina has always been suspected of murdering Claudius by poisoning in 54, presumably so that Nero might succeed while still a youth, and she, as empress-regent, might exercise power.

Nero as Apollo, the god of music. 'No one', says the historian Suetonius, 'was allowed to leave the theatre during his recitals, however pressing the reason, and the gates were kept barred. We read of women in the audience giving birth, and of men being so bored with the music and applause that they furtively dropped down from the wall at the rear, or shammed dead and were carried away for burial'.

The Despot Nero

Nero's succession was undisputed; Burrus, the Praetorian prefect, secured the requisite military support and in the senate the influence of the philosopher Seneca commanded acceptance. Agrippina's attempts to concentrate power in her own hands roused her son's resentment as time wore on, and in 59 she was assassinated at his instigation. The death of Burrus in 62 and the prudent retirement of Seneca freed Nero from all restraint, both personal and political. His inordinate love of and personal participation in musical and theatrical contests as well as chariot racing shocked the staider strata of Roman society. In politics the principate became more and more a despotism. Nero's half-brother Britannicus had perished early in the reign, his mother Agrippina had been murdered, and now his wife Octavia was first divorced and then put to death. The discovery in 65 of a conspiracy to replace Nero by the senator Calpurnius Piso unleashed terror and persecution which eventually in 68 sparked off revolt in Gaul, Spain and Africa. Nero had forfeited the favour of all classes and found support in no quarter. He fled from Rome and in despair committed suicide.

Against the picture of violence and intrigue emphasized by the senatorial, if not Republican, bias of our ancient sources for this and earlier reigns must be set the record, attested by archaeological sources, of a steady tradition of government, of general peace within the empire, and steadily improving economic conditions. In Rome itself, the destruction caused by the great fire of 64, the responsibility for which has also been placed on Nero, presented an opportunity, readily used, for replanning and rebuilding. Nero built his huge palace, the Golden House, on a vast area cleared by the fire.

The peaceful progress of events of the western provinces was disturbed only in the recently conquered province of Britain. Disaffection came to a head AD 61 in a revolt in which the Iceni and their queen, Boudicca (Boadicea) played a part which has become a legend of British history. St Albans and London suffered destruction and massacre before the rebellion was stamped out and the conquest of the province resumed. In the East, war with Parthia over the status of Armenia was concluded in 66 when Tiridates visited Rome and received the crown of Armenia from Nero. The accompanying settlement secured peace on the eastern frontier for half a century and was reached just in time, for in 66 a Jewish revolt flared up in Palestine. When Nero was overthrown in 68 the country was still only partly subdued and forces under Vespasian were on the point of investing the city of Jerusalem.

The Year of the Four Emperors

Since Nero had made no provision for the appointment of an heir there was no obvious replacement to whom the elements of revolt against Nero could rally. A confused struggle broke out as four different armies each named their commander. The competitors were Galba, Otho, Vitellius and Vespasian. After some very ugly scenes which included the brutal assassination of Galba and Otho and pitched battles between conflicting Roman armies, the last on the sacred Capitol hill in Rome, Vitellius was slain, leaving Vespasian the victor. The senate without delay recognized Vespasian who reached Rome from the East only in January of 70.

The whole affair, after three generations of peace, was a frightening revelation of the insecurity of the imperial system: Actium seemed to have been fought in vain. Suddenly not one, but three civil wars were being fought with the utmost savagery, while fierce outbreaks on several frontiers added to the general alarm. Between the fighting, life was horribly precarious. Anyone distinguished for his wealth, honours or standing was a marked man; murder and assassination were evaded only by flight and exile; Slaves and freedmen were suborned against their masters; to lack enemies was no safeguard for many were destroyed by their friends. And, as we have seen, among the many lessons of this grim outbreak was the sinister realization that emperors now could be created elsewhere than in Rome.

Strong Rule Returns: the Flavian Achievement

The events of the years 68-9 throw a lurid light on the basic weakness of the principate—the lack of assured succession—and Vespasian made clear from the beginning his intention to establish an orthodox dynastic succession. He himself held the office of consul in most years of his reign, and had as his colleague on six occasions his son Titus to whom in 71 he gave the proconsular *imperium* and the tribunician power. Vespasian, recalling the part played by the Praetorian guard when succession was in question in the Julio-Claudian principate, appointed Titus Praetorian prefect. His younger son, Domitian, similarly held office on one occasion as ordinary consul and on others as a suffect consul. To both Titus and Domitian were granted the title *Princeps Iuventutis*, used from this time onward to mark out the heir apparent.

Vespasian, himself owing his elevation to the army, made a point of cultivating the loyalty of the troops, but at the same time he took steps to reduce the hazards of revolt inspired by their

In 68 AD—about 40 years after the death of Christ—the Jews rose in revolt against their Roman masters. It took a three-year campaign to suppress the rebellion. The siege of Jerusalem, begun by Vespasian and continued by his son Titus, ended in the total destruction of the city and the demolition of the Temple. This coin of 71 AD, with the inscription 'Judaea Capta', celebrates the event.

incipient local nationalism. Locally recruited *auxilia* were transferred to more distant theatres and were no longer commanded by native officers. In the chain of legionary camps, on which the vital defence of the empire depended, lay dormant the seeds of precisely this danger of local nationalism, but against this neither Vespasian nor his successors were able to devise a remedy. Though the political importance of the senate was now negligible, membership of it was still the qualification for the great administrative office, and Vespasian, by assuming the office of censor in 73, saw to its replenishment by men of his own choice, many being drawn from the municipalities of Italy and the West. He also overhauled the finances of the empire. Taxes remitted to purchase popularity by the succession of rulers in 68-9 were reimposed, and the tribute payable by the provinces increased. Imperial expenditure was cut, particularly that of the court, but without detriment to public works in the provinces and in Italy.

The reign saw considerable activity in the provinces. The capture of Jerusalem in 70 by Titus finally ended the Jewish revolt and gained for him a triumph in which were exhibited the spoils from the great temple. It was commemorated by the great arch which bears the name of Titus. In the West a nationalistic revolt in Lower Germany under Civilis was subdued, and the frontier was advanced in the angle between the Upper Rhine and the Upper Danube. In Britain the extension of the conquest to the north and into Wales brought the establishment of legionary fortresses at York, Chester and Caerleon, and Agricola began the series of campaigns which were to culminate in his defeat of the Caledonian tribes at Mons Graupius in north Scotland in 84.

Vespasian, unlike so many of his predecessors, died peacefully in 79 at his native Reate and was succeeded without opposition by his son Titus. Titus' generosity has gained for him the reputation of being the most popular of Roman emperors. Two notable disasters occurred at this time. In 79 the great eruption of Vesuvius overwhelmed the towns of Pompeii and Herculaneum, and in the next year another great fire in Rome destroyed the Capitol which had been rebuilt only ten years before, as well as a considerable area of the city. The great new Flavian Amphitheatre, known now as the Colosseum, which had been begun by Vespasian was not involved in the destruction and was dedicated by Titus in 80 to the accompaniment of a tremendous slaughter of gladiators, criminals, captives and wild beasts, reputed to have lasted a hundred days.

Although Titus had not followed his father's example and made it clear that Domitian was to be his heir, Domitian was immediately recognized when Titus died in 81. Domitian was considerably more autocratic. He held the consulship in practically every year of his reign, and in 85 assumed the office of censor in perpetuity. He disliked the senate, so he increased the importance of the equestrian order from whose ranks the heads of the great administrative departments were now appointed. Domitian continued the successful financial policy of his father, but his positive achievements are overshadowed by the terror and treason trials of his latter years, particularly after the unsuccessful revolt of Saturninus on the Rhine in 88.

Domitian is accused by the historian Tacitus in his biography of his father-in-law, Agricola, of recalling Agricola at the height of his success in Britain in 84 merely from jealous spite. It is question-

Roman soldiers tend their comrades after a battle with the Dacians; on the left is a barbarian prisoner. The relief on Trajan's Column (erected in AD 113 to celebrate his campaigns on the Danube) are a unique historical record of the life and work of the army.

able, however, whether the extended conquests in Britain could have been held without a vastly increased force, and meanwhile danger was beginning to threaten other Roman frontiers. War with the Chatti ended with their expulsion from the Main valley in 85 and the establishment of a more advanced and more secure frontier. A Dacian invasion of Moesia was repulsed, but before war could be carried into Dacia, the revolt of Saturninus in 88 made it expedient to come to terms with Decebalus, king of the Dacians. In 92 the Marcomanni and Quadi who had attacked Pannonia were successfully repelled.

The insecurity caused by the indiscriminate terror at Rome led to a conspiracy amongst the emperor's immediate associates, including his wife, Domitia, and his Praetorian prefect, and in 96 Domitian was assassinated.

Domitian had used his office of censor to attempt to improve the standard of public morals, and, after the fashion of Augustus, endeavoured to encourage family life. Renewed attention was paid to the ancient Roman cults: new temples to Jupiter Capitolinus and Jupiter Custos were constructed, and other temples were rebuilt. The cult of Minerva received particularly favourable treatment, for she was regarded by Domitian as his patron goddess, and her image was a favourite reverse type on his coinage.

Fixing the Frontier Defences

The death of Domitian without an heir threatened the empire with a recurrence of the civil wars of 68, but, though the senate's choice of the elderly Nerva was viewed with disfavour by the Praetorians, the respect for the principate which Flavian policy had inculcated in the army gained his acceptance. Generosity in Rome and a series of measures designed to remedy the economy of Italy helped to maintain Nerva. These measures included the abolition of the charge on Italy for the maintainance of the state posting service, and the introduction of *alimenta*. This was a scheme whereby Italian farmers could mortgage a proportion of the value of their land, paying interest to the local municipality to provide a fund for the maintenance of poor children. In 97

Nerva was obliged to yield to the demands of the Praetorians for the execution of Domitian's murderers, and, to secure for the régime the more enthusiastic support of the army, he adopted as his heir the most popular general, Trajan.

The step had been taken none too soon, for within some three months Nerva was dead. The new emperor was accepted without opposition, both by army and senate, though his advent marked a new stage in the development of the principate. The early emperors were of ancient Roman family, the Flavians at least were Italian, but Trajan was of Spanish descent. By scrupulous observance of the senate's rôle in affairs, Trajan gained the favour of that order both for himself and for his immediate successors in the principate, while his great building programme in Rome and lavish games, coupled with an expansionist foreign policy, earned for him the title *optimus princeps*. The most famous of his buildings in Rome was his great Forum in which was erected the Basilica Ulpia and the great column, which still stands, commemorating on its giant spiral frieze scenes from Trajan's Dacian wars. On it, as on so many Roman monuments, are vividly depicted the slaughter and enslavement of Rome's enemies.

In two campaigns in 101 and 105 Trajan overwhelmed the Dacian tribes north of the Danube. Apart from the immediate gain in booty and captives for the ever-greedy slave trade, a new, rich province was added to the empire. No such permanent success attended the emperor's campaigns in the east, aimed at securing once and for all a settled eastern frontier. Armenia and Mesopotamia were annexed and, to protect them, further eastward advances resulted in the creation of provinces of Assyria and Parthia. The Parthian forces retreated before Trajan's advance which reached as far as Ctesiphon, but insurrection on his lines of communication and Jewish revolts throughout the east forced him to turn back. He had reached no further than Selinus in Cilicia when he suffered a fatal stroke, naming on his deathbed his second cousin, Hadrian, as his successor.

The new emperor, considering that Trajan's conquests had over-extended the empire's resources, capitalized the military prestige which Trajan had won and concentrated on organized frontier defence. The new province of Dacia was retained, but the eastern conquests were abandoned. In pursuit of his policy Hadrian undertook extensive tours of his empire, inspecting the organization and efficiency of the armies, and investigating provincial administration. No emperor before or since made himself personally so familiar with the problems of the empire, and his interest both in the armies and the provinces finds record on two extensive series of coins.

The most striking example of fixed frontier defence in this reign was in Britain, where the forward conquests made by Agricola were abandoned in favour of a great continuous wall, incorporating forts and mile-castles and stretching from Tyne to Solway. More extensive use was made of auxiliary forces in this reign. Their standard of training and armament now approximated to that of the legions and they began to be used as permanent garrisons in frontier forts. Service in the legions was now also raised from twenty to twenty-five years, local recruitment became the practice, even the officers, except for the most senior, being found from non-Italian sources. In the provinces, the greatest problem continued to be the decay in efficiency of local

Roman and barbarian—portrayed together on a relief found in Trajan's forum at Rome. The barbarian, in contrast to the calm and powerful features of the Roman, is shown with an agitated expression, his hair long and disordered. In the background is a circular hut of branches, like those known to have been built at this time in Gaul.

municipalities, and the process, begun under Trajan, of installing imperial controllers was extended. One striking miscalculation in provincial affairs was the decision to build, on the ruins of Jerusalem, a new city to be called Aelia Capitolina, and, on the site of the Temple, a shrine to Jupiter and the emperor. This sparked off in 132 the second great Jewish revolt which was not suppressed till 135.

Careful management of the imperial finances enabled Hadrian to reduce the *aurum coronarium*, the gift made by the provinces and Italy to a new emperor, but he was still able to finance a programme of great buildings, including a temple dedicated to Venus and Rome in 135, the rebuilding of the Pantheon, and his own mausoleum, which still survives as the Castel Sant' Angelo. At Tivoli he constructed a huge palace, lavishly laid out with gardens.

Hope for an After-life: New 'Mysteries' from the East

Throughout the early empire and indeed on through the 2nd and 3rd centuries the ancient cults steadily lost their attraction. They had never had much spiritual content and the universal yearning for something higher, and, in times which became increasingly harsh and dangerous, a hope for an after-life which would be more satisfying, turned men to the various mystery worships. The attraction of such cults was that all the worshippers participated, and by various rituals of initiation and progress through various grades they got a feeling of advancement towards a better life.

In Greece one of the chief centres of these mystery worships was at Eleusis. A very popular cult was that of Dionysus, which was taken up in Rome in the early 2nd century, where Dionysus was identified with the Roman Bacchus or Liber. It continued its popularity through the first two centuries of the empire Those initiated into the mystery were sworn to secrecy and the secret was well-kept, but from such hints as have emerged Dionysus was clearly one of the saviour gods, and the initiates were assured of immortality and of a happy release in the after-world.

More popular was the worship of the great Mother-Goddess Cybele, a cult imported from Asia Minor as early as 204 BC. In addition to the attraction of the element of protection and guidance of the great Mother herself, there was incorporated in this cult a great ceremonial ritual celebrating each year again the death and regeneration of Cybele's consort, the young Attis. The symbolic death of Attis was accompanied by fasting and mourning, and the announcement of his re-birth was celebrated with orgiastic frenzy, inspired by the release from the fear of eternal destruction and the hope of immortality. An unusual feature of the lavish ceremonial was the self-flagellation and laceration of the priests of the cult, culminating, in the frenzy of the ritual, in self-castration by the novices, an act which has been regarded as the greatest sacrifice to the goddess, short of death itself. Associated with the worship and ceremonial of Cybele was the *tauroboliam*. This rite involved the sacrifice of a bull and the drenching of the initiate with the blood, believed to have tremendous powers of rejuvenation, if not regeneration.

The cult of Cybele was rivalled in popularity by that of the Egyptian goddess, Isis. Her worship came to Rome in the later Republic, but it was only in the early empire that it became well established. Such was its appeal that it was one of the last great pagan religions to survive in the late empire. This again was essentially the cult of a saviour god, of hope for mankind, of eventual triumph over death. The centre of the worship of Isis, celebrated in solemn ritual, was the story of the death of Isis' consort Osiris, his dismemberment by his enemy, Set, the search by the devoted Isis for the remains, and finally the regeneration of Osiris. The gift of immortality which this religion offered its adherents required of them conformity with a code of conduct, and the elaborate ritual of her worship contained many hymns of penitence and contrition. Isis, often represented with the child, Horus, in her arms, personified maternal love and care. A particular aspect of Isis was her association with the sea, and every year, in the early spring, when it was again possible for ships to sail, particularly the vital corn ships, their release was celebrated by the Isis festival.

Restricted to Men: the Cult of Mithras

Another mystery cult which found favour, especially with the military, and enjoyed widespread popularity particularly in the 3rd century was that of Mithras. Unlike the other mystery cults, whose central theme of immortality was enshrined in the drama of the death and regeneration of the saviour god, be he Dionysus, Attis or Osiris, Mithraism promulgated a different belief. Mithras, whom the Romans regarded as Persian, was the personification of the spirit of good. The legend, in brief, held that Mithras was created by Ahuramazda, the power of good, from a rock, or as he is sometimes represented, from an egg. The central theme, represented in many paintings and sculptures, is the struggle of Mithras with the bull, the first of living creatures, and his eventual slaughter of it. From the sacrifice of its blood came the harvest of nature, and thus, by association, Mithras came to be regarded as the renewer of life. He guarded the first humans against the machinations of the spirit of evil, and then was taken up to heaven in the chariot of the Sun. He was worshipped as the ideal of manly valour; Mithraism was a faith which placed value on endurance and effort, and inculcated the moral qualities and virtues required for such ideals.

Mithraism, which was restricted to men, appears to have had no priesthood, but for the initiates themselves there was a hierarchy of grades—soldier, gryphon, lion, raven, sun-runner and father. The initiates progressed through the grades by submitting themselves to a series of tests and ordeals, and these ceremonies and the worship of Mithras were conducted in underground shrines. The widespread popularity of the cult is evident from the records of Mithraea which have been identified all over the empire, and which are still coming to light. One of the best preserved, under the church of St Prisca on the Aventine in Rome, excavated over the last ten years, retains wall-paintings showing the ceremonial dress of some of the grades and in a side chapel is a pit which played a part in the ordeals. In recent years the remains of a Mithraeum and the sculptures which adorned it have come to light at the Walbrook in the City of London; and the popularity of this cult with the soldiery is evidenced by Mithraic shrines in isolated frontier posts, as at Dura Europus in the East and at Carrawburgh on Hadrian's wall, the most northerly frontier of the Roman world.

Mithras as a god of light was to some extent identified with Sol, the sun-god. Sol was worshipped under various forms in the East, as for instance Baal or Elagabalus at Emesa in Syria. Transferred to Rome by the emperor of the same name, this particular worship did not survive his short reign, but Sol Invictus continued to attract attention throughout the 3rd century, finding particular favour with the emperors Aurelian and Constantius Chlorus. Indeed Sol was the favourite deity of Constantine the Great in his early reign. The monotheistic tendency in this belief undoubtedly contributed something to the more ready acceptance of Christianity in the 4th century.

The Persecution of the Faithful

The young Christian church in the years immediately following the Crucifixion was fortunate in not attracting the attention of officialdom to any great degree, and on such occasions as it did come under scrutiny it was regarded as a sect of the Jews and shared in the toleration accorded to that faith. The first persecution came in the reign of Nero, when the emperor, looking for scapegoats to meet the charges of starting the Great Fire at Rome being levelled at himself, found them in the Christians. The toleration previously extended to them was withdrawn, and, in the harrying of the faithful which followed, both St Peter and St Paul suffered martyrdom. Persecution flared up again under Domitian, and it is against the background of these events that the Book of Revelations was written.

The continuing precariousness of professing Christianity is illustrated by Pliny's famous despatch from Bithynia, seeking the guidance of Trajan on dealing with the Christians. Trajan's reply instructing him to spare those who recanted but to pursue those who persisted and to ignore anonymous accusations laid down the conditions of the uneasy truce which lasted down to the mid-3rd century. A fresh wave of persecution came in the reign of

The Emperor Marcus Aurelius enters Rome. The figure behind him is Victory, holding a crown. Heralded by a trumpeter, the ornate chariot is about to pass through a triumphal arch. This panel, dating from the end of Marcus Aurelius' reign, comes from a now vanished memorial erected in his honour, possibly a triumphal arch.

Trajan Decius (AD 249–251) with whose religious policy, requiring recognition and sacrifice to the gods, Christians could not conform; and still further persecution came under Valerian (AD 253–259). The last and greatest persecution came in the time of Diocletian at the very end of the century, but the final triumph of Christianity under Constantine the Great was then near at hand.

Emperor worship which had begun already in the reign of Augustus in the provinces continued to be a feature in the succeeding reigns; but in Rome, at least, worship of the emperor as a god was confined to those emperors who had died and suffered an apotheosis.

The Calm Before the Storm

Although Hadrian had no son to succeed him, and had for some years suffered ill-health, he took no steps to appoint an heir until 136. His first choice, Lucius Aelius, died in early 138. Hadrian promptly nominated Antoninus and required him to adopt as his heirs the young Marcus Aurelius and the boy Lucius Verus, son of Lucius Aelius.

The last years of Hadrian's reign had earned him the bitter hatred of the senate who now tried to refuse to consecrate him, but Antoninus made it clear that he would accept the succession on no other terms. His loyalty to his adoptive father earned him the title of Pius. There was no change in the policy of good careful government, though Rome and Italy got more attention than the provinces. Such wars as were waged concerned frontier defence, as in Britain, where a new defensive wall was constructed between Forth and Clyde. This was on the whole a reign of peace, usually regarded as the apogee of imperial rule, but it was the calm before the storm which was to break in the next reign. Symptoms of decline were already apparent. The economy of the empire was stagnating; the continued policy of *alimenta* in Italy was indicative of the plight of the small farmers in hopeless competition with the spread of large estates worked by slave labour, while the increasing necessity of state participation in local government was a vicious spiral leading to bureaucratic stultification of ever more aspects of ordinary life. But for the moment circumstances were tolerable, and it is easily understandable that the crisis-ridden centuries which followed would look back on the reign of Pius as a Golden Age.

It was the misfortune of Marcus Aurelius, who succeeded in 161, to have to devote the greater part of his reign to slaughtering and enslaving barbarians rather than to the pursuit of philosophy which was his natural bent. Although himself the nominated heir of Pius, Marcus immediately adopted Lucius Verus as his co-emperor. In 162 Verus left for the East, where the Parthians had invaded Syria, and, after initial setbacks, Roman arms prevailed

and the two emperors celebrated a triumph in 166. The army returning from the east brought with it a terrible plague which spread throughout the empire and greatly hampered the preparations to meet a new danger. The Marcomanni, Quadi and Sarmatians, native tribes from across the Danube, invaded the empire and reached north Italy. Verus died in the early stages of the campaign in 169, and it was not until 175 that Marcus succeeded in crushing the invaders, some of whom he settled within the frontier. This partial solution of the problem of barbarian invasion began the process of barbarization of the frontier provinces which was to have dire consequences for the later empire.

In the same year Marcus had to hasten to the East to put down the revolt of his general, Cassius, and on his return he was faced with a renewed war on the Danube. Marcus, accompanied by Commodus, his son and heir, now appointed joint emperor, again defeated the Marcomanni, but before he could accomplish his intention of creating a new Danubian province he died at Vindobona in 180.

Now, for the first time since the Flavians, there was a dynastic successor, but the failure of Commodus contrasted lamentably with the succession of good emperors hitherto provided by adoption. Peace with the Marcomanni was quickly patched up, and Commodus returned to the more congenial life of the capital. The direction of affairs was left to a succession of favourites, first Perennis and then, after his fall, Cleander, both Praetorian prefects while Commodus devoted his interest to the games of the Circus in which he himself performed as a gladiator, and represented himself as a new Roman Hercules. An unsuccessful conspiracy against Commodus provoked a reign of terror and, as in the case of Domitian, led to a further conspiracy of those in the immediate court circle who felt themselves threatened. This time it was successful and Commodus was assassinated on 31 December 192.

The Storm Breaks

The Praetorian prefect Laetus, who had headed the conspiracy, procured the proclamation of the prefect of the city, Pertinax, and it seemed for a time that the rôle played by Nerva in 96 might be repeated. The Praetorians, however, discontented at the austerity and discipline which Pertinax tried to impose, murdered him. They then literally put the empire up to auction and proclaimed the highest bidder, Didius Julianus, as emperor. Other claimants quickly appeared. The army in the east proclaimed Pescennius Niger governor of Syria, the troops in Pannonia saluted Septimius Severus and in Britain Clodius Albinus advanced his claim. Severus quickly seized Rome, having reached an accommodation with Albinus, whereby he was recognized as Caesar and heir, and in a swift campaign in the East overcame Pescennius Niger. Severus began a further campaign against the Parthians who had supported Niger, but had to turn back to deal with Albinus, who, mistrustful, had crossed to Gaul to claim his rights. The two forces clashed near Lugdunum, Albinus was slain, and Severus was left sole emperor. Severus returned to the East to defeat the Parthians who had resumed the offensive in his absence, and it was not until 202 that he returned to Rome.

To repair the ravages of the Civil War, Severus stole the property of the supporters of Niger and Albinus. From this point the principate became more of a ruthless monarchic despotism. The senate and the senatorial order declined in importance and influence, while the equestrians secured easier access to posts of importance, particularly in the army. It was to the army which Severus looked for his principal support and he sought to maintain its loyalty by raising the soldiers' pay to 500 *denarii* per annum. Severus crossed to Britain in 208 with his two sons, Caracalla and Geta to restore the province which had suffered tribal invasions in the north. In a series of campaigns the barbarians were expelled and the defences of Hadrian's wall restored, but in the midst of preparation for further campaigns, Severus died at York in 211.

The empire was left to the two sons, but shortly after their return to Rome Caracalla had Geta murdered. The continued support of the army was secured by increasing the soldiers' pay by fifty per cent, and to meet the cost the citizenship was extended in

212 to all the free population of the empire by the *constitutio Antoniniana*, for duty on inheritance was payable only by Roman citizens. After campaigns in Germany against the Alemanni, Caracalla, emulating the feats of Alexander the Great, set off to conquer the East, but before a conclusive battle was fought he was murdered at the instigation of his prefect, Macrinus, who believed his own life in danger from Caracalla.

The army proceeded to salute Macrinus as emperor and the senate also extended recognition, though Macrinus was only an equestrian, a member of the order which was able to fill only the second flight of important administrative and military posts. The Parthians were bought off with a huge indemnity. Macrinus' attempt to economize on the soldiers' pay opened the way for intrigue by Julia Maesa, sister of Severus' empress, Julia Domna. She successfully purchased the army's support for her grandson. Proclaimed emperor as Marcus Aurelius Antoninus, he is better known to history as Elagabalus, the name of the sun-god at Emesa, whose high-priest he was. This revived Severan dynasty continued the policy of Severus, what rule there was being exercized by Maesa. Elagabalus, a vicious and fanatical pervert, imported to Rome the cult of his sun-god, but this oriental despotism proving too much even for the army, Maesa engineered the removal of Elagabalus and his replacement by his cousin Severus Alexander.

The cult-stone of Baal is solemnly introduced into Rome by the Emperor Elagabalus, who reigned for only three years (from the age of 14 to 17). A cruel and unbalanced pervert, he was finally murdered by his own guards in AD 222.

There was some attempt in this reign to return to the policy of the 2nd century emperors and to hold the army in check. The consequent half-hearted support of the army rendered inconclusive the campaigns of Alexander in the East against the new, virile, Sassanian empire which had replaced Parthia. Discontent came to a head in 235 in the midst of preparations on the Rhine for a campaign in Germany, when Alexander and his mother, Mammaea, were murdered and the army proclaimed its own choice, the general Maximinus.

One of the results of the civil war in AD 193 and the emergence of Septimius Severus as victor in the struggle was to increase the dependence of the emperor on the support of the army. To secure the loyalty of the troops Severus not only raised army pay but relaxed conditions governing the soldier's freedom to instal his wife and family in the settlement outside the legionary fortress. From confiscated properties Severus formed a new fund, the *res privata*, which he used largely to meet increased expenditure on the army. The army was increased by two legions at this time and for the first time a legion, the II Parthica, was stationed in Italy, on the Alban Mount. The advice of Severus to his sons, 'enrich the army; despise the rest of the world' was only too well followed by the emperors of the 3rd century, so that the army became the master rather than the servant.

The character of the army also changed. Its efficiency deteriorated in the 3rd century, for the main source of recruits became increasingly the peasantry of the frontier provinces. The *numeri*, the local militia, instituted by Hadrian to round off his system of frontier defence, were by their nature tied to the soil. The *auxilia* also developed stronger ties though these troops, despite their Romanization, continued to be developed as special arms—archers, slingers and cavalry—and to be used on occasion in other theatres. In the 3rd century the javelin and short sword of the legionaries was replaced by the longer *spatha*, previously used by the *auxilia*, and by the lance. The greatest change was the development of the cavalry into a force of cataphracts, or mailed horsemen, who were eventually formed into a new special, mobile, army under Gallienus.

From recruitment from the peasantry of the frontier provinces it was but a short step to the recruitment of their barbaric kinsmen from across the frontiers. As the Roman element in the army declined, the army became more and more barbarized, became more of an alien element within the empire, but yet was the force which made and unmade emperors. It was left to the reforming hand of Diocletian to reduce the army again to an instrument of state rather than controller of the state.

Anarchy, the Plague, Barbarian Attack

The principate, however much Augustus tried to disguise it and to make use of existing institutions, was essentially an autocracy. After two and a half centuries, far from having engendered widespread interest in and shared responsibility for government, the principate had become more and more autocratic. It had become a dominate with hardly any pretence of shared rule, and to maintain himself the emperor had come to rely more and more on the army. For the next half-century few emperors were of requisite calibre to command the loyalty of all the armies for any length of time, and with a few exceptions emperors came and went in rapid succession as the several army groups, prompted by local nationalism or the desire for a donative, proclaimed each their own commander. It was a miserable time of bad government, oppression, misery and despair.

Maximinus, the second equestrian to become emperor, never visited Rome but was engaged for the three years of his reign in wars in Germany and on the Danube. Exactions to meet military requirements roused resistance in North Africa, where the elderly senator Gordian I, was proclaimed emperor, together with his son Gordian II, in 238. They were quickly suppressed but they had already been recognized at Rome by the senate. Aware that Maximinus was already on his way from the Balkans to deal with this defection, the senate hastily chose two of their number, Balbinus and Pupienus as emperors. Maximinus' army, delayed in conditions of near famine by the lengthy siege of Aquileia, turned against him and slew him. Before the year was out the two senatorial emperors were slain by their German guard and Gordian III, grandson of Gordian I, was proclaimed in their stead. The young Gordian found in his prefect and father-in-law, Timesitheus, a sturdy adviser, but when a fresh war with Persia required Gordian's presence, the sudden death of Timesitheus betrayed his patent inability and the army replaced him by his new prefect Philip.

The reign of Philip was marked by the great celebrations of Rome's thousandth year in 248 and the Secular Games of that year find record on a whole series of coinage. Such occasions for rejoicing were exceptional, for the next few years saw a bewildering turn-over of emperors. Decius, sent to quell revolt in Moesia, was hailed emperor by his troops, and turning about defeated Philip at Verona. Two years later he fell in battle against the Goths, one of the warlike tribes now pressing forward against the northern frontier, at Abrittus in Lower Moesia. Trebonianus Gallus, governor of Moesia, succeeded him for a brief reign of two years, during which plague from the East again swept the empire. A fresh usurper from Moesia, Aemilian, defeated Gallus at Interamna, only to suffer the same fate after a few months at the hands of Valerian who joined his son Gallienus with him as co-emperor.

Now, at a time when Roman strength had been drained by plague, misgovernment and economic decline, the full fury of incessant barbarian inroads broke along the whole northern frontier and Gallienus established his headquarters in Gaul to combat this invasion, while Valerian departed for the East, where the Sassanians under Sapor I had begun fresh invasions. The unprecedented disaster of the capture of Valerian by the Persians in battle before Edessa in 259 alarmed and appalled the Roman world. The eastern armies proclaimed their own emperors, Macrian and Quietus; the governor of Gaul, Postumus, successfully revolted and established a separate empire which controlled Britain and Spain as well as Gaul, and which lasted under Postumus' successors until 274. Gallienus for a time controlled only the central empire and had to suppress a succession of usurpers in the Danubian provinces. Macrian was defeated in the Balkans by Aureolus, commander of the new field army formed by Gallienus from vexillations or detachments from the legions and stationed as a central force in north Italy. In the East, Odenathus of Palmyra suppressed Quietus and turned back the Persian invaders. Rewarded with the title *Dux Orientis*, Odenathus preserved a nominal loyalty to Gallienus, but exercised effective control over most of the eastern provinces.

The part played by Gallienus in the preservation of the empire has been minimized by ancient pro-senatorial sources, for in his reign the significance of the senatorial order was further reduced by its exclusion from important military posts. Though Gallienus was not able to recover the western provinces or to gain real control over the eastern provinces and Egypt, he succeeded in putting down all revolts in the Danubian and Balkan provinces and prepared the way for reunification by his successors. In 268 his general, Aureolus, in Milan, declared for Postumus. During the subsequent siege of Milan, Gallienus was assassinated, and one of his senior staff, Claudius, proclaimed emperor in his stead.

Claudius' great defeat of a Gothic invasion at Nish in the Balkans earned him the title of Gothicus, but in 270 he was carried off by the plague, being replaced for a few months by his brother, Quintillus, until the army fixed its new choice on the general Aurelian. Invasions of Alemanni, Goths, and Vandals were repelled, but continuing threats made it necessary for Rome and other cities once again to rebuild walls and fortifications that had been almost forgotten in the long imperial peace. The province of Dacia was now finally abandoned. Aurelian had initially been compelled to continue recognition of Palmyra's rulers, Zenobia, the widow of Odenathus, and her son, Vaballathus, but in 272–3 he embarked on war against Zenobia and succeeded in recovering all Rome's eastern provinces. The successors of Postumus had continued to hold a separate Gallic empire, but in 274, Tetricus, beset with difficulties both from barbarian invasions and the indiscipline of his own troops, made overtures to Aurelian, who now invaded Gaul. At the battle of Châlons in 274, Tetricus went over to Aurelian, his leaderless troops were defeated, and the western provinces were reunited with the empire.

Even such a victorious general as Aurelian could not for long command the loyalty of his army; a group of officers murdered him as he was on his way to war with Persia in 275. For once the army proclaimed no new emperor immediately, and the senate nominated the elderly Tacitus. He, too, fell victim to the army who proclaimed the prefect of the guard, Florian, who suffered the same fate when the Syrian legions fixed their choice on Probus. The empire, reunited by Aurelian, was further strengthened by Probus whose reign was spent in repelling barbarian invasions and restoring the frontiers on the Rhine and Danube. Again the army turned on its emperor, when Probus tried to divert its military strength to other, more constructive labours, such as planting vineyards, and replaced him by the Praetorian prefect, Carus, in 282.

Carus left his son and Caesar, Carinus, to watch over Gaul and the West, while he himself, accompanied by his other son, Numerian, on whom he conferred the title of Caesar, departed for the East and the Persian war. On the march back from a successful campaign which had carried him to Ctesiphon and had gained much booty, Carus was allegedly killed by lightning which struck his tent. Numerian, who like his brother Carinus in the West had in the meantime been advanced to the rank of Augustus, was

shortly afterwards murdered by Aper, the prefect of the guard, whose hopes were, however, disappointed when the army proclaimed Diocletian as the new emperor. Carinus, after defeating the usurper Julian at Verona, marched to meet Diocletian. The armies clashed in the valley of the Margus in Moesia in 285. The battle was won by Carinus, but he fell by the hand of one of his own men, and the final victory went to Diocletian.

The Last Great Figure: Diocletian

Diocletian, reserving to himself the ultimate authority over the whole empire, took as his particular responsibility the eastern provinces, and in 285 appointed Maximian to take charge of the West, first with the rank of Caesar, then with that of Augustus. This delegation of part of the imperial power was something new. It was further elaborated in 293 when each of the Augusti appointed a Caesar as his second-in-command to take charge of a specific portion of the empire. There was Galerius in the East, Constantius in the West. The prime necessity was to strengthen the empire itself, particularly in the West, where in 287 a usurper, Carausius, had set up an independent empire consisting of Britain and the north coast of Gaul. An abortive attempt to recover Britain was made by Maximian, but it was not until Carausius had been replaced by his *rationalis*, Allectus, in 293 that a more determined invasion launched by Constantius recovered the province of Britain in 296. Campaigns by Constantius on the Rhine, by Maximian in North Africa, by Galerius against the Carpi, and by Diocletian in Egypt completed the process of reintegration. A successful campaign by Galerius against the Persians fixed the frontier on the upper Tigris and, for the time being, settled the eastern question.

In an overhaul of the provincial system, the provinces were reduced in size, and the consequently increased number of 101 provinces organized in larger units called dioceses, of which there were twelve, each in charge of a *vicarius*. Military command was now removed from the governor of a province and entrusted to an independent commander with the title of *dux*. The distinction between offices which could be held by senators and equestrian officers disappeared; there remained now only the one imperial civil service with its strictly ordered hierarchies.

On the economic side Diocletian conducted a new survey of the empire on which a new taxation was based. About 295 the whole coinage system was reformed, introducing new weight standards of gold and silver. By an edict of maximum prices in 301 attempts were made to check inflation.

The old religious cults continued to attract at least nominal adherence. Diocletian and his Caesar, Galerius, considered themselves under the special patronage of Jupiter, while Maximian and Constantius looked to Hercules. Christianity, which had enjoyed a respite from persecution since the time of Valerian and had flourished, was now to face its last and most serious attack. Diocletian, as part of his general scheme for the regeneration of the older Roman virtues, was prepared to champion the old cults against the new, particularly when the new cult could be seen to be universal in the empire and organized in such a way that it might well prove a dangerous rival to the state.

The reign of Diocletian is one of the last great milestones in the history of Rome, for there was hardly one aspect of imperial civilization that the reforming hand of Diocletian left untouched, and what he created or refurbished provided the political, military and economic institutions by which the empire survived in the West for close on another two centuries, and in the East in the guise of the Byzantine Empire, for another millennium. Something of Rome survived in human memories yet longer still. Even today men's thoughts about the meaning of Empire, the rule of law, the treatment of subject-peoples, the unity of Europe and their hopes for the future are inevitably coloured by some recollection, however dim, that these problems are all ones with which the Romans grappled before them, not indeed with complete success, but yet with sufficient skill and energy to make the story of Rome an abiding possession in the annals of humanity.

VIII POETRY, PROSE, AND RHETORIC

The riches of the Roman language

MICHAEL GRANT

'I pass to the satisfaction which eloquence affords.

It is not for a single instant only that its delights are ours,

but almost every day of the week, indeed

every hour of the day.'

TACITUS, DIALOGUE ON ORATORS, VI

The living inspiration

of Latin literature, from its beginnings until the rise of Christianity, was Greece. In lyric poetry, drama and epic, no less than in painting and sculpture, Greek models provided the encouragement which spurred Romans to develop their own talents. Virgil looked back to Homer—utterly different from Homer though he was—Seneca to Euripides, Plautus and Terence to Menander. Many Greek myths and legends were taken over intact; the Olympian hierarchy, with some changes of name but none of substance, became the official religion of the state; and the nine Muses presiding over the arts were invoked in Rome as frequently as in Athens. The mosaic (right), of the 2nd century AD, once formed the floor of a villa at Trier. Six of the Muses can be named with some certainty. Top row: Thalia, Muse of Comedy, with comic mask, ivy-wreath and shepherd's crook; Terpsichore, Muse of the Dance, with a lyre; and Clio, Muse of History, with a scroll. Middle row: Euterpe, Muse of Lyric Poetry, possibly originally holding a double flute (this panel has been much restored); one unidentified Muse; and Erato, Muse of Love Poetry, holding a lyre, but smaller than Terpsichore's. Bottom row: Urania, Muse of Astronomy, with a celestial globe; and two more. The three unidentified ones must be Calliope (Epic), Melpomene (Tragedy) and Polymnia (Sacred Song).

But while the forms and often the standards of Latin literature were derived from Greek—which was, after all, the only previous literature there had been—its character was uncompromisingly Roman and individual. Its greatness has the same qualities as the greatness of Rome itself—a constant and serious moral concern; an observant, almost clinical, attitude to the emotions (which makes some Latin literature more *personal* than Greek); and a solid respect for the reasonable and the practical. In the Latin language, too, the Romans found their perfect instrument of expression—terse, forcible and precise. It became the language of the whole western world (many of the greatest Latin writers were in fact from outside Italy), and retained its usefulness as the *lingua franca* of scholarship until the 18th century.

At the end of the classical period, Latin took on yet another lease of life by becoming the language of the Catholic Church, which it still is. St Augustine belongs almost equally to the ancient and the modern world. In the medieval church, both great traditions, pagan and Christian, were preserved. Copied and re-copied in beleaguered monasteries, the classical texts precariously survived until the 'Renaissances' of the later Middle Ages and the 15th century, and the invention of printing, made them once more a vital force.

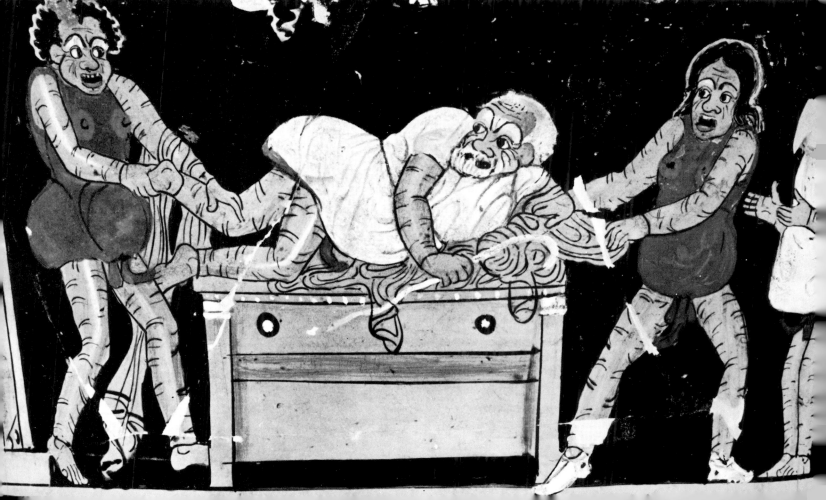

Latin comedy was closely based on the Greek 'New Comedy' established by Menander, a comedy of stock types and farcical action. The angry father was a popular type of this kind. In the relief (*above left*) he is rushing out of his mansion with a stick. His son has just come home from a party, accompanied by a girl playing the flute and his slave, half supporting him, half hiding behind him. *Above*: slave mocking two lovers; a wall-painting from Pompeii.

Grasping misers, cunning thieves and dishonest slaves appeared in the south Italian farces; and they were taken over by Plautus and Terence. On the *left* two thieves are trying to drag the miser Charinus off his money chest, while his slave stands by ineffectually—a scene that occurs again with small variations in Plautus' *Comedy of Pots*.

Popular farces in the Greek cities of south Italy also made burlesque use of stories from the epics. On the vase (*right*) Odysseus is seen arriving at the court of the King of the Phaeacians (Nausicaa's father) and his formidable queen.

The national epic of the Romans was Virgil's *Aeneid*, and it was national in a sense that Homer was not. Virgil himself (1st century BC) is shown in this Tunisian mosaic (*left*), holding a scroll of the *Aeneid* (*Musa, mihi causas memora*) between the Muses of Epic and Tragedy. The story tells how Aeneas, prince of Troy, escaped from the captured city and set sail to found a 'new Troy' in Italy. In the Second Book he relates to Dido, Queen of Carthage, the story of Troy's fall. A wall-painting from Pompeii (*above*) shows the Trojans dragging the fatal Wooden Horse. The tragic love-affair between Dido and Aeneas is told in a mosaic from Low Ham, Somerset (*above right*). On the right the Trojan ships approach Carthage. Faithful Achates takes a diadem as a gift to Dido. Next (going anti-clockwise), Venus and Cupid enflame Aeneas and Dido to *vivus amor*. Then the Royal Hunt—Dido, Aeneas and Ascanius on horseback. A storm breaks out, the lovers take shelter together, and Dido surrenders. In the central octagon is Venus, mother of Aeneas, with two cupids. In Italy Aeneas is received by King Latinus (*right*, a manuscript of the 4th century AD).

The later Roman drama produced little that was original. In tragedy the only great name is Seneca. His themes are all adapted from the Greek, but his talent was more rhetorical than dramatic: the Romans loved melodrama, violence, ghosts, murders and prodigies. Even now, in some of the masks and pictures that survive, it is possible to catch an echo of the horror that was aroused. *Right*: mosaic of a female mask from Pompeii. The relief (*below*) possibly illustrates scenes from Seneca's *Phaedra*. On the left Phaedra, whose advances to her stepson Hippolytus have been repulsed, accuses him of the very crime of which she was guilty. Theseus, his father, calls down vengeance from Neptune, and Hippolytus is dashed to pieces when a sea-monster terrifies his horses.

In Horace (*left*), whose compact felicity of language is unequalled, lyrical inspiration initiates displays of flawless technique. He can be passionate and urbane, cynical and romantic, sensuous and sophisticated. His *Odes* cover many themes and many moods—love, wine, the good life, the gods, moral virtue, the absurdities of men, the munificence of patrons. This early manuscript (10th century, *right*) includes a panegyric of his friend and patron Maecenas.

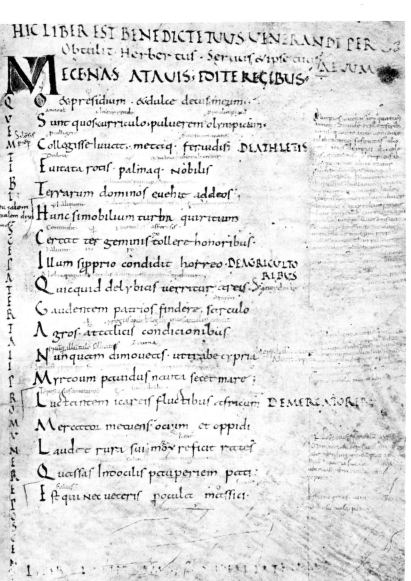

The violent gestures and distorted features of this ivory statuette (*above*) convey something of the power of Roman acting. The actor's mouth can be seen through the mask, which represents an elderly woman, possibly Clytemnestra.

The last notes of a dying culture sounded amidst the increasing chaos of the barbarian invasions. Here and there men like Ammianus Marcellinus or Claudian continued to celebrate a way of life that was passing away, while the Latin fathers of the Christian church began to explore areas of experience left untouched by paganism. The tortured conscience of St Augustine (*right*) gives his *Confessions* a Proustian modernity; his *City of God* both summed up the ancient world for the Middle Ages and helped to give it its death-blow. This fresco is the earliest known representation of him; it is in the Lateran Library and dates from about AD 600. The enigmatic ivory relief (*below*) is symbolic of its time (*c*. AD 500). Is it Christian or pagan? Philosopher or poet? Claudian or Ausonius? or Boethius with the Lady Philosophy?

The riches of the Roman language

MICHAEL GRANT

SUCH EARLY REMNANTS of the Latin tongue as have come down to us are fragmentary and of a clanking uncouth quality that needed the touch of Greek standards and Greek culture before, at the hands of writers from many different races, this literature could give birth to its own specific achievement. Rustic farces (now lost) with stock characters, known as Atellan Fables after Atella in Campania, owed something to Greek colonies on the nearby coast such as Cumae and Neapolis (Naples), with the local tribes as intermediaries. A tradition of chanted spells, too, added a quasi-literary element to drama; they were called 'Fescennine verses', perhaps from Fescennium—in Etruria which, itself under Greek influences, played so large a part in Rome's early development.

The most prosperous Greek community of the peninsula was Tarentum (Taranto) in the south, and this was the Greek city which first encountered the naval and military opposition of the Romans—and provides them with their first identifiable literary figure. The former event (282 BC) led to the Roman campaigns against Tarentum's ally Pyrrhus of Epirus, and the literary figure was a freed prisoner of war, Livius Andronicus. Probably a Greek or half-Greek, Livius wrote Latin plays that were performed at Games celebrating Rome's victory over the Carthaginians in the First Punic War (240). His plays included comedies, apparently modelled on the Athenian New Comedy of Menander and other 4th-century playwrights—the most readily available and attractive Greek exemplars—and tragedies based on Sophocles, Euripides and their successors, but without their choruses which were by now no longer performed. Tragic subject-matter from the Trojan cycle shows how the Romans were now 'discovering' their origins from the heroes of Troy—the enemies of Greece as, in many clashes from Pyrrhus onwards, Rome itself was. Livius Andronicus also translated or paraphrased the *Odyssey* into the much cruder 'saturnian' metre of native Italian origin.

His younger contemporary, Naevius, boldly adapted this epic tradition to a national Roman theme within recent memory, the First Punic War (261–41). Like the works of Livius Andronicus, this epic is almost entirely lost, but its preface may perhaps have offered an early version of the mythical link between Rome and Carthage, later enshrined by Virgil in the tragic romance of Aeneas and Dido. Naevius also wrote a number of plays—some again on historical Roman subjects—which included certain references to leading Roman statesmen, so adverse that he was for a time imprisoned.

Another whose output included both plays and epic poetry was Ennius (c. 239–169 BC), from Rudiae (near Lecce) in Calabria. Subsequent Romans revered him as the father of their poetry and above all of its pre-eminent epic, by virtue of the *Annals* in which, adapting the Greek hexameter to a Latin form of the same metre, he chronicled the course of Roman history up to his own day. Ennius exercised a profound effect on subsequent historiography. The six hundred lines that have survived shew a rough, grand vigour which earned him the sometimes rather perfunctory veneration of later critics. Ennius had been grounded in Greek as well as Latin and Oscan culture; adapting the Greek philosopher Euhemerus, he devoted a poem to rationalizing the traditional mythology—and particularly the father-figure Jupiter. A poor man but convivial, Ennius is said to have died of gout. However, his output was at least partly owed to this trouble, for 'unless I have the gout', he is on record as remarking, 'I never write poetry'.

Explosive Comic Genius

Among his works were also comedies and tragedies, but in these fields he was outshone by his older contemporary Plautus. With Plautus (c. 254–184), who came from Sarsina (Mercato Saraceno) in Umbria, we have reached the zenith of Latin comic drama—and a writer whom we can judge for ourselves, from 20,000 of his verses, since twenty complete comedies (and one incomplete one) by his hand have come down to us. Plautus adapted a famous Greek *genre* to an almost totally different Roman dramatic purpose. His models, like those of Livius, were the complicated, soft and sophisticated plays of the Athenian New Comedy familiar by now to Roman soldiers and others who had seen it acted on their travels in south Italy and Sicily. Plautus rewrote these plays and made them almost unrecognizable in the process. In the first place he performed an astonishing *tour de force* by welding the rock-like, gracelessly cumbrous Latin of his day (of which the verse may well have been naturally guided by stress-accent like our own) into the quantitative sort of metre, with its formal longs and shorts, that had been employed in the suppler Greek language. Thereby—despite the retention, discarded by later poets, of an undercurrent of stress accent—he permanently divorced Latin poetry from the spoken tongue. Unfortunate though some of the consequent artificialities may have been, this prepared the way for Roman literature's specific glories that were to come.

The spirit of Plautus, too, was very different from the Attic, and evidently owed something to the rudimentary Italian song-and-dance and dramatic sketches of the past. For while retaining the complex trickeries and misunderstandings and changes of fortune and sexual double standard of his originals, he abandoned their subtlety in order to give free rein to his own explosive comic genius and racy, slap-stick energy; and so his plays proliferated in the belly-laughs and puns and farcical quick-firing situations needed to keep the attention of a Roman audience. Theatres were only temporary structures still, and audiences, often rowdy, had to be forcibly attracted from adjacent boxers, dancers and charioteers who formed part of the same programme of Games. It is an effort for us to enjoy Plautus today, because ancient jokes are no longer funny (until good modern acting makes them so), and also because of the unfamiliar conventions of his day—the explanatory Prologue, the backcloths of traditional town-scenery, the difficult metres; to which would have been added, on the stage, the 'types' recognizable—in the absence of programmes—by costume, wigs, beards and even music and gestures, and the small number of actors (not yet an influential profession) employed to double or treble the parts.

Plautus rose above these formidable hazards; and in the future theatre of Europe, almost every sort of comedy is his debtor. Ariosto's *Casaria*, which acted at Ferrara (1508) led the Renaissance of ancient drama, blended three plays of Plautus, and Shakespeare's *Comedy of Errors* is largely modelled on Plautus' *Menaechmi*, with borrowings from his *Amphitryo*. This was also adapted by Molière (1668)—leaning on the humorous irony of which Plautus was the prototype—and by Giraudoux (1929). The latter added '38' to his title, to show how many times this Plautine dramatic theme, of Jupiter's love for a woman, had been attempted.

For all his careless good humour, Plautus spoke for the generation that overcame Hannibal. His successor among comic dramatists, Terence (c. 195–159 BC), though he may have come from humble origins in North Africa, wrote for a more cultured age, and especially for the exclusive phil-Hellene circle of Scipio Africanus the younger (Scipio Aemilianus): indeed, according to rumour, Scipio was part-author of Terence's plays. All six of these survive; they reflect the new epoch, as well as his own gentler and more literary talent. Their writer is much less robust and more contemplative than Plautus, and so closer to the original New Comedy—although Caesar, for all his admiration of Terence's pure Latin, found him less *comic* than Menander. Yet the improbable plots, with their amoral young men about town tinged by the fashionable Stoic humaneness, are sensitive in their deft use of charac-

AESCHINUS ADULES CENS · CIESI · PHO II · SYRUS · SERUUS SANNIO

iest ille sacrilegus SAN men querit nu quidnam effert occidi nihil uideo,

A scene from Terence's 'Adelphi'. The drawing was made in the 4th century AD, though it survives only in a later manuscript. Aeschinus and Ctesiphon are the 'brothers' of the title. Aeschinus has just carried off a girl belonging to the slave-dealer Sannio, beating him in the process, and has sent his slave Syrus to placate him without actually paying him money. Here he has just entered from the house on the left, saying 'Where is this impious specimen?' Sannio (on the right): 'It's me he means. Anything in his hand? Damn! I can't see anything—nihil video.'

ter contrasts and of suspense. But it is above all their skilful construction which has stamped his influence upon Italian, Spanish, French and English drama. Molière's *Ecole des Maris* and *Fourberies de Scapin* are funnier versions of Terence's *Adelphi* and *Phormio*, and the *Woman of Andros* has had a long English career from 16th-century translations (some intended for schools) right down to the adaptation of Thornton Wilder (1934).

Merit, fashion and chance have all played a part in deciding why some ancient works should have survived and others perished; the tragic drama, which at Rome reached its climax at the same time as comedy, has almost all been lost. Ennius' nephew Pacuvius (c. 220–130 BC) from Brundisium (Brindisi) was not only a distinguished painter but a tragedian. Cicero called Pacuvius 'first' in tragedy as Ennius was in epic—though the style he employed to deal with his Greek and Trojan (and on one occasion Roman) subjects was less vigorous and perhaps more diffuse, and his strength seems to have lain rather in metre. Roman tragedy, in all its branches, culminated in Pacuvius' younger friend and rival Accius (170–c. 85 BC) from Pisaurum (Pesaro), a master of tragic debate and repartee who lived long enough to discuss literary matters with Cicero. Three of Accius' contemporaries made their names by specializing in comedies 'in Roman dress' *(togatae)*.

A Ruthless Private Eye
Slightly older than any of these was Lucilius from Suessa (Sessa) Aurunca (c. 180–102 BC), who turned his own exceptional gifts into the channel of satire. Literary satire had waxed among Hellenistic Greeks, and Ennius had moralized in this vein, but it was Lucilius who brought his varied and salty mockery to bear upon contemporary life and letters. One of the most highly educated men of his time, Lucilius, like Terence, belonged to the circle of Scipio Aemilianus. Although his verse was later regarded as slovenly, it was he who set European satire on the lines which made Boileau, Dryden, Swift and Pope his direct successors. It can be seen, from the 1,300 lines which survive out of his 30 books, that Lucilius believes in Cynic and Stoic doctrines of directness and simplicity, but his own contribution is a ruthless private eye which, sensing the democratic ideas that were current in this epoch of the Gracchi, saw unerringly through futilities and shams. Later Roman critics saw something specially Roman about this spicy branch of literature which derived from Lucilius.

The generations which produced Plautus and Ennius and tragedians (whose works are lost) also gave Rome its first great prose-writer, Cato the elder (234–149 BC) from Tusculum (Frascati). No less versatile, in his way, than the poets, Cato was nevertheless a conservative Roman who probably thought the poetic art fit either for foreigners or clerks. The arts in which he excelled were oratory and history, both closely linked with the government and way of life of the Roman Republic. Public speaking was its mainspring,

and although Cato as a champion of the Roman nobility was outwardly anti-Greek, yet—as his sponsorship of the phil-Hellene Ennius suggests—he was not entirely immune from the Greek rhetorical 'art of persuasion', and the innumerable technicalities which it imparted. These influences blended with the urgent practicality of Roman speaking at the Assembly and the Bar to create that formidable instrument, Latin oratory. Cato, with his recurring refrain 'Carthage must be destroyed', was the first of its exponents who can be disentangled from myth. A hundred and fifty of his speeches were known to Cicero, and their surviving fragments show that shrewd, terse punch of his which played so great a part in 2nd-century affairs. Cato also produced the first great Roman historical achievement, his seven-book *Origines* (now lost).

The Exploration of Emotion
Cato did not live to see what would have pleased him, the downfall of the Gracchi and the conservative reaction which followed. Henceforward there was a greater precariousness and ruthlessness about the new mighty imperialist state. As wealth and culture increased, an artistic, aristocratic coterie at the turn of the century made poetry socially 'smart'. This circle of the consul, orator and poet Quintus Lutatius Catulus went back for its inspiration to the Alexandrian school whose learned, individualistic, sentimental tendencies had characterized Hellenistic culture during the previous two centuries. And so Lutatius and others adapted to Latin various kinds of Hellenistic poetry—including the fashionable miniature brand of epic, and elegiac and erotic epigrams and trifles which were new to the language. Yet the Greek and Roman Alexandrian movements differed markedly, for in Greek lands this had served to inject new, topical elements into a tired culture past its zenith, whereas Latin literature, despite its achievements, was still raw and unrefined when these influences overtook it. They played their experimental part, in an age which was less despairing and escapist than that of Alexandria, in preparing for the technical perfection that was to come.

This type of poetry was absorbed and transfigured by a man who, like some of its earlier practitioners, came from the north Italian countryside: Catullus (c. 84–54 BC). The manuscript of his surviving 2,300 lines was discovered at his native city Verona. They comprise nine long and 109 short poems, including epigrams, elegies, hymns, miniature epics and diatribes against his enemies. The havoc that this output played with traditional genres cost him his esteem with ancient critics who could not decide how to categorize him. But it is as a love-poet of heart-broken and heart-breaking intensity—as the lover of the hopelessly unfaithful Lesbia—that he reigns supreme in Latin literature.

> All gentle things a man can say or do
> In love, by you have all been said or done:
> All, to a thankless heart entrusted, perished . . .
>   Was my life honest?
> Then snatch away this plague and ruin from me. . .
> I ask no longer this: for my love, her love:
> Nor wish she'd wish, though vainly, to be chaste.
> I want mere health: to lay down this vile sickness.

Though his work fluctuates greatly from one level of intention and degree of intensity to another, at times the excitement he feels and the excitement he generates are alike irresistible: and none the less so for the sober precision of his language. Yet the belief, attractive to 19th-century romantics, that these outbursts are 'spontaneous' vanishes before the technical virtuosity, the masterly exploitation of the epic-tragic and elegiac and comic-satiric traditions of Greece and Rome, which gained him the epithet 'learned' and, like the learning of John Donne, gave him all the greater power to express unquenchable feelings. For Catullus is the product of agonizing tension between a powerful mind and tortured emotions. He takes love seriously, with an unprecedented responsiveness to its demands ranging between ecstasy and desperation, and conveying these passions with a frank intimacy possible in poetry intended only for a circle of close, like-minded friends.

In its less poignant moments this elegant society, to which he and Lesbia belonged, was frivolous and uninhibited. Its poets were 'new men', revolutionary devotees of art for art's sake delicately adapting the metres of their Greek Alexandrian forbears, while excelling them in the portrayal of urgent human feeling. Traditional large-scale epic was taboo, but its jewel-like miniature form, the epyllion, was modernized by Catullus in a brilliant, rather cloying *Marriage of Peleus and Thetis*. More startling, to us, is a Hymn with a racing rhythm which, although this 'kind' of poetry was traditional enough, is dedicated with uncontrolled passion to the bloody, horrific cult of Attis, associate of the Asian mother-goddess Cybele. But it was the other, less morbid poems of Catullus which by their freshness inspired the Renaissance humanists; and this same immediacy, this maintenance of personal life in a time of flux, makes Catullus above all others a poet for the twentieth century.

'On the Nature of Things'

So, in an utterly different way, is his contemporary Lucretius. Taking as his incongruous model the quiet Greek prose in which Epicurus had tried to prove that the universe consists solely of atoms and of the space in which they move, Lucretius converted this material into a burning impassioned Latin poem, the *De Rerum Natura*. The physics of the work now only retain a historical interest, as a link between the early Greek atomism of Democritus and Leucippus and their European followers from Newton to our own day. But Lucretius' exposition is presented with a sharp, visual vividness and the overpowering conviction of a poet who was also, perhaps, Rome's greatest intellectual. These descriptive and mental gifts were combined with an intense urge to communicate what seemed to him the all-important truths: namely that, as Epicurus had said before him, fear of death, and of the gods, is utterly unjustified and pointless. The picture with which he replaces them, demonstrating the triumphs of the human brain and will that had enabled the world to develop, is one of the supreme expositions of the capabilities of man. For, in a deterministic world, man, by the occasional unpredictable swerve of atoms, remains a free agent: his purpose should be happiness, and that he should achieve by the traditional Hellenistic and Epicurean means of freedom from disturbance (*ataraxia*).

Poetry of this philosophical and informative kind, cast (like Lucretius' poem) in hexameters, possessed a long Greek pedigree—not least among the Alexandrians—and it was well suited to the gravity which played so persistent a part in the Roman character. Lucretius owed technique to his Greek and Roman forerunners, but the rapid fiery grandeur and human pathos of this magnificent poem were his own, and they give him a strange, unique place in the history of poetry and thought. We have no idea who he was, and few early traces of his poem's impact, other than the certainty that it influenced Virgil. There is also an isolated cryptic tribute to its genius by Cicero.

Philosopher, Orator and Statesman

Marcus Tullius Cicero of Arpinum (106–43 BC) was Lucretius' contemporary, but like most Romans in public life he instinctively liked the Epicureans less than their Stoic rivals whose doctrines were more moral and less materialistic, being centred upon a belief in Providence. Cicero wrote his ethical treatises mostly at times when he was excluded from political life, or to console himself in a bereavement such as the loss of his daughter. Among the most perpetually famous of these moral essays are *On Duties (De Officiis)*, *The Boundaries of Good and Evil (De Finibus)*, *On Old Age*, *On Friendship* and the political studies *On the Laws* and *On the State*. Though these are for the most part unphilosophical practical popularizations of Stoic ethics, presented with the undogmatic modesty which was the special feature of Cicero's own instruction by the successors of Plato's Academy, the doctrines which they presented so attractively were the most civilized the world had seen. To use his own word, they show *humanitas*—enlightenment of mind and character. A man should treat his fellow-men decently because Man himself is of value. This basic assumption of western thought derives, through Cicero, from the Stoic idea that all men share a spark of divinity which makes them akin to one another, irrespective of race or degree in the universal Brotherhood of Man. And he stressed that right is right and wrong is wrong, objectively; and that no law-making can make them otherwise. Pagans and early Fathers, Dante and Petrarch and Luther and Montaigne, Bolingbroke and Locke and Bossuet and Hume, all turned to these guides to human behaviour.

To Cicero, living in an age when liberal education as well as public life was permeated by Greek-taught rhetoric, it seemed that the man best equipped to teach and preach the good life was the *orator*. For he, in addition to mastering elaborate techniques, must himself be a man not only of wide and liberal culture but of virtue: the Whole Man whom the Renaissance was so greatly to admire. That is the viewpoint of a number of rhetorical treatises in which Cicero gives us unique insight into this all-important branch of ancient life.

He himself was one of the most brilliant, successful and persuasive orators who have ever lived. The combination of his native gifts with an elaborate education and training furnished him with every weapon that a speaker in Senate, Assembly or lawcourt could need, and empowered him to speak and write that unprecedentedly eloquent language which is the foundation of Europe's subsequent prose and has only very recently ceased to echo in the cadences of its orators. Though striking, in the ancient view, an effective mean between the flamboyant Asianic and plain Attic dictions, to us northerners this style, in most of its variations, seems rotund; nor can we recapture the electric atmosphere at these gatherings of Romans (who were so much more excitable than their portrait-busts look). Nevertheless, it is possible for

Specific illustrations of Latin narrative poetry in painting and sculpture are naturally rare, but this sarcophagus relief showing the wedding of Peleus and the sea-nymph Thetis (note the dolphins along the top) might well have been inspired by Catullus's poem: 'Now when the longed for *day, in time fulfilled, had come for them, all Thessaly in full assembly crowds the house, the palace is thronged with a joyful company. They bring gifts in their hands; they display joy in their looks.' The sarcophagus is now in the Villa Albani, Rome.*

us to comprehend dimly from the fifty-eight surviving speeches of Cicero (more than half of his total output) why none except the Athenian Demosthenes was thought fit to compare with him.

The story they tell is the story of his times and of the stresses and strains of the mighty Republic on the verge of succumbing to autocracy. In this painful process Cicero played, for three or four decades, a leading part. Hardly anyone has written so well about his own work at the centre of events; hardly anyone has revealed so much about himself. The man who emerges is vacillating, extravagant, as unable as anyone else to see how to make a city state rule an empire, conceited about his success in stifling Catiline's rather feeble *coup d'état*, and over-respectful to the high nobility to which he did not belong. Yet, once or twice he stood up against tyranny; and it cost him his life. A supporter, always, of the rising business class, which was regarded by him as one of the pillars of Republican 'freedom' such as it was—a freedom he attributed to unity and *co-operation* among the governing groups—Cicero sourly and reluctantly endured Caesar, who forced everyone else into obvious subordination; but against Caesar's less imposing would-be successor Antony he came out openly. His impassioned *Philippics* were unendurable to Antony, who in collaboration with Octavian—the young Augustus, mistakenly regarded by Cicero as his admiring pupil—had him proscribed and put to death.

Although no medieval epoch was unaware of Cicero's speeches, Petrarch, in the 14th century, was more determined than anyone before him to see Cicero as the paragon of eloquence and the guide to past and present alike. Petrarch also studied the wealth of autobiographical (as well as historical) information provided by Cicero's incomparably vivid personal letters to Atticus and other friends. Out of the eight hundred of these that survive, half were seen by him at Verona and brought to the world's notice. Their revelations shocked him because of Cicero's 'rash' return to public life. But what fascinated the 15th century that followed was the patriotic responsibility shown, above all, in his speeches. Later, again, the French and American revolutions admired their political Republicanism, while the analogies of House of Commons debates and trials by jury made the English also interested in Cicero's evidence for the Roman precursors of these institutions. It was not until nowadays—despite the special interest for our own times, of a timid man's brave actions—that surfeit of admiration has turned to excessive neglect.

The 'Official' Histories of Caesar and Sallust

Next to Cicero, his political enemies Caesar and Antony were among the ablest orators of the 1st century BC, the former adopting a simple, direct style and the latter preferring the more emotional methods which made his speech, imaginatively reconstructed by Shakespeare, more effective than the plain delivery of Brutus in the days following the Ides of March. None of Antony's pronouncements (except a few letters) have survived. But Caesar's style of narrative, if not of oratory, is represented by his masterly, rapidly moving accounts of the *Gallic War* and *Civil War*. These two components of what he modestly called the *Commentaries*—'Memoirs' or 'Notes'—present not only a disarmingly reasonable evasion of political war-guilt (which shows that the Romans had nothing to learn about propaganda) but an unequalled picture of the workings of Roman discipline and efficiency in war and administration. Caesar's deliberate abstinence from rhetoric was too plain for ancient tastes, but throughout European history the wonderful sinewy Latin of his *Commentaries* has been pored over by many a despot and commander—and innumerable schoolboys too.

One of Caesar's supporters in the Civil War against Pompey was the historian Sallust, from Amiternum (San Vittorno) in central Italy, who served him as governor of Numidia. Surviving charges of embezzlement, he acquired a splendid estate at Rome, on which he created the sumptuous 'Gardens of Sallust'. His masterpiece the *Histories*, covering the years 78–c. 66 BC, exercised a profound influence upon Roman writers living a century and a half after his death, in the archaizing Hadrianic age. But hardly any of it has survived. Two of Sallust's works, however, have come down to us. They comprise the first important historical monographs in Latin—the *Catiline*, describing the conspiracy in

terms which favour Caesar (and the staunch stoic Republican Cato the younger) rather than Cicero; and the *War against Jugurtha*, the Numidian king defeated by Marius—who was Caesar's uncle. Sallust has a profound, emotional insight into national and moral decline, and expresses it with fervour: he is at one and the same time politician and propagandist, moralist and philosopher, and master of stylistic effects. Even ancient critics, accustomed to moralizing and rhetorical history, saw him more as an orator than a historian. Yet the superb rapidity of his artificially rugged and semi-archaic Latin, the product of a powerful and crystal-clear brain, seemed at last to have elevated Latin historiography to the status that belonged to it. Erasmus was one of many who have found him more worth reading than any other Roman historian.

The Supreme Master of Latin Poetry

During the years immediately before and after the death of Sallust (34 BC), the ultimate winner of the Civil Wars, Augustus, himself the author of a skilfully composed political testament—his *Res Gestae* inscribed on an Ankara temple—was fortunate and clever enough to attract to his circle the greatest writers of the age. Virgil, born near Mantua in 70 BC—of uncertain and probably mixed race—and resident in the region of Naples, astonished literary circles at Rome by the novelty of his ten short *Eclogues*, transmuting into a melodious, evocative Latin the Greek pastoral 'bucolic' themes of Theocritus. This is a timeless, unreal Arcadia blended with Italian elements—an Arcadia for city-dwellers—conflicting in the poet's heart with the need to come to terms with imperial Rome. The fourth of these poems (40 BC) reflects the widespread belief that a Saviour was about to appear and to rescue the world from its miseries. The Fourth Eclogue's expression of this feeling was to make medieval Christendom take Virgil as their prophet. The other Eclogues are responsible, along with other classical traditions, for the innumerable manifestations of Arcadia which have produced some of the masterpieces (notably Milton's *L'Allegro*, *Il Penseroso* and *Comus*, and Claude's nostalgic landscapes), as well as some of the tritest 'shepherdess' themes, of later European culture.

The four *Georgics* that followed are dedicated to the politician and literary man Maecenas, the friend both of Augustus and of Virgil. The *Georgics*, favourite reading of Montaigne and Dryden, hymned in hexameters of a new sensitive flexibility the antiquarian past and rich natural gifts of the Italian countryside, the beauties and labours and rewards of the rustic life, and the glory of the Augustan peace. Strangely enough, much of this lore was derived from a recent text-book for farmers by Varro (116–27 BC), the outstanding encyclopedic scholar and polymath of the age. The fourth Georgic, about the lives of bees as symbols of the lives of men, rises far above its theme to culminate in that poignant myth, the snatching away from Orpheus, greatest of singers, of his wife Eurydice.

Next Virgil turned to epic, but the subtleties of his romantic *Aeneid* are far removed from Homer's ballad-like extroversion, and so is the hitherto unimaginable rhythmical elaboration and sonorous majesty of the poem. Aeneas escapes from captured Troy, to many wanderings and adventures. He encounters Queen Dido of Carthage, whose tragic poignancy owes more than incidental debts to Alexandrians such as Apollonius, gathered up and magically changed by Virgil's far greater gifts. Finally Aeneas reaches Italy: battles end in peace, he marries a Latin bride, and

'ARMA VIRUMQUE CANO TROIAE'—'*Arms and the man I sing, [who first from the shores] of Troy—*' The opening words of the Aeneid have been found painted or scratched at least three times on the walls of Pompeii—for reasons which remain obscure. It is, however, a measure of the fame achieved by Virgils' poem by the mid-1st century AD.

The walled city is Troy at the moment of its capture by the Greeks. Amidst scenes of slaughter Aeneas (behind the wall, centre left) gives his household gods to his father Anchises, then escapes through the gate carrying Anchises on his shoulders and leading his son Ascanius by the hand. Hermes conducts them. Bottom right, they embark on a ship which, says the inscription, 'sets out for the West.' To the left are the Greek ships at anchor, and behind them the tomb of Hector, with members of his family mourning beside it. Several of these Roman relief tablets showing the story of Troy and the wanderings of Aeneas have survived; this detail is from the best preserved (1st century AD). They were possibly used for teaching Homer and Virgil to schoolboys.

Rome's foundation will follow. The turning-point is reached in the sixth book of this twelve-book poem, when Aeneas, guided to the Golden Bough by the Sibyl, descends with her through Lake Avernus to the Underworld. This conscious echo of the *Odyssey*, in which, likewise, the hero had communed with the shades, is profoundly interwoven with a thousand other intimations of tradition, philosophy, legend, emotion and religious belief.

The theme is mainly war—the *Aeneid* is, to this extent, an *Odyssey* followed by an *Iliad*, the latter indebted to the national epic tradition of Ennius and Naevius. Augustus' feat in bringing peace seemed to Virgil, after generations of civil strife, the greatest of national gifts. Yet Aeneas does not become a successful emblem of Stoic virtue until he has bitterly suffered, and his enemies such as Turnus are given almost more than their share of nobility.

Accursed war they will have, at once, flying into the face of
Omens and oracles, impelled by a power malign . . .
Latinus made many appeals to the gods, to the deaf, blind heavens:
'Oh! We are pounded by doom, adrift at the storm's mercy!
It is you, poor souls, who will pay in your own blood for this
                                                                    sacrilege.
Yours is the guilt, Turnus; punishment most severe is
In store for you: too late shall you turn to the gods with prayer.'

Wars turn to weariness, dust and ashes—though with a radiant future ahead—and Virgil at last, melancholy but unembittered, seems to reckon military conquest lower than the conquest of his own soul by man: whose goal, and place in the Universe, remain mysterious. These shifting nuances are conveyed at different levels simultaneously, with an astonishing complexity of art and feeling and sound, wringing from the Latin language its ultimate potentialities.

Virgil is at the head of those Latin writers who are noteworthy not only because they transmitted Greek culture, or influenced later cultures, but because of the supreme quality of what they themselves wrote. And yet to say that Virgil 'influenced later cultures' would be a monumental understatement about the poet whose achievement seemed to the Middle Ages miraculous, to Dante the supreme source of guidance, and to many in every epoch the bringer of comprehension and insight into the splendours and tragedies of our mortal condition. As the somewhat retiring 'poet-laureate' of Augustus, Virgil confounds all answers to the question whether state-patronage is good for writers: would he have written even better without it (if this is possible), or would he not have written at all? He himself, when he was dying (19 BC) without having quite finished the poem, is said to have wanted it destroyed; but his executors, at the emperor's request, did not carry out his wishes

Sense and Sensibility

One other Augustan poet rose to a universal understanding of human problems, or at least of those which affected his own community and society. This was Horace of Venusia in southern Italy (65–8 BC). The son or grandson of a slave (perhaps a prisoner of war), his racial origins are as obscure as those of Virgil; with whom, after serving on the frustrated anti-Augustan side in the Civil Wars, he shared the friendship of Maecenas and Augustus. After the bitter *Epodes* of his early years—his own term was *iambi*, this being the metre traditionally employed for invective—Horace's *Satires* modernized the tradition of Lucilius in fast-moving, informal hexameters humanely presenting the poet's famous commonsense. The *Epistles* which then pursued similar themes, with additions (including literary criticism) and in maturer vein, have made a strong impact on generation after generation as the well-turned products of a mildly philosophical mind and a civilized, humorous taste. At the end of this collection is the *Ars Poetica*, a series of notes on poetry which Horace cleverly adapted—again with topical additions—from the Alexandrian Greeks. Misunderstood as a systematic treatise, the work has gained powerful authority among European poets and dramatists. Of this, as of the other *Epistles*, Alexander Pope could rightly say,

Horace still charms with graceful negligence,
And without method talks us into sense;
Will, like a friend, familiarly convey
The truest notion in the easiest way.

There were satirists and poetic epistle-writers after Horace, but his lyrical *Odes* were too good ever to have a pagan successor. Ancient critics, ignoring Catullus, regarded them as virtually the only Latin lyrics. Although he wrote for a small and highly educated circle, Horace knew he would become a school-book, and this forecast was accurate; but that is only the smallest part of the fame of the *Odes*, which is second only to the renown of the *Aeneid*. They came into their own with Petrarch, and every epoch since then has found something different in them to admire; except perhaps our own, which is irritated by their smooth quietism. These poems are cast in a variety of Greek lyric metres, imposed upon the far more solid Latin tongue by marvels of invisible ingenuity: so tight is the structural compactness that every word, as Nietzsche put it, 'by sound, by position and by meaning, diffuses its influence to right and left and over the whole'. The *Odes* often begin with a strong impulse of inspiration which, as in Donne and Baudelaire, then turns into something more calculated and elaborate. Their clever surprises, pointed to the utmost by a bold astute word order, are a long way from the spontaneous productions of Alcaeus and Sappho; though Horace—following the custom that required Latin poets to develop their originality (however marked) within the tradition—claimed to be their Romanizer. Unlike them, again, he nearly always wrote for recitation rather than song.

Agreeing with Virgil that Augustus had performed wonders by bringing peace, Horace signalized his own succession as 'poet laureate' by writing the praises of the *princeps* in his formal Secular Hymn (17 BC). Yet his specific note remains a polite and humorous detachment which never forgets the operations of Fate or Fortune. However, Horace asserts his power to withstand the onslaught of these, and holds to the dignity and freedom of will which enables him to do so.

> Not the rage of the million commanding things evil,
> Not the doom frowning near in the brows of the tyrant,
> Shakes the upright and resolute man
> > In his solid completeness of soul.

With such thoughts in mind he ranges over many matters; the transience of human life and the futility of exaggeration, the glory of Rome and its virtues and gods, the familiar beauties of its countryside (for Horace has a very Roman sense of home) and the pleasures and annoyances of love. But Horace, though occasionally profound on this last matter, has like his emperor a double standard of feminine values: one for the freeborn Roman ladies whose morals Augustus was seeking to elevate, and quite another for the Greek-named girls, unsuitable for marriage, who are treated in his verses with a tenderness that easily turns to ridicule.

The 'Tearful' Elegy, Expression of Unhappy Love

Love is the main theme of the elegiac poets who also reached their zenith in this Augustan age. The metre after which they are named consists of couplets, a hexameter followed by a line two syllables shorter (the pentameter) which interrupts and lightens the heroic grandeur but encourages sentiment and point. After a long and varied Greek history, the elegy had become in Roman hands 'tearful', the expression of unhappy love—a branch of Latin poetry which has exercised an incalculable effect on later literatures. Though Catullus had experimented brilliantly in this medium, its first serious exponent was held to be Cornelius Gallus from Forum Julii (Fréjus), a friend of Virgil—and also of Augustus until, as first Roman governor of Egypt, he fell into fatal disgrace.

Unlike Virgil and Horace, elegiac poets were of good birth and well off, these being helpful preconditions for the 'studied wistfulness and self-pity' involved in this genre. The gentlest of its practitioners was Tibullus (c. 48–19 BC). A true Augustan in his love of peace—perhaps it is what he loves more than anything else—he does not specifically mention the emperor; the circle to which he belongs is of the somewhat independently minded (though acquiescent) soldier statesman Messalla. Tibullus writes of his love for 'Delia' and 'Nemesis' (of the non-Roman half-world like Horace's women) and of a boy-love Marathus. He is sensitive, reflective, softer than other Romans, yet strikes an authentic note as, in a hard world, he seeks an endurable place. For his analysis of love as it affects him, his private background is the countryside; but it is a nostalgic, rather vague countryside,

akin to the pastoral world of the *Eclogues*. Tibullus is haunted by a feeling of loss, an instinct that happiness, the possession of country and love, was precarious and perhaps irretrievably doomed. His quiet but articulate appeal caused the leading critic Quintilian to rank him first among Roman elegists.

'But', he adds, 'there are some who prefer Propertius'; and, although virtually untranslatable, Propertius would come at the head of most poets' lists to-day. He was an Umbrian, probably from Asisium (Assisi), impoverished like Virgil and Horace by the Civil Wars. He joined Maecenas' pro-Augustan circle, and yet remained for a long time wholly immersed in the theme of love: thereby, despite his conventional claim to be the Romanizer of Alexandrian elegists such as Callimachus, endowing this sort of poetry with a novel subjectivity. His passion for Cynthia is intense, all-absorbing and catastrophic. Veering rapidly—though with the occasional saving grace of irony—from ecstasy to depression, Propertius extracts from the elegiac metre new potentialities of strength and feeling as his rich, sombre, often obscure imagery (anticipating the tortured syntax of some modern poets) explores the depths of neurotic self-abandonment—what the Romans called *mollitia*. The mythology which was the life-blood of the ancient literatures, but which so often delays our own understanding of them since we cannot at once grasp the allusions as the ancients did, was in Propertius' poetry always integral and deeply felt (as others, such as Titian, have felt it deeply since) and never merely decorative. Towards the end of his career, when love was ended, Propertius wrote more public sorts of poem, in his final book; they dwell on that blend of myth and patriotic antiquarianism which had fascinated Virgil. But the last poem of all is a superb epitaph to the lady Cornelia.

> And if you grieve, let them not see you grieving;
> > When they approach, receive them with dry eyes.
> Enough for you to wear the nights with sorrow,
> > To dream of phantoms with Cornelia's face;
> And, when you talk in secret to my image,
> > Speak every word as if I might reply.

Imaginative History

The antiquarian love of Italy which had shone through the other poems in that book is again evident throughout the moralizing, emotional history of Livy of Patavium (Padua) (59 BC—AD 17). His History of Rome from the earliest times (*Ab Urbe Condita*) is a mighty, unparalleled historical feat which took him forty years to complete; it consisted of one hundred and forty-two 'books' (nearly one hundred and seven are lost), which would have filled twenty or thirty modern volumes. Written in rich, fluent prose, and making loftily imaginative use of many sources without too much critical analysis, his poetical evocations of Rome's beginnings and heroic age—reanimated in the nineteenth century by Macaulay—and his rousing narrative of Hannibal's invasion are masterpieces of dramatic art.

Rome, as the chosen object and instrument of providential destiny, receives its supreme glorification from Livy. Its heroes and their actions served as models for Renaissance historians and educationalists and have been handed down by them, as revelations of the human spirit and its capacities, to many a modern school and college. Livy's account of the young Roman Republic also became a favourite reference-book of the French Revolution. Yet the most favoured among his heroes was that destroyer of the Republic, or its 'restorer' as he preferred to call himself, Augustus —who had himself, converting Livy into sculpture, placed statues of all the victorious generals of earlier Roman history in his splendid new Forum. However, the historian retains a certain independence, for in the prologue of his work, although the Augustan régime is by now under way, he expresses a traditional pessimism about the inferiority of modern to ancient times.

The Supreme Story-Teller

Ovid of Sulmo (43 BC–c. AD 17) was only sixteen years younger than Livy. But he belongs to a very different generation, no longer brought up amid Civil War, no longer much interested in serious pro-Augustan patriotism or even in serious love. Ovid, therefore,

Latin drama leant heavily on Greek models, although in the design of theatres, in costume, scenery and spectacular effects the Romans made original contributions. Looking at the bare ruins of today it is easy to forget the gaiety and splendour of these entertainments, but a series of wall-paintings at Pompeii show the 'scenae frons' as it must actually have appeared. There are three entrances, with hinged doors and steps leading

down to the stage and another space running behind them. The back wall is painted with perspective architecture. Everything is profusely decorated in paint, bronze ornament and sculpture. The play, or mime, includes a young hero (centre) and two older warriors. Two slaves in the background with torch and wine-jar are preparing for a banquet. The setting corresponds closely to the real theatres of Pompeii and Herculaneum.

was an elegiac poet of a more worldly kind than Tibullus or Propertius. His principal collections of poems in this metre are the *Amores*, the *Heroides* (mostly epistles from mythical women to their absent husbands), the *Art of Love*, the *Tristia* and *Letters from Pontus*—the last two composed after his exile to Tomi (Rumania) for 'a poem and a mistake', the latter perhaps connected with the disgrace into which, for alleged immoralities, the daughter and grand-daughter of Augustus fell. These collections of adroit dexterous couplets reflect a smart, rather antisocial metropolitan society.

> Jove swore to Juno falsely by the Styx:
> Now he aids those who imitate his tricks.

Ovid looks at men and especially women with not unfriendly or unhumorous or altogether untender gaze, yet with a certain professional cold-bloodedness. Yet this does not strike a chill because of the poet's incomparable genius for vividly descriptive narration. His quality as a playwright we cannot judge since his famous *Medea* is lost, but his gifts as a teller of stories attain their fullest expression in another major work, not in elegiacs but in a lightened version of the epic hexameter. This is the *Metamorphoses*, a vast Latin Arabian Nights of every sort of myth, legend, folk-tale and anecdote. The link, real or artificially contrived, between all these stories is the theme of magic change of shape, familiar to literature since Homer—and to folklore no doubt much earlier—and the subject of learned collections of material by Alexandrian poets. Ovid seems at times to be deliberately, as an academic exercise, inviting comparisons of earlier treatments with his own.

His talent for telling a colourful tale, though censured as uneconomical by some ancient critics and un-Roman in its graceful agility of gesture, has been one of the greatest influences upon European culture. In the 12th and 13th centuries Ovid's poems largely created the ideal of Romantic Love, in the 16th century they inspired many of the supreme achievements of Venetian painters, and thereafter the greatest of Poussin's pictures and Bernini's statuary.

> Arachne shows the gods in various guise;
> And first the bull that cheats Europa's eyes,
> So skilfully depicted, you would swear
> A living bull, a moving sea, was there.
> The girl herself was seen to watch dismayed
> The fast-receding shore, and call for aid,
> And draw her feet back, fearing to be caught
> By mounting waves—so well the weaver wrought.

In England Arthur Golding's popular translation of the *Metamorphoses* (1565–67) was familiar to Shakespeare, who owes it many allusions. Ovid was the favourite Latin poet of Goethe, absorbed like himself in changes of shape; and Keats, too, found in his writings an unending supply of material. Classical mythology, never absent for long from the European tradition, has generally meant Ovid, the last great writer of the Roman Golden Age.

Models for the West

There were many other Latin authors of comparatively minor talent writing under Augustus: for example Vitruvius, whose ten-book treatise on architecture, of Hellenistic inspiration, guided Renaissance architects. Writers who extended their activities into the reign of Tiberius included Seneca the elder of Corduba in Spain (a country now rapidly becoming a centre of Latin culture), expert critic and historian of the ever more flourishing study of rhetoric, much admired by Ben Jonson; Celsus, whose attractively written encyclopedia, of which medical sections survive, was one of the first books printed in the 15th century; and Phaedrus (c. 15 BC–AD 50), a Macedonian slave whose popular fables in the Greek tradition of Aesop (basic to Roman education) provided a model for greater writers such as La Fontaine.

But the most versatile talent of the later Julio-Claudian period belonged to another Spaniard Seneca the younger (c. 4 BC–AD 65), son of the authority on rhetoric. In contrast to earlier Roman tragic drama, of which almost all is lost, we have nine tragedies written by Seneca, and there is much of him in the phantoms, madmen and tyrants of Shakespeare, as well as in the plots of innumerable other European playwrights. Seneca set the tone of the new Silver Age of Latin by developing the sparkling verbal tricks and ingeniously vivid epigrams of the Pointed Style—into which the Latin language, with its lapidary conciseness and alliteration, naturally falls. The characters breathe the enlightened tolerance and humanity of Stoicism—which included sympathy for slaves. This same spirit, more explicitly expressed, likewise pervades his thirteen ethical treatises, his 124 moralizing 'letters' ostensibly addressed to one Lucilius, and his scientific work the *Naturales Quaestiones*. The fame of the treatises has earned Seneca a forged correspondence with St Paul. They have also given him (along with Plutarch) a unique place as moral guide for the Renaissance and the centuries that followed it.

And yet Seneca must have had to trim his sails as Nero's chief minister; though not enough, for Nero compelled him to die. In the same year (AD 65) the emperor also caused the suicide of Seneca's nephew Lucan. This was a young poet who had adapted the scintillating style and Stoic morality of the Silver Age to national epic, in his poem *Civil War* or *Pharsalia*, which tells of the strife between Pompey and Caesar. For all its exaggerated rhetoric and delaying digressions, this mordant, powerful poem won fame in the Middle Ages for its history and philosophy and earned its author a place as one of Dante's four 'lords of highest song'. It was also particularly admired (for a time) by Shelley; but thereafter its purple patches fell into disrepute. Lucan was one of those whose philosophical standpoint, tending towards anti-monarchist views, had increasingly estranged him from the emperor. His friend, Persius (AD 34–62), another young Stoic, turned his own gifts to a private, rarified brand of satire, terse and cryptic yet lively and famous both in his day and in Elizabethan times, when he was one of the models for angry young men like John Donne.

> Flash these crow-poets and magpie-poetizing
> Females one glimpse of the ready cash, and you'd swear
> The Muses' nectar was no sweeter than their song.

A more remarkable talent was that of Petronius, variously identified with Nero's 'arbiter' of court fashions (who incurred his master's fatal displeasure in 65) or with a little-known contemporary consul. His name is associated with a lively, scandalous, partly colloquial picaresque novel known to us as the *Satyricon*. The preceding centuries had seen many sorts of Greek fiction including pseudo-biography, travellers' tales, the romantic novels or novelettes which flourished in the Greek world's eastern borderlands, satirical sketches in mixed prose and verse, and pungent, sexual 'Milesian tales' (introduced to Latin by one Sisenna). Petronius gathers these threads together in his adventure-story of three disreputable young men on the move round south Italy. The work, of which a good deal but nothing like all survives, contains poems, digressions on literary criticism, and parodies (perhaps the whole theme parodies epic). It also includes set-pieces or short stories, of which the most famous are *The Widow of Ephesus* and the long and highly entertaining *Dinner of Trimalchio*. The host at the dinner is a self-made ex-slave industrialist living near Naples, whose banquet and reminiscences (like the remarks of his friends) are first-class historical material. Petronius has played a great and varied part in the mixed beginnings of modern fiction, particularly since the *Dinner* first came to light in 1650.

Another prose-writer of a much less frivolous character, who was likewise at work during the reign of Nero, was Pliny the elder (AD 23/4–79) from Comum (Como). Before becoming prominent in public life under Vespasian, Pliny first served as a cavalry officer, and then wrote, among much else, a *Natural History*. Its 37 books contain a vast mine of curious information about the ancient world and its sciences (especially medicine) interspersed by vivid descriptions and by shrewd comments about Roman affairs. Veering between the fabulous and sceptical, it played a major part in the transmission of classical learning through the Middle Ages.

Pliny uses many a rhetorical device, but for expertise in this field he yields to his younger contemporary Quintilian of Calagurris in Spain (Calahorra) (born c. AD 35), lawyer, the first state-paid professor of rhetoric at Rome, and tutor to the grand-nephews of Domitian. Quintilian's twelve-book treatise on the *Training of an Orator (Institutio Oratoria)* is a sensible, practical and revealing restatement of the classical system of education at various levels. This system was still unremittingly, and even increasingly, based upon instruction in public speaking but, by Quintilian as by Cicero, was linked with the improvement of the Whole Man: and so the *Institutio* became staple diet of Renaissance schools directed towards the character-training of an *élite*. The writer also advises his pupils on Greek and Latin authors deserving study, in a section which, brief and casual though it is, has attracted great attention, for example from Alexander Pope in his *Essay on Criticism*.

Less fame has fallen to men of the same period who continued the tradition of epic poetry, such as Statius of Naples (c. AD 45–96) whose *Achilleid* was much admired in the Middle Ages: but it is his thirty-two fluent and polished occasional poems, the *Silvae*, rediscovered in 1417, which, by virtue of their miniature scale and occasional haunting unfamiliar note, exhibit the gifts of Statius at their best. A far more original talent, however, was that of his Spanish contemporary Martial of Bilbilis (Calatayud) (c. AD 40–104), the foremost epigrammatist of the ancient world, who has imprinted his definition of the term on subsequent European literatures. As Byron translates his appeal to the public:

> He unto whom thou art so partial,
> Oh, reader! is the well-known Martial,
> The Epigrammatist: while living
> Give him the fame thou wouldst be giving:
> So he shall hear, and feel, and know it—
> Post-obits rarely reach a poet.

Martial's 1561 witty, direct, humane but frequently obscene little poems, some merely descriptive and others reminiscent of the pungent sayings *(sententiae)* that were a feature of Silver Age rhetoric, cast a vivid light upon the contemporary Roman scene.

Masters of Denunciation

Juvenal, born in about AD 50, at Aquinum, strikes a harsher and also a grander note in his sixteen poems, which show him to be not only without an equal among Roman satirists, but one of the outstanding masters of the Latin language of all time. Neither forgetting nor forgiving the relative poverty, as a not very successful practising declaimer, from which he had emerged, he castigates the evils of contemporary Roman life with a pessimistic irony and invective none the less savage and crushing for their ostensible direction against persons belonging to the past. Although he lived and wrote under Trajan, in times much more agreeable than those of the hated Domitian, the empire still seemed to him a sick, maladjusted organism, full of stupid, ugly, vicious individuals, especially women. Adding to the heritage of Ennius, Lucilius and Horace a fierce conception of the satirist's task and a formidable equipment for giving it effect, Juvenal is the true founder of the *genre* as a continuous European tradition. Dryden, Pope, and Samuel Johnson are his debtors, as well as Byron and Victor Hugo. But although satire is fashionable today Juvenal's weighty impact is no longer *à la mode*.

An equally damaging view of Roman society, despite current improvements, was implicit in the work of Tacitus (c. AD 55–? c. 120), the greatest of Roman historians. Perhaps the son of a tax-officer in one of the Gallic provinces, he became a well-known pleader, and is probably the author of one of the most reasonable and readable treatises on rhetoric, the *Dialogue on Orators*—in which it is explained that in times of imperial peace forensic pleading can no longer flourish as it did. The hazards of official life under Domitian deeply affected Tacitus, and that emperor is posthumously criticised in his biographical sketch of his own father-in-law Agricola, governor of Britain. Germany, too, was the subject of a special study, in the form of a moralizing essay of much ethnological interest.

Then Tacitus turned to his major life-work, the history of Rome from Tiberius to Domitian. Of the *Histories* (about AD

The tale of Cupid and Psyche is the most famous of the stories included by Apuleius in the 'Golden Ass'. To Apuleius, as to the artist of this terracotta group from Tanagra, Cupid still has something of the power of the ancient Eros, the procreative force of the sexual instinct, and is far from the pretty winged boy that he later became.

68–96) only the first part, describing the Civil Wars, has survived, but we have most of the subsequently published *Annals*, dealing with Augustus' Julio-Claudian successors (AD 14–68). These unequalled works with their haunting, penetrating studies of the doom-laden monsters of the imperial court, form our earliest account indeed our only extensive account of this decisive period in the history of the western world. Their claim to impartiality, however, seems scarcely acceptable; in particular, among other hidden allusions to the emperors of Tacitus' own lifetime, his hatred of Domitian overflows into bias against earlier rulers such as Tiberius. This exciting, incisive, moral-pointing narrative is written in an increasingly individual style of an abrupt, tortured, un-Ciceronian point and brevity—which might seem a little less novel to us if his immediate predecessors had survived. Often poetical in vocabulary and construction, the *Annals* echo tragic drama in their emphasis upon the overbearing rather than the constructive aspects of the imperial régime, and upon the implacability or even malevolence of fate.

Nevertheless, Tacitus was sure, even among the horrors of civil strife and the obvious degeneration which accompanied them, that the nature of man has the capacity of rising to remarkable heights of heroism; and he expresses this conviction, at times, with an almost Virgilian compassion. Although the repute of this most difficult writer long remained in abeyance, and the High Renaissance preferred Livy who provided easier paragons, Tacitus' belief in the enduring human spirit proved extremely attractive to the Cinquecento humanists who rediscovered him. Then and since then, autocrats and revolutionaries alike have found his attitude and personality versatile and enigmatic enough to provide text in support of any or every political cause.

Among Tacitus' friends was Pliny the younger (born AD 61–2), a pupil of Quintilian and well-known public speaker, nephew of the elder Pliny whose death in the eruption of Vesuvius he interestingly describes. This is one of the varied themes in his ten books of humane, cultured literary letters, early representatives of a form which, although alien to the twentieth century, has been one of Rome's gifts to European literature. 247 of these letters, addressed to 105 recipients, form the first nine books, and the tenth contains correspondence of great historical importance exchanged by him—as a conscientious if somewhat fussy governor of Bithynia in northern Asia Minor—with Trajan. This exchange includes enquiries from the man on the spot and imperial decisions concerning the treatment of Christians, who should, Trajan directed, not be hunted out—but ought to be punished if they were recalcitrant.

A slightly younger contemporary Suetonius (AD 69–c. 140) wrote far less elegant and thought-out prose in his biographies of *Famous Men*, which are lost, and the *Twelve Caesars*, which have survived and (together with the moralizing Greek studies of Plutarch) laid the foundation for all subsequent biography. His material is wonderfully varied and gossipy, and presented with an indiscriminate, dead-pan lack of prejudice or philosophical preconception which is rare in Latin literature. Suetonius was able to draw upon the memoirs of imperial personages which have now disappeared, and perhaps he also got to know some of his spicy facts about earlier court-happenings, as well as acquiring something of an official's viewpoint, while serving in various ministerial capacities under Hadrian.

From Africa Something New

That emperor, whose own most famous composition is a moving little poem from his death-bed, was a distinguished connoisseur and patron of literature as well as other arts; and yet in the wearying Roman society of his day this latter-day Augustus, as his propagandists regarded him (in contrast to Trajan, a latter-day Caesar), did not inspire a revival of the Augustan literary age. Under his Antonine successors, when the lecturers in popular philosophy (sophists) characteristic of this century reached the height of their fashion, there was an archaizing movement, the 'New Speech' *(elocutio novella)*, led by Marcus Aurelius' tutor Fronto from Numidia. His letters to that ruler, apart from some literary judgments, are unstimulating, but the features of the movement reappear in a writer of genius—Apuleius from Madaura in Algeria (born c. AD 123). Sophist and lawyer, lecturer and devotee of the Egyptian goddess Isis whom he passionately praises, poet and lavish manipulator of a new sort of Latin prose that in its combination of the archaic and the luscious looks forward towards the Middle Ages, Apuleius provides in his *Apologia*—one of the few Latin speeches, other than Cicero's, that have come down to us—a fantastically exuberant defence against charges of magic: and a magician was what Augustine believed him to be! The *Metamorphoses* of Apuleius is the only Latin novel which has survived intact; any Greek model on which it may have been based has been wholly eclipsed by Apuleius' effervescent story-telling, the inspiration of many a Renaissance writer and painter. The work is also called the *Golden Ass*, its theme being the adventures of Lucius who has been turned into a donkey. The many stories that it incorporates include the Cinderella folk-tale of the fairy bridegroom, *Cupid and Psyche*, the object of numerous allegorical interpretations from late antiquity onwards.

The characteristic of African Latin was vividness and excitement, but this took a sombre and passionate turn in the writings of Tertullian (c. AD 160–225). Pagan by birth, excellently educated for the legal profession at his native Carthage, Christian by conversion, he finally became an adherent of the austerely remote Montanist sect. Of the thirty of his works which survive, the best-known is the *Apologeticus*. In this he strongly defends his faith in terms designed to persuade Roman officials, while refuting attacks on Christianity: his pupil Origen did likewise in Greek. In these and other writers, notably the 'Christian Cicero' Lactantius, there was already apparent the dilemma which exercised the early church and provided some of its most interesting subject-matter: should it reject pagan culture (as one of its early poets Commodianus rejects classical metres), or welcome it as a foundation to build upon?

The Last of the Pagans

The continued survival of that pagan culture, in modified forms, is recalled by a mysterious hymn to Venus (the *Pervigilium Veneris*), unique among ancient poems in the nostalgic, romantic gracefulness of its appeal to nature and love. Perhaps it was written early in the 4th century, which likewise witnessed the extensive but more stereotyped poetic output of Ausonius (c. 310–395), a professor from Burdigala (Bordeaux) in Gaul which despite lowering politics was now a leading cultural centre. Among his works—carefully insulated in an ivory-tower from which the menacing Goths are forgotten—the most attractive today, with its not too classical love of natural scenery, is a poetic guide to the river Moselle. As the first professing Christian writer whose works do not centre upon Christianity, Ausonius has been called the ancestor of Christian Europe's secular literature.

But this was also the age of the last great Roman historian, a pagan, Ammianus Marcellinus. Latin was not his first language, since he was born in the Hellenized East at Antioch (c. 330). Yet it was in Latin that he wrote—a rather clumsy Latin, overloaded with ornament, Graecisms and bombast. His work is a continuation of Tacitus' history extending from AD 96 to 378. Its first thirteen books have perished, but the last eighteen, dealing in unprejudiced detail with the events of 353 to 378, have survived. To us, looking back, these harsh years seem like the beginning of the end; but Ammianus, for all his wide travel in west and east—including service against the Persians—remains a senatorial historian in the old tradition, pitting his hopes for moral reform upon the senatorial class.

The century that followed witnessed the last noteworthy pagan poet, Rutilius Namatianus who held high office under Honorius. His account in verse of a journey to his native Gaul includes a full-blooded, profoundly felt eulogy of Rome—which had been sacked by Alaric the Goth ten years earlier (410).

The Latin Roots of Christian Thought

More original is the writing of contemporary Christians. Ambrose (c. 337–397), another Gaul, was famous alike as theologian and preacher, letter-writer, orator and poet. By compelling the emperor Theodosius to repent publicly for murders committed on his responsibility, he set the pattern for all subsequent prelates who have stood against the civil power. His treatise *On the Duties of Priests* Christianized Cicero *On Duties;* his hymns in un-rhymed stanzas, which have had many imitators, created the hymnology of western Christianity, and the prose lyric *Exsultet* is probably also by him. The greatest scholar of the early Christians was Jerome (Hieronymus) from Stridon in Dalmatia (c. 348–420). His translation of the Bible, the Vulgate that is the basis of the official Catholic version today, has exercised incalculable influence upon the form and spirit of European literature; and his period of ascetic retreat in the desert was, as countless European paintings bear witness, the prototype of the medieval monastic discipline.

Augustine of Thagaste in North Africa (354–430) illustrates no less thoroughly the two currents, biblical and pagan, blending or warring in Christian thought, to which like Jerome he was a convert. His enormous output is equally conspicuous for the revolutionary talents that it displays and for their canalization into an urgently orthodox theology, inspired—against his contemporary Pelagius—by the conviction of original sin, as well as of predestination. One of the greatest autobiographies of all time is the passionately introspective and self-critical *Confessions* in which Augustine is almost Proustian in his endeavour to recapture successive mental states. The more massive *City of God*, in its twenty-two books which passed on to medieval times a large proportion of all they knew about the ancient world, calls upon the resources of pagan philosophy, transformed by Christian doctrine, to distinguish between the earthly city (founded by fallen angels) and its counterpart in heaven—whose citizens live on earth as prisoners. This work also dwells on the greatest secular event of the age, the collapse of Rome in the West, and asks the vital question that it raises: why was the coming of Christianity to the empire accompanied by disasters—why is there such a gap between the worlds of the spirit and of earthly life, and how can it be bridged? The catastrophe of the Roman Empire, he answered, could not touch a true Christian—and so this man, heir to all the pagan traditions, gave warning that the exaltation of Rome's commonwealth as an ideal was at an end.

Prudentius (AD 348–c. 405) from Spain was a lawyer and civil servant who withdrew from the gathering clouds of governmental life to write religious poetry inspired by a dedicated faith in Christ, and sometimes foreshadowing the origins of the medieval ballad. The most significant of his works, historically, is the two-book poem *Against Symmachus*, urging against a prominent pagan of the day that in spite of all reverence for the destiny of Rome the Altar of Victory should be expelled from its senate-house.

> This was achieved by the great success, the triumphs
> Of Roman Power: —Christ even then was coming
> (Believe it), and the way made ready for him.

Prudentius' contemporary Paulinus of Bordeaux (353–431), Bishop of Nola in Campania in honour of whose patron saint Felix he wrote, renounced inherited wealth and the comfortable culture of his teacher Ausonius for a monastic Christianity which gives his poems a far greater emotional force than his master's. They include the first Christian wedding-hymn, the first Christian elegy and the forerunners of many poems in praise of saints and martyrs.

The poetry and prose of Venantius Fortunatus (c. 530–600), who was born near Treviso, contains the mysticism and pathos of a new age.

> Altar and victim, hail to you!
> O glorious was His abject pain!
> Life out of death His victory drew,
> And life in death is made our gain.

A Bridge to the Middle Ages

Prose writers as well as poets provided the Middle Ages with a bridge from the classical past. The *Marriage of Philology and Mercury* by Martianus Capella of Madaura, cast in the allegorical shape that from now onwards played a great part in literature and thought, became one of the six most widely circulated books in the Middle Ages and a major formative element in European education. It includes, following an old tradition, passages of verse to vary the prose. Of the same mixed genre is the *Consolation of Philosophy* by Boethius (c. 480–524). Condemned to death by his former friend Theodoric the Ostrogoth, Boethius faces the fact that, although God governs the world, evil men prosper in it; and so he imperturbably sets out the pleasures of the contemplative life, together with his continuing hopes for the human race. Although the philosophy of this work does not incorporate any of the Christian doctrine found in Boethius' other treatises, it soon became immensely popular. Its translators included King Alfred, Chaucer and Queen Elizabeth I; the *Consolation* is often quoted by Dante, and it was one of the first Latin books to be translated into Italian. Gibbon described it as 'a golden volume, not unworthy of the leisure of Plato or Tully (Cicero)'.

Cassiodorus (c. 487–583) from Scylaceum (Squillace) in Calabria produced an extensive literary output, which throws much light on the Ostrogothic régime at Rome. Then he left the city and founded two monasteries, at one of which, Vivarium, he introduced the copying of manuscripts which played so decisive a part in the transmission of pagan and Christian literature alike. His own *Institutiones* provided the monks with a compendium of the wordly sciences. Further links between antique learning and the centuries to come were supplied by Tribonian of Side (Manavgat) in southern Asia Minor, who edited an immense codification of the classical Roman Law (the *Corpus Iuris Civilis*) for the Byzantine emperor Justinian, and Isidore bishop of Seville (AD 602–36) whose *Etymologies* are an encyclopedic summing-up of all that seemed to him worth knowing in the ancient world. And so the stage was set for a new age—still using Latin, although vernaculars would soon gain ground; still dependent upon the writings of those people from many countries who had written in the language of ancient Rome.

IX THE VISION TURNS INWARDS

The art and architecture of a world empire

MORTIMER WHEELER

*'But I observed that you cared both about the common life of
all men and the constitution of the state, and also about
the provision of suitable public buildings, so that not only was the
state made greater through you by its new provinces but also
the majesty of Empire was expressed through the eminent dignity of
its public buildings.'*

VITRUVIUS TO THE EMPEROR AUGUSTUS
TEN BOOKS ON ARCHITECTURE,
PREFACE

The artists and the art of Rome

have long lacked proper appreciation through invidious comparisons with Hellenic and Hellenistic masters and masterpieces and through failure to follow the evolving trends of what was a strong and competent native Roman creative impulse. Such relative neglect of Roman achievements is understandable; within the limits to which it aspired, Greek art reached perfection. Some of its qualities endured into Roman times by the looting and copying of priceless Greek originals and by the enslaving or hiring of artists from the Greek world.

Difficult although it has been to follow the specific Roman contribution through the welter of the accumulated treasures of the Greek heritage, a new and gratifying vision of a sturdy, rational and aesthetically satisfying achievement by the Roman genius rewards us when we do so.

The emphasis must be strongly upon their practical achievements: upon their clean, decent and well-ordered cities with their rational layout, their convenient markets, meeting halls, theatres, public baths, roads, aqueducts, bridges, temples, houses and palaces; marked by an impressive dignity merging occasionally into the flamboyant.

Not everything was made for the hard usage of daily life. Romans sought beauty in their surroundings and also in their possessions, in the decoration of their homes, in the design of their household furniture and utensils, their plate, their jewels, coins and gems, just as they did in the embellishment of their public buildings and monuments with their beautiful, forthright inscriptions cut in marble. Many of them were keen collectors and discerning patrons of artists and craftsmen. From thousands of portrait busts, themselves not least among their artistic legacy to later ages, they look out at us today, strong, forceful, purposeful folk who conquered the world and impressed their image vividly upon it; with what success we may gather from the examples presented in these pages and even more clearly from the abundant endeavour of countless later craftsmen, particularly from the Renaissance onwards, to expand and exploit the Roman achievement now two thousand years old.

Soaring columns sixty-five feet high that still remain of the Temple of Jupiter at Baalbek are eloquent of the creative impulse of the Roman spirit. They are of the 1st century AD.

The chessboard pattern that now seems so Roman was in fact a Greek invention of as early as the 6th century BC. The Romans saw it in south Italy before the end of the 5th century BC. The chessboard was quartered by two main streets, the *decumanus* tending to run east and west and the *cardo* north and south. From these sprang straight streets, dividing the buildings of the town into square or oblong blocks, the *insulae*.

The Roman stamp is clearly shown at Timgad in North Africa (*right*). It was founded in AD 100, an outpost town, built on military lines for time-expired legionaries. In the centre, south of the *decumanus*, was the large, paved, rectangular forum, surrounded by porticos, and with the town-hall, *basilica*, on its eastern side. Further south lay the semicircle of the theatre (AD 161–9). The short *cardo* terminates at the forum.

Roman Paris is rarely remembered by the hundreds of thousands who now visit it, yet the road that takes them across the Seine to the middle of the island on which stands Notre Dame is the Roman *cardo*, the main north-south road through *Lutetia Parisiorum*, and the island itself was the nucleus from which the Roman city grew. As it spread over the south bank uphill to get clear of the marshy river bank, a forum (a) was made about where the rue Soufflot branches from the rue St Jacques. The Forum Baths (b) were close to the present Luxembourg métro station. There were two other baths: under the Collège de France (c) and the Cluny baths (d), the latter being of considerable pretension. An amphitheatre (e), partly restored, lay to the east.

Verona's ancient city, whose chessboard plan can still be discerned in this aerial view, was bounded on three sides by the river Adige, which has since slightly changed its course. The probable site of the city wall is outlined, with Gallienus's extension to include the well-preserved amphitheatre.

The heart of Imperial Rome as it would have looked in the 4th century AD from the air. Immediately below on the left is the great Circus Maximus (a). Beyond rises the Palatine Hill (b), on which are the imperial palaces. To the right the arches of the great Claudian aqueduct (AD 36) snake their way into the city. The huge Colosseum (c) draws all eyes. Between it and the sacred Capitoline Hill (d) lies the Roman Forum traversed by the Sacred Way as it passes by the arch of Constantine (e), the arch of Titus (f), and the Basilica of Constantine (g). Beyond is the arch of Septimius Severus (h) and the vast Forum of Trajan (i).

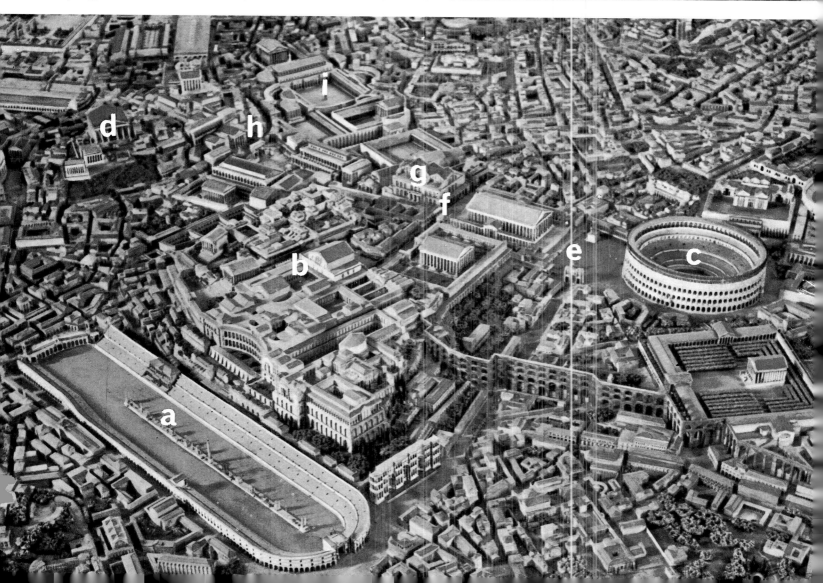

One of man's rare masterpieces, the Pantheon in Rome (*left*), was reconstructed by Hadrian (AD 120–4), and dedicated to the seven planetary deities. Strong in the powerful lines of its superbly coffered dome, and united with the dome of heaven itself by the bold opening in its summit, it still looks today as it did when Pannini painted this elegant scene about 1750.

The horrors of the arena could nevertheless produce splendid architecture. The Colosseum (*right*), begun by Vespasian and finished by Titus, held 45,000 spectators. Its exterior is articulated by superimposed Doric, Ionic, Corinthian and Composite columns—a sequence that was to remain orthodox for all classical buildings.

Roman theatres are not hollowed out of hillsides, like Greek, but are free-standing, usually in the centre of cities, and have elaborate *scenae frons* behind the acting area. *Below left*: the auditorium at Aspendus, Asia Minor. *Below right*: the stage at Sabratha, North Africa.

Stupendous edifices for purely secular use of a size, solidity and magnificence of construction such as mankind had not previously seen in the West, were among the triumphs of the architects and builders in Rome's service. The *Basilica Nova* of Maxentius, or of Constantine, who completed it around AD 313, seen in the reconstruction *above*, had a vast central hall or nave whose three huge cross-vaults carried on four great piers rose 114 feet above floor level. Eight monolithic marble columns stood in front of the four piers and at the corners of the nave. The apse at the west end contained a statue of the Emperor. Longer than the nave and choir of Westminster Abbey, more than three times as wide, the Basilica glowed with rich colour from its marble walls and floors.

The triumphal arch was a particularly Roman type of building. Arches were erected all over the Empire as symbols of Rome's power and as aspects of the personal cults of the emperors. The Arch of Constantine (*above*) is the grandest of them all, but to build it Constantine pillaged the works of his predecessors, so that it is almost a museum of late Roman sculpture. The Arch of Titus (*right*) spans the Sacred Way to the Forum. It celebrates the conquest of Jerusalem and contains famous reliefs (see p. 214) showing the treasures of the Temple being carried in triumph through Rome.

The vast palace at Spalato, or Split, (about AD 300) across the
Adriatic on the Dalmatian coast, to which Diocletian retired,
filled about eight acres and was almost a small town in itself. Set
within massive fortifications it forms a rectangle, 575 by 460 feet,
walls 60 feet high and 7 feet thick. Its sixteen towers are

rectangular except for those at the landward gates which are octagonal. Colonnaded streets divide it internally. South of the centrepoint the columns were capped by arches. To the east, the octagonal Mausoleum of the Emperor stands upon an 11 foot podium. The octagonal pyramid roof covers an internal dome. To the west is a vaulted Corinthian temple. The southern or seaward side had a great covered gallery with loggias at either end and in the centre, and intervening arched openings divided by columns on plain corbels—an architectural innovation. Sufficient of it survives to make this reconstruction basically certain.

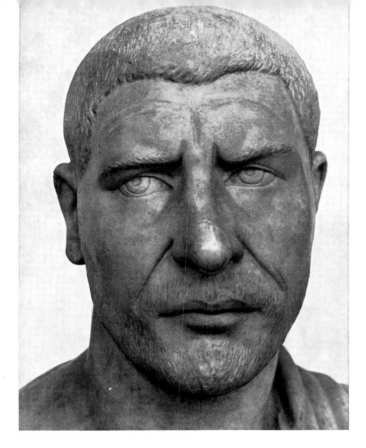

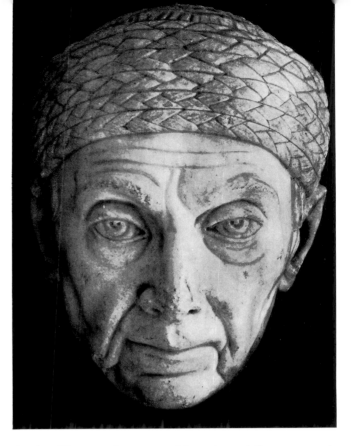

The Roman portrait-sculptor was no flatterer, and it is to the credit of his subjects that flattery was not exacted. *Above left* is Philip the Arabian, son of a notorious Arab brigand and Emperor of Rome from AD 244 to 249. During his brief reign was celebrated the thousandth anniversary of the founding of the city. The portrait expresses his anxious, shifty, opportunist character. The other portrait of an aged woman, from Tripolitania, shows some of the realistic devices that had become normal by the 3rd century AD, such as the lighting of the pupils by means of small wedges.

Ampudius with his daughter (*above*) was a corn-merchant, sufficiently prosperous to afford this sculptured memorial.

Roman artistic genius comes out strongly in the remarkable skill with which, from the 2nd century BC onwards, their sculptors carved strikingly realistic, thoughtful likenesses of countless individuals, in contrast to the almost passionless, idealized faces by Greek sculptors of the classical period.

A conscious touch of the grotesque is to be found in this bust of Commodus (*right*), unworthy son of the great Marcus Aurelius and Emperor from AD 180 to 193. The artist's skilful rendering of the curled hair and beard of this sadistic pervert is subtly mocked by presenting him in his favourite rôle of Hercules, holding the club and the apples of the Hesperides and wrapped in the lion's skin.

The state procession (*below*) was recorded for all time on the great Altar of Peace in Rome. The Imperial family, with the senators, magistrates and officials shown on this north side, are 'caught' in marble, just as they were at a given moment on 4th July, 13 BC. The life-size figures are aloof in the calm, unanxious society which they represent, their dignity and actuality enhanced by the small child who tugs at the toga next to him.

Richly decorated walls were a striking feature of the houses of wealthy Romans. Beginning with simple colour schemes, they developed, as we know from many examples which have survived in Pompeii and Herculaneum, into elaborate pictorial scenes. The picture from Stabiae (*opposite left*) shows Roman skills in depicting sunlight on the sea and on wharves, columns, boats and jetties. The handling of the paint is remarkably free and confident, conveying (almost in the manner of Pissarro) the passing play of light and movement. The masterpiece of Roman wall-painting is the 'Garden of Livia' (*above*) found at Prima Porta near Rome. In Bernard Berenson's words: 'How dewy, how penetratingly fresh the grass and trees and flowers, how coruscating the fruit. Pomegranates as Renoir painted them. Bird songs charm one's ears. The distance remains magically impenetrable'.

The new appreciation of nature evident in some Roman art has been thought to have been a Hellenistic influence brought to Rome from Alexandria, where all manner of craftsmanship flourished including the production of great Nilotic mosiacs. The mosaic (*left*) shows the influence of Egypt and its great river. *Right*: a bucolic scene painted on the wall of a house at Pompeii.

The absence of perspective in the work of Roman artists is only surprising because the problem seemed so often on the brink of being solved. In the famous reliefs on the Arch of Titus a procession of soldiers (*top left*) returning with booty after suppressing a Jewish revolt in Palestine (AD 70) swings through an arch—and perspective seems almost discovered. But in the opposite panel (*centre left*) failure is complete; the Imperial chariot faces to the front and the horses are in awkward echelon.

The Romans excelled in telling a continuous story in stone, a narrative of actual events in their history illuminating the prowess of the supreme Roman, the Emperor. The outstanding example is the famous pictorial chronicle (*opposite*) of Trajan's campaigns in Dacia, which winds spirally up a huge Doric column 100 feet high. The carved band, 3–4 feet wide, and some 650 feet in length, recalls incidents of the war, showing in all some 2,500 figures. A spiral staircase winds inside to the top, which has been crowned successively by a bronze eagle, a bronze statue of Trajan and the present statue of St Peter. The ashes of Trajan once lay beneath.

Landscape settings in stone (*left*) on mythological and secular themes, appear in shallow, pictorial relief on wall-panels carved by the artists of Alexandria in Hellenistic times.

The art and architecture of a world empire

SIR MORTIMER WHEELER

'IN GREEK ARCHAEOLOGY, any object you turn up is beautiful: in Roman, you are delighted if you can argue that it is second-rate.' Thus the late Arnold Gomme, who long professed Greek with distinction at Glasgow. There was something more than mere naughtiness in the remark; it reflects a traditional misunderstanding of major issues, and must be traversed at the outset of any account, however summary, of the Roman achievement.

The Hellenist, who is customarily responsible for this kind of misunderstanding, is the heir to a young world in which cultural values were sharp and explicit. There were the Greeks (the most splendid snobs in history), and beyond the Greeks were the Barbarians, the rest. Between the two stretched an intellectual barrier more impenetrable than the social barriers which isolated classes in Victorian England. It is easy enough to draw a pencil-line round the Hellenes and to find within that frame an essential community of aspiration and attainment; even—to use a highly dangerous word—an essential community of race.

Not so with the Romans. Their political genius enabled them to assume control of the civilized West, including Western Asia, to enlarge it to the Danube, the Sahara and the shores of Ocean, and to provide the means and opportunity for an equivalent expansion of ideas and forms. But these ideas and forms were no more theirs, or theirs alone, than were they themselves all Latins or Italians. Indeed the whole concept of Empire, in which Roman politics culminated, had already been given vivid expression by Alexander the Great before he died in 323 BC at the age of thirty-three. His transit marked the end of the old Hellenic isolation before ever the Romans came upon the international scene. It would be more exact to say that by the end of the 4th century BC Western civilization was intellectually ripe for the change of which Alexander and Rome were the successive instruments.

Between 'Greece' and 'Rome', therefore, can be no sort of opposition in any intelligent and historical sense. They are related but sequential phenomena. Roman art and architecture are not *bad* Greek art and architecture; they are different in aim and achievement, based upon evolving, not merely repetitive values. So also within the wide geographical scope of the Roman achievement itself it is wholly fallacious to think, as a former generation of scholars tried to think, in tendentious local terms: to speak of 'the Orient *or* Rome', for example, as though these were viable alternatives in the make-up of Roman culture. Of course they were not. To speak of the Orient *and* Rome would be an over-simplification but would more nearly approach a truth. The 'Roman' emperor himself might be an Italian; he might equally be a Spaniard, a North African, an Illyrian, a Syrian, a Gaul, the son of an Arabian brigand, a Low Country adventurer. Rome was an amalgam: its importance to us is that of a political label which may conveniently be attached to a great formative phase in the history of thought, a phase in which, at its best, the ideas perfected in their primal shape by 5th-and 4th-century Greece were developed into something new and more complex, though also with new simplifications, as is the proper habit of evolving thought.

In the summary which follows I have begun with the over-all shape of the towns, as the nuclear element in classical civilization. Then follows a brief account of some of the public buildings and private houses which were the substance of these towns, with passing reference also to the buildings of the countryside. Thereafter in a narrow space something must be said of the sculpture and painting to which the Roman contribution was of outstanding significance. And finally some attempt must be made to define in general terms the qualities which mark the Roman episode and constitute its importance in the history of art and architecture as the expression of evolving ideas.

THE SHAPE OF THE TOWNS
The Greek Pattern Persists

It is common knowledge that the political focus of the Greek mind, from its emergence somewhere about 700 BC until its adjustment to wider vistas in and after the time of Alexander the Great (died 323 BC), was the individual city. Within the cultural limits of the Greek world, you owed your allegiance to your own paternal city or *polis* and so gave to politics its initial and homely meaning.

When the Romans began to take over the Greek world from Alexander's successors in the 2nd century BC the civic idea was, in form, merely enlarged. You now owed your allegiance to the ultimate city, Rome. But the substance behind the civic idea had changed. You might now be a 'Roman citizen' without ever setting eyes upon the Eternal City. At the same time you remained functionally a citizen of your own particular city or province. A sort of differential focus had entered into your thinking; for even when the Roman Empire had begun to harden into a disciplined universal state, strong local elements continued to dominate and diversify local life behind the formulae which tended, and still tend historically, to overlay and conceal them. Not the least important of these formulae is an astonishingly tenacious adherence to the urban pattern established by the Greeks in the early days of Hellenic and more particularly Ionian civilization.

In the classical world there were no pre-Hellenic towns in any viable sense. The Mycenae of Agamemnon, for example, was not a city; it was a fortified feudal palace with little scattered communities of farmers and traders in the surrounding countryside. No doubt Mycenaean Athens was the same. Essentially these were lordly strongholds, with an economy based upon agriculture, commerce and piracy. Not until the 8th–7th century BC do we encounter visible vestiges of a co-ordinated civic life, and then, perhaps significantly, on the coast of Anatolia: at Old Smyrna, where a temple and houses defended by a wall and flanked by alternative harbours have been partially excavated by J. M. Cook. There is enough to show that Smyrna in the time of Homer had an orderly civic aspect of a kind and shape remarkably reminiscent of the Phaeacian city of King Alcinous in the *Odyssey*, with its walls, its houses, its market-place (*agora*), its fine stone temple of Poseidon, and 'an excellent harbour on each side'. The persistent tradition that Homer was born in Smyrna fits happily into the picture. In short, on the threshold of the Greek world the literature and archaeology of Ionia converge upon the primary condition of the Hellenic way of life—the city.

The Chessboards of Hippodamus

It is unnecessary here to pursue the civic idea through the details of its early growth. But the Greek coastline of Asia remains in the picture. At the end of the 6th century planning of a chessboard kind appeared at Olbia in south Russia, a colony of Miletus, and at Miletus itself the famous and eccentric Hippodamus, probably after 466 BC, systematized the chessboard plan; according to Aristotle (*Politics* II, 5), who cannot be strictly correct, he 'invented' the division of cities into blocks. At the invitation of Pericles, he subsequently introduced the principle to the Piraeus—in Aristotle's phrase, he 'carved up' the Piraeus. More immediately relevant to the present context, in 443 BC he accompanied Athenian colonists to Thurii in south Italy and there again applied his chessboard scheme. At Thurii, Diodorus (XII. 10) tells us that 'they divided the city lengthwise by four streets, the first of which they named Heracleia, the second Aphrodisia, the third Olympias, and the fourth Dionysias, and breadthwise they divided it by three streets, of which the first was named Heroa, the second Thuria, and the last Thurina. And since the blocks formed by these streets

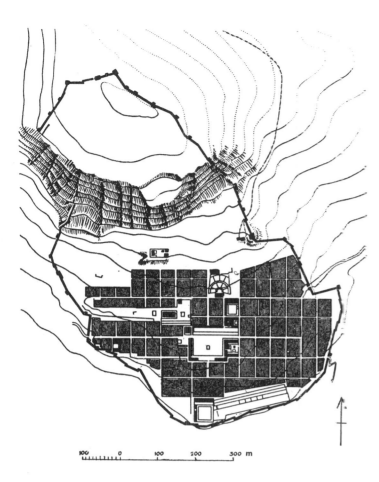

Priene—a classic example of the Hellenistic town-planning which was taken over by the Romans. Steep cliffs rise to a high acropolis in the north. On the slopes below, contained within the irregular outline of a hillside defence system, the town was laid out on a strictly geometrical plan more suitable for a level site.

were filled with dwellings the city had a well-built appearance.' No doubt, in addition to the main streets the plan was amplified by minor streets and lanes conforming with the over-all design.

Strabo (XIV. 2.8) avers that Rhodes, founded in 408 BC, was also built by Hippodamus. The time-factor is against this, but air-photography has shown there in astonishing detail the rectilinear lay-out of the large Greek town, with blocks about 105 yds by 55 yds in extent. These may be compared with the 99 by 44 yd blocks of the residential extension built at about the same time at Olynthus in Macedonia where, as at Thurii, main streets from north to south were crossed by others from east to west. It is to be presumed that both at Rhodes and at Olynthus the Hippodamian example may be recognized. A century later Priene, beside the Maeander valley opposite Miletus, was rebuilt on the slopes below a sheer acropolis, and its lay-out, a chessboard within the irregular outline of a contour-defence, is the classic example of Hellenistic planning. In the application to a hillside of a geometrical plan more suitable to a level site, Priene constitutes almost a *tour de force*, and emphasizes the prestige which now attached to the conventions of the rigid Hippodamian scheme.

The First Roman Planning

From western Asia Minor to Italy. There in general terms the Graecized south, with its fertile sea-plains, offered a contrast to the Italic centre, with its hills and marshes; a contrast expressed, for example, by Cicero in his *De Lege Agraria* (II. XXXV. 95–6). 'The Campanians', he says, 'are inclined to boast of the excellence of their fields and the abundance of their crops, of the healthfulness, orderliness and beauty of their city . . . They ridicule and despise Rome with its hills and close valleys, its garrets hanging up aloft, its poor roads and miserable lanes, in comparison with their Capua spread upon the level plain and most admirably laid out.' And Strabo (V. 3.8) a generation later says much the same thing.

Of the progress of town-planning in the Greek towns of southern Italy from the 5th century BC onwards, our knowledge is at present slight. We have seen that in the latter half of that century Hippodamus himself was at work at Thurii in the extreme south. But at Pompeii in the small nucleus which represents the town prior to the Samnite invasions of the late 5th century BC the planning was sketchy and not (as preserved) up to Hippodamian standards. In contrast, the very symmetrical plan of Paestum, south-east of Salerno, has not been well dated but may well not be earlier than the planting of the Roman colony there in 273 BC, although Axel Boëthius would like to date it to the age after the Lucanian invasion, about 400 BC. In this uncertainty it is to Ostia, at the mouth of the Tiber, that we have to look for the earliest clear example of truly geometrical Roman planning, and that of an interesting and remarkable kind.

The core of Ostia, the port of Rome, is a fort (the *castrum*) forming a rectangle some 5 ½ acres in extent within walls 20 ft high. The enclosure was quartered by straight streets which passed out through gates set at or near the centre of each side. The date of the work, as reviewed by Russell Meiggs, lies within the years following 349 BC, when Rome was troubled along the coast by Greek raiders. The garrison may have consisted of about 300 military colonists.

This *castrum* raises a question which cannot at present be answered. Was its geometrical planning derived from the Greek mode, or was it of independent Italian origin, influenced just possibly by the procedures of Roman augury, the marking out of oriented squares of sky or ground in which to await signs? In general, did the military plan precede and inform the civil plan, or, as Polybius (VI. 31.10) thought, was the military plan derived from the civil plan? Did the Romans on the other hand adapt their military planning from that of the Greeks? So Frontinus (IV. 1.14), who held that the Romans copied the organized Greek camp of Pyrrhus of Epirus which they captured in south Italy in 275 BC, whereas previously they had been content with mere huts (*mapalia*)

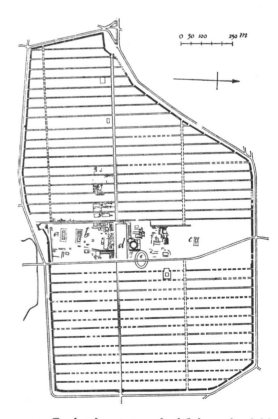

Paestum was a Greek colony just south of Salerno, founded by Greek colonists before 600 BC. Its chequer-board plan may be Greek or may date from the Roman occupation about 273 BC. The three Greek temples for which it is famous do not seem to be part of the regular lay-out: the so-called 'Basilica' (a); the 'Temple of Neptune' (b); and the 'Temple of Ceres' (c) (the real dedications are probably to Hera and Athena). Roman times saw the development of a forum (d) and an amphitheatre (e).

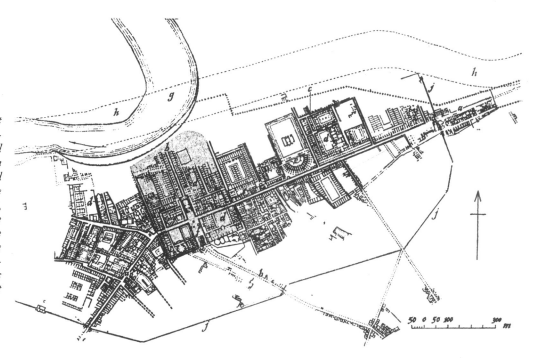

Ostia, the port of Rome, began as a fort (the stippled rectangle). By the 2nd century BC most of the original features had been rebuilt and the town had expanded on all sides: decumanus (aa), cardo (bb), and forum with a temple at each end (f). The most orderly development was to the east, on the northern side of the decumanus. Here were barracks for the vigiles (c), a theatre (e) and one of the many baths (d). In the time of Sulla the growing town was surrounded by defensive walls (j). On this plan g marks the present and h the ancient course of the Tiber.

for their soldiery. But this event was something like three quarters of a century *after* Ostia, so that the sequence does not work. We have no firm answer to these queries; indeed there may be no firm answer to seek. Etruscan art and architecture were interpenetrated with Greek ideas; other Greek ideas arrived more directly from the Greek colonies of southern Italy, and to both of these formative influences Rome added mutations contributed by its own powerful mind. In these complex circumstances the extent to which (if at all) Roman military planning influenced early Italian town-planning baffles definition.

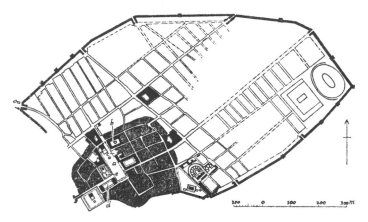

The growth of Pompeii: shading marks the oldest part of the town, which contained the forum and public buildings. From the late 5th century onwards, it was progressively enlarged, the new portions following the familiar grid-pattern. Features of the earlier town include the forum (a), with the Temple of Jupiter at its north end; a market (b); the Temple of the Lares (c); a basilica (d); and a temple to Apollo (e).

Setting aside the disputed case of Marzabotto near Bologna, thought by some to have been laid out on a rectangular street-plan as an Etruscan colony not later than the early 5th century BC, but by others (including G. Lugli) to be a Roman plan of the 4th century or later, the earliest known rigid urban lay-out in Italy is to be seen at Pompeii. Here, sometime after the Samnite raids of the late 5th century, the original Oscan town with its indifferently co-ordinated plan was progressively enlarged by rectilinear suburbs. In this development of the town, the older nucleus, including the forum and public buildings, was retained as a peripheral unit; so that we have not here an integral Greek plan comparable

with Miletus or Priene. For the rest, the new residential enlargements accorded with the Greek mode. They compare in essence with the residential New Town at Olynthus, built about the same time and in the same presumed Hippodamian tradition.

For the most part, by the beginning of the 3rd century BC the basically Greek plan came naturally to the builders or rebuilders of Roman towns in Italy—using 'Roman' in the widest sense. There is little, for example, in a plan such as that of the Roman colony founded at Etruscan Cosa in 273 BC that can be ascribed to other than Hellenistic patterns. But for the most ample example of Roman planning at present available on home ground we must return to Rome's port, Ostia.

The Port of Rome: Ostia

By the 2nd century BC Ostia had submerged its nuclear *castrum* and was a burgeoning commercial city. The initial urban development would appear to have been of a gradual and piecemeal character; the resultant plan is a mosaic of partially organized fragments with no over-all scheme. Only in one area was there fully effective co-ordination: east of the *castrum*, between the main east-west street conventionally known as the *decumanus maximus* and the Tiber to the north, stood a regimented group of public buildings, including extensive blocks of store-houses, the offices of the shipping merchants, baths, the barracks of the *vigiles* or firemen and, from the time of Augustus, the theatre. Five identical stones along the northern edge of the *decumanus* proclaimed that this land was under public control; a natural provision since it bordered upon the all-important river. The stones date probably from the latter part of the 2nd century BC.

It may have been in the time of Sulla, about 80 BC, that the town was given the defensive walls which were to serve it for the remainder of its days. By that time it occupied some 160 acres, and the main limits of its growth had, it seems, been determined. Scattered structures of one kind and another, including baths, lay beyond the perimeter, and of course the harbour and its attendant works. But of the buildings within the walled city of the Republican period little is at present known. The private houses would appear to have approximated to the spacious Pompeian type with *atrium* and peristyle garden. With the growth of population under the Empire these tended to be replaced by blocks of flats, such as also characterized the capital. Residences of one kind or another were of varying quality, but there is no district that can be written off as a 'slum'; no doubt because most of the grades which in a freer society might have produced the slums were absorbed anonymously into the main body politic under the guise of slavery. On the other hand, there is evidence enough of genuine slums in Rome itself.

Two miles to the north of the town of Ostia lay its successive harbours, rendered necessary under the early Empire by the growing volume of sea-borne trade; first the wide Claudian harbour, which was not, however, gale-proof, and then under Trajan (probably about AD 112) a more compact and sheltered basin, hexagonal in plan, with a connecting canal. At some late Roman period the Trajanic basin and its adjacent buildings were enclosed by a wall, and in the 4th century AD the whole complex became a small independent town under the name of Portus. In this character its importance outlasted that of its parental Ostia.

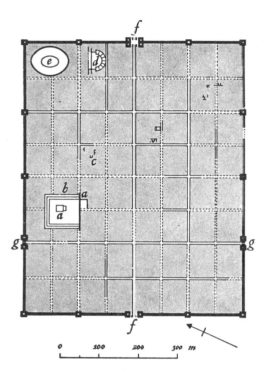

Aosta, near the foot of Mont Blanc, in general reflects the basic castrum lay-out. Excavated buildings include temples (a), storehouses (b), baths (c), theatre (d) and amphitheatre (e). There were four main gates in the rectangular wall, at each end of the decumanus (ff) and the cardo (gg).

Copybook War-Office Fortress-Towns

Elsewhere in Italy type-sites are most readily chosen from the colonies established under the Republic and the Principate (Augustus to Nero) as a means of diverting veterans and disbanded armies—a dangerous potential—into a settled and productive civil life. At the same time these new foundations served a continuing military purpose in tracts of country still liable to disturbance, where a community accustomed to discipline and adequately fenced was an economic substitute for scattered garrisons of serving soldiery. In no instance have we anything approaching a complete town plan; but the evidence is sufficient to indicate that the Greek chessboard tradition, now thoroughly naturalized in Italy, had here been in some measure stiffened by the Roman military mind. Whereas a Hellenistic town like Priene was essentially a civic chessboard within the rambling fortifications of an older tradition, a Roman colony such as Aosta or Turin or Verona was primarily a copybook war-office fortress ameliorated by an urban content.

Aosta (Augusta Praetoria) was founded by Augustus in 25 BC for 3,000 discharged soldiers of the Praetorian Guard. Its situation, 50 miles north of Turin near the foot of Mont Blanc, was of a tactical importance reflected in its severe military outline. The walled colony was about 100 acres in extent and was planned in sixteen large blocks (145 by 180 yds) which were doubtless subdivided. The identified buildings include two temples, storehouses, baths, a theatre and an amphitheatre; the last, normally outside the walls, was here placed within them, presumably for local reasons of security on the fringe of the mountainous terrain.

Of Turin (Augusta Taurinorum), founded as a colony by Augustus in 28 BC, less is known. Its outline, nearly a square,

though with one angle cut off, enclosed about 125 acres, and the general arrangement of its interior has survived in the modern street-plan. Its buildings were partitioned by straight streets into seventy-two blocks, mostly about 80 yds square. Of the town's Augustan architecture, the remarkable Porta Palatina with its sixteen-sided brick towers, the foundations of the east gate, and part of the theatre in the gardens of the Palazzo Chiablese, are the most notable survivals.

The unusual polygonal towers recur at Spello (Hispellum), another Augustan colony, in the fertile valley of the Chiaggio. These and other resemblances within the Augustan series have suggested the existence of a school of northern town-planners such as is testified epigraphically elsewhere in Italy, at Puteoli, Cumae, Formiae, and Terracina; whilst another group, perhaps under the great Vitruvius himself, has been suspected at Verona, which was in fact almost a duplicate of Turin. It is likely enough that, in a period of active urban development under official stimulus, regional planning and building would tend to acquire something of a 'Ministry of Works' imprint.

Africa's Rich Urban Life

For examples further afield we may turn first to North Africa, rich in corn and, later, in olives, rich also in the Saharan trade which brought gold and ivory, slaves and show-animals to the Mediterranean ports, and proportionally rich in its urban life. From great Carthage, 1,000 or 1,500 acres in extent, to little towns such as Timgad (originally 34 acres) or Tiddis which, in spite of a mere 9 acres, numbered amongst its citizens Lollius Urbicus the Antonine conqueror of Scotland, its seven provinces teemed with Romanized communities and produced a fair share of the intelligentsia of the Roman world. Here a brief sketch of two of its towns must suffice.

First Timgad: the ancient Thamugadi, a dozen miles east of Lambaesis, fortress of the IIIrd Augustan Legion, exhibits Roman town-planning in its simplest terms. It was founded as a *colonia* by Trajan in AD 100 to house the legion's veterans in a suitably regimented environment. Its familiar shape was at first nearly a square, with rounded corners to its stone defences, main gates in the centre of three (possibly all four) sides, and two posterns. Subsequently public and private buildings spread loosely and even untidily about the surrounding landscape in the common fashion of Roman towns; we have seen an early example at Ostia.

Beside the main east-west street (the *decumanus maximus*) at the centre of the town lay the forum, a large paved rectangular space surrounded by porticos. On its eastern side stood the *basilica* or town-hall, with an apse at one end and an oblong alcove (probably law-court) at the other. A range of rooms at the back no doubt accommodated civic officials. At the opposite end of the courtyard were the *curia* or council-chamber and a temple. The other sides of the courtyard included shops and a public lavatory containing rows of stone seats of the sociable kind which was a normal feature of Roman towns. Nearby a step bore a scratched gaming-board and the inscription *venari lavari ludere ridere occ est vivere*—'to hunt, to bathe, to play, to laugh, that is to live'. In one way and another, the forum was the central and catholic expression of civic life.

Adjoining the forum stood the theatre, built in AD 161–9 with a seating-capacity of 3,500–4,000, and manifestly designed to accommodate both town and country. Amongst other public buildings more than a dozen baths show that one at least of the scribbled conditions of the full life was adequately fulfilled at Timgad.

The hint of an intellectually fuller life is perhaps contained in an interesting library-building which occupies an *insula* or block near the forum. Behind a forecourt, colonnaded on three sides and flanked by small rooms, opens a hall, formerly half-domed and surrounded by steps (or seats) and niches, and in turn by flanking rooms. The recesses round the hall were presumably used for storing scrolls or books. One would give much to know the nature of the contents of Timgad's library in its prime. Respect for it was not always universal; there are signs that hopscotch was played in its courtyard, and its columns bear graffiti of a highly unacademic kind.

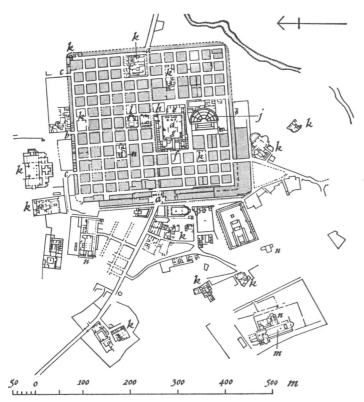

Timgad, in modern Algeria, was built in AD 100, on the basically Greek 'chessboard' plan. The almost square defences are pierced by two main gates (a) on the line of the decumanus, a north gate (b) and two posterns (c). The west gate was later a triumphal arch. The forum (d), town-hall (e), curia (f), temple (g), public lavatory (h), theatre (j), and library (l) occupy the centre of the town. Both within the walls and outside are numerous baths (k). Christian churches (n) were built in the 4th century and to the west a large cathedral (m) of the Donatist sect.

For the rest, the churches of Timgad form a notable series. They lie mostly outside the original plan, and at least three of them are of the 3rd–5th century; the largest, an aisled basilica 100 yds long, adjoins the house of the bishop, identified as an adherent of the Donatist heresy which arose at Cirta and Carthage after the Diocletianic persecutions at the beginning of the 4th century.

The second of our African examples is the city of Lepcis Magna, on the coast of Tripolitania, built on the site of a Phoenician settlement and developed on a chessboard pattern in the time of Augustus and his immediate successors. The early forum lay at the base of the promontory which formed one side of the harbour, and was flanked by a basilica which had a four-sided internal colonnade, no doubt with clerestory, and rectangular exhedrae at one end. The opposite side of the forum was occupied by three temples, of which the central was dedicated in AD 14–19 jointly to Rome and to Augustus with other members of the Julio-Claudian family. It had two shrines, and stood on a high podium which could serve also as a platform for oratory. Further to the south-west stood the market (9–8 BC) and the theatre (AD 1–2), both built by the same benefactor whose munificence is recorded in Latin and Neo-Punic over the two main entrances of the theatre. The market is noteworthy, with its two polygonal halls and its stones bearing the standard measures of length and volume.

These two buildings marked the junction between the earlier chessboard and its southerly extension, which hereabouts changed direction in conformity with the bending line of the main north-south road that was also its *cardo*. The extension resumed the rectilinear plan with elongated *insulae* on the new alignment, and shortly absorbed the arterial coast-road (north-west to south-east) as its *decumanus maximus*. The full southerly extent of the city—then as later—has not been ascertained, but a line of earthwork appreciably further south may have been designed in the 1st century AD to include also the surrounding countryfolk with their livestock in an emergency.

In AD 109–110 Lepcis received the rank of *colonia*, entitling it to the Italian franchise. Shortly afterwards, under Hadrian (in AD 127), a fine large bath-building on an imperial scale was erected beside the Wadi Lebda on the east of the city. But it is to the time of Septimius Severus that the buildings belong which give the place its outstanding distinction. Severus was born at Lepcis and died at York (AD 211), his life-span thus literally reflecting the span of his Empire; and he lavished upon his birthplace a wealth of artistry in excess of its economic significance. Near the Hadrianic baths a new colonnaded street, of a kind particularly characteristic of the Roman cities of the Near East, is one of several architectural links at the same period with the eastern Mediterranean. Above all, Severus created a new and splendid forum and basilica which are, both architecturally and sculpturally, of outstanding distinction amongst the buildings of the Empire. The forum, 1,000 by 600 ft, was surrounded by colonnades, with arches springing from stiff-leafed capitals of an East Mediterranean type. At its south-western end is the podium of a temple; at its north-eastern end, set askew as a compromise with the two directions of the main civic plan, is an imposing basilica, a three-aisled hall with an apse at each end and a former height of not less than 100 ft. Its columns were of red Egyptian granite and green Euboean marble; and pilasters of white marble at both ends were carved with the adventures of Dionysus and Hercules, the patron deities of the Severan family. The building was completed by Caracalla in AD 216, and was turned into a church in the 6th century.

Another Severan structure, dating probably from the visit of the emperor to his native city in AD 203, was a four-way triumphal arch set across the junction of the *cardo* with the *decumanus maximus*. As reconstructed, the arch was of remarkable design, and it carried a notable series of sculptures with sharply drilled and incised carving in a Near-Eastern mode (below, p. 313).

Yet another architectural achievement of this period of inflated aggrandisement was the reconstruction of the harbour at the mouth of the Wadi Lebda, a basin 24 acres in extent, flanked by quays carrying warehouses, a temple and a watch-tower, with a lighthouse on the northern promontory. But here the city overreached itself. The pierced mooring blocks on the quays show no signs of use; the whole scheme was still-born, and the harbour quickly silted up as it is today.

Lastly, the so-called 'Hunting Baths' on the western fringe of the city are of an architectural interest which far outstrips their small

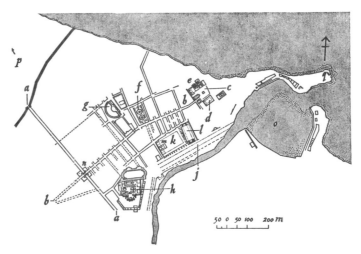

Lepcis Magna belongs to two phases. During the reign of Augustus and Tiberius the Roman town was built on a promontory—the old forum (c), basilica (d) and temples (e); its southernmost and latest limit was marked by the market (f) and theatre (g). About a century later, under Hadrian, and later again under Septimius Severus, many sumptuous new buildings were added: the new Severan forum (k) with its basilica (l) and temple (m), the magnificent Hadrianic baths (h) and colonnaded street (j), and at the meeting point of the new cardo (bb) with the decumanus (aa), a four-way triumphal arch (n). At the same time the harbour (o) was extended and refitted with quays, warehouses and a lighthouse (q). To the north-west (off the plan, p) the 'Hunting Baths' are still almost intact.

size. Their domes and vaults, disinterred from the dunes which had long protected them, are nearly intact. A wall-painting in the main barrel-vaulted hall suggests that the building was the property of a guild of hunters whose trade was to supply wild beasts to local and Italian amphitheatres.

In summary, Lepcis Magna shows the processes of growth which other Roman town-plans have made familiar: a nuclear chessboard with divergent though mostly rectilinear enlargements. Its principal interest to us today arises from the political circumstance which led to its extravagant development under its most distinguished son, Septimius Severus, and made it the greatest surviving example of the transitional art and architecture of his epoch.

The Stronghold of the Parisii

Unlike London, Paris has an assured pre-Roman ancestry. It enters history in 53 BC when Julius Caesar, with an air of proprietorship, transferred to 'Lutetia, town of the Parisii', his assembly of Gaulish representatives which enabled him periodically to assess the attitude of the tribes to the fluctuating success of Roman arms and diplomacy. The Parisii themselves were neither a large nor a powerful state, but situated around the junction of arterial rivers they occupied a position of strategic and commercial importance which eventually encouraged the upgrowth of a considerable Roman town and even the inclusion of an imperial residence. In Caesar's day, as he tells us, Lutetia was 'an *oppidum* (stronghold) of the Parisii, placed upon an island in the Seine' and connected by bridges with both banks; in fact, the Ile de la Cité of the modern map. Subsequently it passed without distinction into the highly Romanized tribal system of Gaul as the *chef lieu* of the Parisii and, like other Gaulish centres of the kind, bequeathed the tribal rather than the local name to later history.

Of the nuclear town on the island nothing is known save for a few fragmentary walls recorded long ago during building-operations, and traces of the fortification which was thrown up round the periphery, here as elsewhere in Gaul, at the time of the Germanic break-through prior to AD 276. But the line of the main north-south street or *cardo* is certain; it followed the lines of the Petit Pont and the Grand Pont (Pont Notre Dame) and between the two is now the Rue de la Cité. Thence on the north it mounted the rising ground towards Senlis, and on the south it proceeded towards Orleans straight up through the Latin Quarter under the Rue St Jacques, where considerable stretches of it have been noted. It was here, on the slopes of Montparnasse, that dry ground clear of the marshy fringes of the river attracted urban expansion from the confines of the island. Here in the 1st and 2nd centuries AD the principal public buildings of the city were laid out within the framework of a grid-plan.

West of the Panthéon, between the *cardo* (Rue St Jacques) and a parallel Roman street represented by the Boulevard St Michel, stood the forum, consisting of a large enclosure, some 530 by 330 ft, with a high external wall and internal shops and porticos framing an oblong open court. At one end of the court was the basilica or town-hall with an internal colonnade, and towards the opposite end was the podium of a temple. The whole lay-out is of a recognized imperial type.

In the next *insula* to the south a public bath-building has been sufficiently preserved by good solid masonry to attract attention. At the eastern end of the *insula*, beside the *cardo*, ran the aqueduct which brought water from a source ten miles to the south. Of two other bath-buildings, one lay on the eastern side of the *cardo*, under the Collège de France. The other, 300 yds to the north-west, beside the Boulevard St Michel, is still one of the most famous Roman buildings of western Europe: the so-called 'Palace of the Baths', known as such since the early Middle Ages and, as a traditional palace, incorporated at the end of the 15th century in a splendid Gothic mansion, the Hôtel de Cluny. The Roman plan, bounded on all four sides by drains or conduits, covered an area approximately 330 by 200 ft, and was roughly symmetrical. Its sequence has not been worked out, but an imposing vaulted central hall built over cellars, with a cold bath in an alcove, may be recognized as the *frigidarium*, and from it access was obtained to warmed and heated rooms of considerable pretension.

Two other public buildings help the picture of a town fully equipped with the normal urban amenities. A hundred yards south-west of the Cluny baths, slight indications of a small theatre—perhaps rather an *odeum* or music-hall—have been observed; and on the eastern fringe of the ancient city restored remains of an amphitheatre can still be seen beside the Rue Monge. The plan shows a stage on one side of the oval arena; so that the structure falls into the class of 'cock-pit theatres' or 'amphithéâtres à scène' which is characteristic of central and northern Gaul, with an outlier at Verulamium in Britain. In Gallia Comata ('Shaggy Gaul') and beyond, the combination of a dual function—stage buffoonery and arena bloodshed—in a single building was no doubt a desirable economy.

Of the private houses of Roman Paris, nothing of value is known. In the absence of town-walls—save on the island, none were built—we are left with an inchoate skeleton of *insulae* which, in the neighbourhood of the forum, seem to have measured 100 by 600 ft. The limit to the west has not been fixed, and to the east we can only say that the town stopped short of the amphitheatre and the burials in its neighbourhood. To the south, an extensive cemetery near the Port Royal marked the bounds of occupation in this direction in the 2nd and 3rd centuries, a little below the summit of Montparnasse and about a mile from the Petit Pont.

'Capital of the Gauls': Trier

Anciently of far greater magnitude and importance than Paris was Trier (Augusta Treverorum) beside the Moselle. It became the headquarters of the so-called 'Empire of the Gauls' established by Gallienus's general Postumus in AD 260, and was more formally

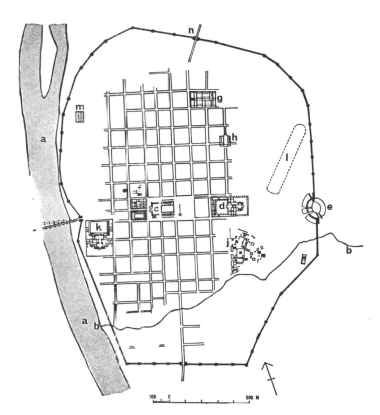

Roman Trier, 'Augusta Treverorum', situated where the river Moselle (a) is joined by a small stream called the Altbach (b), was the third largest town in the western Empire. The forum (c), the Constantinian Baths (d) and the amphitheatre (e) lie along the line of the old decumanus. One of the houses (f) near the forum belonged to the Emperor Victorinus. The Constantinian palace was a large complex of buildings stretching south from the present Cathedral (g), and included the spectacular Aula Palatina, or audience-hall (h). On the banks of the Altbach lay a confused collection of temples (j). Another large bath-building, the 'Barbara Baths' (k), possibly a race-track (l), and warehouses (m) can also be identified. The grandest surviving feature of the town-defences is the Porta Nigra (n), the old north gate.

recognized as the capital of the Western provinces when the Caesar Constantius made it his residence in AD 293. The site had been partially occupied in pre-Roman times, and under Augustus a regiment of Spanish cavalry was stationed here. Its special association, however, with the powerful Celto-German tribe of the Treveri was expressed in its name from the outset, and was not forgotten when it was given colonial status shortly after AD 41 by Claudius, in whose reign Pomponius Mela could already describe it as 'a city of great wealth amongst the Treveri'. Imposing Roman buildings of a later age are still standing, and buried streets and buildings have been noted by local scholars.

The urban centre, the forum, lay 500 yds east of two successive Roman bridges and occupied four *insulae* of the *colonia*, a total space of about 690 by 450 ft. It consisted of an oblong court divided north and south by arcades from double rows of shops, whilst a further courtyard to the west presumably contained the basilica. Adjacent *insulae* to the west and north-west were occupied by residences of considerable pretension. In one of them a mosaic bore the name of M. Piavonius Victorinus, emperor in AD 269–270.

The early lay-out seems to have extended for nearly a mile southwards from the cathedral and to have covered some 200 acres. It consisted of rectangular *insulae* with an average of 330 ft square; most of them were probably subdivided. To the south-east, on the banks of the Altbach, lay a closely-built temple-quarter in which the dominant type was the so-called Romano-Celtic temple with a square shrine surrounded on all four sides by a portico or verandah. Both the deities worshipped here and the unclassical environment in which they were cultivated hark back to pre-Roman days, and the area lay, as might be expected, outside the colonial plan.

In the original scheme the forum area may have been quartered by the *cardo* and the *decumanus maximus*, but in the expanded town of the 2nd and later centuries the axes appear to have moved somewhat east and south. In any case they were probably of no special importance. The famous Constantinian baths on the eastern flank of the city were centred on the hypothetical *decumanus* of the colonial lay-out, and approximately in the same line is the amphitheatre, which was built in stone early in the 2nd century perhaps on the site of a timber predecessor. It could accommodate some 7,000 spectators, and until a relatively late date continued to fulfil its bloodthirsty function; in the time of the first Christian emperor Frankish prisoners were slaughtered there in shoals, whilst it served also as a strongpoint and gateway on the line of the late Roman town-walls. North of it within the defences is the possible site of the circus.

The date of these defences and of their grandest surviving feature—the north gate or Porta Nigra—has been disputed. They enclosed an area of no less than 700 acres—the largest city of the provincial West. The likelihood is that they were built mostly in the time of the 'Gallic Empire' but that the Porta Nigra is a 4th-century addition.

Four other buildings of distinction are included on the plan. Near the successive bridges across the Moselle, and near also to the probable site of the Augustan fort, are the so-called Barbara Baths, an extensive public building of symmetrical plan ascribed to varying dates in the 2nd century. South-east of the cathedral stands the much-patched brick 'basilica', one of the landmarks of the city and now recognized as the *Aula Palatina* or audience hall of the Constantinian palace. It is an aisleless apsidal building 220 ft long and 106 ft high, heated originally by a hypocaust with wall-flues which opened through the outer walls at the level of the lower of two ranges of windows. The windows of both ranges were fronted by balconies. Beneath the hall, forming part of the pre-Constantinian palace which was probably destroyed by the Alemanni in AD 275–6, was a smaller predecessor, also with an apse. The Constantinian palace extended as far as the present cathedral where, incorporating part of it, a double church with intervening baptistry was built in AD 326. Lastly, reference must be made to a pair of Roman *horrea* or warehouses, probably of the 4th century, which have been identified near the river in the north-western quarter.

In general, Trier expanded symmetrically along the lines of its grid but without overmuch attention to *cardo-decumanus* domina-

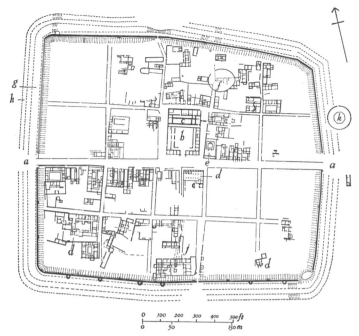

Caerwent, a frontier town in South Wales. Enclosed by a wall with inner and outer ditches (g and h), it was based on the familiar chessboard pattern. There is a decumanus (aa) but no obvious cardo. Near the centre is the forum (b), basilica (c), one of the three baths (d) and a temple (e). The later amphitheatre (f) is within the walls. A rambling building near the south gate (j) may have been an inn, and a polygonal temple (k) stood beyond the east gate. The hollow polygonal towers in the stone wall were a late addition.

tion. Round the periphery large public buildings grew up in orderly fashion; but finally the defences abandoned all pretence of military tidiness and rambled round the landscape, incorporating river and hills and other vantage-points with the unregimented opportunism of a native *oppidum* or fortified settlement. Once again we may look back through the centuries to Hellenistic prototypes, and find little that is very specifically Roman in the general scheme of a great Roman city.

'Beyond the Inhabited World'

From the ultimate north-western province of the Empire, 'beyond the inhabited world' as it seemed to the anxious army of invasion, two very different Roman towns are here taken briefly for their planning. One of them, *Venta Silurum* or the modern Caerwent (Monmouthshire), is tucked away in the western frontier-zone. The other, Londinium, was one of the great peripheral ports of the Empire. We begin with Caerwent.

Caerwent, some 45 acres in extent, lay seven miles behind the frontier-fortress of the IInd Augustan Legion at Caerleon-on-Usk (Isca), astride the main road back into the province. Its essentially regular lay-out, framed by an earthen bank in the 1st or early 2nd century AD, might seem to add point to this proximity, and to recall the conjunction of the fortress of the IIIrd Legion at Lambaesis in North Africa and its cantonment-town twelve miles away at Timgad. The analogy would be only in part correct. Timgad was established as a colony mainly to house retired legionaries amidst urban amenities within a day's walk of the parent-fortress. Caerwent, though laid out doubtless by legionary surveyors, was essentially a tribal capital disguised in attractive Roman dress.

The oblong enclosure was divided symmetrically by the east-west highway, which formed the *decumanus maximus*. North and south of it were ten fairly regular *insulae*, each about 260 ft square. There is no clearly recognizable *cardo*; the street to the south gate flanks one side of the central forum, whilst that to the north gate flanks the other. The forum itself is of a widespread provincial type; an open market-place bordered on three sides by porticos and shops and on the fourth side by the basilica. This was 176 ft long, three-aisled, and had rectangular alcoves at each end for judicial or other uses. At the back, a range of six or more rooms may be regarded as municipal offices.

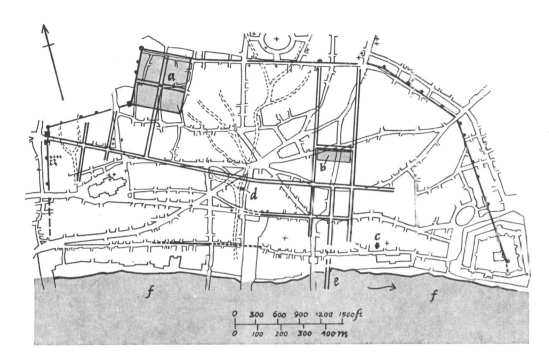

Roman London was one of the largest towns
of northern Europe. It was begun soon after
the invasion of AD 43, and grew rapidly. A
wooden bridge (e) crossed the Thames (f)
slightly to the east of the present London
Bridge. Boudicca destroyed the old town in
60–61, but subsequent re-building included
the huge basilica (b, see below) and the
forum to the south of it, a spacious market-
place 500 feet across. Towards the end of the
1st century Cripplegate Fort (a) was
constructed in the normal Roman plan; it
served as a garrison or transit-camp, conveniently near the port. A century later the
whole city was surrounded by a substantial
defence wall some three miles in length, with
gateways opening on to the principal highways of Britain, and later with numerous
bastions. Among the few Roman buildings
so far identified in London are the Mithraeum (d), on the bank of the Walbrook
(shown by dotted lines), and a bath-building
(c) near the Thames. Crosses indicate
burials of Roman date.

In the next block to the east was a small, square 'Romano-Celtic' temple, with a northern apse and surrounding portico. Other public buildings include substantial baths opposite the forum and two further bath-suites elsewhere; recalling that baths were amongst the seductions mentioned by Tacitus as a means of Romanizing the natives. Shops and workshops, especially in the earlier periods, were undistinguished oblong structures, their longer axes at right-angles to the streets; but the better private houses were of a civilized courtyard plan derived from familiar classical prototypes. A large, rather rambling building beside the south gate is reasonably identified as an inn. The simple bank of the original town-defences was reinforced by a stone wall, probably at the end of the 2nd century; and this in turn was armed with hollow polygonal towers not earlier than AD 330. At some late period, too, when the coastal regions were increasingly harassed by Irish and other raiders, the north and south gates were blocked.

As a whole, the plan of Caerwent bears a closer imprint of official Rome than is generally apparent in the more leisurely and local pattern of the foundations of the English lowlands.

'A Hive of Commerce': Roman London

To turn from this small border-town to Roman London, with its 330 acres (one of the five largest Roman cities north of the Alps), is to enter a different world. Londinium was established beside the Thames at the lowest point at which opposed gravel banks facilitated a permanent crossing; in all probability also near the tidal limit of the period. Here cargoes, brought far inland with a minimum of effort, could be dispersed equally from both banks, linked by an easy bridge. Only one further condition was necessary: the provision and maintenance of highways through the deep woodlands which then imprisoned the London Basin. For these, skills and funds on an imperial scale were necessary. It is understandable therefore that, for all its Celtic name, there is no conclusive evidence for a pre-Roman Londinium. Equally it is understandable that the site should have been developed as a first priority of the new province. Within seventeen years of the Claudian invasion, Tacitus could speak of Londinium as 'crowded with traders and a hive of commerce'.

The city at first occupied the hill (Cornhill) north of the river and east of the Walbrook, and its *cardo* was no doubt a continuation of London bridge, which was about 60 yds below the present bridge. On the southern bank a bridgehead settlement underlay Southwark. The summit of Cornhill was crowned by the basilica, of which enough is known to indicate that it was triple-aisled and had the astonishing length of 500 ft. At one end (possibly both) the 'nave' ended in an apse, and at the back was a

range of some eighteen rooms, probably offices rather than shops. The magnitude of this central official building, combining the functions of town-hall, law-courts and general business centre, is itself sufficiently eloquent of the administrative and commercial importance of Londinium. The great Basilica Ulpia at Rome was a mere 40 ft longer.

Hints here and there show that the city centring upon the basilica was laid out in chessboard pattern with large *insulae* some 480 ft square, subdivided perhaps into units of half that dimension. By the second century, occupation had spread westwards across the Walbrook, along the divergent lines of the main roads and over early cemeteries and kilns in the vicinity of Ludgate Hill. The progress of growth may have been stimulated rather than hindered by the celebrated burning of the unwalled city—built mostly, no doubt of timber—by Boudicca's tribesmen in AD 60–1. And it may or may, more probably, not have been as a sequel to that episode that in the latter part of the century a fort, some 11 acres in extent, was built on the highest available site in the neighbourhood of Cripplegate, within the purlieus of the growing city. This fort had walls 4 ft thick, built of ragstone without bonding-courses and backed by an earthen bank. One of the rounded corners retained an internal turret and there were intermediate turrets along the sides; the position of the west and south gates is known, and a wooden bridge had carried the approach-road to the southern gate across an unemphatic ditch.

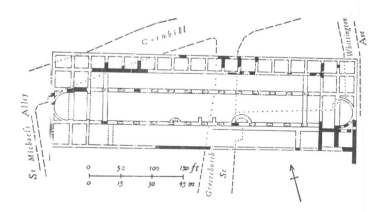

*The administrative centre of Roman London was a huge basilica 500 feet
long with a central 'nave', two aisles and a row of eighteen offices along one
side. Most of the above plan is fairly certain, though there may have been
no apse at the west end. Some idea of its size may be gathered by the fact
that two Wren churches can comfortably share one half of its site.*

The specific function of this fort, entrenched in the civilian zone of the province, can only be guessed. It may be recalled, however, that from the time of Tiberius the Gaulish capital of Lugdunum or Lyons had for upwards of two centuries a succession of urban cohorts of 1,000 to 1,200 men, the only permanent garrison in Gaul; and when in AD 197 the XIIIth *Cohors Urbana* took the losing side of Albinus against Septimius Severus in the contest for empire at Lyons, it was replaced by a new composite unit made up of drafts from the Rhenish legions. An inscription records that amongst the special functions of the Lyons cohort was the guarding of the mint. Tasks of a parallel kind can be envisaged for a similar unit in London; equally a military depot at the great port may have been useful as a staging-camp for men and stores in connection with the considerable military activity in progress or prospect at this time along the northern frontiers.

In the last years of the 2nd century the city as a whole was walled. The fort was now incorporated in the north-western corner of the new defences, much as the praetorian fort was incorporated as a rectangular projection in the outline of Aurelian's Rome. Subsequently (extending into the post-Roman period) round-fronted towers were added to the defences.

Amongst other Roman structures, a bath-building has long been known on the site of the former Coal Exchange and close to the line of the river-wall. But the most notable recent discovery is that of a well-preserved *Mithraeum* beside the Walbrook near the Mansion House. As the god alike of manliness and fair-dealing, the Persian Mithras was no less appropriate to a commercial community than to the soldiery with whom his worship is frequently associated. The Walbrook temple, built probably in the 3rd century AD, was about 60 ft long by 25 ft wide, with an apse at the western end and a narthex at the eastern. The interior included a nave divided by sleeper-walls from raised aisles, upon which the initiates reclined. The sleeper-walls each carried seven brick columns, perhaps with reference to the seven Mithraic grades. In its final form the building was certainly active after AD 310. Whether the burial of some of the numerous sculptures recovered from it at various depths reflects Christian iconoclasm is less certain. But like other late Roman shrines it would appear that in its latter phases the *Mithraeum* accumulated a wide range of divinities and became something of a pantheon. In addition to the normal evidences of Mithraism, the sculptures included Minerva, Serapis, Mercury and Dionysus, mostly of marble and of continental workmanship.

The general story of the town-plan of Londinium is thus a familiar one. From a nuclear chessboard it spread along the adjacent highways and, at a suitable moment, the amalgam was enclosed in defences which, with little regard to geometry, compromised between the existing pattern of occupation and tactical command. We have seen something of the sort, with variations, in several of our other samples of planning, beginning with Ostia. And beyond Ostia there are Hellenistic cities which tell much the same tale. Save for a tendency to emphasize the major axes of a plan—and here the influence of the augur and the soldier may be suspected—the Roman planners added surprisingly little in principle to the Greek tradition. It was rather in the design and construction of individual buildings that Roman individuality expressed itself, and to some of these we must now turn.

THE SUBSTANCE OF THE TOWNS
The Buildings of the Latin World

From the 7th century BC onwards the typical Greek temple consisted of an oblong sanctum with a porch at one or both ends and a surrounding colonnade. The basis of the building was a low stone platform with continuous steps. Variations on this nuclear plan do not here concern us, nor do the problems of its ancestry. Suffice it that the Greek temple offered an essentially symmetrical all-round elevation with no external emphasis on particular function, save for an adjacent altar.

Similarly generalized, the Roman temple, manifestly derived from the same tradition, was of a very different mind. It was raised upon a lofty podium 9 or 10 ft high, and above this it presented a deep and dominating colonnaded porch, often with

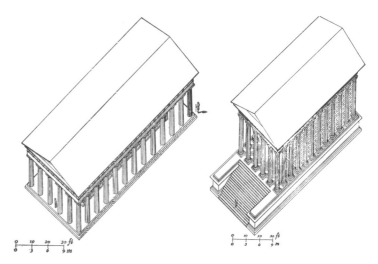

Typical Greek and Roman temples compared: left, the Temple of Hephaestus, Athens (5th century BC) and, right, the Maison Carrée, Nîmes (16 BC). The Greek temple stood on a low base of two or three steps, and had a continuous colonnade round all four sides. The Roman was raised on a high podium and approached by steps from one direction only; it was entered by a deep porch which was not duplicated at the other end, and had attached half-columns instead of a colonnade round the sides and back.

no more than a vestigial continuation in the form of attached columns along the sides and back of the shrine. Compared with the Greek pattern, the Roman was two-dimensional. The back was of no account; it might even be masked by an adjacent wall at the extreme inner end of a forum or *temenos*. The expressed function of the Roman temple was to command the assembly in front of it, whether for religious ceremony or for the more secular purposes of public oratory from its towering podium. This might be approached by a central staircase between flanking platforms, or even by almost secret lateral stairs as in the Temple of Rome and Augustus at Lepcis Magna.

It is not profitable to dispute how far these or other variations upon the Hellenic pattern were imposed by Etruscan middlemen or by the 'Romans' themselves in any narrow sense of the term. The differences fall well within the range of specific variation attributable to transplantation from one environment to another. They are no more (nor less) mysterious than are the specific and regional variations amongst the medieval Gothic cathedrals of western Europe. Suffice it to observe the differences with a proper thankfulness for diversity.

The largest of the early temples of Rome was that which was dedicated in 509 BC to the Capitoline Jupiter in the first days of the Republic. It was often burned and refashioned, but it was apparently about 185 ft wide and 200 ft long, and had a porch of eighteen columns arranged in three rows of six, with a line of columns along each side meeting lateral extensions of the back wall, which was plain. In these flanking colonnades it differed from the Vitruvian type of Tuscan temple, which lacked them. Otherwise it generally resembled the Vitruvian scheme. A sculptor from the Etruscan city of Veii made terracotta sculptures for its adornment.

Here we have then a Graeco-Etruscan temple planted suddenly in an immature Rome but already with a hint of that emphasis of the thickly pillared entrance-façade which was to become a characteristic Roman feature.

As a typical example of a later age we may take the well-known temple, the Maison Carrée, built at Nîmes in Provence in 16 BC. Externally it is complete save that, in some ancient period, the surviving podium stood on a platform surrounded by porticos. Its deep porch has six columns across the front, three open bays on each side, and attached columns extend round the sides and back of the shrine; in other words, it is hexastyle pseudo-peripteral. It is of the Corinthian order, well carved in the local limestone, with an admirable frieze of tendril pattern. The whole building is unimpeachable, if also unexciting.

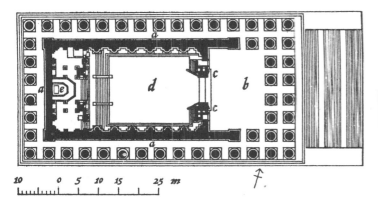

The Temple of Bacchus at Balbek is unusual among Roman temples in being surrounded by a colonnade (a). The approach to the interior, or cella (d) is through a wide porch (b), flanked by staircase-towers (c). At the extreme western end stood the cult-image (e) within a baldachin on a platform.

One other temple of the Graeco-Roman tradition, but very different in detail and implication, may be cited: the so-called 'Temple of Bacchus' at Baalbek in the Lebanon. It is in a sufficiently complete state of preservation to enable the visitor to reconstruct it visually, and a very singular building it is. The famous group to which it belongs was completed in the time of Caracalla (AD 211–217), and the temple itself is probably of the second half of the 2nd century. It stands on a high podium; its peripteral colonnade is of unfluted Corinthian columns and it has a deep porch, six fluted columns in width. The surrounding portico is roofed with a convex ceiling of monolithic blocks richly carved with framed busts of Mars, Ganymede, Ceres, Vulcan, a city-goddess and others. But it is the interior of the building that mostly matters, in contrast with the more austere or extrovert Greek tradition. The entrance, surrounded by almost riotously ornate frames, is flanked by two towers which carry stairs up to the roof level. Within, the *cella* is flanked by Corinthian pilasters set on a dado and enlarged by fluted Corinthian half-columns on pedestals. Between the pilasters are two tiers of niches, the lower round-headed, the upper with triangular pediments; the higher niches formerly contained statuary. At the inner (western) end, a monumental stair approached an elaborate baldachin which contained the cult statue. The whole concept was astonishingly ornate, and, as the most nearly complete surviving example of its kind, the building holds a unique place in the history of architecture.

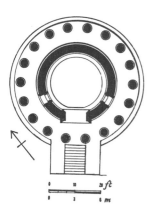

The Temple of Vesta (so-called) at Tivoli, early 1st century BC. The shrine is approached by a flight of steps, and was surrounded by Corinthian columns. Circular temples have a remote ancestry, doubtless going back to primitive huts of prehistoric times.

Two circular temples may here be mentioned as a preface to a third of singular importance. The so-called 'Temple of Vesta' at Tivoli, near Rome, is a good example of Corinthian of the early 1st century BC. The column-capitals are an individual variety which was copied by Sir John Soane at the end of the 18th century for the façade of the Bank of England. The temple was of tufa, travertine and concrete; but another familiar circular temple, now the church of S. Maria del Sole, beside the Tiber in Rome,

is of marble save for the tufa podium which, unlike the Tivoli podium, is completely surrounded by steps in the Greek manner. The entablature has gone and the dating is uncertain.

But of all circular Roman temples the outstanding survivor is of course the Pantheon at Rome; a building indeed which ranks with the Parthenon and St Sophia as one of the landmarks in architectural history. Details of its structure and discussion of the chronology of its parts lie outside this context. It must suffice to record that, approximately as we see it now, the building is the work of Hadrian, about AD 126. It was dedicated to the seven planetary deities and was in effect an architectural simulacrum of the all-containing cosmos.

Externally, even allowing for the removal of stucco veneer, it is a building of no special account. The disharmony of portico and rotunda is indeed thoroughly uncomfortable. It is as an interior that the Pantheon is unsurpassed, and it was as an interior that the structure was conceived. Lightened by its wall-recesses, strong in the powerful lines of its superbly coffered dome, and united with the dome of heaven itself by the bold opening in its summit, this interior is one of man's rare masterpieces. And it is the first of its kind: a point to be re-emphasized on a later page.

The round Temple 'of Venus' at Baalbek, showing the bold use of conventional classical elements in the late Roman period—the broken pediment on unfluted Corinthian columns, the niches, reflected as 'bites' out of the entablature, and the circular cella with domed roof.

An Architectural Discipline: the Baths

Technically, the Pantheon owes its design and quality to the use of concrete and brickwork for the structure of its immense dome. Vaults of masonry, on a small scale, had been constructed here and there by the Greeks or their neighbours as early as the 6th century BC (Pyla in Cyprus), and were used shyly for basements and tombs by the Pergamenes. But the dome was a Roman contrivance, and owes its substantive introduction into architectural design to the development of concrete, or stiffly mortared rubble, in the 2nd century BC. The earliest certain surviving example is in the *frigidarium* of the Stabian Baths at Pompeii, where the conical dome had a circular opening that anticipated the central opening of the Pantheon some two-and-a-half centuries later.

It is an axiom of architectural history that the innumerable public baths of the Roman Empire made an outstanding contribution to the general development of plan and structure. Their elements of course recur in other settings; in basilicae, for example, and other public buildings, and in the palaces of which surviving witness is less ample. But even a small town might well have two or more communal baths on an appreciable and even lavish scale, and the implied assemblage of rooms of varying size and shape within the discipline of a systematized function provided a recurring creative exercise of far-reaching consequence. At first the resultant plan tended to lack coherence; the Stabian Baths themselves illustrate this immaturity, and so do the Forum

Baths of Pompeii early in the 1st century BC, though already with a hint of greater symmetry. It would appear that sometime in the 1st century AD—evidence is incomplete—the general lines of the vast symmetrical establishments of the middle and later Empire were worked out in principle, and it may be that Apollodorus of Damascus, who was employed by Trajan, had a final hand in this. Certainly by the time of Hadrian the pattern was set, and can still be seen in admirable shape in his great baths at Lepcis Magna (AD 126–7).

This building may be taken as a sample of the manner in which a succession of interiors of wide diversity was reconciled in an over-all harmony by means of vaulted and colonnaded vistas and a wealth of connecting or diverting ornament. The outermost compartment was an open-air swimming-bath surrounded on three sides by Corinthian porticos and flanked by pairs of colonnaded halls. Beyond these on each side was a latrine in which the occupants sat on marble seats on three sides, regarded by a statue in a niche on the fourth. From the swimming-bath four doors opened on to a corridor surrounding the cold room or *frigidarium*, a splendid hall paved and panelled with marble and roofed by three concrete cross-vaults springing from eight Corinthian columns. At each end of the hall arched doorways opened on to cold plunge-baths. A central door at the back connected the hall with the warm room or *tepidarium*, with a large central bath and two smaller lateral baths of later date. Beyond again was the hot room or *caldarium*, a large barrel-vaulted room with arched windows which were presumably glazed. On each flank was a pair of superheated rooms which later became the *laconica* or sweating-baths. Other apartments in the periphery of the plan are of uncertain purpose, but the greater baths, such as these, not infrequently included a library and exercise-rooms.

The Heart of the City

The market-place—Greek *agora* and Roman *forum*—was the centre of the business and social life of the classical town, save in so far as in Roman times the public baths usurped elements of social interchange. An essential feature of the agora was the *stoa* or colonnaded shelter where conversation might continue undeterred by rain or shine. At Athens and elsewhere these *stoae* tended to frame the *agora*; and from this principle developed the normal Roman forum, laid out with a portico on three sides and, on the fourth, a *basilica* or town-hall, which was essentially a roofed extension of the forum.

Colonnaded halls were not unknown to the Greeks, but the regular provision of an urban centre of this kind was essentially a Roman innovation. The earliest known examples go back to the formative 2nd century BC, when, as we have seen, the use of concrete and the dome, with the parallel development of ambitious vaulting, marked the beginning of a new era in architectural thinking. In 184 BC the elder Cato added the Basilica Porcia to the Roman Forum, and a few years later the Basilica Aemilia was built nearby. The latter was an oblong hall with an internal four-sided colonnade which probably carried a clerestory. One of the longer sides of the building opened through a colonnade upon the forum. A similar basilica on a small scale, dating from the middle of the 2nd century, has been excavated at Cosa in southern Etruria; in the back wall, opposite the entrance, was a projecting tribunal for the presiding magistrate. The whole scheme resembles that of the basilica built by Vitruvius at Fano about 27 BC and described by him (V. I. 6).

Differing from this 'Vitruvian' model was another series, represented by the basilica at Pompeii, built prior to 78 BC. Here the oblong hall with its internal ambulatory is entered through one of the short sides, and the tribunal is demarcated within the far end; so that the functional axis is that of the length, not the breadth, of the hall. The early basilica at Lepcis Magna (before AD 53), is of a similar kind, and it is clear that, whatever their mutual relationship, the two types—the 'Vitruvian' and the 'Pompeian'—were in vogue side by side at the end of the Republic and the beginning of the Empire.

To these archetypes may be added a number of variations, ranging from the great basilicae of Rome, which might have four internal colonnades and great terminal apses, to relatively modest

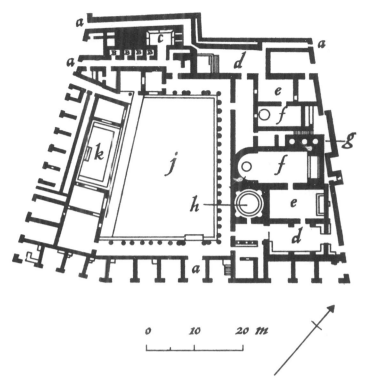

The Stabian Baths at Pompeii were begun at an early period and the plan lacked overall coherence. The oldest corner is the north-west, where there are two entrances (a), narrow passages, small private baths (b), and a latrine (c). Next came the east side, divided into men's (to the south) and women's baths (to the north), each with its changing room (d), tepidarium (e) and caldarium (f)—the last with a fountain. The heating plant (g) was between the two. The men's bath also included a domed frigidarium (h) with a circular opening, foreshadowing the Pantheon. The west side, across the spacious palaestra (j), was the last to be built and included a swimming-pool (k). The west and south sides had shops opening on to the street.

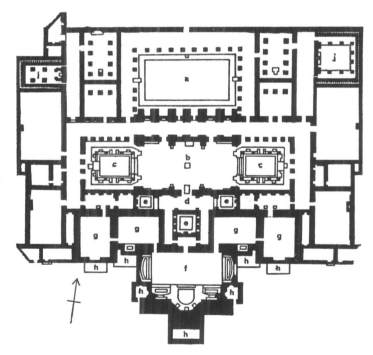

The baths built by Hadrian at Lepcis Magna in AD 126–7 show a more developed phase. The plan is now almost perfectly symmetrical. Entering from the north, the visitor came first to the big open-air swimming-bath (a), surrounded on three sides by a colonnade. Beyond this was the frigidarium (b), a splendid paved and vaulted hall with plunge-baths (c) at each end. Beyond this again was the tepidarium (d) containing a large central bath and three smaller ones (e). And finally the hot-room, the caldarium (f), from which smaller super-heated rooms (g) opened. The whole building was heated by numerous furnaces (h), and included several other spacious rooms (libraries or gymnasia) and two latrines (j).

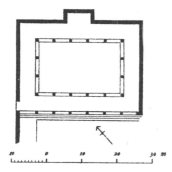

Roman basilicas (town-halls, law-courts) were normally oblong halls with an internal colonnade round all four sides. The tribunal, or seat of the magistrate, was placed opposite the entrance. In one type (the 'Vitruvian', as at Cosa, above), these occupied the two long sides; in the other (e.g. Pompeii, below), the shorter. It was this second type which later influenced the design of Christian churches.

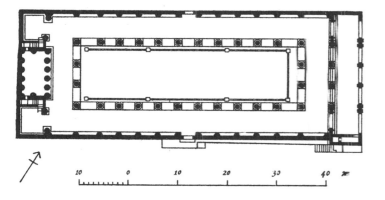

halls with no internal colonnade at all, as at Doclea in Dalmatia or Timgad in Africa (both 2nd century AD).

In the western provinces, and not least in Britain, there was a tendency under the Empire to adopt a simple, closely co-ordinated plan, consisting of a square or squarish forum bounded on three sides by porticos and on the fourth by a basilica, its long axis parallel with its side of the forum. The basilica itself would normally have a range of offices at the back, a tribunal (sometimes apsed) at each end, and entrances in the long side facing the forum. This combination of hall and courtyard was likewise the conventional plan of the headquarters of a Roman fortress, and the respective share of military and civil influences in the evolution of the design is a part of an inconclusive argument which, indeed, goes back in principle to classical times. It is likely enough that the military headquarters owed its plan to a regimentation of civilian practice; but that in the remoter provinces, where military engineers must have had a considerable hand in laying out the first civil buildings, it was the military version which provided the standard model.

Of all surviving, or partially surviving, basilicae, the most imposing is the fragment of the great hall, the Basilica Nova, begun by Maxentius and finished after AD 313 by Constantine in the Roman Forum. The three massive cross-vaults of its nave rose to a height of 114 ft above the floor, and their lateral thrust was eased by partitions carried across a broad aisle on each side. The western end was strengthened by an apse, the eastern by a narrow entrance-lobby pierced by five doorways. The original splendour of the structure, when its walls and floor were still veneered with marble and glowed with kaleidoscopic colour in the varying light, must have been memorable indeed.

For Spectacle, Slaughter and Sport

Briefly, it may be said that the Greek theatre was essentially a structure of the open air, whilst the Roman theatre, whether it had or had not a permanent roof, conformed with the Roman trend towards enclosed interiors. Its *scaenae frons*, the elaborately adorned back-wall of the stage, rose to the full height of the semi-circular auditorium, and was joined to it by lateral returns, so that audience and actors were entirely withdrawn from the world

without. If the theatre was a small one, as were many of the so-called *odea* or concert-halls, it would normally be completed by a timber roof. A large theatre could, when necessary, be sheltered by awnings, and in some cases at least there was a permanent pent-roof above the stage.

The orchestra, which in the earlier Greek theatres was circular with a central altar and was used by a part of the cast during the performance, was in Roman theatres reduced to a semicircle, embodied in the auditorium and reserved for movable or semi-permanent 'stalls'. The change from Greek to Roman usage reflects sharp changes in function, with religious ceremony and epic drama on the grand scale at the one end and intimate burlesque at the other. In this sense, although based upon Greek prototypes, the Roman theatre was a Roman creation. For a long time it was restricted structurally to temporary wooden booths and staging; Vitruvius (v. 5. 7) speaks of 'many theatres set up at Rome every year'. Not until 55 BC was a stone theatre built in the capital—by Pompey, who had been impressed by the Greek theatre at Mytilene. The outstanding feature of the major imperial theatres was the back-scene, the *scaenae frons*, which, as at Aspendus in Pamphylia or Sabratha in Tripolitania or Orange in Provence, might be sumptuously enriched by tiers of colonnaded niches with statuary: an elegant background for what must often enough have been a not particularly edifying entertainment.

Less edifying still, however, were the spectacles offered to the Roman public in the amphitheatres or oval (rarely circular) enclosures which, under the Empire, were a normal emblem of Romanization outside the more Hellenized eastern provinces where, to the credit of the humane Greek tradition, they never took firm root. The various forms of brutality for which they were the setting were originally practised in the open market-place (Vitruvius v. 1. 1), and the earliest structural amphitheatre is that at Pompeii, built after 80 BC. The first stone amphitheatre at Rome was not erected until nearly half a century later; but perhaps the greatest work of architectural engineering left to us by Roman antiquity is Rome's Colosseum, built by the Flavian emperors within the last quarter of the 1st century AD on the site of the lake of Nero's Golden House, and designed to hold 45,000 spectators.

Of the circuses, used for chariot-racing, little need here be said. Their general shape in Roman times reflected that of their Greek predecessors. Built on large tracts of eligible flat ground, few of them have survived save as the most shadowy of ghosts amidst modern streets. One of the best of them can be seen today at Perge, near the southern coast of Turkey, where the sloping stone subvaults built probably in the 2nd century AD to carry the seating have survived in a remote countryside, and show the normal plan of the elongated racecourse, rounded at one end and open or squared at the other. Down the centre formerly stood the dividing *spina*, marked by monuments such as still indicate the axis of the famous circus of Constantinople (Istanbul) or, in the form of a pyramid, the circus which underlies a residential suburb of Vienne in Provence.

Town and Country Houses

Roman town-houses represent diverse traditions and adaptations of which only a brief sketch can be attempted here. The basic scheme of the average classical dwelling, as of far earlier houses in the orient, was that of an unroofed courtyard surrounded by rooms, of which one might be of dominant size. In the present restricted context, Roman variations on this theme, and one or two other types, will be illustrated by examples from key-sites.

First, Pompeii. The oldest houses here, going back to about 300 BC, consisted of rooms grouped with an un-Greek symmetry round a court or *atrium*, which usually contained a tank for rain-water. Beyond the *atrium* was the principal room, the *tablinum*, open-fronted or at most screened by a curtain; and beside this, right and left, were two *alae* or recesses from which access could be obtained to the back rooms without traversing the *tablinum*. Between the *alae* and the front of the house were ranges of private rooms. Except above the *tablinum*, there was an upper storey of limited height, sometimes with balconies, and at the back there might be a small garden. Where, as in the wealthier houses, this

garden was a sizeable one, it might in the 2nd century BC or later receive a peristyle in the Greek mode, commonly with rooms around it.

Outside Italy, the *atrium* house scarcely existed. On Delos, where a considerable community of Roman traders flourished in the trade-boom which followed the capture of Corinth in 146 BC and even survived awhile the destruction of Delos itself by the fleet of Mithradates in 88 BC, the houses of the Roman quarter are of Greek types. Amongst them are good examples of the pattern known to Vitruvius as the 'Rhodian': in which the inner or northern range of a colonnaded courtyard was higher than the flanking porticos, and the roofs of the latter rested on brackets projecting from its lateral columns. This contrivance emphasized the importance of the innermost, southerly-facing room, which thus in effect equated with the *tablinum* of the Pompeian scheme.

In the great cities the end of the Republic marked for a time the end of the widespread construction of spacious private houses of the Pompeian kind. In Rome and Ostia the busy days of the early Empire meant concentrated populations and rising ground-rents, and, as in the comparable circumstances of far more modern times, buildings tended to grow vertically rather than laterally. At Rome indeed high tenements were no novelty. They had been known as early as the 3rd century BC, and Vitruvius (II. 8. 17), remarking upon the use of brick and concrete in their construction, considered that they were not only a necessity in the face of a growing population but were not unworthy of the capital. Others, including Strabo, held an opposite view. Certainly, dangers from fire and collapse, culminating in the great fire of Nero's principate, had to be countered by building-restrictions; Augustus limited the height to 70 ft, Trajan to 60 ft. Even so, blocks of five or six storeys came easily within the law.

It is at Ostia that the most ample material evidence of these tenement-buildings survives. Externally their aspect was for the most part severely functional. Normally they were built of unfaced brick which might, however, be enriched on the arches or lintels of doorways and windows by vermilion paint, and might

be further varied by a plain string-course and by pillars or pilasters at the main entry. Balconies, carried on projecting timbers or stone corbels, more rarely on brick corbel-vaulting, were also a feature of some of the blocks; though the curious observation has been made that these balconies did not, at least in some instances, conform with floor-levels and were actually non-functional—a whimsy hard to parallel until the days of Edwardian baroque in England. The flats or apartments were reached from courtyards or from the street by stairs often set between ground-floor shops. A recurrent apartment-plan comprises five or six rooms served by a spacious corridor overlooking the street and terminating in a room larger than the rest. Walls and ceilings in the better establishments were elaborately painted, and a fair measure of comfort is implied, though there is an absence of structural heating and, usually, of private sanitation.

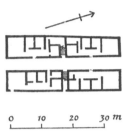

Tenement-buildings at Ostia followed a standard plan, varied according to circumstances. Each flat normally consisted of four or five rooms, the smaller ones opening off a wide corridor and a large one at the end taking the whole width of the apartment. There would be two or more flats per storey. The ground-floor was often used for shops. In this plan, from a small housing estate on the west of the town, flats (not shops) occupy the ground-floor and stairs between each pair lead to other flats above.

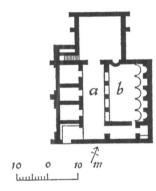

In the later Empire more luxurious houses were being built at Ostia. The house of Amor and Psyche, one of the best to have survived, contained a wide central corridor (a) opening through an arcade to a small garden (b) backed by a nymphaeum—five niches in the outer wall fronted by brick arches.

When the population-problem began to ease at Ostia under the later Empire, houses of an individual and attractive kind reappeared in the more peripheral quarters. Unlike the tenements with their substantial windows, these late houses tend to look inwards and, again unlike the tenements, to have structural heating with wall-flues. They seem normally to have been of a single main storey with minor rooms above. One of the best of those which have survived is the House of Amor and Psyche in the western part of the town. Its principal feature is a wide central corridor opening on one side through a Corinthian arcade on to a small garden backed by a *nymphaeum*, which consists of five alternately round and rectangular niches fronted by brick arches springing from smaller Corinthian columns. On the other side of the corridor are small rooms, a staircase and a lavatory; and at the end is a large room with a niche in one wall. The whole effect is one of graciousness, charm and comfort with a hint of the almost 18th-century elegance that sometimes marked the later days of the Empire.

The House of Pansa, one of the most magnificent houses at Pompeii. The main entrance was in the south (left on the plan) and the rooms were grouped round two courtyards (atrium and peristyle), the latter with a sunken pool in the centre. The shaded areas on the plan show rooms which, though under the same roof, were not parts of the house but formed separate, self-contained premises, mostly shops. The house itself was entirely inward-looking; at the back (the north side) was a large garden. House, garden and shops together occupied the whole insula.

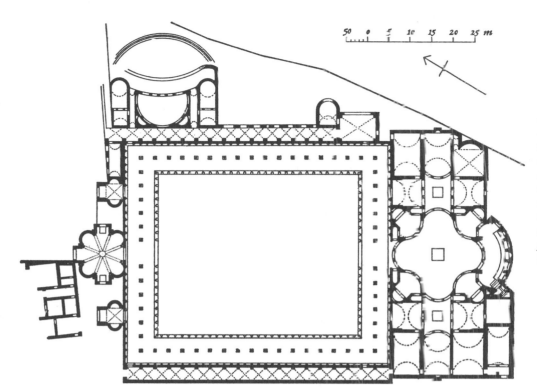

Hadrian's villa at Tivoli, just outside Rome, is the most elaborate of the imperial retreats. The largest feature—an immense colonnaded courtyard—is known as the Piazza d'Oro. On the left is an eight-sided apartment with alternate apsidal and rectangular bays once covered by an octagonal dome. On the right is a large hall, also originally with a dome carried on eight piers. Around the central space colonnades wave in and out between the piers.

From the constricted environs of the city we turn to the countryside. There, ranging from crofts to immense palaces, were the houses of the small farmers, the agents, and the rich owners for whom the country was part occupation and part *divertissement*, a quiet setting for good food and good talk. As far away as Glamorgan, on the ultimate shores of Ocean, a country-house spread, with its outbuildings, across three-quarters of an acre of coastal plain amidst fields and, no doubt, a great spread of golden gorse. Gaul was particularly rich in large country-houses, some of them almost small towns. The famous establishment at Chiragan, beside the Garonne between Toulouse and Dax, covered 40 acres; it comprised a complex residence and three regimented lines of cottages, barns and other outliers, all framed by a long boundary wall. Again, at Anthée, near Namur in Belgium, a country-house with lines of cottages occupied 30 acres. In a number of instances, periods of insecurity, such as the Frankish invasions of 275–6 or the Vandal inroad of 408, induced the owners of these mansions to fortify them in substantial fashion. For example, Sidonius Apollinaris (*Carm.* XXII, 117) tells of a land-owner who built his house so that 'neither engine of war nor opposing *agger* nor heavy catapult-shot nor massed attacks nor scaling ladders could shake the walls'; and the well-known remains of a fortified mansion can still be seen at Thésée, between Tours and Chabris.

Minor country buildings were subject to many variations, such as the inclusion of a cellar, or the elaboration of one or both wings into a tower, but they bear the stamp of Romanization, even to the frequent provision of tessellated or mosaic floors. At the same time, to complete the picture we must visualize here and there upon the landscape a scatter of primitive round huts of the prehistoric kind, where, as in much later centuries, herdsmen and charcoal-burners continued to live traditionally on the fringe of the forests and the downs.

The Imperial Retreat

Certain of the larger Gaulish mansions might be described as palatial in size and quality, and a large villa of the 4th century at Welschbillig near Trier was in all likelihood built actually as an imperial country-residence. In the centre of Sicily the villa probably of Maximian near Piazza Armerina, with its diverting mosaics, again sets the imperial standard of elegant luxury. But the most extravagant of all Roman country-palaces was Hadrian's great villa which stretched for a mile across the slopes below Tivoli, 15 miles from Rome. Stripped and shattered though it be, it remains the most fantastic material creation of the Roman

genius: of a particular Roman genius, which had travelled far and experienced much, and had learned to temper affairs with sentiment, sentiment with reason. With its 'Poikile', its 'Prytaneum', its 'Academy', its 'Canopus', its miniature 'Vale of Tempe', it fed the nostalgia of the aging emperor; with its 'Styx' and its 'Elysian Fields', it lent an indulgent melancholy to the prospect of old age. It cannot here be described in any detail, but at every turn it offers interest and intelligence in plan or contrivance. For example, at the ends of an immense colonnaded courtyard known as the Piazza d'Oro are apartments of remarkable plan. One is eight-sided with alternate apsidal and rectangular bays, covered by a dome which, like the Pantheon, has a central opening. Between each bay are piers connected by arches; above each of these is a segment of concrete vaulting which merges into the central dome.

At the other end of the courtyard is a larger hall of equally unusual shape. Eight main piers support arches which must have carried a central dome. Between the pairs of piers are recesses with alternately concave and convex fronts on plan, each front supported by columns which thus waved in and out around the central space. Adjacent rooms assist this decorative alternation of supports to distribute the thrust of the dome.

Another charming feature, adjacent to the 'Poikile', is a small island carrying a building approached by little bridges across a surrounding canal within a marble Ionic peristyle: a cool and private retreat which may have been one of the Emperor's studies. The whole palace was enriched with statuary, much of it no doubt imported from Greek lands; and the combination of new and ingenious craftsmanship with traditional features epitomized the outlook of Hadrian and his epoch.

Of later palaces the most remarkable is that which still stands in tolerable preservation at Split or Spalato, on the coast of Yugoslavia and on the outskirts of the ancient town of Salona. It was built by Diocletian at the beginning of the 4th century and is a material symbol of the later Empire; combining with the apparatus of a remote and splendid pageantry the guarded withdrawal from an increasingly alien and uncertain world. It is framed by massive fortifications on a rectangular plan, 575 by 460 ft, with walls 60 ft high and 7 ft thick, and with square towers save at the landward gates, where they are octagonal. The enclosure was quartered by broad colonnaded streets, interrupted behind the sea-wall by the Emperor's apartments and by a great hall with a domed vestibule on the line of the north-south street. Between the vestibule and the central crossing the street was flanked by tall Corinthian colonnades with arches springing from

the capitals. To the east at this point is the Emperor's Mausoleum, standing on an 11 ft podium and externally octagonal within a peristyle of Corinthian columns on isolated pedestals. The massive walls are reduced internally by deep niches alternately round and rectangular; between the niches Corinthian columns on a circular plan carry the projections of an engaged entablature and are surmounted by smaller columns, alternately Corinthian and Composite. The dome, of elaborate brickwork, is round internally and an octagonal pyramid externally. Opposite the Mausoleum is a tetrastyle prostyle Corinthian temple, standing on a vaulted podium and roofed with a coffered barrel vault of stone.

On the southern or seaward face of the enclosure a great gallery extended continuously between the corner towers, with a loggia at each end and in the centre. The gallery had forty-two arched windows; between them plain corbels carried engaged Corinthian columns supporting an entablature normally horizontal but arched at two points. The use of corbelled columns appears here for the first time in the history of architecture. Features such as this, or the adoption on a monumental scale of arches springing direct from capitals—a device in fact shown as early as the 1st century BC in wall-paintings of the Villa dei Misteri at Pompeii and represented structurally both at Pompeii (Casa della Fortuna) and at Herculaneum (the Shore Baths) during the following century but not fully exploited until much later—place the Spalato Palace on the threshold of a new phase in architectural thinking. Roman is sensibly merging already into Romanesque.

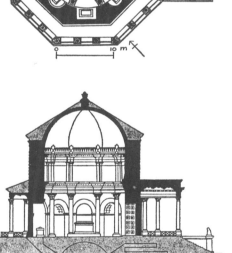

Plan and section of the Mausoleum of the Emperor Diocletian, in the midst of his huge palace at Spalato. The tomb-chamber itself, octagonal outside, circular within, had two tiers of columns and was surrounded by an octagonal peristyle.

THE ART OF AN EPOCH
Some Achievements of the Roman World

Roman art, interpreted as sculpture and painting, must here be treated very selectively. But a glance at certain of its outstanding achievements or experiments in sculpture, wall-painting and mosaic may suffice to hint at something of its contribution to certain evolutionary trends in art-history. The course of evolution, whether physical or intellectual, never did run smooth; the failures of Roman art were admittedly as signal as its successes. But its successes were remarkable and important.

Let it be re-emphasized at the outset that the phrase 'Roman art' is essentially an abstraction and a misnomer. It is a clumsy symbol for the composite effort of minds ranging through a wide variety of environments, from the Atlantic mists to the hard

sunlight of Asia, and through a changing complex of ideas, from the comfortable fruition of Hellenism to the uneasy aspiration of the Middle Ages. It is really valid only in so far as it represents an epoch and an encompassing economy which assured to that epoch the needed means and opportunity. It has nothing like the simple connotation of the term 'Greek art', which is integrated alike by a narrower geography, cultural uniformity, and the more restricted aesthetic concepts proper to an earlier phase.

I propose to select for illustration three of the principal achievements of Roman art in this qualified sense: the development of portraiture, the development of narrative, and the development of landscape.

The Roman Portrait: a Revealing Image

'One cannot imagine any Greek statue carrying on an intelligent conversation.' This traditional *mot* contains an important truth: the Hellenic ideal was the perfect *shape*, with little or no actively intellectual or emotional content. A Medusa or a centaur might wear a grimace as a sort of theatrical property; just as an actor in a Sophoclean drama might wear an unresponsive tragic mask. Equally unresponsive are the handsome young men of the Parthenon frieze; they do not share a mental reaction between them, even when struggling with a refractory bull. They have not forgotten that child-art, to which, for all their technical sophistication, they are still very near, is concerned with generalized outline, not with individual thought.

So too in Hellenic portraiture. The Pericles of Cresilas, as he comes to us, is intellectually a barber's dummy. He is not the individual creative intellect that gave us 5th-century Athens. The first specific hint of Greek portraiture in any modern sense is, if we may believe a remark doubtfully ascribed to Lucian, the portrait by the 4th-century sculptor Demetrius of the Corinthian general Pellichus, who was represented as 'high-bellied, bald, his clothes half off him, his veins prominent'. Demetrius, adds the so-called Lucian, was a 'maker of men' rather than 'of statues'. If so, he marked a new phase in the evolution of aesthetics.

But he was not alone. The 4th century BC did in fact coincide with a new appreciation of the individual. In 351 some of the foremost Greek sculptors of the day set to work upon the great monument to Mausolus, ruler of Caria on the coast of Asia Minor—a monument destined to become one of the 'Seven Wonders of the World'. Amongst surviving vestiges is the fine large statue probably of Mausolus himself, showing his calm, strong, majestic presence almost with a Hadrianic verisimilitude. Idealized though the portrait be, we are already moving away from the brain-washed Pericles of Cresilas in the direction of robust factual statement. The trend received a wider sanction a few years later when Lysippus and his colleagues gave universal currency to the aspect of Alexander the Great. His vital features, set upon an abrupt neck beneath a shock of stormy hair, are convincingly those of the destroyer of the nondescript egalitarianism of the Greek city-state and the real architect of the personal authoritarianism of the Roman world-state. Not for nothing was he destined to a firm place amongst the Personalities of history who became the Nine Worthies of the Middle Ages.

As in so much else, the Hellenistic age was to find its logical sequel aesthetically in the later Republic and the Empire of Rome. It created the climate in which Rome, in the widest sense, was to cultivate the seeds of new ideas. Those seeds were gathered from many sources; of course from Greece itself and from the East, and, in uncertain measure, from Etruria which had in turn borrowed and transmuted Greek skills and notions. But once again let there be no attempt to define too closely the origins of the 'Roman' complex. A composition is liable to be something more than the aggregation of its parts: and in any event time and evolutionary change have to be added as controlling if less tangible factors.

So when in Roman portraiture, which is amongst the greatest portraiture in the history of art, some specifically Etruscan inspiration is adduced, as it not infrequently is, we may well be wary. No doubt the oft-quoted Italic custom of storing death-masks was an appreciable contribution to the cult of the portrait. 'In the halls of our ancestors, wax models of faces were displayed to

furnish likenesses in funeral processions; so that at a funeral the entire clan was present' (Pliny, *N. H.* xxxv, 2). The custom epitomizes the realistic interest of the Roman in the personality as distinct from the type.

But all this might well have lacked appreciable influence upon the history of art, had it not been for the fact that the mind of the classical world from the latter half of the 4th century BC onwards was increasingly ripe for a new individualism, whether in politics, in religion, or in aesthetics. After Aristotle philosophy too 'became more and more concentrated on the individual rather than the community'. It was 'mainly concerned with finding the right way of life for individual men' (A. H. Armstrong). In terms of aesthetic form, the generalized and idealized outline was beginning to dissolve or evolve quite logically into the more wayward shapes imposed by individual thought and emotion and experience. By the end of the 3rd century BC the Roman portrait had arrived, and thereafter for six centuries there accumulated an astonishing gallery of revealing images of men and women of all degrees, from emperor to tradesman. The examples illustrated may recall their range and vitality.

To the Glory of Rome: the Narrative Reliefs

Greek art in celebrating historical events had tended to think in terms of symbolism and analogy. Battles of Athenians against Persians, of Pergamenes against Galatians, had merged in battles of Athenians against Amazons and gods against giants, culminating in the great gigantomachy on the altar of Pergamum, about 180 BC. The Romans, though not averse from the occasional and subordinate use of allegory, were essentially factual, or at least secular, in the depiction of historical events. They were interested in the prowess of the supreme Roman, the Emperor, who represented the grandeur that was Rome but was also intensely individual. Rome indeed took upon herself the image of the Emperor. Thus Roman narrative sculpture (the equivalent painting has almost entirely vanished) was a particular extension of the trends more widely exhibited in Roman portraiture.

The outstanding example is the famous carved band which winds spirally for 215 yards up the shaft of Trajan's Column in the Forum and was set up in AD 113 to commemorate and illustrate his Dacian campaigns. It marks the moment when the Empire reached its vastest extent and, within the limits of certain conventions, is the masterpiece of Roman historical art. Its conventions are not in fact exacting, and it must be remembered also that anciently the great relief was tricked out with colour and could be seen at easier range from the roofs of two adjacent libraries. The principle is that of a strip-cartoon, in a fashion to which the term 'continuous style' has been applied; it is that of an undivided panorama in which the successive incidents run continuously but are punctuated by the recurrent appearance of the Emperor at focal points. The technique may have been suggested or encouraged by the *rotulus* or scroll-book in which such histories may often enough have been recorded. In sculpture the germ of the convention, as of so much else in Roman art, is found already in the Hellenistic period. On the Pergamene altar referred to above (c. 180 BC) a minor frieze relates the story of Telephus, the legendary founder of Pergamum, by repeating the same characters from scene to scene in a single undivided composition. Ultimately the convention may have been derived from the East, where it was already used in Indian Buddhist sculpture at least as early as the 2nd century BC. But it remained for Trajan's sculptors nearly three centuries later to exploit the method on the grand scale.

Their chronicle begins at the foot of the Column with the emergence of the Roman army from a fortified city and the crossing of the Danube in two columns, one of them led by Trajan himself. The busy life of the river is vividly shown, surveyed unostentatiously by Father Danube from a nearby cave. Then the Emperor is seen outside his camp. A few moments later he is holding a council of war. Thereafter, veiled as a Pontifex or High Priest, he is present at the solemn sacrifice which marks the beginning of the campaign. He is on an eminence giving orders and surveying the scene. He harangues his troops whilst fortifications are being built beside the river. He is in the fortress; he

leaves it on reconnaissance; a captured spy is brought before him. And so on, through the long succession of mounting episodes in which the details of the campaign down to the most ordinary routine are shown with an authority and liveliness that incidentally have taught us more about the Roman army in the field than any other single document. Action flows unhesitatingly from episode to episode, and the stone-cutting shows a complete sureness and much sensibility. The strange convention of the 'continuous style' works; so too does that other convention whereby the further figures rise head and shoulders above the nearer ones. Indeed, all perspective is at sixes and sevens, but the curious effect of this is to add to the tumultuous vivacity of the scene. We find ourselves committed to the midst of a crowd of men hurrying about their ordered and urgent business, always with the calm, commanding figure of the Emperor close at hand. It is history scribed around the presence of one great man—the apotheosis of the individual.

Throughout the remainder of the Empire the 'continuous style' reappeared on friezes and columns, and it lingered on into the Middle Ages and later. In the cathedral of Hildesheim in Hanover a bronze pillar made in 1022 bears a spiral relief illustrating the life of Christ in conscious imitation of the Trajanic prototype. And the Vendôme Column in Paris revives the device in the time of Napoleon.

'The Pleasant Fashion': Landscape Art

The cult of the individual implies an awareness of the individual's spacial setting. The high gods can be envisaged in an airy environment of nothingness; not so the butcher, the baker, the candlestick-maker, or even—save in some moment of theatrical apotheosis—the Emperor himself. Landscape, in however subordinate a role, is an inevitable counterpart of the portrait and the historical narrative.

Not that the Romans *invented* landscape, any more than they *invented* portraits. As early as the Old Kingdom the Egyptians had used landscape on a sufficient scale to indicate the lifetime occupations of their dead: cutting a field of corn, fishing in the river, shooting wildfowl in the marshes. But here landscape was little more than a sort of pictograph, designed to convey a message rather than an aesthetic impression, and the difference is a substantial one. The 5th-century Greek artist was not interested in landscape. It was not until the 4th–3rd century BC that landscape began to enter into the consciousness of the poet and the artist in its own right, as an active element in the mental or even sentimental reactions of their characters. Note how closely these developments tally in time: the emergence of portraiture and the new status of the individual; the New Comedy and idyllic poetry; and over all the personality cult of a supreme ruler.

It has been conjectured that Alexandria took a lead in the new appreciation of Nature. This may be so, though the evidence is very incomplete. True, Alexandria was already the cultural centre of the Mediterranean. Hither came Theocritus from the vivid life of his Sicilian hills and pastures to the no less vivid life of the Alexandrian streets. Here in due course all manner of craftsmanship flourished, including the making of great Nilotic mosaics—landscapes indeed—and, in all probability, the stone wall-panels of which a number survive in museums, showing in shallow, pictorial relief secular scenes or assemblages from the minor mythology in a considerable landscape setting.

And with the advent of the Empire this trend continued apace. The *emblemata* or central panels of mosaic, made by skilled artists in specialized workshops and traded for setting in locally-made mosaic floors, might illustrate farm-scenes (as in the Roman villa at Zliten on the coast of Tripolitania) or more rugged landscapes (from the Villa of Hadrian). Behind the *emblemata* lie vanished paintings, represented by fragments here and there (e.g. in the Trier Museum, W. Germany, in the Tripoli Museum, N. Africa, and above all at Naples), and by one masterpiece. This is the great Augustan fresco of the so-called Garden of Livia, from Prima Porta near Rome and now in a special room at the Museo delle Terme. It shows a gentle woodland beyond a low garden-paling, and its subtle gradation of blues and greens, with birds here and there amongst the leaves, has something of

Stiff figures staring straight out at the spectator, typical of western Asiatic art, mingled with Roman naturalism at Palmyra and Dura Europus, and there is a hint of this 'frontality' in Roman work as early as the reliefs on the Arch of Titus. This hybrid style remotely heralds Byzantine art. The bas-relief (right) from Palmyra, and dating from the first half of the 1st century AD, represents three Palmyrene gods, Aglibol, Baalshamin and Malakbel.

the melancholy graciousness of the age of Corot. Bernhard Berenson in his diary wrote well of it: 'How dewy, how penetratingly fresh the grass and trees and flowers, how coruscating the fruit. Pomegranates as Renoir painted them. Bird songs charm one's ears. The distance in the 'Garden of Livia' room remains magically impenetrable, veiled as it was in the gardens of Lithuania where I lived when I first came to awareness.' Such gentle landscapes were indeed the mode of the time; no doubt with excessive precision, Pliny (*N. H.* xxxv. 16) ascribes to a certain Spurius Tadius, in the time of Augustus, the introduction of 'the pleasant fashion of painting walls with pictures of country-houses and porticos, landscape gardens, groves, hills, fish-ponds, canals, rivers, coasts, ... with sketches of people going for a stroll or sailing, and approaching country-houses on asses or in carriages, and fishing or fowling or hunting or gathering the vintage . . . .'

Here and there indeed, amongst the carved and painted landscapes of the end of the Republic and the earlier Empire, we have something strangely akin to the Romantic Movement of the 18th and 19th centuries. There can of course be no complete identity between one age and another; but the conscious cult of Nature, seen somewhat as an elegant curiosity from the window of a comfortable and sophisticated room, is in harmony with the spirit of both 'Augustan' periods.

A Near Miss on Perspective

The strange failure of classical art to work out the mechanism of perspective, even when. as under the early Empire, the time was aesthetically ripe for it, may have helped a little to frustrate the further development of landscape as a mode in its own right. This failure is the more remarkable in that as far back as the 5th century BC the mathematical ingenuity of the Greek mind had nearly solved the problem. Vitruvius (VII, Preface, 11) records how Agatharchus, concerned with the mounting of a tragedy of Aeschylus, had considered the matter, and how his ideas were developed by the philosophers Democritus and Anaxagoras. The words of Vitruvius are difficult but may be rendered as follows: 'It behoved that a certain spot should be determined as the centre in respect of the line of sight and the convergence of lines (*ad aciem oculorum radiorumque extentionem*), and we should follow these lines in accordance with a natural law, so that the appearance of buildings may be rendered conventionally in stage-scenery and that what is figured on simple plane surfaces may seem to be in some cases receding, in others projecting'.

That, however interpreted in detail, appears to have been a near miss. And in practice very much later it seemed again for a moment that the discovery was about to be achieved. In the famous reliefs of the Arch of Titus in the Roman Forum, the procession swinging through the Triumphal Gate, shown in three-quarter view, is nearly right; and the figures at the back are shown effectively in sensitive low relief. But the opposite panel, with the imperial chariot facing to the front and its horses in awkward echelon, fails utterly to comprehend the spacial problem. The failure was final. Thereafter, figures at the back were shamelessly projected upwards in a convention that had long prevailed in the East and now remained unquestioned. And at the beginning of the 3rd century Septimius Severus, albeit carved with the aid of new techniques, is content at Lepcis Magna to ride in a chariot which suffers from a similarly undisguised distortion; thus incidentally, with the flanking figures, conforming frankly with the principle of frontality which, under Eastern pressures, was already anticipating the convention of a subsequent age.

On the Fringes of the Empire

In this slight and highly selective sketch no mention has been made of Roman art in the outer fringes of the Empire. This might be of three kinds: essentially classical work *in partibus*, essentially local work, or an attempted mingling of the two. The last might at its worst represent unmitigated incompetence. It might on the other hand produce something new and intriguing if not necessarily successful; the man's head from Gloucester is an example showing not ineffectively the Celtic artist's instinctive schematization of a Roman subject. In the Near East this kind of commingling was more fructuous. There the rigidity which came naturally to western Asiatic art, associated in sculpture with a predilection for the sharply chiselled lines which produced effective contrasts in the hard light, fused on occasion to good effect, and, as far east as the Indian subcontinent, transmitted an intelligent intermingling of Persian and Roman concepts. And incidentally that frontality which we have already noted in the sculptures of the arches of Titus at Rome and Severus at Lepcis, and was indeed already hinted at in the essential frontality of the Roman temple, was at home in the east. By the 1st century AD at Dura Europus on the Euphrates and at Palmyra it was firmly established by Parthian sculptors or closely under their influence; lines of stiffly identical figures in harshly linear drapery facing uniformly to the front. Here are the roots of much that was to flower in late Roman and Byzantine art from the 4th century onwards.

THE ROMAN CONTRIBUTION

If we add up the selected achievements which have been outlined in this summary survey, what is the order of their magnitude? How far are they coherent and creative? Their main external source lies within the Hellenistic world; the stream flowing first through Etruscan and colonial Greek channels and later, after the 2nd century BC, directly from metropolitan Greece itself. That is, however, only a part of the story. Alexander the Great had already given political expression to that widening of the Greek mind which was in fact becoming generally manifest in the latter part of the 4th century. Aristotle is the father-figure of this age of change, and Alexander was a pupil of Aristotle. Alexander's own greatness, as is the proper habit of successful men of action, was due in the first instance to good timing; his epiphany occurred at precisely the right moment. In a world subconsciously prepared for him, his theatrical success marked, for all to see, the beginning of a new international concept, which led directly on to the Roman Empire and, on the way, fed into the Hellenistic tradition all manner of variant or alien ideas and attitudes. In so far as these new ideas fitted into the orderly evolution of human comprehension, they gradually and logically reshaped that tradition and, amongst much else, eventually gave us 'Roman' art and architecture.

In measuring this metamorphosis, let us first glance for an instant at essential aspects of the Hellenic achievement, as yet untroubled by Hellenistic mutation. It is fair to say that on the Acropolis of Athens in the latter half of the 5th century BC the Greeks said practically all that they had to say about architecture; in the Doric Parthenon, in the Ionic Erechtheum and temple of Athena Nike, in the Doric and Ionic Propylaea, all between 447 and 405 BC. And the first point about all this masterly construction is that it is essentially extrovert. The Parthenon is probably the most intelligent extrovert building that the world has seen. True, it imprisoned in its crepuscular interior the massive gold-and-ivory bulk of Athena, just as it imprisoned the more secular tribute of the faithful; it was a religious safe-deposit. But to the world it showed a plain and sturdy exterior set squarely and possessively on its rock and owing its sturdiness to infinite judgment and finesse. And, secondly, it showed too in its external sculptures an impersonal pageant of heroic but utterly extrovert mimes, impeccably wrought, chiselled (at their best) as marble may never be chiselled again, but with nothing whatever in their heads. Neither the building nor its decoration had any inner life; it was a perfect exterior, a perfect piece of man-made geology, and *because* it was, within its proper limitations, perfect it marks an end. The finality of the Parthenon, architecturally and sculpturally, is its defining quality.

Only at Bassae, far off in the Peloponnese, is there a contemporary building, made perhaps by the chief architect of the Parthenon himself, with a hint of things to come. Here, within, was the first Corinthian capital; here too the sculptured frieze was carried round the *inside* of the shrine, not the outside. For the first time here was a major classical temple with an *interior* as well as an exterior. But the revolutionary innovation was not pursued. Bassae long remained in Greece a desolate and untimely pioneer of the rich order and the rich interior that between them were to dominate the architecture of the Roman Empire: an architecture that was to look more and more inward, to become more and more—in a crude usage of the term—introvert.

For the Roman problem was above all to create and adorn *interiors*, larger and more magnificent interiors to match imperial pride and the growing self-consciousness and importance of the individual. New techniques—particularly, from the 2nd century BC onwards, the increasing exploitation of concrete and brick-work—stimulated and were stimulated by this endeavour. By the

end of the 1st century AD the whole complex process was approaching its early prime. But its oldest surviving triumph is Hadrian's Pantheon. 'The Pantheon is perhaps the first major monument to be composed entirely as an interior' (J. B. Ward-Perkins). This superb interior is one of man's rare masterpieces. They were right to bury Raphael within it.

Now what has happened in the five-and-a-half centuries between the Parthenon and the Pantheon? Bluntly, architecture has been turned outside-in. The mind of man has itself been turned outside-in. Philosophy and religion and politics have combined to alter the shape of the world and man's relationship to it. The world has ceased to be a collection of disjected phenomena, expressed politically by a scatter of city-states; it has become a coherent cosmos, expressed politically by an empire. Its encompassing vault finds a proper symbol in the Pantheon, which stands for Rome just as the objective Parthenon, perched on its Acropolis like a (very distinguished) ornament upon a mantelpiece, stands for Hellas.

'My intention had been that this sanctuary of All Gods should reproduce the likeness of the terrestrial globe and of the stellar sphere, that globe wherein are enclosed the seeds of eternal fire, that hollow sphere containing all.' That is Hadrian speaking of his Pantheon; he is using the words of Madame Yourcenar, but it is the authentic voice. It is the voice of the cosmos, but it is also Hadrian's. And that is of course the nub of the matter. To vary the picture, the Roman Empire was in large measure monolithic; it was a monarchy; its ultimate doctrine was monotheism. But, of no less importance, its monarch was, for good or ill, an intensely human individual, and it discovered its crowning god in a Man.

We are back once more in that milieu wherein the art of portraiture and historical narrative, the cult of particular men and women of all degrees in the circumstances and landscape which environ them, are in context and inevitable. Our journey from the Parthenon to the Pantheon has taken us from the pageant to the personality. Strangely enough, yet quite rationally, the growth and the growing coherence of the civilized world had found a counterpart in the growing importance of the individual. And that—to revert—is why the insides of buildings are now so important. In place of the milling crowd of anonymous spectators outside the temple, the individual devotee now goes inside his *Mithraeum* or his chapel for personal interchange with his deity; and, where old extrovert temples were used for this intimate purpose, the open colonnades were now to be walled up, as in the cathedral church (ex-temple of Athena) at Syracuse, or formerly in the Parthenon itself; to ensure privacy within for the mysteries of the initiate. The temples were literally turned outside-in.

And alongside godliness we have the claims of cleanliness—surely a tolerably individual virtue. It has already been remarked as an axiom of architectural history that the great public bath-buildings which constituted the social rendezvous of the Roman world were a leading stimulus in the development of spacious and ornate interiors. You went to the baths in great numbers to talk to and about your friends and to work off the night-before. But one thing you certainly did not do; you never glanced at the untidy complex of domes and gables outside as you entered. (For a small example, look again at the confusedly functional exterior of the substantially complete 'Hunting Baths' at Lepcis Magna.) It was the *inside* of the building that mattered, with its towering wall-spaces that stretched the minds of architect and sculptor and gave a sense of self-importance and well-being to patron or client. We may appropriately leave our Roman within the great hall of the Baths of Diocletian, which Michelangelo and Vanvitelli have preserved for us by enshrining it with fitting splendour as Santa Maria degli Angeli in Rome.

Select Bibliography

I Introduction

BOLGAR, R. R. *The Classical Heritage and its Beneficiaries* (Cambridge, 1954)

BUSH, J. N. D. *Mythology and the Renaissance Tradition* (Minneapolis, 1932)

GOMBRICH, E. H. *The Story of Art* (London, 1962)

GRANT, M. *Myths of the Greeks and Romans* (London, 1962)

HIGHET, G. A. *The Classical Tradition* (Oxford, 1949)

MANUEL, F. E. *The Eighteenth Century Confronts the Gods* (Cambridge, Mass., 1959)

PANOFSKY, E. *Studies in Iconology* (New York, 1939), *Renaissance and Renascences in Western Art* (Stockholm, 1956)

SCHERER, M. R. *The Legends of Troy in Art and Literature* (London, 1963)

SEZNEC, J. *La Survivance des Dieux Antiques* (English eds; London, 1953, 1961)

WEITZMANN, K. *Greek Mythology in Byzantine Art* (Princeton, 1951)

WITTKOWER, R. *Architectural Principles in the Age of Humanism* (London, 1949)

YOUNG, A. M. *Legend Builders of the West* (London, 1959)

II The Troubled Birth of a New World

ARRIAN *The Life of Alexander the Great*, trs. A. de Sélincourt (London, 1958)

BOWRA, C. M. *The Greek Experience* (London, 1957)

BURN, A. R. *Alexander the Great and the Hellenistic Empire* (London, 1947)
Pericles and Athens (London, 1948)
The Lyric Age of Greece (London, 1960)
Persia and the Greeks (London, 1962)
A History of Greece (London, 1964)

BURY, J. B. *A History of Greece to the Death of Alexander the Great* (3rd ed.; London, 1951)

CARY, M. *A History of the Greek World from 323 to 146 BC.* Volume III of Methuen's *History of the Greek and Roman World* (London, 1932)

GROTE, G. *A History of Greece* (12 vols; London, 1846–56)

HAMMOND, N. G. L. *A History of Greece to 332 BC* (Oxford, 1959)

HERODOTUS *The Histories*, trs. A. de Sélincourt (London, 1954)

PLUTARCH *Lives* in *The Rise and Fall of Athens. Nine Greek Lives*, trs. I. Scott-Kilvert (London, 1960)

ROBINSON, C. E. *History of Greece* (latest ed.; London, 1957)

TARN, W. *Hellenistic Civilisation* revised ed. by Tarn and G. T. Griffith; (London, 1952)

THUCYDIDES *The History of the Peloponnesian War*, trs. R. Warner (London, 1954)

XENOPHON *The Persian Expedition*, trs. R. Warner (London, 1949)

ZIMMERN, A. *The Greek Commonwealth* (Oxford, 1911)

III The Voice of Greece

ARNOTT, P. D. *An Introduction to the Greek Theatre* (London, 1962)

BALDRY, H. C. *Greek Literature for the Modern Reader* (Cambridge, 1951)

BIEBER, M. *The History of the Greek and Roman Theater* (Princeton, 1961)

BOWRA, C. M. and HIGHAM, T. F. (eds) *The Oxford Book of Greek Verse in Translation* (London, 1938)

BOWRA, C. M. *Greek Lyric Poetry* (2nd ed.; London, 1961)
Tradition and Design in the Iliad (London, 1930)

BURY, J. B. *The Ancient Greek Historians* (reprint; New York, 1958)

DOBSON, J. F. *The Greek Orators* (London, 1919)

KIRK, G. S. *The Songs of Homer* (Cambridge, 1962)

KITTO, H. D. F. *Greek Tragedy* (2nd ed.; London, 1950)

KÖRTE, A. *Hellenistic Poetry* (Columbia, 1929)

LUCAS, D. W. *The Greek Tragic Poets* (London, 1950)

MURRAY, G. *Aeschylus, the Creator of Tragedy* (London, 1940) *Aristophanes, a Study* (London, 1933)

ROSE, H. J. *A Handbook of Greek Literature* (4th ed.; London, 1950)

IV The Revolution in the Mind

ALLAN, D. J. *The Philosophy of Aristotle* (London, 1952)

ARMSTRONG, A. H. *An Introduction to Ancient Philosophy* (London, 1947)

BURNET, J. *Early Greek Philosophy* (4th ed.; London, 1930)

CLAGETT, M. *Greek Science in Antiquity* (London, 1957)

COHEN, M. R. and DRABKIN, I. E. *A Source Book in Greek Science* (New York, 1958)

CORNFORD, F. M. *Principium Sapientiae. The origins of Greek philosophical thought.* (Cambridge, 1952)

FARRINGTON, B. *Greek Science: its meaning for us* (2 vols; New York, 1944 and 1949. Single vol. ed. 1953)

FIELD, G. C. *The Philosophy of Plato* (London, 1949)

GUTHRIE, W. K. C. *A History of Greek Philosophy* Vol I: *The Earlier Presocratics and the Pythagoreans* (Cambridge, 1962) *The Greeks and their Gods* (London, 1950)

NEUGEBAUER, O. *The Exact Science in Antiquity* (Copenhagen, 1951)

NILSSON, N. M. P. *Greek Popular Religion* (New York, 1940)
The Minoan-Mycenaean Religion and its Survival in Greek Religion (2nd ed.; Lund, 1950)

ROBIN, L. *Greek Thought* (New York, 1928)

SAMBURSKY, S. *The Physical World of the Greeks* (London, 1956)

WAERDEN, B. L. VAN DER *Science Awakening* (Gröningen, 1954)

V The Sublime Achievement

ARIAS, P. E., HIRMER, M. and SHEFTON, B. B. *A History of Greek Vase Painting* (London, 1962)

BEAZLEY, J. D. *The Development of Attic Black-Figure* (London, 1951)

BERVE, H., GRUBER, G., and HIRMER, M. *Greek Temples, Theatres and Shrines* (London, 1963)

BIEBER, M. *Sculpture of the Hellenistic Age* (New York, 1954)

COOK, R. M. *Greek Painted Pottery* (London, 1960)

DINSMOOR, W. B. *The Architecture of Ancient Greece* (London, 1950)

HIGGINS, R. A. *Greek and Roman Jewellery* (London, 1962)

LAMB, W. *Greek and Roman Bronzes* (London, 1929)

LAWRENCE, A. W. *Greek Architecture* (London, 1957)

LULLIES, R. and HIRMER, M. *Greek Sculpture* (London, 1960)

PAYNE, H. and YOUNG, G. M. *Archaic Sculpture of the Acropolis* (Oxford, 1950)

RICHTER, G. M. A. *Kouroi: Archaic Greek Youths* (London, 1960), *The Sculpture and Sculptors of the Greeks* (Oxford, 1950)

ROBERTSON, C. M. *Greek Painting* (Geneva, 1959)

WYCHERLY, R. E. *How the Greeks built Cities* (London, 1949)

VI The Ancient Life

ANDREADES, A. M. *History of Greek Public Finance* Vol. I (Cambridge, Mass., 1933)

APICIUS *The Roman Cookery Book*, trs. B. FLOWER and E. ROSENBAUM (London, 1958)

CARCOPINO, J. *Daily Life in Ancient Rome* (London, 1941)

COWELL, F. R. *Everyday Life in Ancient Rome* (3rd ed.; London, 1964)

EHRENBERG, V. *The People of Aristophanes* (London, 1943)

FRANK, T. *An Economic History of Rome* (2nd ed.; London, 1933). *An Economic Survey of Ancient Rome* (5 vols; Baltimore, 1933–40)

FRIEDLÄNDER, L. *Roman Life and Manners under the Early Empire* (London, 1913)

JOLOWICZ, H. F. *Historical Introduction to Roman Law* (Cambridge, 1939)

JONES, A. H. M. *Athenian Democracy* (Oxford, 1957)

MARROU, H. I. *History of Education in Antiquity* (London, 1956)

MIREAUX, E. *Daily Life in The Time of Homer* (London, 1959)

PAOLI, U. E. *Rome. Its People Life and Customs* (London, 1964)

RICHTER, G. M. A. *Ancient Furniture* (Oxford, 1926)

ROSTOVTZEFF, M. *The Social and Economic History of the Hellenistic World* (3 vols; Oxford, 1953)

SINCLAIR, T. A. *History of Greek Political Thought* (London, 1961)

ZIMMERN, A. *The Greek Commonwealth: Politics and Economics in Fifth Century Athens* (5th ed.; London, 1931)

VII 'A City of the Scattered Earth'

BLOCH, R. *The Origins of Rome* (London, 1960)

Cambridge Ancient History Vols I–XII (Cambridge, 1923)

GJERSTAD, E. *Early Rome* (3 vols; Lund, 1956–60)

HEYDEN, A. A. M. VAN DER and SCULLARD, H. H. (eds) *Atlas of the Classical World* (London, 1959)

MARSH, F. B. *A History of the Roman World from 146 to 30 BC* (London, 1935)

MATTINGLY, H. *Roman Coins from the earliest times to the fall of the Western Empire* (2nd ed.; London, 1960) *Roman Imperial Civilisation* (London, 1957)

NASH, E. *Pictorial Dictionary of Ancient Rome* (2 vols; London, 1961–62)

PARKER, H. M. D. *A History of the Roman World from AD 138 to 337* (London, 1935) *The Roman Legions* (Oxford, 1928)

ROSE, H. J. *Ancient Roman Religion* (London, 1949)

ROSTOVTZEFF, M. *Social and Economic History of the Roman Empire* (2nd ed., revised by P. M. Fraser, 2 vols; Oxford, 1957)

SALMON, E. T. *A History of the Roman World from 30 BC to AD 138* (London, 1944)

SCULLARD, H. E. *A History of the Roman World from 753 to 146 BC* (London, 1935)

VIII Poetry, Prose and Rhetoric

BEARE, W. *The Roman Stage* (London, 1950)

BOWRA, C. M. *From Virgil to Milton* (London, 1945)

FRAENKEL, E. *Horace* (Oxford, 1957)

GRANT, M. *Roman Literature* (London, 1954)

GRANT, M. (ed.) *Roman Readings* (London, 1958)

HADAS, M. *A History of Latin Literature* (New York, 1952)

KNIGHT, W. F. J. *Roman Vergil* (London, 1944)

LAISTNER, M. L. W. *The Greater Roman Historians* (California, 1947)

LÖFSTEDT, E. *Late Latin* (Oslo, 1959)

SYME, R. *Tacitus* (Oxford, 1958)

THOMPSON, J. A. K. *The Classical Background of English Literature* (London, 1948)

WILKINSON, L. P. *Golden Latin Artistry* (Cambridge, 1963)

IX The Vision Turns Inward

BOËTHIUS, A. *The Golden House of Nero: Some Aspects of Roman Architecture* (Michigan, 1960)

GRANT, M. *The World of Rome* (London, 1960)

GRIMAL, P. *The Civilization of Rome* (London, 1960)

KÄHLER, H. *Rome and her Empire* in 'Art of the World' Series (London, 1963)

MAIURI, A. *Roman Painting* (Geneva, 1953)

ROBERTSON, D. S. *A Handbook of Greek and Roman Architecture* (2nd ed.; Cambridge, 1943)

ROSTOVTZEFF, M. *Dura-Europos and its Art* (Oxford, 1938)

STRONG, D. E. *Roman Imperial Sculpture* (London, 1961)

STRONG, EUGÉNIE *Roman Sculpture* (London, 1907, 1911)

TOYNBEE, J. M. C. *Art in Roman Britain* (London, 1962) *The Hadrianic School* (Cambridge, 1934)

Sources of Illustrations

Ashcroft, Diana: 97
Athens, Acropolis Museums: (Photo Hoegler) 96
    Agora Museum: (Photo American School of Classical Studies) 102 (top left and bottom)
    American School of Classical Studies: 136 (centre)
    Ceramicus Museum: (Photo Deutsches Archäologisches Institut) 31 (bottom left)
    Deutsches Archäologisches Institut: (Photo E. M. Czako) 94 (bottom right)
    National Museum: 76 (top), 91 (top centre), 99 (top); (Photo Roloff Beny) 25; (Photo V. and N. Tombazi) 53 (top left), 99 (bottom); (Photo Max Hirmer) 72 (top), 90 (top), 91 (top left and bottom); (Photo Martin Hürlimann) 100 (bottom left)
Avezzano, Villa Torlonia:

(Photo Mansell-Alinari) 125
Avignon, Musée Calvet: 125, 128 (centre)
Beny, Roloff: 104 (bottom left)
Berlin, Staatliche Museen: 50, 53 (centre) 105, 106 (top left), 135 (centre), 182 (bottom); (Photo Jutta Tietz) 94 (centre)
Boston, Museum of Fine Arts: 102 (top right)
Cefalù, Coll. Mandralisca: (Photo Leonard von Matt) 128 (top left)
Chatillon-sur-Seine, Musée: 95 (top right)
Colchester and Essex Museum: 15
Compagnie Aérienne Français: 202 (top and bottom)
Copenhagen, Carlsberg Glyptotek: 155 (bottom left)
Delphi, Archaeological Museum: (Photo G. Farnell): 72 (bottom)
Farnell, G: 54 (bottom left), 55

(bottom), 205 (bottom left and right)
Ferrara, Museo Archeologico Nazionale: (Photo Max Hirmer) 52 (top); (Photo Manlio Agodi) 73 (bottom)
Florence, Galleria degli Uffizi: (Photo Mansell-Alinari) 129
Foligno, Museo Civico: (Photo Deutsches Archäologisches Institut, Rome) 132 (bottom)
Fototeca Unione: 215
Frankfurt, Städelsches Kunstinstitut: (Photo Kurt Haase) 76 (bottom)
Geneva, Coll. Robert Boehringer: 74 (top left)
Harrissiadis, D. A.: 54 (top)
Hébrard, Ernest: 208–9
Italian Air Ministry: 203 (top)
Johnson, Pamela: 160 (bottom)
Leningrad, Hermitage: 12 (bottom left), 102 (top centre)
London, British Museum: 12 (top left and right), 16 (top), 30

(top), 31 (top left), 49, 50 (bottom), 53 (top left and bottom), 54 (bottom right), 71, 74 (bottom), 78 (top and bottom right), 90 (centre), 92 (bottom left), 94 (top right), 95 (left top and bottom, and bottom right), 102 (right centre), 103 (top and bottom right), 104 (left centre and right), 135 (bottom), 136 (top left and right), 154 (centre), 155 (bottom right), 156–157, 158 (top right), 159 (bottom left), 160 (top), 186 (centre), 210 (bottom left), 214 (bottom left), 216 (bottom)
    Ministry of Works: 158 (top left)
    Royal Greek Embassy: 26
Lucca, Museo Civico: (Photo Mansell-Alinari) 13 (top left)
Madrid, Museo del Prado: 11 (bottom), 14 (left)
Mainz, Altertumsmuseum:

Index

The renowned Gemma Augustea, carved in onyx, shows Augustus on a bench with the goddess Roma, being crowned by the *Orbis Romanus*, symbolizing the civilized world. Above is the sign Capricorn representing the month (January) in which the Emperor received his title. This gem (about AD 10) commemorates victories won over the Pannonians by Tiberius, who is descending from his chariot on the left. Below, a trophy is being erected.

A sort of status symbol in the later Republic and Empire, ornamented silver plate was avidly collected. Army commanders used to travel on campaigns with lavish supplies of it. In an emergency, one of these hoards might be buried for safety by its owner and never recovered. The finely chased and engraved Great Dish, platter, bowl, goblet and spoon are part of a collection found intact at Mildenhall, near Cambridge.

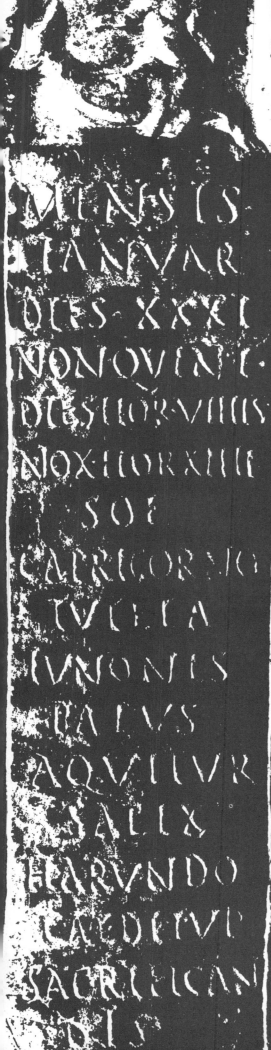

MENSIS	MENSIS	MENSIS
IANVAR	FEBRAR	MARTIVS
DIES·XXXI	DIES·XXVIII	DIES·XXXI
NON QVINT·	NON QVINT	NON SETTIMAN
DIES HOR VIIIIS	DIES HOR X S	DIES HOR XII
NOX HOR XIIII	NOX HOR XIIII S	NOX HOR XII
SOL	SOL AQVARIO	AEQVINOCTIVM
CAPRICOR NO	TVTELA IVNII	VIII KAL APR
TVTELA	SEGETES	SOL PISCIBVS
IVNONIS	SARIVNTVR	TVTELA MINERVAE
PALVS	VINEA CVM	VINEA GRADITVR
AQVITVR	SVPERFICIE	IN PASTINO
SALIX	ARBORIBVS	PVTANTVR
HARVNDO	INCIDVNTVR	
CAEDITVR	PALI VIMINA	
SACRIFICANT	LVPERCALIA	SACR MAVRIS
DIS	CARA COGNATIO	